CC20236

W9-BKK-420
3 1702 00038 0221

Learning Resources Center
Collin County Community College District
SPRING CREEK CAMPUS
WITHDRAWN
Plano, Texas 75074

DATE DUE

MAR 0 5 1989	
APR 6 '89	
APR 2 7 1989	
FEB 1 6 1990	
MAR 1 5 1990	
APR J 3 1990	
NOV 2 9 1994	

JK
1929
A2
G37

Garrow, David
J. 1953-

Protest at Selma

$10.95

© THE BAKER & TAYLOR CO.

PROTEST AT SELMA

Martin Luther King, Jr., and the
Voting Rights Act of 1965

David J. Garrow

New Haven and London   Yale University Press

Copyright © 1978 by Yale University.
All rights reserved. This book may not be
reproduced, in whole or in part, in any form (beyond
that copying permitted by Sections 107 and 108 of the
U.S. Copyright Law and except by reviewers for
the public press), without written permission
from the publishers.

Designed by John O. C. McCrillis
and set in VIP Times Roman type.
Printed in the United States of America by
The Vail-Ballou Press, Binghamton, N.Y.

Library of Congress Cataloging in Publication Data

Garrow, David J   1953–

    Protest at Selma.

    Revision of the author's senior honors thesis,
Wesleyan University, 1975.
    Includes bibliographical references and index.
    1. Afro–American—Southern States—Politics
and suffrage.   2. Voters, Registration of—Southern
States.   3. Selma–Montgomery Rights March,
1965.   I. Title.
JK1929.A2G37   324'.15   78–5593
ISBN 0–300–02247–6 (cloth)
ISBN 0–300–02498–3 (paper)

13   12   11   10   9   8   7   6   5   4

To EOG and the CSS

Contents

Illustrations

Tables

Preface

On August 6, 1965, the Voting Rights Act of 1965 was signed into law by President Lyndon B. Johnson, an event to which the newspapers of August 7 devoted headline coverage. On the same morning front-page stories also informed readers that voter registration officials in Sumter County, Georgia had dropped their opposition to a black registration drive that had been going on for some two weeks, and that some three hundred new black voters had been registered in Sumter County on August 6 alone.[1] While at that time the second story and its timing were not especially notable, from the perspective of November 1976 the coincidence was noteworthy and perhaps rather ironic.

A decade after its enactment the Voting Rights Act was being called "the most successful piece of civil rights legislation ever enacted" by a former attorney general and "one of the most important legislative enactments of all time" by a leading educator who had served previously as chairman of the U.S. Civil Rights Commission.[2] Perhaps surprisingly, these ten years had passed without the publication of even one book that told the story of the Voting Rights Act. This volume is in large part an attempt to fill that void.

This study had its origins in a tutorial paper written for David A. Titus in the College of Social Studies at Wesleyan University late in 1973. At his urging, and with the support provided by a Summer Study Grant from Wesleyan, I pursued the subject in my senior honors thesis. Throughout the drafting of that manuscript I benefited from the counsel of John G. Grumm, Herbert H. Hyman, Leon V. Sigal, and Clement E. Vose, as well as Professor Titus. My deepest thanks also go to my other tutors in the College of Social Studies, Eugene O. Golob, Richard V. Buel, and Jon Rasmussen. Valuable help at Wesleyan also was provided by a number of Olin Library's professional staff members, especially Brian Rogers and Bill Dillon.

The initial suggestion that I revise the thesis manuscript for publication came from James David Barber of Duke University, and I shall remain in his debt. Valuable critical comments on the thesis manuscript were made by Russell D. Murphy of Wesleyan and David L. Paletz, David E. Price, and Ole R. Holsti of Duke. Sheridan Johns, Peter G. Fish, and Lester M. Salamon of Duke also provided assistance, and the

Duke University Political Science Department graciously provided me
with financial support while I revised the manuscript. Duke also provided me with the funds to travel to the Lyndon B. Johnson Library
in Austin, Texas, where Martin I. Elzy, Tina Lawson, and Claudia
Alexander were of great help.

At Duke, the Interlibrary Loan staff, headed by Emerson Ford, has
provided almost continuous assistance for more than two years. I also
have benefited from the perhaps unknowing assistance of many other
friends, including the Sheplers, Karla Bell, Jacqueline Connelly, my
sister Holly, and my parents. Marian Neal Ash of Yale University
Press has provided invaluable counsel on numerous occasions. Bowden
Anderson did a superb job of copyediting the manuscript.

The irony now visible in the front pages of the newspapers of August
7, 1965, is merely one small facet of a story that in large part reflects just
how great the direct and indirect effects of the Voting Rights Act of 1965
have been upon the South and its politics. In 1965 few could have imagined that little more than a decade later a white former governor of
Georgia from Sumter County would accept the presidential nomination
of the Democratic party on a platform containing the Reverend Martin
Luther King, Sr. and Coretta Scott King, and to the strains of the civil
rights movement's favorite anthem, "We Shall Overcome."

In the wake of the strong support accorded Jimmy Carter in the 1976
general election by southern black voters, a number of political commentators have noted that any study of his success must take account of the
substantial increase in the number of southern black voters that followed
the enactment of the Voting Rights Act of 1965.[3] Informed observers
attributed Carter's margins in Louisiana, Mississippi, North Carolina,
and South Carolina to the votes of their black citizens, and many found
it ironic that it was Mississippi that put the former Georgia governor
over the top in electoral votes early Wednesday morning. Reliable estimates indicated that Carter had polled well over 90 percent of the black
vote throughout the South, and that black turnout all across the region
had been heavier than at any time in the past.[4] Black political figures
were not reticent at noting the importance of that support to Carter's
victory, and in large part their assertions that without the Voting Rights
Act and the growth of the southern black electorate there would have
been no Carter presidency are correct.[5] The movement, and Lyndon
Johnson, do deserve some of the credit for what has come to pass, and
there can be no real doubt that the Carter candidacy and victory sym-

bolize much of the change that the Voting Rights Act has brought to the South and southern politics.

In the wake of that triumph, however, it would be wrong for observers to conclude that the long voting rights struggle has ended. Even in November 1976 several hundred federal observers were deployed in almost one dozen southern counties where black citizens feared that local white election officials would strive to dilute their votes, and in the aftermath of those elections charges of widespread irregularities were made in at least one locale.[6] In other areas of the rural South black fear of economic retaliation by whites still represents a substantial barrier to black voting.[7]

While some notable victories were won by blacks in the South in 1976, such as the election of South Carolina's first black county sheriff,[8] the continuing black political struggle in the South is better seen in the strong but ultimately unsuccessful race that an admirably qualified black candidate made for the Democratic nomination for lieutenant governor in North Carolina. Although Howard Lee managed to capture some 25 percent of the white vote in the runoff primary against a veteran state legislator, after having led his opponent narrowly in the first primary, Lee went down to defeat with some 44 percent of the vote in the runoff. While that showing was the strongest by a black candidate in a major statewide race in the twentieth-century South, observers attributed Lee's defeat in the second primary to the disinterest and low turnout—some 35 percent—of North Carolina's 265,000 black voters. Figures suggested that a turnout of slightly more than 50 percent of those black Democrats would have given Lee a victory.[9] Thus, actual black political participation in the South is still far from what it might—and should—be.[10] If the victory of Jimmy Carter is heralded as indicative and symbolic of how much southern politics has changed since the Voting Rights Act of 1965 became law, the defeat of Howard Lee indicates how far black southerners and the South as a whole still have to go.

Introduction:
Voting Rights and Protest

This book is about voting rights, but it is also about protest, because the story of how southern blacks finally won equal voting rights cannot be fully appreciated without an understanding of how the dynamics of protest helped them to achieve the remarkable gains that they made.

The reason why the voting rights story cannot be understood without an appreciation of the dynamics of protest can be summarized in one word: Selma. In the long saga of southern blacks' efforts to win free and equal access to the ballot, no one event meant more than the voting rights campaign in Selma, Alabama, in the first three months of 1965. Those three months represent the key period of time in the voting rights story, for it was during those weeks that the bill that was to become the Voting Rights Act of 1965 was drafted and began its path through the Congress.

The Voting Rights Act of 1965 revolutionized black access to the ballot throughout most of the Deep South. In so doing, it changed forever the politics of those states and, indirectly, those of the entire nation. While a subsequent chapter will detail the effects of the Voting Rights Act and how the enforcement of that law has proceeded, my main concern is *how* the Voting Rights Act of 1965 came into being. This is not, however, a book about "how a bill becomes a law," a simple legislative history. Instead, it focuses on how the strategy of protest employed by the Southern Christian Leadership Conference and its president, Dr. Martin Luther King, Jr., influenced the emergence of the Voting Rights Act. The central episode in the voting rights story is the story of that act, and the story of the Voting Rights Act is inextricably tied to the story of the SCLC's protest campaign in Selma. Selma is the nexus at which the voting rights story and the dynamics of protest come together so vividly.

Chapters 2 and 3 relate that story, which began late in 1964 when the SCLC initiated its plans for a major campaign focusing upon voting rights and when serious discussion about drafting a voting rights bill in 1965 began within the Johnson administration.[1] It continued on through January and February of 1965 as both the Selma campaign and the drafting of the administration's bill proceeded, and it climaxed on Sunday, March 7, when a column of voting rights marchers was violently attacked by a large group of state and local lawmen on a highway just east of Selma. A tense and hectic week followed, and then, on March 15, Lyndon Johnson went before the Congress to urge passage of the voting rights measure his administration would soon introduce. Less than five months later, in early August, Johnson signed the Voting Rights Act of 1965 into law.

My account of Selma and the birth of the Voting Rights Act focuses on several particularly important aspects of the story. First are the strategic and tactical considerations of the Southern Christian Leadership Conference. The SCLC went to Selma with one goal in mind: to win a strong federal voting rights law that would provide for executive branch enforcement of southern blacks' constitutionally guaranteed right to vote. For the SCLC, success at Selma would be determined by whether or not such an act was won from the federal government. In the four years that the SCLC had been active in civil rights campaigns in the South, Martin King and his associates increasingly had come to understand the potential national effects of their efforts, and they had learned that several things were necessary for a protest to receive the national coverage, attention, and support that would help to bring about federal legislation. Foremost of these was unprovoked white violence aimed at peaceful and unresisting civil rights demonstrators.

Prior to the end of the SCLC's first substantial campaign, which took place in Albany, Georgia, in 1961 and 1962, the SCLC's philosophy of protest had centered on nonviolent persuasion aimed at their immediate opponents. The protestors' goal, King had written, should be to change the hearts and minds of their opponents and oppressors, to convince these purveyors of racial injustice that true human respect, love, and equality should not be limited by the color of one's skin.[2] The Albany campaign, however, was judged a dismal failure. The local police chief had coped with the movement's protest marches by repeatedly jailing the participants; no great national interest had been aroused, and no gains had been won for the local black community. Racism in Albany had given no sign of responding to moral and religious persuasion, and racism's most ugly aspects had remained hidden from the national audience whose attention the SCLC had hoped to draw.

In early 1963 the SCLC chose Birmingham, Alabama, as the site for its second major campaign. Birmingham was known as a tough town, "the most segregated city in America," but among black activists it was most notorious for its violent-tempered police commissioner, Eugene "Bull" Connor. In Connor the SCLC had someone who would represent southern racism at its worst, and as events in Birmingham unfolded,

Connor obliged by living up to his reputation. Few who saw photos of Connor's men using police dogs and water hoses ever completely forgot them.

Birmingham showed King and his associates that a violent white opposition could do much good for the movement; national interest heightened in the wake of Birmingham. But two things had hindered the movement's effort to win greater national support for the civil rights cause. First, the effort there, as at Albany, had lacked a clear, single goal that could be easily conveyed both *to* and *by* the news media. The movement had had five or six specific aims in Birmingham, and they were not susceptible to a quick and simple presentation. One clear, simple aim would be easier to get across to that important national audience, and that single goal would be received most positively by the audience if it was one that embodied and appealed to some of the nation's most widely-shared values.

The second problem at Birmingham had been that on several occasions black citizens not formally involved in the movement had themselves employed weapons or violence against white officials, one substantial clash occurring immediately after several racist bombings on May 11. These actions, King and his associates realized, served only to alienate possible supporters of the blacks' cause across the nation. If these two difficulties could be overcome in future SCLC campaigns, only one other requirement for success would remain: white violence against the peaceful protestors.

The contrast between the failure of the peaceful, undramatic Albany effort and the substantial though qualified success of the eventful and often violent Birmingham campaign indicated to the SCLC that unprovoked white violence was to the movement's advantage. When white lawmen used tactics such as Connor's against demonstrators, national attention was quick to focus on the protestors' cause. Nothing could stimulate a heightened national interest in new voting rights legislation more than white violence against blacks peacefully seeking to register and vote.

The choice of Selma as the focal point for the 1965 SCLC voting rights effort thus was the outgrowth of this evolution in the SCLC's approach to nonviolent protest. Albany had shown that nonviolent persuasion was ineffective, and Birmingham had indicated that white violence redounded in the movement's favor. Selma was famous within movement circles for the vicious and violent behavior of the local county sheriff, Jim Clark. Past conduct indicated that Clark was more likely than most southern lawmen to lose his temper and respond violently when confronted with determined protestors. If peaceful protests could evoke such a response from Clark and his assistants, the SCLC effort to draw national attention to the need for stronger voting rights legislation would benefit immensely. Thus, a strategy that bordered on nonviolent provocation supplanted the earlier belief in nonviolent persuasion. In chapter 7 the SCLC's development and use of this strategy is analyzed in depth.

A second focus of this account of Selma and the birth of the Voting Rights Act is the national news coverage the events in Alabama received. If the SCLC's goal for the Selma campaign was to stimulate national support for a new federal law, the news media would provide the crucial link between the conflict in Selma and the national audience that the SCLC hoped to reach. The way in which the news media portrayed the Selma struggle was thus of the utmost importance. The SCLC leadership understood well what would appeal to the national audience and what sort of conduct by the movement's opponents would most greatly activate support of the SCLC's efforts. Chapter 4 analyzes the ingredients of this appeal and the responses that it was able to stimulate. Contrasting the Selma campaign with the earlier Birmingham effort helps explain why the "audience reaction" to Selma was far greater than in the campaign two years earlier. Certain components of the American "political culture" influenced the national reaction to both Birmingham and Selma and account for the sharper reaction to Selma.

The third focus of this account of Selma is the reactions that the news coverage provoked throughout the country, and especially in Washington. Since the SCLC sought a new federal law, presidential and congressional reactions to the events in Selma and to the movement's calls for new voting rights legislation were of the greatest importance. The tone and quantity of the congressional reactions can be examined easily because of the many congressional statements made about the subject at the time, and chapter 5 considers why members of Congress reacted as they did. The character of the administration's reaction and response is recounted in chapters 2 and 3 and at the outset of chapter 4.

Throughout this recounting and analysis of the story of Selma and the birth of the Voting Rights Act, my most central concern is the dynamics of protest activity. Within the arena of protest there are, generally speaking, three important sets of actors: the protestors, their immediate opponents, and the larger "audience" which is not directly involved in the conflict at the outset. Much of this book focuses on that audience, especially on the Washington portion. Only rarely have political scientists given such third-party audiences the attention they so often deserve. Nearly two decades ago one of this country's foremost political analysts,

E. E. Schattschneider, upbraided the profession for its failure to perceive the crucial role that such initially uninvolved audiences could and often did play in determining the outcomes of political conflicts.[3] Schattschneider's perspective on the dynamics of political conflict unfortunately has not been employed to anywhere near the extent that it should be, and it is one of this volume's goals to make clear to its own "audience" how increased attention to Schattschneider's writings can infuse new life into much political analysis. This argument is articulated in greater detail in the concluding portion of chapter 7.

In addition to the primary focus upon Selma, the creation of the Voting Rights Act, and the dynamics of protest activity, two chapters depict the course of the voting rights struggle both before and after Selma. One of these, chapter 6, traces the effects of the Voting Rights Act on southern politics in the first decade following its enactment. Passage of the Voting Rights Act, this discussion shows, did not signal the end of the voting rights struggle. Instead, it merely signaled a crucially important shift in that struggle by providing southern blacks for the first time with effective enforcement by the federal executive branch of their right to register and vote. These new methods of enforcement, such as federal registrars, federal poll watchers, and the suspension of the numerous tests and requirements that long had been used to hinder or prevent black registration, proved to be far more effective at protecting the right to vote than had the judicial enforcement employed with little success in the years prior to 1965.

The voting rights story in the pre-1965 period is the subject of chapter 1. After briefly charting the course of black political participation in the South in the 1940s and 1950s, I discuss the first federal attempts to protect southern blacks' right to vote. These first federal efforts, based upon the Civil Rights Acts of 1957 and 1960, employed a litigative strategy of enforcement which placed much faith in the federal courts' ability to rectify racial discrimination in the electoral process. As we shall see, this faith was badly misplaced. Recalcitrant, obstructionist judges in most southern jurisdictions all but stifled the Justice Department's attacks on voting-related racial discrimination and harassment. Only minute gains in black registration and voting resulted from the Justice Department's long and costly attempts to eliminate racial discrimination in the electoral processes of several dozen southern counties. Recently one scholar has asserted that the courts eventually would have proven successful in effectively enforcing southern blacks' right to vote.[4] Consideration and analysis of this claim shows how erroneous it is.

1 Black Voters and the Federal Voting Rights Enforcement Effort in the South, 1940–1964

As the starting point of the civil rights movement, many writers have chosen either May 17, 1954, the day on which the Supreme Court handed down its historic ruling in *Brown v. Board of Education of Topeka*,[1] or December 1, 1955, the day on which Mrs. Rosa Parks's refusal to move to the rear of a segregated bus ignited the Montgomery bus boycott.[2] The true beginning of black southerners' political emergence, however, goes back to a day in early April of 1944, when another Supreme Court ruling signaled the culmination of one effort and, in certain ways, the beginning of another. *Smith v. Allwright* represented the next to last installment in a series of rulings that have come to be called the Texas white primary cases; it was the first instance in which the Court ruled that black citizens could no longer be prohibited from participating in political party primary elections on account of their race.[3] It made possible "the initial political mobilization of Negroes" in the twentieth-century South.[4]

When the Supreme Court's ruling in *Smith v. Allwright* was handed down, black voter registration in the eleven southern states stood at a level not substantially higher than that to which it had been reduced by the disfranchising efforts of the late nineteenth and very early twentieth centuries.[5] Black registration in 1940 was estimated by the foremost expert of the period to be no more than 151,000, which represented only 3 percent of the approximately 5 million southern blacks of voting age. In three states—Alabama, Louisiana, and Mississippi—the estimated statewide black registration totaled only two thousand in each.[6]

With the downfall in 1944 of the white primary, which a number of authorities have characterized as "the most effective" barrier to black registration and voting,[7] "the number and proportion of Negroes registered to vote in the southern states increased with startling speed."[8] The effects were first seen in the elections of 1946, and nowhere were they more noticeable than in Georgia, where the incumbent governor, Ellis Arnall, was ineligible to succeed himself. Arnall and the Democratic State Committee worked to facilitate black registration and voting in the

TABLE 1-1

Black Voter Registration in the Southern States, 1940–1952

	Estimated Percentage of Voting-Age Blacks Registered			Estimated Number of Black Registrants		
	1940	1947	1952	1940	1947	1952
Alabama	0.4	1.2	5	2,000	6,000	25,224
Arkansas	1.5	17.3	27	4,000	47,000	61,413
Florida	5.7	15.4	33	18,000	49,000	120,900
Georgia	3.0	18.8	23	20,000	125,000	144,835
Louisiana	0.5	2.6	25	2,000	10,000	120,000
Mississippi	0.4	0.9	4	2,000	5,000	20,000
North Carolina	7.1	15.2	18	35,000	75,000	100,000
South Carolina	0.8	13.0	20	3,000	50,000	80,000
Tennessee	6.5	25.8	27	20,000	80,000	85,000
Texas	5.6	18.5	31	30,000	100,000	181,916
Virginia	4.1	13.2	16	15,000	48,000	69,326
All Southern States	3.0	12.0	20	151,000	595,000	1,008,614

Sources: The 1940 and 1947 totals and the 1947 percentages are from Luther P. Jackson, "Race and Suffrage in the South Since 1940," *New South* 3 (June-July 1948): 1-26, at 3-4. The 1940 percentages have been calculated from the statistics supplied by Jackson. Jackson's figures previously have been adopted by V. O. Key (*Southern Politics in State and Nation* [New York: Alfred A. Knopf, 1949], p. 523); Margaret Price (*The Negro Voter in the South* [Atlanta: Southern Regional Council, 1957], p. 5, and *The Negro and the Ballot in the South* [Atlanta: Southern Regional Council, 1959], p. 8); and Florence B. Irving ("The Future of the Negro Voter in the South," *Journal of Negro Education* 26 [Summer 1957]: 390-99, at 391). The 1952 totals appear in both of Price's pamphlets and in Irving's article, and the 1952 percentages appear in Donald R. Matthews and James W. Prothro, *Negroes and the New Southern Politics* (New York: Harcourt, Brace & World, 1966), p. 148, and in Richard Claude, *The Supreme Court and the Electoral Process* (Baltimore: Johns Hopkins Press, 1970), p. 107. It should be stressed that the accuracy of many of these estimates is open to question, but no figures of greater reliability are available.

hope that such votes would aid the candidate of the Arnall faction, James V. Carmichael, in his primary race against the well-known white supremacist Eugene Talmadge. Their effort centered on Atlanta, where they openly funded a black registration drive headed by the NAACP state secretary, A.T. Walden, and carried out by the Georgia Association of Citizens' Democratic Clubs, a group of black political clubs whose total membership exceeded 15,000. As a result of that drive, approximately 100,000 new black voters were registered, and some 85,000 black citizens cast ballots in the Democratic gubernatorial primary, which Carmichael nevertheless lost to Talmadge.

Two years later, in the 1948 Democratic gubernatorial primary, some 65,000 to 70,000 blacks turned out in an unsuccessful effort to defeat Talmadge's son, Herman. Despite this second loss to their most vocal opponents, Georgia blacks could take some comfort in the fact that some 125,000 of them, almost 20 percent of those of voting age, were now registered, a more than sixfold increase in eight years.[9]

These record black turnouts in Georgia were mirrored in several other southern states, such as Texas, where 75,000 voted in the 1946 Democratic primary, and North Carolina, where 40,000 turned out in that same year. But in each of at least four Southern states—Alabama, Louisiana, Mississippi, and South Carolina—less than 5,000 black citizens voted. Georgia's reaction to *Smith* v. *Allwright* thus was unrepresentative of suffrage developments in the other four Deep South states.[10]

Throughout much of the South, *Smith* v. *Allwright* stimulated a "search for a legal substitute for the white primary and precipitated a crisis in southern politics."[11] In several states the initial reaction was to devise some means for continuing the white primary in spite of *Smith*. Without exception, however, these attempts were struck down by the federal courts, and southern legislators were forced to adopt other tactics.[12] Most turned to the many opportunities for discrimination available in discretionary registration systems administered at the county level. By giving substantial discretion to the local white registrar, who was, as Key noted, "a law unto himself in determining the citizen's possession of literacy, understanding, and other qualifications," legislators could restrict black registration with a minimum of effort.[13]

The first and most extensive effort to revise and expand the qualifications for voter registration came in Alabama in 1946, where first the legislature and then the state electorate in a referendum approved an alteration in the state constitution known as the Boswell Amendment. This provision specified that all future applicants for registration be able to read and write, to understand and explain any portion of the United States Constitution, to demonstrate their understanding of the duties and obligations of citizenship, to prove that they possessed "good character," and to prove that they had been regularly employed for the past year. Although this package of new requirements soon was ruled unconstitutional by a three-judge federal court, the failure of the Boswell Amendment signaled not the end but the beginning of southern legislatures' attempts to devise new methods by which black applicants for registration could be rejected.[14]

While the majority of Deep South registration officials strove to minimize black registration in their jurisdictions, their application of the discretionary tools that their legislatures provided proved to be a good deal more porous, especially in urban areas, than the white primary had been. Black registration figures for late 1947, the first area-wide compilation done in seven years, reflected that fact clearly. Whereas the 1940 southern black registration total had barely exceeded 150,000, within seven years it had grown to just short of 600,000, and within five more years it grew to slightly more than one million. While the 1947 figures showed that two states, Alabama and Mississippi, had managed to keep their black registration totals at approximately 5,000, within five years black registration was to increase no less than fourfold even in these more restrictive southern states.[15]

As the 1952 registration totals partially reflect, black registration in the South continued to increase at a moderate rate throughout the early 1950s. While this progress, given its very gradual nature, went almost without public attention, the southern racial climate experienced a quantum change literally overnight as a result of the Supreme Court's May 17, 1954 ruling in *Brown*.[16] Within one to two years after the *Brown* ruling, southern politicians and state officials developed a sharpened appreciation of the growing black electorate and its possible influence. Hence, for the first time in several years southern legislators once again began to devote substantial attention to the possible ways by which this growth could be halted or even reversed.

The two states in which this reaction to increases in black registration was most pronounced were Mississippi and Louisiana. In the former, legislators added a literacy requirement to the state's existing provision that each applicant be able to interpret to the registrar's satisfaction a section—any section—of the lengthy and complex Mississippi state constitution. Needless to say, the great majority of black applicants had found that the registrars, who seemed always to present blacks with particularly difficult sections, were impossible to please. While this added literacy test further hindered prospective black registrants, local Citizens' Councils in a number of cases managed to "persuade" those blacks already registered to "voluntarily" remove their names from the rolls. The classic case of this sort of "persuasion" occurred in Sunflower County, where within a few months black registration fell from 114 to zero. All in all, in 1955 fourteen rural Mississippi counties had not a single registered black voter.[17]

In Louisiana a more extensive and organized effort to purge the names of black voters from the rolls was conducted under the direction of a state senator who headed a legislative committee designed to foster segregation. Beginning late in 1954, the senator and his chief counsel traveled the state distributing a pamphlet, "Voter Qualification Laws in Louisiana—The Key to Victory in the Segregation Struggle," and encouraging parish registrars and local political leaders to reexamine previously approved registration applications for errors and omissions on the basis of which a voter's registration could be revoked. Their recommendations were adopted most enthusiastically in the north-central parishes of the state. In twelve such parishes during 1956 and 1957, between 10,000 and 11,000 black voters were removed from the rolls, with parishes such as Red River, Bienville, and Webster experiencing up to 99 percent "success." In Ouachita Parish, black registration dropped from 5,782 to 595 in two months in 1956. East Feliciana Parish's 1956 black registration total of 1,361 had declined to 82 by 1960. All in all, between 1956 and 1959 black registration dropped in forty-six of Louisiana's sixty-four parishes, and the decline in the statewide total registration was minimized only by the fact that some 50 percent of Louisiana's black voters lived in or about New Orleans.[18]

While the black registration situations in all of the other southern states during the years of "massive resistance" were not all similar to that in Louisiana and Mississippi, throughout the South in the late 1950s black progress in adding voters to the rolls was very limited at best, with only sizable gains in North Carolina and Tennessee enabling the southern total to continue its slow creep upward. Throughout the long swath of the Black Belt, running from southside Virginia to northern Louisiana and southeastern Arkansas, where the black percentage of the population was highest and black registration historically the lowest,[19] reported incidents of economic and physical intimidation of prospective black voters increased. The economic dependence of most rural blacks on local whites not only often dissuaded many blacks from attempting to register in a hostile climate; it also made the use of physical force unnecessary in quieting those who did undertake political activity. Physical threats, however, and actual murders, such as that of George Lee in Mississippi, were certainly not rare. Potential black voters in Mississippi's Lowndes County in 1956 received anonymous death-threat letters, while a year later a series of bombings and burnings in northern Florida's Liberty County convinced nine of the ten registered blacks to remove their names from the rolls. As Margaret Price observed at the time, "For Negroes in some sections of the South, an attempt to exercise their right of franchise as Americans seemed a greater risk in 1958 than at any time since the outlawing of the white primary in 1944." Looking beyond those hard-core areas and surveying black registration

TABLE 1-2

Black Voter Registration in the Southern States, 1956–1960

	Estimated Percentage of Voting-Age Blacks Registered			Estimated Number of Black Registrants		
	1956	1958	1960	1956	1958	1960
Alabama	11	15	13.7	53,366	70,000	66,009
Arkansas	36	33	37.3	69,677	64,023	72,604
Florida	32	31	38.9	148,703	144,810	183,197
Georgia	27	26	29.3	163,389	161,958	180,000
Louisiana	31	26	30.9	161,410	131,068	159,033
Mississippi	5	5	5.2	20,000	20,000	22,000
North Carolina	24	32	38.1	135,000	150,000	210,450
South Carolina	27	15	15.6	99,890	57,978	58,122
Tennessee	29	48	58.9	90,000	185,000	185,000
Texas	37	39	34.9	214,000	226,818	226,818
Virginia	19	21	22.8	82,603	92,172	100,100
All Southern States	24.9	25	29.1	1,238,038	1,303,827	1,463,333

Sources: The 1956 and 1958 percentages appear in Matthews and Prothro, *Negroes and the New Southern Politics*, p. 148. The 1960 percentages appear in William C. Havard, ed., *The Changing Politics of the South* (Baton Rouge: Louisiana State University Press, 1972), p. 20. The 1956 and 1958 totals appear in Price, *The Negro and the Ballot in the South*, pp. 8-9; and the 1960 totals are from "Southern Voter Registration in the 1960s," *VEP News* 2 (April 1968): 3. Havard adopts most of them as well. Also see "Negro Voter Registration Remains Constant in the South," *New South* 14 (January 1959): 8-9. Some of the fluctuations apparent in these totals, and in those portrayed in other tables, are the result not of drastic changes in actual registration levels but of overly optimistic estimations made in one year and more sober estimates made several years later. Witness South Carolina's totals between 1947 and 1958—especially 1956 to 1958—and Tennessee's between 1960 and 1962. A particularly good reflection of the problems involved in such estimates is M. Jerome Diamond, "The Impact of the Negro Vote in Contemporary Tennessee Politics," *Tennessee Law Review* 34 (Spring 1967): 435-81, at 435-37.

levels across the South, Price concluded, "Currently, it cannot be said that either the proponents or opponents of equal suffrage are winning."[20]

Such was the black registration situation in the South in the mid and late 1950s when the federal government began to exhibit its first real interest in eliminating or at least reducing the barriers to political participation faced by southern blacks. Although the Roosevelt and Truman administrations had made some efforts in the civil rights field,[21] as of mid-1955 the Eisenhower administration had taken few steps in civil rights and had shown no discernible interest in black southerners' voting rights.[22] Late in 1955, however, a group of urban Republicans, looking ahead to the 1956 elections and the growing number of votes being cast by northern blacks, urged Attorney General Herbert Brownell to consider the introduction of some civil rights legislation by the administration. Throughout the first several months of 1956 the possibilities were discussed within the administration, and after some jockeying among liberal Republicans in Congress, Brownell, and various White House officials, all of the provisions drafted by the Justice Department were presented to the Congress, in spite of some apparent White House objections, in the second week of April.

The complex and hazardous legislative journey experienced by the provisions that ultimately emerged on September 7, 1957 as the Civil Rights Act of 1957 has been detailed by a number of other writers.[23] The law as enacted had five titles. The first established for two years a United States Commission on Civil Rights. The second established a Civil Rights Division and a new assistant attorney general within the Justice Department. The third provided for Justice Department intervention in civil suits brought by private citizens alleging denial of their civil rights. The fourth outlined the attorney general's authority to file civil suits in federal district courts seeking injunctive relief against violations of the Fifteenth Amendment's prohibition of racial discrimination in voting. The fifth dealt with criminal contempt proceedings and jury trials in cases where a violation of an injunction was alleged.[24]

Some commentators complained that whatever muscle the original provisions had possessed had been deleted by Congress.[25] The heart of the act as passed, however, was title 4. It amended section 1971 of title 42 of the United States Code by adding three subsections that prohibited actual or attempted intimidation or coercion of potential registrants or voters, gave the attorney general the power to institute civil actions seeking injunctive relief in voting rights cases, and gave jurisdiction over such suits to the federal district courts.[26]

Almost an entire year passed before the newly constituted Civil Rights Division of the Justice Department filed its first voting rights case under title 4. In that action, *U.S.* v. *Raines*, the government sought to end discrimination by the Terrell County, Georgia, registrar of voters. Six months later the department filed a second suit, *U.S.* v. *Alabama*, aimed at the board of registrars of Macon County. On the heels of that action came the initial ruling in the *Raines* case, in which District Judge T. Hoyt Davis held that the 1957 act was unconstitutional.[27] Shortly thereafter another setback was suffered when, in the wake of the resignations of the Macon County registrars, District Judge Frank M. Johnson, Jr. denied relief on the grounds that the state of Alabama, which the department sought to cite in the absence of any registrars, could not be sued under the provisions of the 1957 act, which had spoken of actions against "persons."[28]

A more positive result was obtained in the department's third suit, *U.S.* v. *McElveen*, when in January 1960 another federal district court upheld the constitutionality of the 1957 act and ordered the restoration of the names of 1,377 purged black voters to the voting rolls of Louisiana's Washington Parish.[29] One month later the Supreme Court affirmed that ruling at the same time that it reversed and remanded Judge Davis's order in the *Raines* case.[30] In April of 1960 the Justice Department also was able to settle a fourth case, *U.S.* v. *Fayette County Democratic Executive Committee*, which had sought to end a white primary conducted by that organization in southwestern Tennessee, with the entering of a consent decree.[31]

This limited record of voting rights litigation during the last three years of the Eisenhower administration soon came under strong criticism. Some of the blame was apportioned to the Justice Department's implementation of the provisions of the act, but inherent weaknesses in those provisions were also cited. Allan Lichtman, for instance, placed most of the blame on the assistant attorney general for civil rights, Wilson White. Under White's leadership, Lichtman wrote, the division "adopted a narrow, inflexible approach which precluded a full exploitation of the powers provided by the legislation." Instead of seeking to learn of discriminatory registrars, the division authorized an FBI investigation of a particular county's registration system only upon receipt of a formal, written complaint from someone in the locale alleging violations of federal law. Given the extremely limited, in many cases simply nonexistent, legal knowledge and advice available to rural southern blacks in 1960, such formal complaints were few indeed.[32]

While the Civil Rights Division adopted a more activist posture in regard to voting discrimination after Harold Tyler succeeded White as assistant attorney general in January 1960, such a personnel shift was irrelevant to those whose criticisms of voting rights enforcement centered on what they regarded as the severely limited tools provided the department by the 1957 act. The majority of critics focused on the fact that "not a single Negro who had not been previously registered was enabled to register to vote by federal action during the three-year period" following the 1957 act's adoption.[33] A number of legal practitioners and scholars were quick to point out the "inherent defects" of an enforcement method that relied solely upon the federal courts in the South. Those defects included the limited scope of any one case, which would apply to only one of the dozens of discriminatory southern counties, the cost and effort of the hundreds of man-hours necessary to gather and analyze the great amount of factual and statistical data necessary for proving racially discriminatory application of voter qualifications, the difficulties in obtaining access to the necessary registration records, and, most important, the almost limitless opportunities for delay in the judicial process. As Ira Heyman summed up, "The prosecution of individual suits is a cumbersome and slow means for protecting the voting rights of significant numbers of qualified Negroes who are the victims of discrimination."[34]

Not only legal writers noted the limitations of the judicial approach to voting rights enforcement. Within the Justice Department itself Civil Rights Division officials were confronted with severe difficulties in obtaining registration and voting records from noncooperative southern registrars, records that the department considered "essential to proving racial discrimination in the voting field."[35] By mid-1959 numerous members of Congress too were aware of the problems. Although a number of relevant bills were introduced, and although two subcommittees held hearings on several of them, no legislation reached the floor of either house of Congress in 1959. Further attention was drawn to voting rights enforcement problems when the Civil Rights Commission issued its first report in September, which among other recommendations called for legislation that would allow the president to appoint federal registrars to examine those applicants rejected by local registrars in counties where voting discrimination complaints had been made.[36] Shortly after that proposal, the Justice Department itself proposed that federal district judges be allowed to appoint a voting referee responsible to them once the court had found a "pattern or practice" of discrimination in a county's registration system. There the matter stood until legislative action began in the Senate in mid-February 1960 at the instigation of the majority leader, Lyndon B. Johnson.

As with the 1957 act, the story of the passage of the Civil Rights Act of 1960, which became law on May 6, has been told adequately elsewhere.[37] As with the 1957 act, many commentators regarded the final version of the legislation as more of a victory for southern segregationists than for those members seeking more stringent protection of black southerners' rights.[38] Of the 1960 act's six titles, which covered a variety of subjects, the third and the sixth were the most important. Title 3 provided for the preservation of registration and voting records and stated the Justice Department's clear right to examine them upon demand. Title 6 outlined the attorney general's power to request a "pattern or practice" of discrimination finding from a federal district court and provided for the optional appointment of a voting referee by the judge following such a finding. The referee, a resident of that federal court district, would reexamine voter applicants rejected by the county registrar and recommend to the judge the registration of those whom he found possessed the qualifications set down by state law. The judge could then enter an order specifying such registrations. The 1960 act also made it clear that a state, as well as individuals, was suable under the provisions of section 1971(c), and pursuant to that the Macon County, Alabama, case was remanded to the district court for trial on the merits.[39]

In the wake of the enactment of the 1960 act, many of the criticisms that had been aimed at the 1957 act were renewed, as observers once again noted the serious limitations of the judicial approach to voting rights enforcement.[40] Also in the months immediately after enactment, the Civil Rights Division chief, Harold Tyler, instituted five more voting suits, including one aimed at ending a purge of black voters in Bienville Parish, Louisiana, organized by the Citizens' Council, and four aimed at acts of economic intimidation against prospective black voters in southwestern Tennessee and Louisiana. Tyler also requested the registration and voting records of some twenty-three southern counties.[41]

Before many of these efforts had a chance to come to fruition, a new administration with a new attorney general—Robert F. Kennedy—and a new assistant attorney general for civil rights—Burke Marshall—took office. A good measure of continuity was achieved by Marshall's retention of Tyler's second-in-command, John Doar. More important, the new team displayed none of the hesitancy in aggressively prosecuting voting rights cases that had characterized the earlier years of the Eisenhower administration. With little delay, however, Marshall and Doar were brought face to face with two problems that were to plague severely the administration's unspoken policy of "litigate rather than legislate" in the civil rights field. In time a third and more crucial barrier to the successful use of the judicial approach to voting rights enforcement would emerge as well.[42]

The first problem emerged from the aftermath of Tyler's requests for the registration records of some two dozen southern counties. Most of the counties in Alabama, Louisiana, and Mississippi simply refused to provide them, despite the explicit language in title 3 of the 1960 Civil Rights Act. This continuing series of refusals, which eventually totaled fifty-eight of the 140 counties from which the department requested records up through mid-1964, soon constituted a major litigative burden on the division, while also assuring lengthy delays in the acquisition of substantive decrees reducing voting discrimination.[43] Southern officials understood clearly the benefits of such resistance, for they could not even be charged with discriminatory registration practices until the proof of those actions—the registration applications of black and white applicants and the registrar's evaluation of them—were in the Justice Department's hands. An entire series of actions was filed simply in pursuit of such records, and in at least one case the department was forced to appeal a district court ruling to the Fifth Circuit Court of Appeals before an order mandating the handing over of the records was entered.[44] In another case, U.S. v. Cartwright, the Justice Department moved against an Elmore County, Alabama, registrar who had destroyed his records upon learning of the department's interest in them.[45] Even a Supreme Court ruling implicitly affirming the court of appeals' endorsement of the constitutionality of title 3 of the 1960 act did not fully stem the problem.[46]

The second problem for the Civil Rights Division in voting rights litigation involved the difficult degree of proof required to demonstrate that actions by private individuals constituted violations of section 1971(b), which prohibited the intimidation or coercion of potential registrants or voters. The provision was designed expressly to protect politically active southern blacks from economic retaliation, a favorite tool of the southern whites upon whom so many blacks were almost completely dependent for income, employment, and housing.

The first four suits under 1971(b) were filed in the last months of the Eisenhower administration but were not adjudicated until Marshall took over from Tyler. All four aimed at halting blatant acts of economic retaliation. In the first case, U.S. v. Deal, Joseph Atlas, a black farmer from East Carroll Parish, Louisiana, had testified before the U.S. Civil Rights Commission about the deprivation of voting rights in the parish, where not one black was registered. Soon after, Atlas discovered that no merchant in the area, all of whom were white, would gin his cotton or sell him supplies. His previous dealers now told him to take his business elsewhere. After some delay, and considerable economic and personal hardship for Atlas, the white merchants involved agreed to a consent decree specifying no further boycotting.[47]

Also in late 1960, three interrelated 1971(b) cases were filed in response to the economic harassment and intimidation of newly active blacks in Fayette and Haywood counties in southwestern Tennessee.[48] These black citizens, many of whom were sharecroppers, were not only subjected to the same tactics employed against Atlas, but in a substantial number of cases also were put off the land on which they long had resided. Their resultant effort to form a tent city on other land in the area drew both publicity and support in the North and physical attacks by local whites.[49] Injunctions against the white merchants involved in boycotting the blacks were entered by the district court in December 1960, and in early April 1961 the Sixth Circuit Court of Appeals extended them to cover the white landowners as well. All three suits were eventually settled by consent decrees in May and July of 1962.

While the Justice Department was successful in each of these first four cases, subsequent 1971(b) cases proved far more difficult to prosecute successfully. One of the clearest examples involved the firing of a black school teacher, Mrs. Ernestine Talbert, by the Greene County, Mississippi Board of Education shortly after she had attempted to register to vote in her home community, located in neighboring George County, and had testified in a federal court regarding voting discrimination there. The Greene County school board stated that Mrs. Talbert's George County political activities had not been a factor in its decision not to renew her contract, and the Justice Department was unable conclusively to prove otherwise, despite local blacks' belief that the firing was in direct retaliation for Mrs. Talbert's registration activity. The district judge held that there was no clear proof of a connection between the two events and refused to order that Mrs. Talbert's contract be renewed.[50] As the *Yale Law Journal* observed early in 1962, while 1971(b) seemed "adequate to combat blatant instances of economic coercion" such as those experienced in southwestern Tennessee, in other cases, such as that of Mrs. Talbert, "where the violations are less obvious, the government may have difficulty in proving intent to interfere with voting rights."[51] As a number of writers noted at the time, and as the outcomes of a number of additional 1971(b) cases showed, the extreme difficulty of proving *intent* to interfere with voting rights through a variety of private economic relationships all but thwarted the Justice Department's ability to prosecute successfully those who had employed subtle, but nonetheless all too real, acts of economic retaliation against politically active southern blacks.[52]

More numerous than those cases that alleged harassment and intimidation of potential black registrants were those where the Justice Depart-

WITHDRAWN
Learning Resources Center
Collin County Community College District
SPRING CREEK CAMPUS
Plano, Texas   75074

ment charged southern registrars with discriminating against black applicants by subjecting them to a more demanding interpretation of voter qualifications than was commonly the case with white applicants. By the end of 1964 almost fifty such 1971(a) cases had been filed by the department, compared to some sixteen alleging acts of intimidation that violated 1971(b). In the 1971(a) actions brought against the registrars, the most common allegations were (1) that white applicants had been provided with assistance in filling out the required forms and taking the necessary tests, while blacks had not; (2) that blacks' applications had been rejected for minor and inconsequential errors while whites' had not; (3) that significantly more difficult test materials had been given to black applicants than had been given to whites; and (4) that registration officials had refused to inform black applicants of whether or not their application had been approved or rejected. Other procedures attacked in these suits included the different standards used by registrars in evaluating the oral interpretations of constitutional excerpts offered by black and white applicants; the propriety of any "oral" test in and of itself; and the pernicious effects of the voucher requirement enforced in many Alabama counties and Louisiana parishes, whereby an applicant had to have an already registered voter "vouch" for his identity and residency. In counties where no blacks were registered it proved impossible for black applicants to obtain "vouchers."[53]

As a part of its efforts to promote the registration of southern blacks through the judicial proscription of discriminatory tactics and devices, the Justice Department also employed two somewhat less formal strategies. The first, adopted at the outset of the Kennedy administration by the attorney general and Burke Marshall and adhered to throughout the following four years, specified that before any court suit was brought against a county, Justice Department attorneys would first attempt to persuade local officials to end their discriminatory registration practices. As Robert F. Kennedy stated early in his tenure, "No legal action is brought by the government until state and local authorities have been given full notice and opportunity to avoid litigation by the adoption of corrective measures." Although that same theme was reiterated often by both Kennedy and Marshall, the instances of department-induced registration gains in the absence of litigation were few and far between.[54]

The second of the Justice Department's less formal and more private initiatives consisted of efforts to encourage the civil rights organizations active in the South to emphasize voter registration drives as opposed to other modes of activity. While the civil rights representatives who attended one meeting with Marshall in the spring of 1961 and a second one with Robert Kennedy in August 1962 were receptive to such sugges-

TABLE 1-3

Black Voter Registration in the Southern States, 1962–1965

	Estimated Percentage of Voting-Age Blacks Registered		Estimated Number of Black Registrants		
	1962	1964	1962	1964	1965
Alabama	13.4	23.0	68,317	111,000	92,737
Arkansas	34.0	49.3	68,970	95,000	77,714
Florida	36.8	63.8	182,456	300,000	240,616
Georgia	26.7	44.0	175,573	270,000	167,663
Louisiana	27.8	32.0	151,663	164,700	164,601
Mississippi	5.3	6.7	23,920	28,500	28,500
North Carolina	35.8	46.8	215,938	258,000	258,000
South Carolina	22.9	38.7	90,901	144,000	138,544
Tennessee	49.8	69.4	150,869	218,000	218,000
Texas	37.3	57.7	242,000	375,000	377,000
Virginia	24.0	45.7	110,113	200,000	143,904
All Southern States	29.4	43.1	1,480,720	2,164,200	1,907,279

Sources: The 1962 percentages come from Pat Watters and Reese Cleghorn, *Climbing Jacob's Ladder: The Arrival of Negroes in Southern Politics* (New York: Harcourt, Brace & World, 1967), p. 376. It should be noted that the adoption of new voting-age population figures following the 1960 Census accounts for some of the decline in percentages from 1960 to 1962 experienced by several states. The 1962 totals appear in "Southern Voter Registration in the 1960s," *VEP News* 2 (April 1968): 3, and generally are adopted by Havard. The 1964 percentages reported here are those chosen by Havard, while slightly different ones are presented by Matthews and Prothro and by Claude. See *The Changing Politics of the South*, p. 20; *Negroes and the New Southern Politics*, p. 148; and *The Supreme Court and the Electoral Process*, p. 107. The actual registration totals labeled "1964" are those of the Voter Education Project, which reported that they dated from early November of that year. See *VEP News* 2 (April 1968): 3; Havard, *Changing Politics*, p. 20; and "Estimated Negro Voter Registration," *New South* 21 (Winter 1966): 88. The totals labeled "1965," and absent any accompanying percentages, come from the *New York Times*, 8 August 1965, which reported that they had been obtained from the Justice Department and the Civil Rights Commission and that they dated from late 1964 and, in some cases, early 1965. They also are adopted by Charles V. Hamilton in *The Bench and The Ballot: Southern Federal Judges and Black Voters* (New York: Oxford University Press, 1973), p. 238. The magnitude of the differences between some of these estimates— (e.g., Georgia) once again indicates how unreliable many of these guesses have been. No fully detailed accounting of and explanation for the 1962 to 1964 increases has yet been offered, though it seems clear that they were concentrated in urban areas and in the so-called peripheral states of the South. Nonetheless, as Matthews and Prothro wrote, "The causes of this sharp increase are difficult to untangle" (*Negroes and the New Southern Politics*, p. 18). On the early VEP role in the increase, see Pat Watters, "Negro Registration in the South," *New Republic* 150 (4 April 1964): 15-17.

tions, they went away from those sessions believing that an implicit understanding existed whereby in return for their stress upon registration drives, the federal government in turn would make efforts to assure the physical safety of those persons involved in such drives in dangerous areas of the South. Events soon disabused them of that belief.[55]

The major vehicle by which a number of the nationally constituted civil rights organizations pursued increased black registration in the hard-core areas of the Deep South was the Voter Education Project, formed in March 1962 under the wing of the Southern Regional Council. Throughout the next three years, the VEP bore much of the organizational burden of the voter registration effort in the South, and in turn it received a good deal of the credit for the substantial increase in southern black registration between mid-1962 and the latter part of 1964.

As Watters and Cleghorn, two journalists with close ties to the VEP, described it, "The voter campaigns from 1962 to 1964 were generally of two kinds—those that mainly battled white resistance, and those whose chief problem was called 'apathy' " on the part of local blacks.[56] The drives against resistance—those in the Black Belt counties of Louisiana, Mississippi, and southwest Georgia—received the most resources, despite day-to-day harassment and outright violence by local whites. The first major drives took place in the summer of 1963, with CORE in particular making a heavy effort in the parishes that made up Louisiana's Sixth Congressional District. In much of that area the movement workers often found their efforts opposed not only by local whites, who in some parishes revived the purge techniques of the late 1950s, but also by the more cautious elements within the local black leadership, which feared any open conflict with local whites. This division within the black community limited the results achieved in 1963, when CORE was able to obtain statewide a monthly average of only 150 new black registrants, and in the first five months of 1964, when only 942 black voters were added to Louisiana's registration rolls. A renewed effort in nine parishes in the summer of 1964 succeeded in registering only 1,070 new black voters.[57]

The greatest effort, in both resources and attention, was the 1964 Mississippi Freedom Summer, which had hardly began before three civil rights workers were murdered in Neshoba County. The 1964 summer effort was not formally a VEP effort, as that project had decided to shift its funds to more successful projects elsewhere after a large initial investment in Mississippi in 1962 and 1963 had produced less than 4,000 new black registrants.[58] Instead, officially headed by an amalgam of civil rights groups known as COFO, the largely SNCC staffed effort endured a summer of intense fear and only very limited success in terms of black voter registration gains. The bread-and-butter tactic of the workers, as Watters and Cleghorn relate so well, was door-to-door canvasing. By visiting individual's houses and cabins, and by in some cases assisting the residents with a variety of chores, the workers hoped to build up a degree of trust among the local black citizenry, which in turn would lead to increased attendance at voter education sessions held at local black churches. Once the intricacies of the registration process had been explained, the next, even more difficult step was to persuade several potential applicants to brave facing the registrar.[59]

In all but Panola County, the summer's efforts did not result in an appreciably large number of new black voters in Mississippi. As John Herbers of the *New York Times* wrote near the end of the summer, "There were few tangible results . . . toward giving Negroes more political power." In truth, the campaign, although written about extensively and pursued bravely, produced almost as many acts of violence by local whites as it did new black voters.[60] As Watters and Cleghorn related the tallies, the "Freedom Summer alone produced 35 shooting incidents with 3 persons injured; 30 homes and other buildings bombed; 35 churches burned; 80 persons beaten; [and] 3 other murders" in addition to those of Chaney, Schwerner, and Goodman.[61]

While perhaps the most notable offshoot of the summer was the Mississippi Freedom Democratic party and its challenge to the regular Mississippi delegation to the Democratic National Convention at Atlantic City,[62] the events of the summer also had served to sharpen the anger felt within the movement at the Justice Department's failure to protect visibly and aggressively the workers and their constitutional rights. While a number of movement leaders believed that an implicit promise of protection had been given them by the Kennedy administration, in Mississippi in 1964 they were confronted on virtually a daily basis with instances of FBI agents merely observing and taking notes of violations rather than moving to halt them on the spot. Only in the investigation of the Philadelphia triple murders and on two other occasions did the FBI and Justice move with the vigor the movement desired.[63]

While the antipathy felt within the movement towards the federal civil rights effort increased considerably throughout 1963 and 1964, Robert F. Kennedy, Burke Marshall, and those associated with them offered a somewhat academic and, in the movement's eyes, irrelevant explanation for Justice's lack of front-line involvement and protection. This explanation was rooted in the conception of "federalism" held by Kennedy and Marshall. Marshall voiced the practical effects of this doctrine at a lecture in early 1964: "The national effort is to realize the constitutional rights of Negroes in states where they are now denied, but to do so with the smallest possible federal intrusion into the conduct of state affairs."[64] Foremost of the "state affairs" was, it appeared, law enforcement. Active use of the FBI in protecting the rights of movement workers in the South, it was often said, would lead to the creation of something that no one was thought to desire, a "national police force." Although a number of observers harshly criticized the department's position, calling it "a philosophy of inaction, an ideology of impotence" and "an enlightened apology for the existing social order," it remained unchanged throughout 1963 and 1964, a source of increasingly bitter contention between the movement and the administration.[65]

At the same time, the Justice Department leadership was plagued by a developing problem that was more serious, in their estimation, than either the debate over protection or the difficulties involving access to registration records and the successful prosecution of economic retaliation cases. This greater problem centered around the substantial delays that many Justice Department suits against southern registration officials were experiencing in the federal district courts of the South.

The Justice Department first acknowledged its concern publicly in a politely worded comment issued late in the summer of 1962. "The time from the filing of the complaint to the submission of the case after a trial on the merits has become a serious problem in some jurisdictions," Burke Marshall wrote in his report for fiscal 1962. With the publication of what was to be an influential article on the subject in the November 1963 issue of the *Yale Law Journal*, the problem became a public and professional topic of concern.[66] The delays were centered in the courts of the Northern and Southern Districts of Mississippi, the Southern District of Alabama, and the Eastern and Western Districts of Louisiana. With little dissent, legal observers were quick to attribute the lengthy and unusual delays to the personal political and social views of the judges themselves, for, as Donald Strong put it, "The reliance on equity proceedings accentuates the importance of judicial bias."[67]

Five men whose dockets showed such judicial procrastination and intransigence in voting rights cases soon became the subject of repeated comment in both academic and popular publications. Certainly the most infamous of these recalcitrant federal district judges was William Harold Cox of Mississippi's Southern District. Quoted as having on one occasion called would-be black voters "chimpanzees" from the bench, Cox was involved in more than one dozen voting rights cases in which his conduct was ostentaciously hostile to the Justice Department and the black citizens involved.[68] Perhaps best known was *U.S.* v. *Lynd*, in which over the course of several years the Justice Department sought to end discriminatory registration practices employed by the Forrest County registrar, Theron Lynd. The department first asked to see Lynd's records in August 1960. Following his refusal, in January of 1961 the department petitioned Judge Cox for an order instructing Lynd to comply with the request forthwith, as required by title 3 of the 1960 Civil Rights Act. Cox took no action in response, and in July of 1961 the department filed a further request with him, asking that Lynd be enjoined from continuing certain discriminatory practices. Some seven months later, on February 15, 1962, Cox made his first response, when he dismissed the department's January 1961 request for Lynd's records on the grounds that the July complaint had superseded it. One month later Cox called up for trial the suit filed in July, for which the government had not yet received the necessary records from Lynd. As one might have expected, Cox found against the Justice Department when, lacking access to Lynd's records, the department was unable to meet Cox's demand for detailed evidence of discrimination on Lynd's part.[69]

Many additional such stories could be told about other cases handled by Cox and the four other district court judges whose records reflected outright hostility towards the Justice Department's efforts to win equal voting rights for black southerners through the federal courts: Daniel H. Thomas of Alabama's Southern District,[70] Claude F. Clayton of Mississippi's Northern District,[71] and E. Gordon West[72] and Benjamin Dawkins[73] of Louisiana's Eastern and Western Districts, respectively. More important, however, are the two common themes that run through most of those cases: first, the great degree to which the district judges' actions prevented any substantial judicially mandated expansion of southern blacks' voting rights by failing to halt most of the discrimination to which those citizens were subjected; second, what progress was achieved through the courts was largely the result of rulings issued by the Fifth Circuit Court of Appeals in reversing the actions of the district judges. The record of that appellate court was truly remarkable and was largely the result of the combined presence of four uncommon men: Elbert P. Tuttle, Richard T. Rives, John Minor Wisdom, and John R. Brown. As one attorney intimately involved in the voting rights struggle later wrote, "It was not until cases began reaching the Fifth Circuit that any significant enfranchisement occurred."[74]

The burgeoning controversy in the early years of the 1960s over the malperformance of these obstructive federal district court judges generated a substantial public discussion concerning how the blame for their appointments to the federal bench should be spread. Unfortunately for the incumbent administration, a predominant number of the obstructionists or segregationists had been appointed by the Kennedys. Most notable among these appointments were those of W. Harold Cox, whose long friendship with the Senate Judiciary Committee chairman, James O. Eastland, was widely assumed to have played a substantial role in his selection, and Louisiana's E. Gordon West, a close associate of Senator Russell Long.

All of these segregationist appointments were made within the first fifteen months of the Kennedy administration, and as time passed it became clear that the officials involved had learned from their mistakes and were both investigating prospective nominees' private views more intensively and putting less faith in blithe assurances of future impartiality on civil rights cases. In time, scholars and journalists who studied the circumstances of the early appointments and interviewed the participants concluded that at the outset the Kennedy staffers had been too eager to meet the wishes of southern senators and too naive in evaluating the statements of both the candidates and those who knew their previous records.[75]

While these initial errors were not repeated, the Kennedy administration's record of southern judicial appointments was viewed by friends and foes alike as one of its weakest performances, all the more so because of the administration's decisive choice of a litigative rather than a legislative strategy in the civil rights field. While the Justice Department filed scores of suits throughout the South aimed at securing the rights of black citizens, its overall strategy in effect was self-defeating, for more than one hundred of those suits were rejected by men that it had chosen for the southern federal bench. Within the department, the eventual reaction appeared to be one of "live and learn," coupled with a determination to persevere with the litigation, which in any case would be reviewable by the more receptive appellate judges.

As the Kennedy administration continued, legislative strategists slowly warmed to the proposition of making low-key, low-priority legislative requests in the voting rights field. In early 1962, a limited effort to achieve acceptance of a sixth-grade education as presumptive proof of literacy failed in the face of a Senate filibuster. Greater success was gained that year when Senator Spessard Holland achieved congressional approval of a constitutional amendment banning the poll tax in federal elections. Ratification by the required number of states was obtained within two years.[76] Late in February of 1963, John F. Kennedy sent to the Congress his first major message on voting rights. He emphasized both the "long and difficult" judicial delays experienced in the prosecution of a large number of voting suits and the widespread use of discriminatory registration procedures by many southern registrars. Reflecting his administration's strong belief in the importance of the franchise, Kennedy said: "The right to vote in a free American election is the most powerful and precious right in the world" and "a potent key to achieving other rights of citizenship."

The substantive proposals Kennedy outlined in the message were introduced in legislative form in early April, in a bill containing four major provisions. The first called for the appointment of temporary voting referees responsible to the local district court during the time in which a suit was being adjudicated if the locale in question had fewer than 15 percent of its minority voting-age population registered. The second called for the expedited handling of voting rights suits by special three-judge district courts. The third specified that registration standards be applied uniformly, that only written literacy tests be used, and that applications not be rejected because of minor errors. The fourth declared a sixth-grade education to be presumptive proof of literacy, the same provision that had been proposed the previous year.[77] Although five months later the Kennedy administration greatly expanded its legislative requests concerning civil rights, no substantive changes were made at that time in the voting rights provisions proposed in the early spring. A little more than one year later, on July 2, 1964, the last three of the four Kennedy proposals were enacted into law as title 1 of the Civil Rights Act of 1964. The proposal for temporary referees had been dropped because of Republican opposition.

Although all observers regarded the 1964 act as a landmark law because of its provisions regarding public accommodations and federal funding of schools, at the same time no one denied that its voting rights provisions represented no real change from the judicial approach to enforcement specified in the 1957 and 1960 acts. Even in the substantive specifics of title 1, the 1964 law did little more than codify as statutes doctrines that had already been applied in a number of cases by rulings of the Fifth Circuit Court of Appeals. Hence, like its two predecessors, the 1964 act's voting provisions came under heavy fire from those who argued that the judicial approach to voting rights enforcement was both inefficient and ultimately ineffective. No real improvement, it was asserted, would result from the enactment of the 1964 act's voting provisions. In any event, "before they were tested, a rush of events overtook the voting provisions of the 1964 Act."[78]

Despite the continuing criticisms of the judicial approach to voting rights enforcement, other observers defended the effectiveness of the approach embodied in the 1957, 1960, and 1964 acts. More often than not, they relied heavily upon the record compiled by one southern federal district judge, a man whose aggressive and forthright handling of voting suits led one newsweekly to call him "the foremost champion of voting rights on the southern bench": Frank M. Johnson, Jr., of Alabama's Middle District, sitting in Montgomery.[79] Any account of Johnson's record in the voting rights cases must focus upon both his dogged oversight of the continuing conduct of registrars whose previous practices had led the Justice Department to bring them before Johnson's court, and to the trailblazing role he played in assuring that the real standards applied to past white registrants would be applied to future black applicants until the effects of the earlier discriminatory registration practices had been erased, a procedure that came to be termed "freezing" relief.

Johnson's close and continuing attention to registrars' practices once he initially had commanded them to end discrimination was best reflected in his handling of early suits brought against the registrars of Macon and Bullock counties. The Macon County case, which had begun in 1959 only to be terminated by the resignation of the registrars, was resumed after the passage of the 1960 act and the appointment of a new board of registrars, which approved only ten black applicants in its first seven months. After a trial in early 1961, Johnson quickly entered a "pattern or practice" finding and ordered the registration of sixty-four rejected black applicants whom he had reexamined personally.[80] He followed that up with detailed orders to the registrars concerning the standards to be applied to applicants, and he ordered that monthly reports be made to him.

The Bullock County case was tried shortly after the Macon one, and Johnson again entered a "pattern or practice" finding. As in the Macon case, rather than to appoint a referee, Johnson chose to maintain a close personal supervision of the registrars' conduct. The Bullock registrars proved less cooperative than those from Macon, and throughout 1961 and into early 1962 their less than complete compliance required Johnson's attention. By midsummer of 1962, however, the Civil Rights Division, in a report that otherwise reflected only the delays visited upon its litigation by hostile registrars and judges, was able to crow about how black registration had increased in Macon from 256 to 1,856 and in Bullock from 5 to 915 as a result of Johnson's orders and monitoring.[81]

More important, in the Bullock case Johnson also ordered the registrars *not* to apply strict interpretations of standards to *all* present applicants, as they were doing in place of the racially discriminatory standards employed in the past. Such a shift, Johnson emphasized correctly, merely would serve to continue to exclude from the rolls black citizens whose qualifications were equal or superior to those of some whites who had been registered under the previously lax standards applied to that race. Johnson enlarged upon this reasoning in the Montgomery County case of *U.S.* v. *Penton*, decided in 1962. Future black applicants, he ordered, must be evaluated not in line with the qualifications laid down in state law, but according to the *real* standards applied to white applicants in the past, standards the records revealed were very loose compared to those specified in the statutes.[82] Applying the real standards of the past meant that not only would discrimination be eliminated, but that a serious attempt would be made to erase the effects of past discrimination by requiring black citizens to meet only those conditions previously imposed upon whites and not more demanding ones. This doctrine of "freezing," perhaps the most important product of the voting litigation of the early 1960s, was also employed in several important later appellate court rulings.[83]

While those who endorsed the judicial approach to voting rights enforcement—and who doubtless realized that four sympathetic appellate judges could not hope to make up fully for the malperformance of so many district judges—have relied heavily upon Frank Johnson's record to support their views, they have also on occasion cited the eventual outcomes of two particular suits—*U.S.* v. *Louisiana* and *U.S.* v. *Mississippi*—to buttress their position.[84] In each case the Justice Department challenged the legality of certain state-imposed voter qualifications. In *Louisiana*, filed in December 1961, the department sought to have the state's constitutional interpretation test declared unconstitutional on the grounds that its purpose and its effect were racially discriminatory and that it violated the Fourteenth and Fifteenth Amendments. In the *Mississippi* case, filed nine months later, the department challenged on the same grounds that state's four new voter qualifications enacted in April 1962. The importance of these two cases lay in the fact that of all the suits the department had brought, only they applied to voting limitations in an entire state, instead of merely one county or parish. Their potential impact thus was far greater.

However, the litigation of each case took approximately three years. In addition, although the special three-judge district court that heard the *Louisiana* case struck down the challenged constitutional interpretation test, the state legislature soon replaced that particular statute with another of similar purpose and effect. Hence, as Armand Derfner has written, "the ability of the Southern states to stay one step ahead of federal law" effectively emasculated the impact of a *Louisiana* style suit. When the Supreme Court in March 1965 finally upheld the initial ruling in *Louisiana* and reversed a three-judge court's ruling in the *Mississippi* case that had gone against the Justice Department, the impact of those decisions, state statutory changes aside, was mooted by simultaneous developments discussed in chapter 2.[85]

While the practical effect of the *Louisiana* and *Mississippi* cases was in the end virtually nil for blacks desiring the vote, to argue that defenders of the record of voting rights enforcement achieved by the federal courts between 1957 and 1965 are without solid grounds is not to demean the admirable accomplishments of Judge Johnson and the Fifth Circuit Court of Appeals. What it does do is to stress the unavoidable limitations of scope within which those men operated.

Those who, like this author, have concluded that the "overall progress" achieved through civil suits brought under the voting provisions of the 1957, 1960, and 1964 Civil Rights Acts "proved disappointing" have advanced a number of explanations for this failure.[86] As we have seen, perhaps the most popular of these centered on the malperformance of the majority of southern federal district court judges before whom any appreciable number of voting suits were brought.[87] Often the criticism of the conduct of these men has been coupled with references to related shortcomings for which others bore responsibility, such as the discretionary nature of the relief provided by the 1957 and 1960 acts,[88] or with mention of problems that appeared unavoidable, such as the necessity of prosecuting discriminatory registration practices on a time- and resource-consuming county-by-county basis and the inherent difficulty of securing convincing proof of 1971(b) economic retaliation violations.[89] Others, such as Chief Judge Elbert P. Tuttle of the Fifth Circuit Court of Appeals, focused the blame not so much on those who staffed the district courts as on those who were brought before them. Defendants who employed every possible means for delaying the enforcement of what previous statutes and rulings had indicated clearly was the law not only forced a profusion of suits, such as those seeking registration records, but also significantly postponed enforcement. Delay was important, for in voting and elections, as Tuttle observed, "time is what counts."[90]

Those who have defended the record of judicial enforcement have admitted that the process was far from perfect, and certainly not speedy, but have still sought to stress the positive.[91] At times this tendency has been carried too far, as when Charles V. Hamilton wrote late in 1965, "As a general rule it must be conceded that most of the Southern district judges have done a good job of enforcing the rights of

Negroes.'' Even eight years later, in reviewing the same material, Hamilton was to write, "Many of the apprehensions toward utilizing the federal courts were not justified."[92] Unfortunately, at the district court level, beyond the record of Judge Johnson and the occasional actions of less involved judges such as Louisiana's Herbert Christenberry and Florida's Bryan Simpson, who dealt more with demonstrations than with voting suits,[93] the supporting evidence for Hamilton's claims is weak.

Most persuasive is some evidence that Hamilton did not consider when surveying the possible objections to the judicial enforcement record: the actual effects, direct or indirect, that the profusion of suits in the early 1960s had upon black registration levels in the three states in which the great majority of them were filed—Alabama, Louisiana, and Mississippi.[94] Those effects can be examined at three different levels. First would be an accounting of new black voters registered *directly* as a result of judicial action. In several instances, one of which we noted in discussing Judge Johnson, judges themselves ordered the registration of specific black citizens. All told, however, the actual number of individuals added to the voting rolls in this fashion barely exceeded 1,000, and the great majority were added by one decree issued by Johnson in the *Penton* case.[95] The major provision for such judicially mandated registrations, the referee provision of the 1960 act, went virtually unused by the courts. Only two referees appear to have ever been appointed, and they recommended the registration of no more than several hundred new voters.[96] Two writers were guilty of understatement when they wrote in later years that the referee scheme had proved "ineffective."[97]

Second, one could look at the total registration gains made in counties that were the target of voting suits, for developments in several, such as Macon and Bullock, showed that properly pursued suits could induce local officials to register substantial numbers of new black voters themselves. As Hamilton correctly put it, "All the results of the judicial approach need not come from specific action of the judges alone."[98] However, the figures produced in such a county-level examination show limited increases. Two different sources report that in the forty-six counties or parishes against which a total of seventy voting suits were brought, between 1957 and 1965 only 37,146 new black voters were registered out of a black voting-age population of 548,358. That represents a total gain resulting from all possible influences, and not simply the judicial process, of fewer than 850 new black voters per county.[99]

A third measure of the impact of judicial action is the change in overall registration totals and percentages in the three states in which a total of more than four dozen voting suits were filed. Although different sources report slightly different figures, the overall picture is clear: while, as we noted previously, the South in the early 1960s registered a notable increase in the number of black registrants in urban areas and in the "peripheral" states of the region, no significant increase in black registration occurred between 1957 and 1965 in the three hard-core states of Alabama, Louisiana, and Mississippi against which the Justice Department brought the great majority of its voting suits. Chief Justice Warren, writing in 1966, observed that the percentage of voting-age blacks registered in Alabama had increased only from 14.2 in 1958 to 19.4 in 1964, while in Mississippi and Louisiana the gains had been even more limited: from 4.4 in 1954 to 6.4 in 1964 in Mississippi, and from 31.7 in 1956 to 31.8 in 1965 in Louisiana. Looking back at the impact of the voting rights provisions of the 1957, 1960, and 1964 acts with those statistics in mind, it is not at all surprising that the Chief Justice observed that these "laws have done little to cure the problem of voting discrimination."[100]

The conclusion that the judicial approach to voting rights enforcement proved ineffective is unavoidable. In the absence of judges such as Frank M. Johnson, Jr., the judicial process lacked the "coercive capabilities" necessary for ensuring any meaningful progress in the elimination of racial discrimination in the electoral process.[101] As one commentator phrased it, "Eight years of litigation provided the most persuasive argument that adjudication and court-ordered enforcement tools could not ensure extensive registration."[102] In 1965, however, the adjudicative approach to enforcement was put aside suddenly and supplanted by a new approach which bypassed the courts and shifted the responsibility for voting rights progress to the federal executive branch. "The patience of the nation with the judicial process ran out in Selma, Alabama."[103]

2 Selma and the
Voting Rights Act:
Commencement and Climax

In April 1961, Selma, Alabama, was an inconspicuous city in the heart of the Black Belt. Blacks comprised approximately half of the voting-age population of Dallas County, within which Selma was situated, but only 156 of them, out of 15,000 or so, were registered voters, and only fourteen had been added to the rolls since 1954. Such circumstances had drawn the attention of the Justice Department, and it had charged the Dallas County registrar, J. P. Majors, with employing racially discriminatory procedures and requested access to his registration records. Several weeks later, in May 1961, Majors resigned. Nine months after that, Judge Daniel H. Thomas ordered Majors's three successors, led by Victor B. Atkins, to turn over the registration records to the Justice Department's representatives. Three months later, in May 1962, Thomas called up for trial the case the department had filed thirteen months earlier. Black registration, the trial revealed, now stood at 242 in Dallas County, as the new board of registrars had approved the applications of 71 of the 114 black applicants who had appeared since June of 1961. Six months after the trial, in November 1962, Thomas issued his decision. He denied the Justice Department's request for relief, holding that while discrimination had been practiced by previous registrars, none appeared to have existed since the current board had taken over in mid-1961. Although Thomas did instruct the registrars to allow rejected applicants to reapply after sixty days, he devoted more of his opinion to advising the Justice Department that it should not waste its time on such cases.[1]

While the Justice Department was appealing to the Fifth Circuit Court of Appeals, two young Student Nonviolent Coordinating Committee workers, Bernard and Colia Lafayette, came to Selma in February 1963 to begin a voter education effort.[2] Throughout the spring their monthly Dallas County Voters' League clinics drew an average of forty people, and by mid-June they were able to draw seven hundred to a mass rally at which James Bevel of the Southern Christian Leadership Conference spoke. But such activity soon aroused the strong local chapter of the Citizens' Council, as well as the county sheriff, James G. Clark, Jr. The Lafayettes and their associates were subjected to a series of harassing arrests, and on June 26 the Justice Department filed a request for an ex parte restraining order against Sheriff Clark and the other officials involved, who had begun sending officers to observe the league's meetings as well. Judge Thomas denied the request that same day, and his ruling was upheld by the appeals court the following day. In an atmosphere of heightened fear of economic retaliation from the local whites upon whom so many Selma blacks were dependent, attendance at early July voters' clinics declined dramatically, and they soon were discontinued. The actual trial of the federal government's complaint against Clark began on July 25, but Thomas then delayed further proceedings for several months. Not long thereafter, the Lafayettes, as scheduled, departed from Selma, leaving behind an organized group of black young people and a black businesswoman with an active interest in the movement, Mrs. Amelia Boynton.

Following the arrival in September of a new SNCC representative, Worth Long, some of the youngsters initiated a lunch-counter sit-in, and their arrests were followed by a protest march and additional arrests. Later in the month other SNCC staffers, James Forman and John Lewis, arrived, and the focus of the emerging campaign shifted to voting rights. By early October the total of arrests had climbed to some three hundred, and on October 7 the campaign climaxed in a Freedom Day in which three hundred blacks lined up at the Dallas County courthouse in downtown Selma to register to vote. With four FBI agents and two Justice Department attorneys looking on, Sheriff Clark and his deputies harassed the applicants and prevented workers from bringing them food and water. A mass meeting followed that evening, and the next day SNCC's Atlanta headquarters sent out to northern supporters an "action memo" requesting them to telegraph the Justice Department, the president, and the Civil Rights Commission asking for federal marshalls, court action against Sheriff Clark, and the arrest of local officials guilty of obstructing the right to register and vote. Recipients were urged further to picket federal buildings, to request their local newspapers to provide coverage of the story, and to write their congressmen and ask them to speak out on the issue of voting rights. Despite this plea, however, the campaign petered out almost immediately.[3]

In the midst of this effort, on September 30, the Fifth Circuit Court of Appeals reversed Judge Thomas's decision of a year earlier in the *Atkins* case, ruling that he had abused his discretion by not granting the requested injunction against the Dallas County registrars. No grounds existed, Circuit Judge Richard T. Rives wrote, for denying an injunction against illegal conduct merely because that conduct appeared to have been discontinued. Rives's opinion specified the contents of the order Thomas was directed to enter: that the registration questionnaire not be used as a test or examination, that no oral questions be used, and that no application be rejected because of minor errors or omissions. On November 1 Thomas complied with Rives's directive.[4]

In the meantime, however, the Justice Department on October 8 had filed a mandamus action against Judge Thomas concerning his failure to proceed with the trial of the complaint against the county law-enforcement officials, which had begun in July. One week later Thomas reconvened the proceeding, and five months after that, in March 1964, he handed down his decision, finding that the evidence failed to establish that Sheriff Clark or any others had been guilty of any conduct that warranted injunctive relief in making the repeated arrests in June.[5]

In mid-November 1963, one month after the trial, the Justice Department moved for a temporary restraining order to prohibit Sheriff Clark, state circuit judge James Hare, state circuit solicitor Blanchard McLeod, and the Dallas County Citizens' Council from interfering with the voting rights of black citizens or attempting to intimidate black voter applicants. As part of this request, the department sought to have vacated subpoenas issued for several Justice Department attorneys by a local grand jury acting under Hare's and McLeod's direction which was seeking to investigate allegations that the Reverend Martin Luther King, Jr., had been driven from Birmingham to a Selma speaking engagement on October 15 in a Justice Department car. Thomas rejected the request for such an ex parte order on November 13 and promptly was reversed the following afternoon by the court of appeals. Following the entrance of that order, Thomas held four days of hearings in December on the matter of granting a temporary injunction against McLeod, Clark, and Hare in regard to their alleged use of official powers to harass both the Justice Department attorneys and black applicants for registration. In a decision entered the following March, Thomas found no abuse of powers had taken place. He denied the request for an injunction against the local officials and dissolved the temporary restraining order issued earlier by the appellate court.[6]

While no organized civil rights activities apart from weekly mass meetings were conducted in Selma in the first half of 1964, both discriminatory registration practices and voting rights litigation continued. In March the Justice Department moved to have the county registrars cited for contempt of the November 1, 1963 order, though Thomas, true to form, did not hold hearings on the request until November.[7] After the enactment of the Civil Rights Act of 1964 on July 2, however, civil rights activity soon reappeared in Selma. Stimulated by the act's public accommodations provision, on July 4 several blacks attempted to attend a previously all-white theater and were attacked by whites. Police did not come to their aid. However, four blacks who attempted to desegregate a restaurant were arrested on trespassing charges. The next day a voter registration rally was held, and after it Sheriff Clark's deputies and his volunteer "posse" used nightsticks and tear gas on a crowd of blacks who, they alleged, had been throwing stones. SNCC worker John Love denied that accusation and stated that the deputies had attacked the crowd without provocation. Newsmen and photographers were attacked by the lawmen as well and were then ordered out of town by Solicitor McLeod.

The following day, July 6, some fifty blacks led by SNCC's John Lewis went to the courthouse in search of the registrars. They were arrested by Clark's heavily armed men, who freely used electric cattle prods on their prisoners as they were marched off to jail. With that group in custody events slowed on July 7 and 8, but on the ninth, state circuit judge Hare issued an injunction that named some four dozen blacks and fifteen organizations forbidding public gathering of more than three people [...] n days to have that inju [...] continued enforcement in [...] kly Monday night ma[...] in mid-September on [...] ice again months passed [...] aimed at having the cas [...] o federal court were also [...] rtment in early Septembe [...] ate judge Bernard Reyno[...] ree-judge district court. [...] sion was entered until w[...]

Although Jud [...] vil rights activities in Sel[...] ecoming interested in the [...] isely, its impulsive count [...] in which blacks' voting r [...] f federal litigation. By la [...] were registered in Dallas County, and as the Justice Department's John Doar wrote, even though "the litigation method of correction has been tried harder here than anywhere else in the South," Dallas County blacks still had not been provided with "the most fundamental of their constitutional rights—the right to vote."[9]

[handwritten annotation:] Blacks attend all-white theater, attacked by whites, Police did not help (July 4, 1964) pg. 34 Garrow

Foremost among those attuned to the dismal voting rights situation in Selma were the Reverend Martin Luther King, Jr., and his associates in the Southern Christian Leadership Conference. The SCLC had considered making an effort in Selma earlier in the year, but had chosen to concentrate on St. Augustine, Florida instead. By early November, however, Dr. King was saying,

> We will probably have demonstrations in the very near future in Alabama and Mississippi based around the right to vote. We hope that through this process we can bring the necessary moral pressure to bear on the federal government to get federal registrars appointed in those areas, as well as to get federal marshalls in those places to escort Negroes to the registration places if necessary.[10]

Exactly when the SCLC staff chose Selma as its specific initial target remains unclear, but details of the Alabama voting rights campaign were dealt with in staff meetings during the week of November 9 and again at subsequent meetings in Birmingham in either late November or early December. By the time that King's briefcase was stolen in Anniston, Alabama, however, the plans it contained, which were circulated among Alabama officials, were sufficiently specific to alert the newly hired Selma public safety director, Wilson Baker.

Baker, a former Selma city police captain who had lost a race against Sheriff Clark in 1958 and had gone to teach law enforcement at the University of Alabama at Tuscaloosa, had been brought back to Selma and installed in the new position by Selma's newly elected young mayor, Joseph T. Smitherman, who hoped to replace the hard-line segregationist stance of his predecessor, Chris Heinz, with a lower-key defense of segregation that would not undercut his efforts to attract new industry to the area. By hiring Baker, Smitherman hoped that Sheriff Clark and the tactics Clark had employed against civil rights activists in the two previous years would be less in evidence in Selma in 1965.

Upon learning of King's plans to bring the SCLC to Selma, the businesslike Baker flew to Washington to request Assistant Attorney General Burke Marshall to use his influence to get King to delay his effort or to take his drive elsewhere. As Baker recalled it in later years, Marshall called King, with Baker still in his office, and talked to the SCLC president for some twenty minutes. At the conclusion of the conversation, Marshall reported to Baker that King had said the SCLC had invested too much time and effort in its Selma plans to change course now.[11]

While King continued to speak out in general terms about the problem of voting rights enforcement in the South, a subject which he raised during a meeting on the poverty program with President Johnson on December 18, the SCLC planners were not the only ones looking ahead on the voting rights front.[12] Within the Justice Department thought was being given to whether additional legislative action was necessary to speed up the enforcement of southern blacks' right to vote. Some confusion exists concerning just when consideration of new voting rights proposals was first initiated within the Johnson administration. While some officials were aware of the possible need for new voting rights legislation before the 1964 election,[13] Lyndon Johnson himself was to recall later that soon after the election he had directed Attorney General Nicholas Katzenbach to begin drafting a voting rights measure. Presidential advisor Eric F. Goldman, in his later account, wrote that the instructions had been transmitted in "mid-1964," and that "the assignment was long-range and was to be kept out of the press," for fear that news of it would aid Republican candidate Goldwater in the South. Goldman went on to say that Johnson did not intend to bring up the matter of voting rights in the Eighty-ninth Congress in 1965; he wanted the South to have time to "digest" the 1964 act and feared harm to other legislation in the Senate if he moved for further civil rights legislation in 1965. Recently, an account very similar to Goldman's has been put forward by Johnson biographer Doris Kearns.

> Johnson's sense of timing told him that after the struggle over the Civil Rights Act of 1964, 1965 was not a propitious year to press for more civil rights proposals. He felt that the American people wanted an intermission, a period without renewed conflict, in order to assimilate the political and social impact of the earlier bill. The agencies involved in matters of civil rights wanted time for orderly incorporation of the new people and bureaus and their responsibilities. The Congress wanted time to heal the wounds of division.

Although Johnson instructed Katzenbach in January to prepare voting rights legislation, "no action was expected until the spring of 1966."[14]

While one memorandum written in preparation for the State of the Union and Inaugural addresses supports the positions advanced by Goldman and Kearns (and may well have influenced their accounts), other documentary materials dating from late 1964 paint a very different picture.[15] Johnson's own subsequent assertions that he had requested the Justice Department to begin studying possible legislative proposals concerning voting rights soon after the election is born out by the drafting within the Justice Department in mid-December of a memorandum first sent to Attorney General Katzenbach and then forwarded by him to the president. Completed on December 18 by Harold H. Greene, the chief of the Civil Rights Division's Appeals and Research Section, the memo outlined three alternative "major legislative proposals" which, it emphasized, "must necessarily be considered within the constitutional framework." Most preferable of these three, Greene wrote, was a constitutional amendment prohibiting states from imposing any voting qualification or disqualification other than age, less than two-month's or three-month's residency, a felony conviction, or commitment to a mental institution. While calling it "the most drastic but probably the most effective of all the alternatives," the memo noted that the ratification process was "cumbersome" and could be blocked by the legislatures of only thirteen states.

> It is difficult to estimate the extent of the opposition to this kind of constitutional amendment. In addition to resistance from the South, there may be opposition from sources genuinely concerned about federal interference with a fundamental matter traditionally left to the States. One possible alternative—to follow the poll-tax amendment precedent and limit the reach of the new amendment to federal elections—would tend to decrease the magnitude of the opposition, but it would also impair the effectiveness of the measure.

A second and less preferable legislative proposal, the Civil Rights Division felt, would be "legislation vesting in a federal commission the power to conduct registration for federal elections." Such a body could be either the Civil Service Commission or a new board, and it might be advisable to utilize U.S. postmasters to serve as the actual federal registration officials. While there would be "no substantial constitutional problem" with this approach, the memo went on,

> Opposition to this proposal from Republican quarters may be of two kinds. One faction may argue that such legislation constitutes an unwarranted interference with a state function and provides potential for federal dictatorial control of the electoral process. Others may be expected to espouse the view that the proposal does not go far enough: that it should cover state and local elections as well as federal elections. The first type of opposition can be countered by pointing to the desirability of doing something direct and effective to stimulate voting and combat discrimination. The selection of an impeccably non-partisan body [as the overseeing commission] may also help to alleviate this kind of opposition. The second type of opposition may be met by stressing the constitutional problems,

questions of public policy, and probably loss of legislative support, which would be involved in any proposal for complete federal administrative control of the state registration process.

The third, and least desirable, proposal in the memo called for

legislation granting to an agency of the federal government the power to assume direct control of registration for voting in both federal and state elections in any area where the percentage of potential Negro registrants actually registered is low.

This approach would quickly provide political power to Negroes in proportion to their actual numbers in areas in which they are now disenfranchised. On the other hand, its effect on general voter apathy would be relatively minimal. Among the other objections to this suggestion is that it would recall to members of the Congress a somewhat similar proposal made by President Kennedy as part of the 1963 civil rights bill and rejected because of the opposition of Cong. McCulloch and others. Moreover, its constitutionality is more dubious than that of the preceding suggestion.[16]

That top administration officials were planning in late December 1964 for the presentation of new voting rights legislation early in 1965 is explicitly substantiated by a memo from presidential counsel Lee C. White to Bill Moyers, a Johnson aide, on December 30, two days after Katzenbach had forwarded the Greene memorandum to the president.

If I understood our conversation of the other day correctly, the President has indicated a desire to move forward early next year with a legislative proposal authorizing a Commission to appoint federal officers to serve as registrars for the purpose of registering individuals for federal elections [the second possibility outlined in the Justice Department memorandum].

Certainly I have absolutely no problem with the desirability of such legislation, but I do have a problem about the timing and the approach. This particular proposal is obviously aimed at the problem of racial discrimination in voter registration, and accordingly, will bear the label of civil rights legislation. It seems to me that there are two special burdens attached to such a request at this time: (a) The Civil Rights Act of 1964 is less than a year old and presumably the Congress would have enacted any bill that the President would have requested—in fact, it did have a "voting" title in it; (b) This will be one more proposal when the score sheet is totalled at the end of the year and I would assume that the prospects are not particularly good.[17]

It occurs to me that a slightly modified approach may meet the needs of the situation as well without the foregoing disadvantages. The President could in a speech or statement call attention to the importance of registration and indicate that 1965 was to be a year of test and if there were not any substantial improvements he would feel it desirable for the Congress to consider legislation along these lines in 1966. Presumably this could be done in time for the 1966 elections when there is a greater interest in the registration and voting process.[18]

While administration sentiment at the end of 1964 indicated a definite intention to move ahead with voting rights legislation in early 1965, despite Counsel White's demurral, at the same time Dr. King was completing the final plans to begin the SCLC effort in Selma. In late December, a Committee of Fifteen, formed under the auspices of the Dallas County Voters' League and representing all factions within the black community of Selma, issued a formal invitation to Dr. King to bring his SCLC staff to Selma to assist them in winning the right to register and vote. On December 28, after conferring with other civil rights leaders in Montgomery, the SCLC leadership announced that Dr. King would kick off the campaign with a speech in Selma on the evening of Saturday, January 2. It would be the first mass meeting of Selma's blacks in almost six months. The drive, press reports indicated, was expected to last about half a year. Andrew Young, a King aide, was quoted as saying that Selma was the "most oppressive" city in the South. City officials had made it known, however, that Judge Hare's injunction against civil rights meetings, still pending before Judge Thomas, would no longer be enforced.[19]

On January 2, King arrived in Selma and spoke that evening to some seven hundred blacks gathered in Brown's Chapel African Methodist Episcopal Church. Massive street demonstrations, King told his listeners, would be held if Dallas County did not begin to register its black citizens in large numbers. If appeals to Alabama Governor George C. Wallace and the state legislature went unheeded, King continued, "we will seek to arouse the federal government by marching by the thousands by the places of registration." If that in turn did not succeed, there would be another massive March on Washington "to appeal to the conscience of the Congress." Selma, King stated, had been chosen "for the opening of the drive because it has become a symbol of bitter-end resistance to the civil rights movement in the Deep South." Sheriff Clark was out of town at the Orange Bowl, but the meeting had been both guarded and monitored by city police under Baker's direction. Following a strategy session at the home of Mrs. Boynton, King announced to the press that the drive would concentrate on the larger towns in ten of Alabama's Black Belt counties. It would not fully commence, however, for a week or more so as not to divert press attention from the MFDP challenge to the Mississippi congressional delegation which would take place as the Eighty-ninth Congress opened.[20]

While King was not to return to Selma until January 14, planning by all parties went ahead. In Selma Baker and Smitherman continued their efforts to ensure that Baker, and not Clark, would be in charge of handling the demonstrations when they did occur. This, they believed, was essential to prevent the national newsmen attracted by King's involvement from witnessing Clark's active hostility toward protesting blacks. King and his associates, Baker and Smitherman believed, were hoping that Clark would once again behave as he had in the past. Clark himself, supported by Judge Hare, opposed any diminution of his own role, and the efforts of white moderates, such as the Reverend Ralph Smeltzer, to gain concessions from the county registration board prior to any demonstrations proved unsuccessful.

In Selma's black community a number of SCLC staff members, such as James Bevel and James Orange, continued organizing efforts in preparation for the demonstrations to come. The first step, King's confidant Andrew Young said, was to get large numbers of blacks to the courthouse on registration days, which generally occurred on only the first and third Mondays of each month. "We want to establish in the mind of the nation," Young said, "that a lot of people who want to register are prevented from doing so. We hope this will lead to a revision of the voter registration laws in this state. We feel that action is needed in the courts and in the streets."[21]

In Washington, President Johnson on January 4 delivered his State of the Union address. The seventh item from the top on Johnson's list of domestic conditions in need of government attention concerned voting. "I propose that we eliminate every remaining obstacle to the right and the opportunity to vote." Later in the speech he again spoke of the need to achieve "elimination of barriers to the right to vote" and added that in the next six weeks he would "submit special messages with detailed proposals" in each of the areas of domestic concern.[22]

Two days later there appeared on the front page of the *Washington Post* the first public indication that the administration did intend to move ahead with voting rights legislation in 1965. Johnson, the story said, was "expected to submit to Congress a proposed constitutional amendment that would ban literacy tests as a voter qualification throughout the

United States," in other words, the first proposal that the Justice Department memo of December had outlined. "Sources also said," *Post*
reporter Robert E. Baker went on, "that the White House is considering
legislation to provide federal registrars in Deep South areas as a stopgap
measure to help qualified Negroes register pending approval and ratification of the constitutional amendment," something the earlier administration documents had not mentioned as a possibility. Baker went on to say
that either the federal registrar legislation or the constitutional amendment or both might eventually be proposed. "Winning congressional
approval of either proposal or both," his story went on, voicing an
estimation quite similar to that of Lee White several days earlier, "may
require all the persuasion the President can muster. Many Congressmen
thought no further legislation would be asked until the effectiveness of
the 1964 Civil Rights Act had been thoroughly tested." The present
consideration of voting rights legislation, Baker added, was a reflection of Johnson's "concern over the slow pace in clearing the way for
qualified Negroes to vote," a concern the president reportedly had expressed to Dr. King at their December meeting. "It is reported,"
Baker concluded, that Johnson had "told Dr. King that qualified Negroes who are rebuffed by state registrars should be able to register with
Federal registrars."[23]

On January 8, two days after Baker's story appeared, the Justice
Department completed the draft of a proposed constitutional amendment. Section 1 of the proposal stated:

> The right of citizens of the United States to vote shall not be denied
> or abridged by the United States or by any State for any cause
> except (1) inability to meet residence requirements not exceeding
> sixty days or minimum age requirements, imposed by State law; (2)
> conviction of a felony for which no pardon or amnesty has been
> granted; (3) mental incompetency adjudicated by a court of record;
> or (4) confinement pursuant to the judgment or warrant of a court of
> record at the time of registration or election.

Section 2 specified that the Congress would have the power to enforce
the provisions of section 1 with "appropriate legislation," and the third
and last section noted that the amendment must be ratified by the legislatures of no less than three-quarters of the states within seven years of
congressional passage.[24]

Three days later, in its first weekly Report on Legislation compiled in
1965, the Justice Department reported to the White House:

Draft legislation is being prepared in the Civil Rights Division to implement the President's State of the Union Message remarks with respect to the elimination of barriers to the right to vote. These include a constitutional amendment to prohibit the states from prescribing certain qualifications for voting (including literacy tests) and legislation to provide for Federal registrars to register persons for voting in Federal elections.[25]

In Selma on Thursday evening, January 14, King told a crowd of eight hundred blacks that testing of the public accommodations provisions of the 1964 Civil Rights Act would begin in town on Monday and would be coupled with a gathering at the courthouse for the purpose of making applications to the county registrars. On the following day, the Justice Department filed suit in Montgomery against Alabama's statewide registration test, charging that its difficult standards violated the provisions of title 1 of the 1964 act. By Sunday the seventeenth King's aides were saying that the Selma city administration had assured them that no arrests would be made on Monday at the courthouse gathering and that protection would be given to peaceful attempts to register and desegregate. Sheriff Clark, they said, had been told not to interfere.[26]

On Monday morning seven Selma restaurants were "tested" successfully, and Dr. King and John Lewis of SNCC led some four hundred blacks in the drive's first march to the courthouse in downtown Selma, several blocks from the movement's headquarters at Brown's Chapel. While outside the courthouse, King was approached by several of the right-wing figures who had come to town, such as the head of the States Rights party, J.B. Stoner, and the Nazi party chairman, George Lincoln Rockwell. After a peaceful wait at the courthouse during which Sheriff Clark made the applicants stand in a back alley and no one was registered, Dr. King and his assistants went to the nearby Albert Hotel and registered as its first black guests. In the lobby one of the transient fascists, James Robinson, briefly assaulted King and managed to land one punch before being subdued by Wilson Baker.

Following a rally at Brown's Chapel later that evening, King held a staff meeting at the Albert. According to later reports, the SCLC staff expressed "disappointment" that Sheriff Clark had remained peaceful that morning. They decided to hold another march to the courthouse the next day. If Sheriff Clark again failed to display his expected hostility, they would then shift the drive's focus to the nearby towns of Marion and Camden. That same evening, though, Clark expressed his anger at the position in which Baker and Smitherman were trying to keep him, and the two men became anxious that the next day would fail to be as peaceful.[27] In Washington that Monday the Justice Department had informed the White House that the constitutional amendment had been prepared and that a completed draft of the legislation providing for federal registrars to accept voters for federal elections would be ready early the next week. A presidential message on the subject was also being drafted.[28]

On Tuesday, January 19, in Selma the SCLC obtained the response from the sheriff that it had sought. When the marchers reached the courthouse, they refused to be herded into the alley in which they had spent the previous day. Clark then ordered the group off of the courthouse sidewalk, and when a local leader, Mrs. Amelia Boynton, was slow to move, the sheriff, as the next day's *New York Times* described it, "grabbed her by the back of her collar and pushed her roughly for half a block into a patrol car," which took her to the jail. King, watching the incident from a car across the street, got out and entered the federal building, which was situated directly across from the county courthouse, to ask the Justice Department representative to take court action against Sheriff Clark. The incident was, King later said to the press, "one of the most brutal and unlawful acts I have seen an officer commit." The following morning the *Times* ran a photograph of the incident on page 18, and the *Washington Post* on page 10.

In the aftermath of the scuffle, Clark's deputies arrested sixty seven marchers for refusing to go into the designated alley. That evening another rally was held in Brown's Chapel, and later that night an SCLC staff meeting concluded that the pace of the campaign should be stepped up the next day in light of the success they had enjoyed with Clark. Plans were also discussed for a "freedom registration" effort in which either professors or movement lawyers would "register" local blacks to publicize the large number who wanted to register yet were unable to do so with the county authorities. Later that night, while Baker and Smitherman were describing Clark as "out of control" to newsmen, King departed for a speaking trip of several days.[29]

On Wednesday, January 20, three waves of black marchers confronted Sheriff Clark at the courthouse. Clark insisted to the first group that they use one particular door, and John Lewis responded that they wanted to enter through the front door. Clark then arrested that group and a subsequent one on unlawful assembly charges. When the third wave arrived at the building, Public Safety Director Baker told them that they could use the front entrance so long as they did not block the sidewalk adjacent to it. Clark blocked that move, and for the next few minutes several assistants shuttled between Clark and Baker while the two men glared at each other from a distance of several yards. At the close of that scene, Clark told the marchers they had one minute to move, and when they did not, he arrested them as well.[30]

On Thursday, January 21, the drive slowed, with only a handful of sit-in arrests, but among the white business leadership reporters were now beginning to detect some concern at the publicity engendered by Clark's handling of Mrs. Boynton two days earlier. One prominent white businessman, who requested anonymity, was quoted as saying, "We're sick about what has happened the last few days." He added that some white leaders in town were hoping to arrange an accommodation with the local black leadership, but that they were being "stymied by Clark's attitude and a registration law" that was "unworkable." Also that Thursday, the registration board chairman issued a statement saying that prior to the marches few blacks had appeared to take the registration test, while from within the black community came predictions of more and larger demonstrations.[31]

On Friday, with King back in Selma, occurred an event that Andrew Young termed "the most significant thing that has happened in the racial movement since Birmingham." One hundred and five black teachers, led by the Voters' League president, Frederick D. Reese, himself a teacher, walked as a group to the courthouse late that afternoon to demonstrate their unhappiness with registration procedures. The school board chairman and the superintendent of schools met them on the steps and attempted to persuade them to leave. When they did not, Sheriff Clark and five deputies emerged from the building with their nightsticks in hand and twice pushed those in the forefront of the group off the steps, repeatedly jabbing them in the ribs with the clubs. Upon seeing that no progress could be made, the teachers ended what one reporter termed a "tense confrontation" by walking back to Brown's Chapel, where they were greeted with cheers for the truly courageous display that they had made in the face of their white employers. Later that evening Dr. King spoke at two rallies, while in Mobile movement attorneys filed a request with Judge Thomas for an injunction against Sheriff Clark.[32]

The next day Thomas issued a temporary restraining order prohibiting Selma and Dallas county officials from interfering with voter registration efforts. The judge used the opportunity to criticize both sides in the confrontations. "This court believes," Thomas wrote, "that neither the plaintiffs nor the defendants have made or are making a sincere effort to obtain the registration of qualified voters of Dallas County in an orderly and effective manner. . . . Unnecessary arrests have been made, pro-

voked by unnecessary assemblage of people at improper places."
Gatherings outside the courthouse of true applicants and those intent
upon "vouching" for them were lawful, Thomas emphasized, and
should be protected, not harassed, by officials.

In Selma, meanwhile, King departed for Atlanta and no civil rights
activities were held until a meeting on Sunday night, January 24.[33] On
Monday, the faceoffs resumed with a bang when, during another long
wait on the sidewalk outside the courthouse, a "large," fifty-three-
year-old black woman, Mrs. Annie Lee Cooper, managed to send Sheriff
Clark reeling with a powerful punch to the head. Three deputies then
"grabbed her and wrestled her to the ground, and in the flailing, kicking
struggle that followed Sheriff Clark clubbed her. She was then taken off
to jail in two pairs of handcuffs with a wound over her right eye."

The most important result of this clash was the widely circulated
picture of it which appeared in newspapers throughout the country.
Printed on page 1 of the *New York Times* and page 2 of the *Washington
Post*, the photograph depicted two deputies holding Mrs. Cooper's
hands while Sheriff Clark bent over her with a nightstick, apparently
either just before or just after inflicting a blow with the weapon. Coupled
with the striking photo was the more detailed description offered by
Times reporter John Herbers. "She put up quite a battle as the officers
seized her and threw her to the ground. 'I wish you would hit me, you
scum,' she snapped at the sheriff. He then brought his billyclub down on
her head with a whack that was heard throughout the crowd gathered in
the street."[34] Also on that Monday, the weekly Justice Department report to the White House on pending legislative proposals, unlike the one
a week earlier, made no commitment on when the drafting of federal
registrars legislation would be completed and further indicated that actual work on a presidential message had not yet begun. The text of the
weekly report was to remain unchanged until February 15.[35]

On Tuesday, January 26, the marchers minus King, who had returned
again to Atlanta, appeared at the courthouse, and a U.S. marshall, inter-
preting the details of Judge Thomas's order quite literally, arrested some
thirty applicants whose presence extended the line beyond one hundred
persons, a number the judge's order had stipulated. Also that day some
four dozen Alabama state troopers, reluctantly called in by Baker and
Smitherman at the repeated urging of Clark, arrived in town under the
command of the state public safety director, Colonel Al Lingo, a friend
of Clark's who reportedly had had a falling out with the Governor, of
whom Mayor Smitherman was a protégé.[36]

The next day two dozen more "excess" applicants were arrested, and

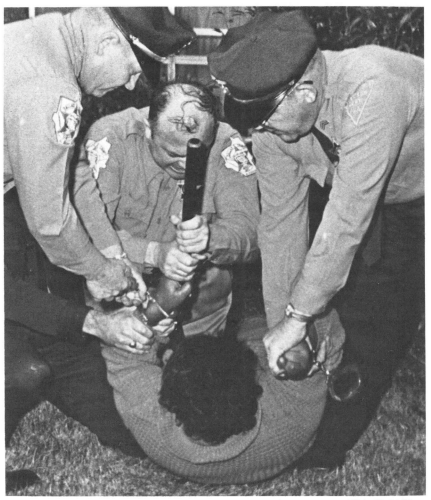

Wide World Photo

New York Times, January 26, 1965, p. 1—

"Violence in Alabama: Sheriff James G. Clark, center, and two deputies struggle with a Negro woman who stepped out of voter registration line in Selma and hit the sheriff."

Washington Post, January 26, 1965, p. A2—

"Dallas County, Ala., Sheriff James G. Clark, at center, uses his nightstick on a Negro woman as she bites and fights back. The sheriff had thrown her to the ground in an attempt to handcuff her after he said she struck him. The woman was in line at the county courthouse in Selma, attempting to register as a voter." (AP) movement attorneys announced that they would ask Judge Thomas for a further clarification of his earlier order. They did so the next day and also asked for a show cause order directed at Clark ordering the sheriff to explain why he should not be held in contempt of the earlier order because of his behavior at the courthouse earlier in the week. Thomas made no immediate response and a quiet weekend ensued. More important, at a special SCLC staff meeting on the night of Thursday, January 28, it was decided that it was now time for King himself, who was due back in town on Sunday evening, to be arrested in Selma—preferably by Baker, and not by the less predictable Clark. Monday, February 1, was chosen for that event. King himself was informed of the decision in Washington, and he mentioned it to supporters there.[37]

Over the weekend the SCLC also laid plans for a voter demonstration in nearby Perry County on February 1, while white Selma officials, learning of the new plan calling for King's arrest through sources in the black community, apparently influenced Judge Thomas to issue on Saturday, January 30, a clarification of his earlier order designed to make it more difficult for King to force his arrest. White moderates in Selma, it was reported, who had "thought they could weather the storm, now feel isolated and believe all is lost. . . . During the past week of registration attempts, pressure mounted from the unyielding segregationists. Moderates watched the deterioration in silence."[38] Also over the weekend, presidential aide Moyers received from Yale Law School's Eugene Rostow a letter surmising that Selma, to which his attention had been brought by the *Times'* front-page photo of Clark and Mrs. Cooper, "may become a test of wills." If it did, Rostow wrote, it would give "the President an ideal issue—the registration of voters." Moyers subsequently showed the letter to Johnson himself.[39]

Upon his return to Selma on Sunday evening, King made one speech to a rally. The following morning he spoke to his fellow marchers before they headed to the courthouse. "If Negroes could vote," King told them, "there would be no Jim Clarks, there would be no oppressive poverty directed against Negroes, our children would not be crippled by segregated schools, and the whole community might live together in harmony." Following those perhaps overly hopeful words, King and more than 250 followers began their march downtown, intentionally avoiding breaking into smaller groups as earlier marches had done to avoid running afoul of the city's parade ordinance. Today, breaking that ordinance and being arrested for it was the SCLC's goal. Within a short distance Wilson Baker halted the column, and following a brief conversation and prayer King and his fellow marchers, as planned, were led off to jail. While local residents were freed without bail, King and his close associate Ralph Abernathy chose to remain in jail. Pictures of the arrest made page 1 of the next day's *Times* and the inside pages of the *Post*. Press reports indicated that segregationist pressure in Selma was such that Baker and Smitherman felt they had no choice but to arrest King when he broke the ordinance. Later in the day some five hundred protesting schoolchildren were also arrested. Some six hundred and fifty blacks also marched in the Perry County town of Marion.[40]

While that was taking place in the streets of Selma on Monday, Roswell Falkenberry, the publisher of the *Selma Times-Journal* and a supporter of Baker and Smitherman, was sending a telegram to President Johnson asking that a special congressional committee be chosen to review the Selma situation. Four days were to pass without a reply. On Tuesday, while King and Abernathy remained in jail, several hundred schoolchildren were arrested by city police, while several hundred other marchers were arrested by Clark's deputies, one of whom was reported to have shocked SCLC staffer Hosea Williams with a cattle prod. Although early that morning Andrew Young had hinted to newsmen that the demonstrations might be halted if the city administration would issue a statement backing the movement's voter registration effort, by later in the day a different tune was being sung. The two-days' arrests, Herbers of the *Times* was writing, had "had the effect of rejuvenating the Negro community just as the campaign seemed to be on the verge of dying. An aide of Dr. King said the civil rights leader now expected to be in Selma for 'some time to come.' " A speech in Selma that evening by Governor Wallace drew no black pickets, as some had suggested, and little press attention, as it was closed to the national press.[41]

On Wednesday, February 3, more than three hundred additional schoolchildren were arrested in Selma, while over seven hundred marchers were taken into custody in Marion. Reporters believed the situation in Selma to be more relaxed than it had been in previous days and that Baker had redoubled his efforts to avoid any violent incidents. King and Abernathy remained in jail, their aides said, to dramatize their "contention that Selma officials should publicly side with" blacks' complaints about the registration process. In Mobile, SCLC attorneys unsuccessfully petitioned Judge Thomas for an order to speed up the Dallas County registration process and to enjoin Baker from interfering with voting rights proponents in the same way that Clark had been restrained. In Montgomery, Governor Wallace appeared with the president of Pennsylvania's Hammermill Paper Company to announce that firm's decision to build a new $30 million plant in Selma, a town the company president said he had heard "nothing but fine reports about."

At that same time SCLC efforts to stimulate Washington's interest in developments in Selma began to pay off. On the floor of the Senate New York's Jacob Javits voiced the first public congressional reaction to the drive, declaring that the hundreds of arrests on Monday and Tuesday were "shocking" because they were of citizens seeking "the most basic right guaranteed by the Constitution," the right to vote. Javits had contacted the Justice Department about his concern and had been assured by officials that they were alert to the situation and possible federal options. The Selma situation should "be watched closely to see whether additional law is now necessary. . . . It may well show that federal legislation is required authorizing the appointment of federal registrars who would themselves be empowered to register citizens to vote."

Also on Capitol Hill it was announced that in response to a letter from Dr. King to the House Judiciary Committee chairman, Emanuel Celler, and to follow-up telegrams from King to a number of liberal representatives stating that "events of the past month here in Selma have raised serious questions as to the adequacy of present voting rights legislation," a group of House members was organizing a visit to Selma for that Friday, February 5. California's Augustus F. Hawkins told reporters that the trip's purpose would be to see whether voting rights legislation was needed.[42]

Also that Wednesday afternoon, presidential counsel Lee C. White received a phone call from Andrew Young in Selma, who told White that the jailed King had asked him to get in touch with the president and pass along three suggestions. As White subsequently conveyed them to Johnson, the suggestions were

1. Send a personal emissary to Selma to evaluate the situation and report back to the President.

2. Make a specific statement supporting the right to register and vote in Dallas County and Selma, Alabama.

3. Through appropriate legislative and executive action secure the right to register and vote in all elections including those controlled by the individual states.

White also told the president that Young was to call back later in the afternoon, and that White's own reactions to each suggestion were:

1. Advise that Assistant Attorney General John Doar (or one of his top aides) is following the situation closely and reporting back to the Attorney General (and through him to the President).

2. In the event that the President is questioned on the situation in Selma, a response, either directly or through the Press Secretary, will be that the President's commitment to securing the broadest possible voter participation and in assuring that all will have the right to vote was

stated in one of the most formal documents the President delivers, the State of the Union Message, delivered in person to the Congress and through the medium of television to the entire nation.

3. Major court cases brought by the Administration [*Louisiana* and *Mississippi*] are pending to remove any obstacles to voting and the additional steps suggested in the State of the Union Message are in the process of preparation and will be submitted to the Congress for consideration as soon as they are ready.

Having recommended these responses, White continued on in a less formal manner.

> I understand from Nick Katzenbach that he spoke to you yesterday [Tuesday, February 2] and indicated that Federal District Judge Thomas hopes to be able to issue an order in the Selma situation that will resolve it satisfactorily, but that the Justice Department's consultation with the Judge is not publicized or generally known. I assume that the basic reason for King's [more precisely, Young's] call is to have a reply that he can publicize and indicate Presidential support of his position. My inclination is to give Young answers to the three points and indicate that you were tied up in meetings and that I have consulted with the Attorney General and did not feel that I wanted to delay responding. An alternative which King would probably find unsatisfactory would be to refer the call to the Attorney General.[43]

Public reports from the White House made no mention of this matter, saying simply that, according to Press Secretary George Reedy, the president had spoken by phone with the attorney general, that Justice was keeping him informed about Selma, and that no decision on any possible federal intervention had been made. Reedy also was reported to have told two Alabama congressmen that publisher Falkenberry's request for a congressional inquiry would have to be sent to the Hill, not to the White House.

While Wednesday's events had signaled some acceleration of the situation, the pace quickened still further on Thursday, February 4. Mayor Smitherman sent President Johnson a telegram endorsing Falkenberry's suggestion of a congressional inquiry to ascertain and publicize the facts of the situation, though not to intervene directly. Smitherman criticized the impending visit by the liberal congressmen as merely a move for "personal publicity" and blamed the current circumstances in his town on "outside influences" and "professional agitation," beginning with King's "invasion" in January.

As the previous day's memo from White to Johnson had suggested, on Thursday Judge Thomas issued a comprehensive decree ordering the Dallas County registrars to discontinue use of Alabama's admittedly difficult "knowledge of government" registration test, to not reject applications because of minor errors, and to process at least one hundred applications each day the board met. If all applicants were not processed by July, Thomas warned, he would appoint a referee. The decree contained a "pattern or practice" finding and further required the board to make monthly progress reports to Thomas. In response, the SCLC staff, although displaying some initial disappointment with the order's contents, suspended street demonstrations while they gave it further study. Justice Department officials made it clear to reporters that they believed "the decision was as favorable to the Negro community as could be obtained."

At Brown's Chapel, SCLC staffers were startled by the appearance of Malcolm X, who told a crowd in brief remarks that he believed one had the right to use any means necessary to gain the right to vote. In Marion, two hundred marchers were arrested, and complaints of overcrowding and lack of food, heat, and bedding began to emanate from the four work camps in which the many arrested demonstrators were being held. In New York City, eleven members of SNCC were dragged from a federal courthouse where they had instigated a sit-in to protest the lack of federal intervention in Selma.[44]

Washington, however, was where Thursday's most important event occurred. While five Alabama congressmen busied themselves with speeches on the House floor criticizing the impending visit to Selma by fifteen of their northern colleagues, at the White House President Johnson appeared before the press, and the third section of his prepared statement concerned voting rights.

> I should like to say that all Americans should be indignant when one American is denied the right to vote. The loss of that right to a single citizen undermines the freedom of every citizen. This is why all of us should be concerned with the efforts of our fellow Americans to register to vote in Alabama. The basic problem in Selma is the slow pace of voting registration for Negroes who are qualified to vote. We are using the tools of the Civil Rights Act of 1964 in an effort to secure their right to vote. One of those tools of course is legal action to guarantee a citizen his right. One case of voting discrimination has already led to a trial which has just been concluded. We are now awaiting a decision in this case [the decision which Thomas issued that same afternoon]. In the meantime I hope

that all Americans will join with me in expressing their concern over the loss of any American's right to vote. Nothing is more fundamental to American citizenship and to our freedom as a nation and as a people. I intend to see that that right is secured for all our citizens.

The SCLC thus received the presidential statement of support which it had sought the previous day. Later in the news conference one questioner asked Johnson if he had any intention of sending federal personnel to Selma. Johnson parried by paraphrasing his earlier statement about the pending decision and the 1964 act.[45]

On Friday morning, February 5, as fifteen representatives headed for Selma in response to the SCLC's letter and telegrams, there appeared on page 15 of the *New York Times* a nine-by-sixteen-inch advertisement headlined in large type "A Letter from MARTIN LUTHER KING from a Selma, Alabama Jail," and dated February 1. The text of the piece is worth quoting in its entirety.

Dear Friends,

When the King of Norway participated in awarding the Nobel Peace Prize to me he surely did not think that in less than sixty days I would be in jail. He, and almost all world opinion will be shocked because they are little aware of the unfinished business in the South.

By jailing hundreds of Negroes, the city of Selma, Alabama, has revealed the persisting ugliness of segregation to the nation and the world. When the Civil Rights Act of 1964 was passed many decent Americans were lulled into complacency because they thought the day of difficult struggle was over.

Why are we in jail? Have you ever been required to answer 100 questions on government, some abstruse even to a political science specialist, merely to vote? Have you ever stood in line with over a hundred others and after waiting an entire day seen less than ten given the qualifying test?

THIS IS SELMA, ALABAMA. THERE ARE MORE NE-GROES IN JAIL WITH ME THAN THERE ARE ON THE VOTING ROLLS.

But apart from voting rights, merely to be a person in Selma is not easy. When reporters asked Sheriff Clark if a woman defendant was married, he replied, "She's a nigger woman and she hasn't got a Miss or Mrs. in front of her name."

This is the U.S.A. in 1965. We are in jail simply because we cannot tolerate these conditions for ourselves or our nation.

We need the help of all decent Americans. Our organization,

SCLC, is not only working in Selma, Ala., but in dozens of other Southern communities. Our self-help projects operate in South Carolina, Georgia, Louisiana, Mississippi and other states. Our people are eager to work, to sacrifice, to be jailed—but their income, normally meager, is cut off in these crises. Your help can make the difference. Your help can be a message of unity which the thickest jail walls cannot muffle. With warmest good wishes from all of us,

> Sincerely,
> Martin Luther King, Jr.

A coupon at the bottom of the ad, giving the SCLC's Atlanta address, read: "I am pleased to contribute $_____ to advance human dignity in the United States."

Although the congressmen arrived in Selma and met with local officials and four Alabama representatives who hurriedly had come to town, as well as with local blacks, their presence was somewhat eclipsed by Dr. King's decision to emerge from jail, after which he met with the visitors from Washington. At the courthouse, Sheriff Clark arrested some five hundred marchers who were protesting the failure of the registration board to open for more than two days a month, a matter overlooked by Thomas's order. After his release, King announced that an "acceleration" of the Selma campaign would begin soon, and he stated explicitly his intent to seek new federal voting rights legislation. Reports quoted King as referring to both a constitutional amendment and legislation providing for federal registrars.

While King's aides sought to arrange appointments for him in Washington early the next week, SNCC's John Lewis called presidential aide Clifford Alexander to complain about the conditions in which the arrested demonstrators were being held. Alexander passed the information along to Lee White, who bucked it to Assistant FBI Director Cartha DeLoach. White himself received a call that day from Falkenberry, the *Selma Times-Journal* publisher, who still was seeking some action on his request for an unbiased congressional inquiry. In reply White wrote a letter to Smitherman, brushing off the inquiry suggestion that both men had made and informing them that Community Relations Service Director LeRoy Collins or Assistant Attorney General John Doar, who was in Selma that day, could perhaps be of assistance.

Later that evening two of the congressional visitors, Republican representatives Charles Mathias and Ogden Reid, told reporters in Washington that their Selma trip had convinced them of the need for new voting rights legislation. Said Reid, "There is a clear need for new civil rights legislation, particularly in regard to federal registrars." Also late Friday afternoon some fifteen SNCC members again clashed with U.S. marshalls at a federal courthouse in New York City after their attempt to enter and begin a sit-in had been blocked. A front-page *Times* account reported: "Hard punches were thrown and found their marks on both sides."[46]

Saturday morning's *Times* also contained a penetrating analysis by correspondent John Herbers. Although Herbers did not indicate that he understood fully just how conscious and well-calculated was the SCLC effort to evoke public nastiness and physical violence from Sheriff Clark and other officials, he did write: "Dr. King's arrest was at least two weeks behind schedule, according to a blueprint his organization drew up before the first of the year." That remark was virtually the only public acknowledgment of the SCLC's highly confidential strategic planning throughout late 1964 and early 1965. As we shall discuss in the concluding chapter, the SCLC leadership believed that its efforts would appeal favorably to more persons if the strategic and tactical considerations underlying those efforts were not made public. Although Herbers did not detail fully just what the SCLC's strategy was, he did offer *Times* readers an interesting commentary on Sheriff Clark, which might have suggested to some just why the SCLC had estimated Selma to be the best possible focal point for its voting rights campaign. Despite all the efforts by some leading Selma whites to deprive the demonstrators of the confrontations with the sheriff which they sought, "observers here detect," Herbers wrote, "something in the white law-enforcement officers . . . that compels the officers to confront the demonstrators. The officers always seem to these observers"—in other words, the national reporters present—"to be out in larger numbers than needed, in riot helmets, with an assortment of nightsticks, electric cattle prods and guns hanging from their belts like so many pendants." Clark, Herbers noted, never failed to be on hand to direct "the defense of the courthouse personally."[47]

At the White House that Saturday morning, Press Secretary George Reedy announced that the president would make "a strong recommendation" to Congress on voting rights legislation at some point in the future, though neither the timing of the message nor the nature of the legislation had been decided. "Mr. Reedy's statement," *Times* reporter John D. Morris wrote, "provided the first official confirmation of reports that President Johnson would definitely press for Congressional action this year to strengthen Federal laws against racial discrimination. Reports of such plans had been circulating since early January." Reedy,

Morris added, "had volunteered the information at a news briefing" at which he had been asked to respond to reports about Dr. King's requests for appointments with several high administration officials on Monday, February 8. King, Reedy told the press, had been advised to talk with Justice Department officials about his ideas on possible legislation, and later that day a department spokesman announced that King would be meeting with Attorney General Katzenbach early in the week. Lee White, Morris reported, had recommended that meeting to one of King's lawyers, Harry Wachtel, and had added that a meeting between King and Johnson in the near future, which all parties understood to be the SCLC's prime goal, remained possible. Reedy had been unable or unwilling to give reporters any details about the legislative options under consideration, but later in the day "other Administration officials said that the main proposals under serious study included legislation for Federal voting registrars as well as a constitutional amendment restricting the authority of states to set voter qualifications."[48]

In Selma, no protests were held on Saturday or Sunday as the SCLC prepared for Monday, February 8, a day the registration board would be in session. Plans were also being made to extend the campaign into adjacent Lowndes County and for a Monday rally in Montgomery. King had left for Atlanta on Friday evening, and his aides concentrated on having the next week's demonstrations articulate their complaint concerning the very limited two-days-a-month openings of the registration office.

On Sunday in Atlanta King made it known that he would meet with Katzenbach, Vice-President Humphrey, and, perhaps, the president in Washington on Tuesday. Also over the weekend a number of Community Relations Service representatives were attempting to reopen communications between Selma city officials and local black leaders. An agreement was reached which provided that an "appearance book" would be available daily in the registration office and that the board when it did meet would process applicants in the order that they had signed the book. While F.D. Reese, the Voters' League president, was satisfied with that apparent concession, SCLC staffer James Bevel viewed it as simply a delaying tactic by the officials. In the North, meanwhile, a number of civil rights and religious organizations publicized the expressions of protest that they had sent to the Hammermill Paper Company concerning its decision to build a new plant in Selma.[49]

Early Monday morning in Selma, Bevel and a small group went to the courthouse and ostentatiously refused Atkins's offer of priority numbers so as to indicate their dissatisfaction with the "appearance book" procedure Reese had endorsed over the weekend. They wanted to undergo complete processing then and there, they said, and they walked out of Atkins's office only to be confronted by Sheriff Clark, who, reporters said, was "shaking with anger" at this intrusion into his headquarters. Clark began "jabbing" Bevel "in the abdomen with his billyclub, then grabbed his shoulders and forced him backward down the [courthouse] steps. 'You're making a mockery out of justice,' Sheriff Clark told him, his voice so tense it was barely audible. 'I have a constitutional right——' Mr. Bevel began. 'You get out of here,' Sheriff Clark said, punching him repeatedly with his club. When Mr. Bevel refused to retreat further, the sheriff called two deputies" and instructed them to arrest him. At the rear of the group a SNCC staffer was also jabbed with billy clubs in a similar scene given detailed description by the reporters present. The whole group of some fifty was then arrested. Later in the day some two hundred students marched to the courthouse to protest the earlier arrests and were dispersed peacefully after thirty minutes of quiet picketing. In Montgomery, King drew a crowd of several hundred as he called for a march the next day.

On the floor of the House of Representatives in Washington, five of the congressmen who had visited Selma on Friday were joined by five other colleagues in calling for voting legislation and commending President Johnson for his expressed intention to make a legislative proposal on voting rights. Two of the representatives, Lindsay and Resnick of New York, each introduced their own bills, and Massachusetts Republican Bradford Morse typified his colleagues' remarks when he stated, "I had hoped that we could wait until we had an opportunity to see the Civil Rights Act [of 1964] in operation before we took up new legislation, but the events of recent weeks have made this impossible."[50]

On the next day, Tuesday, February 9, nineteen representatives delivered comments on the House floor regarding voting rights and Selma. Two of the leaders of the group that had visited the town, Michigan's Charles C. Diggs and New York's William F. Ryan, read from the depositions they had received from Selma blacks and described their meeting with the city's white officials. They and seven others who had made the trip echoed the previous day's calls for new and tougher voting rights legislation, and they were joined by almost a dozen others, such as New York's Lester Wolff and John G. Dow, both of whom attacked the conduct of the local law-enforcement personnel in Dallas County and Selma.

Also in Washington on Tuesday, as expected, King met with Humphrey, Katzenbach, and the president. Earlier he had presided over a disappointingly small crowd of two hundred marchers in Montgomery, while in Selma only one small band of marchers ventured downtown to the courthouse. After meeting with Humphrey and Katzenbach for ninety minutes and with Johnson for about fifteen, King emerged from the White House and termed the sessions "very successful." He reported to the press, "The president made it very clear to me that he was determined during his administration to see all remaining obstacles removed to the right of Negroes to vote." The president had told him that a voting rights message would go to Congress "very soon," and the civil rights leader praised what he called Johnson's "deep commitment to obtaining the right to vote for all Americans." King said that he had described to the president, the vice-president, and the attorney general in greater detail what he hoped the voting rights legislation would include.

> Such new legislation must provide machinery which is virtually automatic to eliminate the interposition of varying standards and crippling discretion on the part of hostile state officials. Only elementary biographical data should be required. It must put to an end the use of literacy tests in those areas where Negroes have been disadvantaged by generations of inferior, segregated education. It must apply to all elections—federal, state or even for sheriff, school board, etc. Enforcement of such legislation must be reposed in federal registrars appointed by and responsible to the president. They must be empowered to act swiftly and locally to insure the nondiscriminatory use of simplified federal machinery. Such legislation at the very minimum should be directed at the most oppressive regions as typified by Selma and other hardcore areas in the South.

While the administration leaders had said they would consider his suggestions but not endorse them at present, Johnson, King added, had mentioned the possibility of registering blacks at U.S. post offices. Others subsequently reported that Humphrey had expressed doubts concerning Congress's interest in passing a voting rights bill at that time, and that King had returned South knowing that further interest in voting rights problems and the Selma campaign needed to be stirred.[51]

One immediate incident that worked to serve that purpose occurred in Selma on Wednesday, February 10, when Sheriff Clark, after arresting 165 marching teenagers, sent them on a forced march, or more precisely a forced run, several miles out into the countryside. While news reporters were blocked from following the procession, youngsters subsequently reported that Clark's deputies had used nightsticks and cattle prods to keep them trotting along. That action provoked a substantial reaction in the black community and generated large turnouts at that evening's two rallies. The following day's news reports stated that the sheriff's action had "revived" the drive, which had "seemed to be losing its spark until" Wednesday's forced march. In the Congress that day, two New Yorkers issued statements supporting the SCLC effort, while four Alabamians rose to defend Dallas County and attack "outside agitators" and unnecessary press coverage. "Registration of Negroes," Representative James D. Martin went so far as to say, "is not an issue in Dallas County."[52]

Thursday witnessed a march by four hundred students and two hundred adults to the courthouse in downtown Selma, and Clark and his deputies did nothing but pace around. That morning's *Selma Times-Journal* had strongly criticized the previous day's forced march, and northern correspondents were writing that whites in Selma had "said Sheriff Clark had yielded to growing pressure in the white community to refrain from making mass arrests," which it was said the city administration and business leaders had come to believe was "a tactical error that gives the campaign more impetus." Press attention was also devoted to the fact that SCLC staffer James Bevel, transferred from the jail to an infirmary when he developed a fever, had been chained to his bed with leg-irons despite doctors' protests.

In Washington that Thursday night, Attorney General Katzenbach met secretly with five senators—Republicans Clifford Case of New Jersey and Jacob Javits of New York and Democrats Philip Hart of Michigan, Paul Douglas of Illinois, and Robert F. Kennedy of New York—and ten staff aides in a conference room off the Senate floor. While Kennedy was sitting in simply to lend support to his successor as attorney general, the other four senators, who had asked for the meeting in the wake of Johnson's press conference statement on February 4 and Reedy's comments two days thereafter, pressed Katzenbach hard for the details of just what legislative ideas the Justice Department had under consideration. Katzenbach, who had been assured of confidentiality, merely reiterated the department's litigative efforts and refused to "go an inch beyond" the public statement Reedy had made several days earlier. The attorney general, columnists Evans and Novak wrote four days later in revealing that the session had taken place, refused to say "when the proposal would be made or what it would contain." Katzenbach simply told the senators to forward their suggestions to the Justice Department, where they would receive consideration. Kennedy, who told his colleagues that the goal of the Selma campaign was not to register black voters but "to influence public opinion," emphasized his belief that the chances for substantial progress in the voting rights field were very poor as long as literacy tests remained in use throughout the South. Kennedy believed those could be eliminated only through a constitutional amendment, and he was reported to have concluded, "It will take many a year for Negro voting rights to be a reality in the South."[53]

Also that day, Diggs and his colleagues who had visited Selma six days earlier sent a telegram to President Johnson urging that Vice-President Humphrey, the administration's designated coordinator for civil rights, "convene a representative group of organizations who will, in cooperation with the Justice Department and certain members of Congress, draft an appropriate bill" to insure voting rights by moving against literacy tests and the poll tax. While noting that "several different measures have already been introduced at this session," the group stated its desire "that legislation should be designed that will not only meet the problem, but represent a consensus of bipartisan support and of course have your endorsement." They asked for a meeting with Johnson at which these possibilities could be discussed.

The following day, Friday, Lee White wrote a letter to Diggs in reply to the telegram. Johnson, White said, suggested that Diggs and his colleagues meet with Humphrey, Katzenbach, and White to discuss their suggestions. "The Justice Department," White added, "is currently considering the subject in detail and is examining the entire range of specific proposals in this field in order to recommend to the President the course of action most likely to achieve the goal of universal suffrage." Also that day, Joseph Rauh, counsel for the amalgam of liberal groups known as the Leadership Conference on Civil Rights, submitted to Katzenbach's office the draft of a bill entitled the "Voting Enrollment Act of 1965." None of its provisions ever were to receive noticeable support from member groups or to be the subject of public discussion.[54]

In Selma on Friday Sheriff Clark entered the hospital suffering from exhaustion, and press attention was focused on black youngsters who came to pray for his recovery in mind as well as body. Judge Thomas ordered the release of some two dozen demonstrators who had been held on contempt charges by Judge Hare, and SCLC attorneys filed with Thomas's clerk a request for a show cause order directed at Clark, contending that Wednesday's forced march had been a violation of Thomas's order of January 23. Thomas did not respond to that request until late March. King left town on Friday for the weekend, and no demonstrations took place on Saturday or Sunday during his absence. On Saturday several local black leaders met secretly with a group of white businessmen at the Albert Hotel, and city officials announced that they would grant a parade permit for a Monday march. A large rally on Sunday evening preceded King's return on Monday.

Also on Sunday the *Times* printed a second analytical piece by John Herbers. "Negro leaders," he observed, "have learned that the White House and Congress act in the field of civil rights in response to a crisis." Herbers wrote that the SCLC apparently had been somewhat disappointed by their reception in Selma, as the town in 1965 was "not the monolithic community that it had been in 1963." As a result, "the campaign did not develop as quickly as had been anticipated." Selma, Herbers predicted, was "not likely to become another Birmingham. . . . The prospect now is that if no further arrests are made here, the campaign will move into surrounding Black Belt counties where the barriers against Negro voting are higher, where white opposition is greater and where community leaders are less sophisticated about law enforcement." Although not saying so explicitly, Herbers now appeared to be aware of what the SCLC's strategy involved, though several years were to pass before anyone suggested in print just what that strategy entailed. But glimmers were emerging, as when Herbers quoted Andrew Young as saying, "We hope that new voting legislation will be written here," in Selma.[55]

On Monday, with Clark out of the hospital, marches were held not only in Selma but in Marion and Camden as well. An SCLC staff meeting that evening decided that further pressure should be applied in Selma in the form of additional demonstrations. In Washington on Monday, the Justice Department reported to the White House that discussions had led to the consensus "that a constitutional amendment would not be a satisfactory approach." Efforts had been concentrated on drafting an actual bill, and it was expected that it would "be completed shortly." A memo written that same day within the Office of Legal Counsel indicated that a number of both political and substantive doubts concerning the constitutional amendment approach had emerged.[56]

In Selma on Tuesday, February 16, occurred perhaps the clearest indication to date of Sheriff Clark's inability to control his temper. Two dozen marchers, led by the SCLC's Reverend C.T. Vivian, appeared on the courthouse steps in the rain and were refused admittance by Clark. They responded by singing, and Vivian took the opportunity to tell Clark that he thought him to be a brute who bore some resemblance to Hitler. Vivian dared Clark to hit him, and Clark, despite his deputies' attempts to restrain him, finally reached out from between the closed doors and sent Vivian sprawling down the steps with a powerful punch in the mouth. Vivian was then arrested. The encounter, one observer noted, "made vivid television."[57]

The following day was relatively quiet, at least until evening. At a rally in Brown's Chapel, King, who had spent the day in bed with a cold, delivered what newsmen regarded as his "strongest" speech of the campaign, calling for more militant demonstrations and civil disobedience, including nighttime marches, and announced that some of the campaign's efforts would be shifted from Selma to other nearby towns. In one of these, Marion, the white leadership, meeting at that same time, decided that Colonel Lingo and his state troopers should be called in the next morning, at which time the SCLC's James Orange, who had been heading the Marion effort, would be arrested as well.[58]

Those two sets of plans made on Wednesday evening collided in a bloody encounter in Marion on Thursday evening. Following a rally in a black church, the Reverend C.T. Vivian lead a column out of the building and down the sidewalk towards the nearby courthouse, their way lit by the glow of the streetlights. Within a block, the head of the column was halted by a sizable detachment of state troopers, who instructed the blacks to turn around and return to the church. At that moment, according to onlookers, the streetlights suddenly went out and the troopers began to rain blows upon those at the head of the column. As the marchers stumbled over each other in an attempt to get back to the church or to seek cover elsewhere, a crowd of white onlookers set upon the press contingent that had been standing across the street. A large head wound was inflicted upon NBC's Richard Valeriani, while at the same time a short distance away a young black man, Jimmie Lee Jackson, was shot in the stomach by a state trooper who had pursued Jackson, his mother, and several others into a cafe. After some delay, Jackson was taken to a Selma hospital where he was to die eight days later.

The evening's events received considerable press attention the next day. Friday's *Washington Post* ran a banner headline on the clash above its page-one masthead and gave a prominent three-column, top-of-the-page layout to UPI reporter John Lynch's account of the clash, which began:

> Club-swinging state troopers waded into Negro demonstrators tonight when they marched out of a church to protest voter registration practices.
>
> At least 10 Negroes were beaten bloody. Troopers stood by while bystanders beat up cameramen.

Friday morning's *New York Times* headlined John Herbers's page-one story "Negroes Beaten in Alabama Riot," and "NBC featured Richard Valeriani in his hospital bed, head stitched up and speech still slow from sedatives, on its evening news."[59]

In Washington on Friday, public reaction in the Congress to the Marion incident was noticeably slight, just as it had been in the wake of the attack upon Vivian. At the White House, Reedy said only that the president was being kept informed of the Alabama situation by the attorney general, though Katzenbach himself told King privately that an FBI investigation of the previous night's attack was underway. In Alabama, Montgomery's leading paper, the *Alabama Journal*, decried the assault as "a nightmare of State Police stupidity and brutality." Observers in Selma on Friday believed that the Marion violence had heightened the tension substantially, and that view received support when a worried Wilson Baker headed off an evening attempt to march to the courthouse, where Clark and his heavily armed posse were gathered. Baker positioned himself on the very steps of Brown's Chapel and threatened to arrest the SCLC's Hosea Williams on the spot if Williams attempted to proceed. A temporary cessation of any night march attempts was agreed to by Williams during subsequent talks with the public safety director in a rear room at Brown's, and in exchange Baker agreed to convey the blacks' demands for city support of changes in registration procedures to Mayor Smitherman.

With King once again out of town for the weekend, no demonstrations occurred in Selma on Saturday or Sunday. On Saturday, however, Governor Wallace issued a ban on any nighttime marches in the Selma area and denounced those seeking to lead them as "professional agitators with pro-communist affiliations."[60] On Sunday, February 21, Vice-President Humphrey told newsmen that the administration had decided that additional voting rights legislation was necessary. That day also witnessed the unheralded release in Jackson, Mississippi, of a lengthy memo on possible voting rights legislation by the Executive Committee of the Freedom Democratic party. Endorsed later in the week by James Farmer, James Forman, and King and circulated extensively thereafter, the MFDP piece focused upon the fear that only token legislation might be enacted. While analyzing the provisions of the bills already introduced by Representatives Lindsay and Resnick, the MFDPers assumed that whatever the administration proposed, whether enthusiastically supported by civil rights groups or not, would be approved by the Congress. The movement's first consideration in seeking to shape the proposals now being drafted, the MFDP argued, should be to oppose completely any provision that provided for federal intervention only if some arbitrary level of black registration, such as 15 percent of the voting-age population, had not been achieved. Also to be opposed would be any clause terminating federal oversight when black registration came to equal or exceed a certain level, such as 50 percent of those of voting age. Federal registrars, the MFDP argued, should be available in any locale where residents requested them and could supply evidence of having been discriminated against by local registration officials.[61]

On Monday, King returned to Selma, led an uneventful march to the courthouse, and visited the wounded Jimmie Lee Jackson. That evening, while former Mississippi governor Ross Barnett was speaking across town at a Citizens' Council dinner, King told his Brown's Chapel audience that they should organize a "motorcade" of "carloads" of disenfranchised blacks that would drive to the state capitol in Montgomery to protest voting barriers. Later that evening King received two calls from the Justice Department, the second from Katzenbach himself, warning of a plot to murder King, of which SCLC staffers had received reports for over a week.[62]

In Washington on Tuesday, February 23, a group of thirty-one Republican politicians, including four senators, five governors, and twenty-two representatives, and organized primarily by Senator Thomas Kuchel of California and Representative Charles Mathias of Maryland, issued a statement criticizing the administration's continuing refusal to announce publicly just what voting rights proposals it would make to the Congress. "How long will Congress and the American people," the Republicans queried, "be asked to wait while this Administration studies and re-studies Dr. King's request for new federal legislation? The need is apparent. The time is now." The next day's *New York Times* reported that one member of the group had said "the television broadcasts and news accounts of Sheriff James G. Clark, Jr.'s treatment of Negroes seeking to register in Selma had been an element in the decision to issue the statement." The Wednesday *Times* also summarized the administration's private response. "White House sources," E.W. Kenworthy wrote, "said today that the Justice Department had nearly completed the drafting of the bill and that it would go to Congress 'in a few days.' The bill has been delayed, the sources said, because of the careful study being given to the route that should be taken—a statute or a constitutional amendment." While only implying that the decision to go with a bill alone had been made, the story did report some disagreement among Justice Department lawyers over the manner in which discriminatory literacy tests should be banned and whether a sweeping ban would require an amendment or could properly be executed in a statute.[63]

While that was Tuesday's public dialogue concerning voting rights legislation, within the Justice Department Solicitor General Archibald Cox sent to Attorney General Katzenbach the initial portions of the bill on which attorneys were working. The proposal began with a draft of suggested "findings" that the Congress would make concerning voting rights discrimination, and a draft title I that would eliminate for ten years all literacy, interpretation, and understanding tests that had been used for the purpose of discrimination at any time in the previous ten years. Prima facie evidence of a test's use for discriminatory purposes, the draft stated, would be (1) its existence and application, and (2) that less than some specific percentage of an area's entire voting-age population was registered to vote as of July 1, 1964, or that, in the absence of reliable registration figures, less than some specific percentage of the actual voting-age population had turned out to vote in the 1964 presidential election. No actual figures as yet were included in the draft, which then went on to say that a state or county seeking to overcome the ban on registration tests would have to demonstrate to the satisfaction of the U.S. Civil Rights Commission that the test in question had not been used in a discriminatory fashion at any time during the previous ten years. The attorney general would be able to contest such claims, and decisions rendered by the Civil Rights Commission would be reviewable in the Federal District Court for the District of Columbia. Cox told Katzenbach that while this draft was not the final language, it did embody the "basic scheme" and the "main outlines" of the approach that had been chosen, and that he would attempt to draft "something on federal registrars" before the end of the week.[64]

In Selma on Tuesday, with reporters describing the town as "tense" and noting the "marked increase in the number of hostile-looking white men" watching the demonstrations, Baker again moved to halt an evening march to the courthouse—this time organized spontaneously by one hundred youngsters—so as to avoid a clash with Clark, Lingo, and the scores of possemen and troopers gathered downtown. Earlier in the day those two officers had announced that any march reaching the courthouse would be broken up. King himself remained at the Torch Motel throughout the day, telling the press that the motorcade to Montgomery and the march on the state capitol would take place on March 8. After that, King said, the SCLC might well go ahead with nighttime marches in Selma despite the governor's ban and despite any adverse ruling from a federal court, in which SCLC attorneys were considering challenging the Wallace edict. That evening King spoke at another rally in Brown's Chapel and told the crowd that he had "been in touch with Washington and I think we are getting near a new voting bill." Later King departed for Los Angeles, from which he was scheduled to return to Selma on Sunday.[65]

With King gone, Wednesday, February 24, was a quiet day in Selma as the SCLC staff devoted its time to strategy sessions. Local black leaders announced that blacks would no longer patronize the white businesses downtown. In Washington, Vice-President Humphrey and Attorney General Katzenbach met at three o'clock with Representative Diggs and his colleagues who had visited Selma. After the session Diggs reported the group's conviction that state and local elections as well as federal ones should be covered by whatever provisions the administration submitted. New York's William F. Ryan added that the consensus had been that literacy tests should be abolished completely. Humphrey and Katzenbach had not agreed or disagreed with their opinions, the members said, but had reminded them of the constitutional questions involved.

Also in Washington, Democratic National Committee Deputy Chairman Louis Martin, reacting to that morning's news stories on the Republican group's Tuesday statement, wrote to presidential counsel White urging that the president have a publicized meeting to discuss progress in expanding minority participation in the Democratic party with Chairman John Bailey and Pennsylvania's governor, David L. Lawrence, who was heading up that effort, so as to even the partisan score.[66]

Thursday was a quiet day both in Selma, where Judge Thomas met with white moderates, and in Washington, where the Civil Rights Division chief, John Doar, testifying at his confirmation hearings, told Senator Javits that additional voting rights legislation that would deal with literacy tests and apply to both federal and state elections was needed, but that he did not know when the administration would submit it. "Meanwhile," news reports stated, "Justice Department sources indicated that the Administration was narrowing its plans for voting legislation to two key areas—a 'localized moratorium' on literacy tests and the limited, last-resort use of some kind of federal registrars where local registrars are shown to discriminate."[67]

Friday, February 26, was a largely uneventful day as well. In Washington a group of Republican senators sent a memo to Katzenbach containing their suggestions for voting rights legislation. They voiced opposition to the constitutional amendment approach and indicated their support for federal registrars appointed by the president. At the White House, Reedy said he still believed a bill would be sent up "within a few days," quite possibly the following week. In Selma, James Bevel was the featured speaker at a rally held in memory of Jimmie Lee Jackson, who had died earlier that day. Bevel predicted that the drive's "tempo" would increase as a result of Jackson's death, and he spoke also of Selma's blacks walking fifty-four miles to the capitol in Montgomery in protest.[68]

Saturday was quiet in Selma as plans were laid for marches on Monday, March 1. In Washington the House Republican minority leader, Gerald Ford of Michigan, issued a statement saying, "The patience of fair-minded people is wearing thin when, after decades of waiting and three civil rights acts, the basic right of citizenship is still denied to a substantial number of citizens in defiance of the Constitution." While this salvo, aimed less at the administration than at black voters whom the Republican congressional leadership feared losing forever in the aftermath of the Goldwater campaign, burst harmlessly, the White House moved ahead with efforts to draft a presidential message to accompany the legislation being crafted in the Justice Department. White House aide Horace Busby, commenting on a preliminary draft message fashioned at Justice and sent to the White House on Wednesday, wrote to White and Moyers, "The message and especially its proposals leave me deeply disturbed." Busby was clearly upset by the proposed setting aside of state literacy tests that had been used for discriminatory purposes, and by the message's failure to acknowledge the Constitution's assignment of the right to set voter qualifications to the states. Southerners, Busby argued, would view the message as signaling a return to Reconstruction, and he feared that it would drive southern moderates back into the arms of the strong segregationists. Additionally, he warned, Johnson would be attacked for advocating voting by illiterates. Saying that he would be "heartsick" to see this proposal go up in its present form, and that if it did, the "political consequences" would be "potentially grave," Busby recommended that instead legislation making it a federal crime to intimidate potential voters or to inequitably administer voting qualifications be sent up. Moyers forwarded Busby's comments to Johnson himself. Busby also continued to work on a draft message that recapitulated the recent history of black suffrage in the South.[69]

Sunday witnessed a service for Jackson in Marion and several quiet meetings in Brown's Chapel, while on Monday morning King led a march to the courthouse in Selma, telling his followers, "We are going to bring a voting bill into being in the streets of Selma." King then visited Camden and Hayneville, the seat of Lowndes County, and departed for Washington, where earlier in the day the Justice Department had informed the White House that the draft of the bill dealing with both

literacy tests and federal registrars was "in the final stages of preparation" and that it was expected to be ready for the White House before
the end of the week.[70]

At the White House on Monday, Lee White, calling it "a legitimate
and good public relations gesture," passed along to Jack Valenti Louis
Martin's suggestion that the president meet with Bailey and Lawrence so
as to display the Democratic party's firm commitment to opening its
ranks to minority participation in all states. White also told Valenti,
"The voting rights message is likely to go to Congress early this week."
Valenti proposed the meeting idea to Johnson the following day, and the
president rejected it.

Also on Monday, Katzenbach forwarded to Moyers and White the
Justice Department's rejoinder to the comments Busby had made on the
voting rights message draft two days earlier. Busby's reactions, Katzenbach wrote, showed that the present draft of the message did not convey
adequately either the inadequacy of remedies presently available for
voting discrimination or the truly limited nature of the newly proposed
remedies. The only alternative to what was now being put forward, the
attorney general said, was to stick with the judicial approach, and that
course, he went on, "will either be ineffective or will take decades of
litigation and effort." Katzenbach added that the comments in the draft
message concerning literacy in voting would be toned down somewhat,
so as to make the message seem "less radical." He too, like Busby,
understood the "political consequences" of the message, but there was
"no real alternative" to it. The task, Katzenbach went on, was to present the message as persuasively as possible so as to establish as great
a consensus in its favor as possible. It therefore would be redrafted to
meet the two main problems noted in Busby's comments. The president
himself, Katzenbach added, had asked him "to discuss the proposed
legislation with the Republican leadership and to attempt to obtain its
support."[71]

Tuesday, March 2, was largely uneventful. No demonstration was
held in Selma, and in Camden, fifty marchers led by John Lewis were
halted by officials while some two dozen armed and mean-looking white
men looked on. In Washington, President Johnson met for almost forty-
five minutes with the NAACP's Roy Wilkins, who had told a Senate
Rules Committee hearing the previous day that civil rights organizations
would insist upon legislation creating federal registrars. On Wednesday,
King returned to Alabama and spoke at one of two funeral services for
Jimmie Lee Jackson, which were attended by a total of over four
thousand mourners. That evening James Bevel told the press that the

walk from Selma to the state capitol in Montgomery would begin on Sunday, March 7, and that it would be led by Dr. King. On Wednesday evening in Washington, President Johnson met for an hour in an "off the record" session at the White House with Alabama senators Lister Hill and John Sparkman and Representative Armistead Selden "to discuss the civil rights situation in Alabama," with Lee White sitting in.[72]

On Thursday, March 4, Alabama Governor Wallace met with Public Safety Director Lingo and his staff for several hours in the evening to discuss how to handle the Sunday march that the SCLC had announced the night before. Wallace's press secretary, Bill Jones, in his subsequent account of the session, asserted that he, Jones, had proposed that the marchers, who would expect to be blocked, be allowed to head toward Montgomery and that the road, U.S. Highway 80, be closed to *all* vehicular traffic except local residents. With no support vehicles and inadequate supplies, the marchers, Jones believed, would fail to get very far. Press coverage would also be hindered greatly.

> When the conference finally ended in the early morning hours of Friday, Wallace was sold on the idea of letting them march. I did not believe—nor did any of us who were present—that King and his fellow travelers could march the 50 miles to Montgomery. I firmly believed my plan could make them the laughing stock of the nation and win for us a propaganda battle.[73]

While Wallace and his staff were making their plans, King himself was speaking in New York before a Jewish women's group. King announced that he would be meeting with President Johnson the next day, and that he would lead the Sunday march out of Selma with the intent of delivering a petition for Governor Wallace. In preparation for the Friday meeting with King, Lee White composed a memorandum for the president in which he reported "general agreement that the Constitutional amendment approach would require too much time and thus we have concentrated on a statute. Key elements under consideration by Justice" included a ban on tests used in a discriminatory manner and provision for the appointment of federal registrars. The Justice Department, White told Johnson, knew of the February 21 MFDP memo whose comments on voting legislation King had endorsed, but had not yet been able to secure a copy to analyze where its views differed from Justice's own thinking. Roy Wilkins, White reported, had informed him—incorrectly, though White did not know that—that the MFDP memo had spoken of thousands of sit-in participants descending upon Congress to lobby for voting legislation, a development that could be extremely harmful to the legislation's chances for passage. "You may wish to refer to the existence of the memorandum," White told Johnson, "and use that as a starting point to stress the need for some restraint on the part of the civil rights groups. . . . There is considerable national interest in voting legislation," White went on, "but it can be drained off by mistakes," such as a congressional sit-in.

Johnson should also impress upon King, White advised, the efforts that the administration had made to collect suggestions not only from civil rights leaders but also from Republican congressional leaders Dirksen, Ford, and McCulloch and from Louisiana senator Russell Long. Johnson should remind King that the coalition that had backed the 1964 bill would have to be recreated, and the president might also refer to the recent appointments of blacks to a number of ranking posts within the administration. Reflecting his own lack of understanding as to just what the SCLC's strategy was, White advised Johnson to remind King that LeRoy Collins of the Community Relations Service was always available to head off any trouble.[74]

On Friday, Johnson and King met from 6:17 to 7:35 P.M., and while providing little substantive detail, White House records do indicate that the two men discussed a wide range of subjects including not only "the voting bill," but also a host of other issues. After the meeting, King told newsmen that any new voting legislation "must" provide for federal registrars, and that Johnson had told him to talk to Katzenbach about the specific language of the bill. King said he had also told Johnson of the need to end literacy tests, but that "Johnson had not told him exactly what would be in the voting proposal and had offered no promises." King also reported, "The President told me that Senator Dirksen had made a commitment to support a voting rights bill." The civil rights leader also mused to newsmen that perhaps he should request federal marshall's to protect Sunday's march, but that he had not voiced that idea to any administration officials.[75]

Earlier on Friday in Alabama, while another group of black marchers were being turned back on the outskirts of Camden, Wallace's office leaked the news that the marchers would be blocked on Sunday on U.S. 80, a leak that Jones's strategy had called for.[76] During the day, however, Wallace reportedly sought the counsel of various legislative leaders and other members from the area through which the marchers would travel. Lowndes County state representative Bill Edwards, Jones later wrote, told the governor that if the marchers made it to his county, which lies east of Selma on the road to Montgomery, they would likely be met with explosives or shootings. Having received that prediction,

Jones later claimed, Wallace's concern for what might happen to the marchers made him reverse his conclusion of the previous evening that the marchers should be allowed to head east towards Montgomery. This was followed by a second meeting between Wallace, Colonel Lingo, and state trooper majors John Cloud and William R. Jones at which methods to be employed in halting the marchers were discussed. What they agreed upon, Jones was to assert, was that unaggressive and nonviolent means would be used to block the marchers.

While discussions were taking place in Montgomery, in Selma Mayor Smitherman, who had been assured that the stoppage would be peaceful and had pledged city cooperation, tried to allay the suspicions of Public Safety Director Baker, who insisted that Clark and Lingo were planning a more violent reception for the marchers. Smitherman then obtained a reassurance from Wallace's staff that that would not be the case.

Within the movement camp the SNCC members attempted to dissuade the SCLC staffers from the march in a lengthy evening meeting. As James Forman later summarized it, "Basically SNCC was opposed to a Selma-Montgomery march because of the likelihood of police brutality, the drain on resources, and the frustrations experienced in working with SCLC." The outgrowth of the meeting was that while SNCC would not formally participate in the Sunday march as an organization, individual members who supported the march idea, such as John Lewis, could participate if they so wished. Also in Alabama on Friday a small group of liberal whites, mostly from the Tuscaloosa and Birmingham areas, announced that they would march in Selma on Saturday in support of the blacks' voter registration demands. In Mobile Judge Thomas issued a brief supplementary order telling the Dallas County registrars to mail rejected applicants a form telling them the reason for their rejection and offering them the opportunity of appealing the rejection to Thomas's clerk, who could pass the appeals along to a referee if Thomas chose to appoint one.[77]

In addition to being a noteworthy day in Alabama and at the White House, Friday also witnessed the completion of the draft legislation and the final analysis of the MFDP memo within the Justice Department. The draft statute was written primarily by Harold H. Greene of the Civil Rights Division's Appeals and Research Section and Sol Lindenbaum, a staff attorney in the Office of Legal Counsel. Like Cox's earlier transmittal to Katzenbach, this proposal too began with a statement of congressional "findings," one of which asserted that the most widespread means of unlawfully denying the right to vote was the discriminatory application of literacy tests. Title I stated the "trigger formula," which mandated the suspension of all tests in all states and subdivisions that used them *and* that had registration *or* turnout levels that fell below 50 percent of the voting-age population in 1964. Basically unchanged from what Cox had detailed to Katzenbach two weeks earlier, the mechanism would eliminate all registration tests in Alabama, Mississippi, Louisiana, Georgia, South Carolina, Virginia, and Alaska, as well as in several dozen North Carolina counties and a handful of other counties across the nation. While this formula left uncovered certain "problem" counties in Arkansas, Florida, Tennessee, and Texas, the Justice Department's goal, as both Katzenbach and John Doar later made clear, was to achieve a concentrated impact on the truly hard-core problem areas. With the burden of dozens of suits against such locales removed from the department's shoulders, its litigative resources could then be directed against whatever pockets of discrimination remained in outlying southern counties. Beyond that very basic trigger formula, title I went on to detail how states, counties, or parishes could go before the Civil Rights Commission and the D.C. federal district court to attempt to prove that despite low registration and/or voting levels their tests had not been used discriminatorily in the past ten years.

Title II outlined the use of federal registrars. The attorney general, at his discretion, could direct the Civil Service Commission to appoint federal registrars for any locale whose tests had been suspended under the provisions of title I. Applicants appearing before a federal registrar, section 203 stated, must prove that they recently had been denied registration by local officials, unless twenty or more individuals so claimed, in which case the requirement for proof of such a recent and unsuccessful attempt to register with the local registrar could be waived for all unregistered individuals by the attorney general. Federal registrars would also be empowered to accept poll tax payments, and a very detailed system of appeals within the Civil Service Commission for hearing challenges to the individual decisions of federal registrars was detailed in section 206. Section 207 made it a federal crime for any person to attempt to block the casting of a vote by a federally registered voter and set maximum penalties of five-years imprisonment and a $5,000 fine. Title III mandated a July 1, 1975 termination date for all the provisions of the bill.[78]

Also on Friday Harold F. Reis of the Justice Department passed along to Lee White the comparison that Justice had made between the MFDP memo of February 21, of which it had finally obtained a copy, and the administration's draft bill. Reis's memo stressed that the main worry of the civil rights groups, that the attainment of a certain registration percentage would allow a locale to "escape" from federal oversight, would not be a problem since no such provision was contained in the Justice draft. A locale that both employed tests and had low registration or voting levels could "escape" only if it proved to the satisfaction of the Civil Rights Commission or the D.C. federal district court that no discrimination in voting had occurred there in the past ten years. Justice also believed, Reis wrote, that the administration draft compared favorably to the two other bills that the MFDP memo had mentioned, John Lindsay's, which retained a heavier reliance on the courts than did the administration's and which also allowed for literacy tests to be given to those applicants with less than a sixth-grade education, and Joseph Y. Resnick's, which Justice believed was "needlessly repressive" and burdened with "many constitutional problems." Neither Lindsay's nor Resnick's had any greater geographical reach than the administration's, Reis added. Hence, it was Justice's expectation that there would be no particular unhappiness with the administration bill on the part of civil rights groups. That, however, was merely a prediction, Reis emphasized, for "in our discussions with the various interested groups, we have avoided being too specific about the details of the draft we are working on."[79]

Saturday, March 6, began in Alabama with a statement from Wallace prohibiting any march on U.S. 80 because such a venture would threaten public safety. Although after reading that proclamation to a group of newsmen Wallace said to a questioner that the state troopers were "to use whatever measures are necessary to prevent a march," gubernatorial press secretary Jones was to claim later that that statement "did not describe the procedures agreed upon in the meeting with the Department of Public Safety the night before."[80]

In Selma early Saturday afternoon some seventy Alabama whites assembled and marched to the courthouse, where their leader, Birmingham minister Joseph Ellwanger, a Selma native, read a statement that was largely drowned out by the taunts of about one hundred hostile whites. Several attempted beatings of the white marchers or supportive blacks were broken up by Wilson Baker. Later that day Baker again told Smitherman, as he had on Friday, that Clark and Lingo intended to turn the Sunday march into a bloodletting and that he wanted no part of it. Smitherman repeated the assurances that Wallace's staff had given him and which Clark himself had offered before leaving town that morning for a trip to Washington from which he was not expected to return until Sunday evening. Baker persisted in his view and reportedly threatened to resign. Several city council members, hearing of the disagreement, stepped in and arranged that the city police would neither halt the marchers before they reached Lingo's troopers and Clark's possemen, as Baker desired, nor participate in halting them along with the others, as Smitherman had told state officials they would do.[81]

In the black community around Brown's Chapel preparations for the next day's march went forward, and late that evening ten doctors and nurses who had flown in from New York arrived. Also on Saturday, Dr. King, in Atlanta, decided not to return to Selma for the Sunday march, as he had previously planned. His absence was to set off an extensive debate after the events as to the true reasons for his avoidance of the venture. While King himself and his wife asserted in their accounts that the SCLC president had felt he could not break his preaching commitments in Atlanta and had expected mass arrests at most to result from the Sunday trek, explanations offered by others who had no direct personal interest in the burgeoning controversy suggested quite persuasively that either King had chosen to heed warnings that his presence in the column might prove fatal to him, or that his staff, entertaining such a fear themselves, had been able to persuade him that there was no need for him to participate while not revealing the true reasons for offering that advice.[82]

In any case, when some six hundred marchers set out from Brown's Chapel in a long double-file column early on Sunday afternoon March 7, in the lead strode the SCLC's Hosea Williams and SNCC's John Lewis, and not Martin Luther King, Jr. Having been informed earlier that morning of the techniques for best protecting one's body from blows and from the effects of tear gas, and with their newly arrived medical corps trailing the procession in four ambulances, the marchers headed down Sylvan Street from Brown's and turned right on Water Street. As they reached Broad Street, on which they would take a left and ascend the arching Edmund Pettus Bridge that spanned the Alabama River on Selma's eastern flank, the marchers passed some three dozen of Sheriff Clark's irregular possemen lounging in the shadows of the *Selma Times-Journal* building. The ambulances were not allowed to follow the marchers onto the bridge.

As the head of the column reached the crest of the bridge, a line of about fifty helmeted Alabama state troopers could be seen deployed several lines deep across the four-lane width of U.S. 80 some three hundred yards beyond the bridge. Behind the troopers were several dozen more of Clark's possemen, about fifteen on horseback. From the sides of the highway, a hundred or so white spectators looked on, while fifty blacks watched beside an old school bus at some distance from the

troopers. Newsmen had been grouped together in front of a car dealership somewhat behind and to the side of the troopers' line, and several
officers had been detailed to assure that none of them ventured from that
position. In a car next to a nearby grocery store sat Colonel Lingo and
Sheriff Clark, who had just arrived from the airport. At a distance of
some fifty feet, Major John Cloud ordered the marchers to stop and
Williams brought the silent column to a halt. Speaking through a bull-
horn, Cloud told them, "This is an unlawful assembly. Your march is
not conducive to the public safety. You are ordered to disperse and go
back to your church or to your homes."

Hosea Williams replied, "May we have a word with the major?"
Cloud replied, "There is no word to be had." The same exchange was
repeated twice more. The major then said, "You have two minutes to
turn around and go back to your church." Approximately one minute

United Press International Photo

SNCC Chairman John Lewis is assaulted by an Alabama state trooper at the
height of the attack upon the column of voting rights marchers. The *New York
Times* printed this photograph in its "Week in Review" section on March 14,
1965. (UPI)

passed in silence and the column did not move. The time was 4:15 P.M.
Cloud then ordered, "Troopers, advance."

> The troopers rushed forward, their blue uniforms and white hel-
> mets blurring into a flying wedge as they moved.
> The wedge moved with such force that it seemed almost to pass
> over the waiting column instead of through it.
> The first 10 or 20 Negroes were swept to the ground screaming,
> arms and legs flying, and packs and bags went skittering across the
> grassy divider strip and on to the pavement on both sides.
> Those still on their feet retreated.
> The troopers continued pushing, using both the force of their
> bodies and the prodding of their nightsticks.
> A cheer went up from the white spectators lining the south side of
> the highway.
> The mounted possemen spurred their horses and rode at a run
> into the retreating mass. The Negroes cried out as they crowded
> together for protection, and the whites on the sidelines whooped
> and cheered.
> The Negroes paused in their retreat for perhaps a minute, still
> screaming and huddling together.
> Suddenly there was a report like a gunshot and a grey cloud
> spewed over the troopers and the Negroes.
> "Tear gas!" someone yelled.
> The cloud began covering the highway. Newsmen, who were
> confined by four troopers to a corner 100 yards away, began to lose
> sight of the action.
> But before the cloud finally hid it all, there were several seconds
> of unobstructed view. Fifteen or twenty nightsticks could be seen
> through the gas, flailing at the heads of the marchers.
> The Negroes broke and ran. Scores of them streamed across the
> parking lot of the Selma Tractor Company. Troopers and possemen,
> mounted and unmounted, went after them.[83]

The remnants of the column began to beat a hasty retreat back across
the Pettus Bridge, with the troopers and possemen on their heels. Some
onlookers joined in as well, and three men were arrested for assaulting
an FBI agent carrying a camera, whom they no doubt had mistaken for a
newsman. From the Selma side of the bridge appeared the three dozen
possemen the marchers had passed on their way over the bridge. The
lawmen, both on foot and on horseback, chased the blacks back into
downtown Selma and then into the black neighborhood and housing

project adjacent to Brown's Chapel, using both nightsticks and whips. Long after the others had fled, five black women remained on the ground at the site of the initial attack. The ambulances were blocked from crossing the bridge to the scene of the attack, and the women, roused by further tear gassing, eventually limped across the bridge after the others.

As the majority of marchers repaired to the area around Brown's, Clark and a dozen of his possemen, plus several troopers, attempted to force those blacks on the street into the church. Several responded by throwing a few bottles and pieces of brick at the officers, and Clark and one possemen were struck by stones, with the latter sustaining a small facial cut. Up Sylvan Street tear gas was fired into the First Baptist Church, and lawmen threw a black teenager through a window. Public Safety Commissioner Baker, furious, arrived at Brown's and persuaded the blacks to enter the building while restraining Clark and his men, who now numbered 150, from any further assaults. Baker was able to force a withdrawal of the officers to a distance of one block from Brown's, but Clark refused to leave the Sylvan Street area. Angry blacks from the neighborhood then gathered in front of the church, and movement staff members moved through the crowd urging calm and nonviolence.

With the battle ended, attention turned to the wounded. The parsonage next door to Brown's Chapel became one treatment center, as the New York doctors and nurses treated the less seriously injured, most of whom were suffering from the effects of the tear gas. At Good Samaritan Hospital several blocks away, fifty to sixty marchers were treated, and seventeen were admitted. Injuries included fractured ribs and wrists, severe head gashes, broken teeth, and what was thought to be a fractured skull sustained by SNCC's John Lewis. More than half a dozen others were treated at the Burwell Infirmary. Estimates of the total number of injured ran as high as ninety to one hundred.

As evening fell upon Selma, officers ordered any blacks they encountered, even in cars, off the streets. The SCLC staff, led by Andrew Young, promptly assembled in the Brown's Chapel parsonage and called King in Atlanta to tell him of the attack, and the conversation went on for over an hour as the SCLC's next move was discussed. A decision was reached to request an injunction prohibiting any state interference with a march to Montgomery from Federal District Judge Frank M. Johnson, Jr., in the state capital the next morning. It was also decided that King would contact SCLC supporters and ask them to join him in a second march attempt, which would take place on Tuesday, March 9. In Brown's Chapel itself an evening meeting of about six hundred blacks, many of them displaying bandages from the events of the afternoon, took place while two carloads of state troopers kept watch outside the front door.[84]

In such a fashion March 7 came to a tense but quiet close in Selma. Outside the borders of Alabama, however, the reactions and responses to what writers would later call "Bloody Sunday"—the climax of the Selma campaign—were just beginning.

3   Selma and the Voting Rights Act: Crisis and Denouement

While the wounded marchers of Selma were having their injuries attended to during the early evening hours, the photographers "who had captured almost the entire attack with their telephoto lenses" were busy as well. Shortly after 9:00 P.M. ABC television interrupted the evening movie, *Judgment at Nuremberg*, "for a long film report of the assault on Highway 80, a sequence which showed clearly the quiet column, the flailing clubs, the stampeding horses, the jeering crowd and the stricken, fleeing blacks." At the same time, telegrams from Dr. King in Atlanta were going out to some two hundred religious leaders known to be sympathetic to the civil rights cause.

> In the vicious maltreatment of defenseless citizens of Selma, where old women and young children were gassed and clubbed at random, we have witnessed an eruption of the disease of racism which seeks to destroy all America. No American is without responsibility. . . . The people of Selma will struggle on for the soul of the nation, but it is fitting that all Americans help to bear the burden. I call therefore, on clergy of all faiths . . . to join me in Selma for a ministers march to Montgomery on Tuesday morning, March ninth.

In Washington, newsmen at the White House were told that the president was being kept fully informed and that Justice Department observers were on the scene. Johnson himself, White House records show, had spent the afternoon and early evening in his office, using the telephone a good deal of the time, as was his habit. Later that evening the president had a late dinner with Lady Bird, aide Jack Valenti and his wife, Texas congressmen Jack Brooks and J. J. Pickle, Brooks's wife, journalist William S. White, and unofficial advisor Clark Clifford before retiring for the night at 11:15 P.M.[1]

It was Monday morning's newspaper headlines that informed most people for the first time of Sunday's events in Selma. In every major newspaper the story was awarded large headlines. Of the papers most read by the Washington political community, Monday morning's *Washington Post* ran a large banner headline proclaiming "Troopers Rout

Wide World Photo

Washington Post, March 8, 1965, p. 1—
    ''Alabama state troopers, wearing helmets and gas masks, drag off a demonstrator after breaking up the voter march in Selma yesterday.'' (AP)

Selma Marchers.'' Under that was printed a large three-column photo showing the gas-masked state troopers dragging off an injured marcher. In the right-hand lead column, under a subheading of "Tear Gas and Clubs are Used, Scores of Negroes Hurt; King Calls For Another Try," the *Post* ran the UPI wire story written by Leon Daniel in Selma:

> State troopers and mounted deputies bombarded 600 praying Negroes with tear gas today and then waded into them with clubs, whips and ropes, injuring scores.
>
> The troopers and possemen, under Gov. George C. Wallace's orders to stop the Negroes' "Walk for Freedom" from Selma to Montgomery, chased the screaming, bleeding marchers nearly a mile back to their church, clubbing them as they ran.
>
> Ambulances screamed in relays between Good Samaritan Hospital and Brown's Chapel Church, carrying hysterical men, women and children suffering head wounds and tear gas burns.
>
> In Atlanta, the Rev. Dr. Martin Luther King, Jr., announced that he would lead a new march from Selma on Tuesday and called on clergymen from throughout the nation to join him.

On page 3, where Daniel's story continued, two additional photos were printed, both showing the injured persons who remained lying on the grassy divider strip after the body of the marchers had been driven back by the onrushing troopers and possemen.

The Monday morning coverage in the *New York Times* was similar to that in the *Post*. Centered on the top of page 1 was a four-column photo of the attack. In its left-hand lead column, the *Times* headlined Roy Reed's story from Selma with the words "Alabama Police Use Gas and Clubs to Rout Negroes." Under that a subhead began "57 Are Injured at Selma as Troopers Break Up Rights Walk."

> Alabama state troopers and volunteer officers of the Dallas County sheriff's office tore through a column of Negro demonstrators with tear gas, nightsticks and whips here today to enforce Gov. George C. Wallace's order against a protest march from Selma to Montgomery.
>
> At least 17 Negroes were hospitalized with injuries and about 40 more were given emergency treatment for minor injuries and tear gas effects.

After noting in his third paragraph reports that some blacks had responded by hurling bricks and bottles, Reed detailed the chronological sequence of Sunday's events. On page 20, where his story continued,

Wide World Photo

New York Times, March 8, 1965, p. 1—
   "Crushing Voter Demonstration: Alabama state troopers break up march by protesting Negroes in Selma."

Washington Post, March 8, 1965, p. 3—
   "A woman demonstrator has fallen to her knees and a state trooper tugs at another felled marcher as the troopers break up yesterday's Selma rights march." (AP)

there was printed an extremely large, six-column photo showing another view of the troopers' advance. Below was a smaller photo showing Clark's mounted possemen after the chase had ended. The AP wire account used by many other newspapers of substantial circulation differed little from those of Daniels and Reed, though it placed somewhat more emphasis upon the use of tear gas.[2]

On Capitol Hill on Monday, six members of the House and the Senate reacted publicly to the news of the previous afternoon's attack. Jacob Javits termed the assault "an exercise in terror," and all of the speakers offered harsh condemnations of the tactics and weapons used by the Alabama lawmen, with several aiming their sharpest barbs at Governor Wallace. Typical of the comments were the words of Texas senator Ralph Yarborough: "I abhor the violent and brutal attack upon Americans who attempt only to march peacefully. . . . These Americans so brutally attacked yesterday sought only their constitutional right to vote." Walter Mondale of Minnesota concluded, "Sunday's outrage in Selma, Alabama, makes passage of legislation to guarantee Southern Negroes the right to vote an absolute imperative for Congress this year."[3]

At the White House on Monday, newsmen who asked George Reedy about the status of the administration's voting rights proposal were told, "That's still down the road a ways." Behind Reedy's response lay the report submitted to the White House by the Justice Department earlier that morning. A new draft of a presidential message, which Katzenbach had spoken of on Friday, "is being polished," the report said, "and the legislation is still in preparation." Because of Johnson's request that Katzenbach discuss the draft proposal with the Republican congressional leadership, it remained conceivable that some changes might be made in both the legislation and the message. "In any event," the report concluded, "there will necessarily be a brief delay before the message and the legislation can be submitted to the Congress." Later that day reporters learned that the Senate minority leader, Everett Dirksen, and three aides were examining the draft proposal, while Louisiana senator Russell Long asserted that he had not been contacted about it.[4]

Also at the White House early Monday morning, President Johnson twice called Attorney General Katzenbach to speak about the Selma situation, and he also called former Tennessee governor Buford Ellington, the director of the Office of Emergency Preparedness, to see if Ellington would contact Governor Wallace. Later in the day Johnson called Alabama senator Lister Hill as well. Wallace himself early on Monday had summoned Sheriff Clark, Mayor Smitherman, and, some reports indicated, Judge Hare to Montgomery. There he gave Clark a heated tongue-lashing on the attack, which served to fuel private speculations in Alabama that Wallace himself had not called for the marchers to be halted in the manner that they were.[5] Also in Montgomery two SCLC attorneys appeared before Judge Johnson in his chambers to present the petition for an injunction against state interference with any subsequent march attempt. Assistant Attorney General John Doar sat in on the meeting, and by late afternoon the word was that Johnson had drafted an order, but that its contents were unknown and that it would not be signed or made public until early Tuesday.

From Selma on Monday morning SCLC attorney Henry Arrington called Louis Martin at the Democratic National Committee to discuss the Selma situation and "the concern of King's aides for his life." Martin himself then called King, who was still in Atlanta, and talked with

him for twenty minutes. When asked for suggestions about what the
federal government might do, King responded, as Martin later recounted
it,

> The President might publicly announce the appointment of a top
> governmental figure to mediate the situation and he suggested
> "someone like Attorney General Katzenbach."
> Such action would give him some reason for calling off the march
> which is scheduled for 10:00 A.M. Tuesday, March 9. He said he
> was "too deeply committed" to call it off unless some such action
> was taken by Washington.
> King suggested also that Federal marshalls to prevent police bru-
> tality were necessary if the march is not postponed.
> King also said that some of his aides are calling on national lead-
> ers of both races to join him in the march tomorrow.

Following his conversation with King, Martin immediately called presidential aide Marvin Watson. Martin suggested that Katzenbach, the
president himself, or Vice-President Humphrey might contact Governor
Wallace in an attempt to mediate. Martin passed along to Watson the
fears that harm might come to King, and Watson's notes further indicate
that King told Martin off the record that he would call off the Tuesday
march. Watson also entertained the idea of having Senators Sparkman
and Hill encourage Mayor Smitherman to request the CRS director,
LeRoy Collins, to intervene, and that if Collins was brought in King
would negotiate rather than march. In a memo sent to Watson after their
call, Martin further informed him,

> King is scheduled to leave Atlanta today at 5:00 P.M. According to
> Attorney General Katzenbach a suit is being filed today by King's
> people and more than likely the Justice Department would join in
> that action. Neither King nor Arrington made any reference to the
> suit in my talks with them and I gather that this action would not be
> reason enough to postpone the march tomorrow.[6]

The question of whether to go ahead with the Tuesday march dominated an almost continuous twelve-hour-long series of discussions which
began among movement leaders in Selma upon King's return there early
on Monday night. The SCLC president met early in the evening, prior to
a rally at Brown's, with SCLC staffers Abernathy, Young, and Williams
as well as the SCLC's Alabama lawyers and civil rights figures James
Farmer and James Forman. The attorneys, led by Fred Gray, told King
and his associates that Judge Johnson had indicated that he would not

grant an injunction against state authorities without a hearing, and that the judge wanted the Tuesday march canceled and no other march to Montgomery attempted before that hearing began on Thursday. James Forman was to recall that Gray had said Johnson expected a reply from the SCLC by 9:00 P.M. as to whether or not it would abide by that informal recommendation. At this early evening session, Forman was to write later, "It was clear that the consensus was to accept Judge Johnson's offer; Hosea Williams was the only SCLC leader pushing for the march. Farmer stated that, while he had come down to march and emotionally understood the position of Hosea, rationally he had to agree with waiting until Thursday." Forman himself opposed accepting the judge's "offer" and reminded the group that the delay involved in waiting for the hearings and a possible final injunction could allow the campaign's spirit to fade. In the end, Forman reports, King "decided to accept the judge's condition. The march would be postponed."[7]

The leadership group then headed to Brown's for a rally made up partially of those who had heeded Dr. King's call and made the journey to Alabama. Many more were still on their way, and the further extensive coverage that Sunday's attack had received on Monday evening's television news shows had moved others to begin the trip. One viewer's account of what he witnessed on the Monday night news is worth quoting at length.

> The pictures were not particularly good. With the cameras rather far removed from the action and the skies partly overcast everything that happened took on the quality of an old newsreel. Yet this very quality, vague and half-silhouetted, gave the scene the vehemence and immediacy of a dream. The TV screen showed a column of Negroes striding along a highway. A force of Alabama troopers blocked their way. As the Negroes drew to a halt, a toneless voice drawled an order from loudspeaker: In the interests of "public safety," the marchers were being told to turn back. A few moments passed, measured out in silence, as some of the troopers covered their faces with gas masks. There was a lurching movement on the left side of the screen; a heavy phalanx of troopers charged straight into the column, bowling the marchers over.
>
> A shrill cry of terror, unlike any sound that had passed through a TV set, rose up as the troopers lumbered forward, stumbling sometimes on the fallen bodies. The scene cut to charging horses, their hoofs flashing over the fallen. Another quick cut: a cloud of tear gas billowed over the highway. Periodically the top of a helmeted head emerged from the cloud followed by a club on the upswing. The

club and the head would disappear into the cloud of gas and another club would bob up and down.

Unhuman. No other word can describe the motions. The picture shifted quickly to a Negro church. The bleeding, broken and unconscious passed across the screen, some of them limping alone, others supported on either side, still others carried in arms or on stretchers. It was at this point that my wife, sobbing, turned and walked away, saying, "I can't look any more."

We were in our living room in San Francisco watching the 6 P.M. news. I was not aware that at the same moment people all up and down the West Coast were feeling what my wife and I felt; that at various times all over the country that day and up past 11 P.M. Pacific Time that night hundreds of these people would drop whatever they were doing, [and head for Selma to place] themselves alongside the Negroes they had watched on television.[8]

As those who had reacted in that fashion to the news of Sunday's assault streamed toward Selma by the hundreds, King himself rose to tell the crowd in Brown's, much to the surprise of Forman and the others with whom he had just caucused, that the second attempt to march to Montgomery would begin early the next morning. Following the rally, both the SCLC and the SNCC staffs came together after midnight at the home of a black dentist, Dr. Sullivan Jackson, to reconsider the earlier decision to call off the march, a decision Forman and his colleagues were arguing strongly against and hinting that they might ignore. After several hours of discussions, by 4:00 A.M. the decision to go ahead with the march had been reached.

From representatives of the Johnson administration the pressure to cancel the march was strong. John Doar had made it clear to King that Judge Johnson would hand down an order barring any march early Tuesday unless he was informed that the SCLC was not going ahead, and Doar emphasized to King that any violation of the judge's order by King and the SCLC could not be supported by the administration and would greatly harm relations between them. CRS officers Fred Miller and James Laue were in attendance at the dentist's house, and Doar, who was elsewhere in Selma, kept in touch throughout the early morning hours with Katzenbach in Washington. Around 4:30 or 5:00 A.M. King spoke personally with Katzenbach on the phone to tell him of the decision to go forward with the march, but Katzenbach, like Louis Martin on Monday, sensed that King was looking still for a way to avoid violating Frank Johnson's forthcoming order. Not many minutes thereafter, CRS Director Collins arrived in Alabama by plane from Washington and was taken to Dr. Jackson's home by Doar to meet with King. Collins talked with King shortly after sunrise and told him that it was President Johnson's wish as well that the march be avoided. Collins was unable to dissuade King, and he departed, telling the SCLC president "that he would call on Colonel Lingo and Sheriff Jim Clark and try to work out an agreement. King wished him luck."

Collins then visited with the trooper commander and the sheriff in the office of a car dealership on U.S. 80 near the spot of Sunday's attack. Collins told them of King's determination to march, and Lingo and Clark replied that they could not let King and the column proceed on towards Montgomery. Collins asked if any contact could be avoided if the marchers turned around when they reached the officer's line, and Lingo and Clark replied Yes. Collins then returned to where King was and told him of Lingo's and Clark's statement. King's response, some say, was noncommittal—perhaps simply a smile. The CRS personnel, however, believed King had accepted the scenario. Collins returned to see Lingo and Clark once again to let them know that he believed a clash could be avoided.

By midmorning Judge Johnson in Montgomery had formally signed and issued a restraining order barring any march prior to the hearing, after reportedly being told by Collins that no firm postponement had been arrived at. Attorney General Katzenbach then called the judge to discuss what steps federal marshalls should take to serve and enforce the order. At Brown's Chapel as the morning proceded, various speakers orated on the protestors' right to march to Montgomery, in spite of Judge Johnson's order, which by then had been served on several SCLC staff members. At 2:25 P.M., Dr. King arrived at the church and announced that he was ready to march. Within a few minutes the column of two thousand marchers, many of whom were now whites, formed and began to move out. As it did so, with King at the head, Collins drove up, told him that "he felt everything would be all right," and handed him a small piece of paper.

Again turning from Sylvan to Water and then onto Broad, the column moved to the foot of the Pettus Bridge, where at shortly after 3:00 P.M. they paused while U.S. Marshall H. Stanley Fountain read to King Judge Johnson's order. Fountain then stepped aside as King indicated that he would proceed on across the bridge. As the column descended the other side of the bridge, several hundred yards ahead of them once again stood Major Cloud and the state troopers. Fifty feet from the officers King brought the column to a halt and requested permission to conduct several prayers. After the singing of "We Shall Overcome" and the leading of prayers by four different individuals, King turned so as to lead the column back across the bridge. As he did so, the troopers, in an unplanned move reportedly ordered over an open phone line from the governor's office in Montgomery, withdrew to the sides of the highway, leaving the road to Montgomery ostensibly open. Although each rank of the column wheeled in turn and followed King back into Selma, the surprise—and anger—at the meek retreat was widespread and strong among the SNCC workers and Selma teenagers, who had not received word of the late-morning negotiations.

Upon the return to Brown's Chapel, King admitted to newsmen, "We agreed that we would not break through the lines. . . . In all frankness, we knew we would not get to Montgomery. We knew we would not get past the troopers." Within the next twenty-four hours, as a result of the turnabout, relations between SCLC and SNCC sank to a new low, and SNCC chose to shift its focus to Montgomery proper.[9]

In Washington early Tuesday morning the editorial reaction to Sunday's attack, which had begun in the previous evening's *Washington Star*, found further voice in the *Times* and the *Post*. The *Post*'s editorial, entitled "Outrage at Selma," was representative of the reactions expressed by all three papers.

> The news from Selma, Alabama, where police beat and mauled and gassed unarmed, helpless and unoffending citizens will shock and alarm the whole nation. It is simply inconceivable that in this day and age, the police who have sworn to uphold the law and protect the citizenry could resort, instead, to violent attacks upon them.
>
> Decent citizens will weep for the wronged and persecuted demonstrators, for the decent citizens of Alabama who must recoil in horror from the spectacle of sadism, for the good name of the nation before the world. This brutality is the inevitable result of the intolerance fostered by an infamous state government that is without conscience or morals.
>
> The situation calls for more than mere reproach and anguish, but it is not easy to say what can be done to prevent the repetition of this scandalous misuse of police power. Congress, as a beginning, must promptly pass legislation that will put into federal hands the registration of voters that the Alabama authorities will continue to obstruct as long as they have any discretion. At least such legislation will put beyond contest the rights that the Negro citizens have been trying to gain by demonstration.[10]

Tuesday morning's papers also provided coverage of the reactions to Sunday's attack in liberal and religious circles and reported that a significant number of church figures had decided to journey to Selma. Western Union was reported to have handled a large number of telegrams to the White House Monday evening demanding federal action in Selma. A number of governors, state legislatures, and city councils also were reported to have issued condemnations of Sunday's violence. Both the *Times* and the *Post* also noted the half-dozen congressional expressions of outrage voiced on Monday, and one northern Democratic senator was quoted as saying that nearly all Democrats were "outraged by what is happening in Alabama" and that unless the administration acted quickly, "northern Democratic liberals will put in a bill of their own."[11]

The best reflection of just how widespread that outrage was within the Congress came on the floors of both houses on Tuesday as forty-three representatives and seven senators rose to condemn Sunday's attack and call for voting rights legislation. Many of the members made reference to editorials from that morning's papers or to telegrams calling for action which they had received from individual constituents or civil rights, religious, and labor organizations. Michigan freshman John Conyers announced that the entire Michigan congressional delegation, including such Republican conservatives as Edward Hutchinson and Gerald R. Ford, had endorsed the text of a telegram sent to President Johnson by the Leadership Conference on Civil Rights, which had urged not only the "immediate" submission of voting rights legislation but also the "maximum use of federal power to prevent further violence and to protect constitutional rights in Selma, Alabama," and had sent their own copy of the message to the White House. Conyers further announced that he would begin circulating the text of an additional telegram to the president among his colleagues for their signatures. It differed little in content from the Michigan-endorsed one, and by the time Conyers forwarded it to the White House early the next day, fifty-two Democrats and eleven Republicans had signed it.[12]

Although a good number of Tuesday's speakers in the House were well-known "liberals," some of whom had been members of the delegation that had traveled to Selma in early February, many others were not. In their comments, the congressmen focused primarily on the officers' weapons and tactics, on the unoffending conduct of the marchers, and on the marchers' laudable goal—the right to vote. The words of conservative Republican representative Carleton J. King of upstate New York are representative of the comments made by more than four dozen of his colleagues.

These Americans, so brutally attacked in Selma, sought only their constitutional right to register and vote. They did not resist arrest. They were, however, gassed, clubbed, and beaten at random in their efforts to pursue equality. While I do not condone lawlessness or defiance of law and order, I am equally appalled at any violent or unmerciful attack upon Americans who attempt only to march peacefully in their quest for civil rights.[13]

Tuesday morning was busy for the administration, too; by 8:30 A.M. the president had twice called Attorney General Katzenbach for the latest word on the Selma situation and King's likely course of action. The attorney general told the president that his conversations with Judge Johnson had led him to believe that the march would be authorized some time in the very near future. The president subsequently met with the congressional leadership for forty minutes, and George Reedy recommended to Johnson that a statement be issued saying that the Selma situation could be settled adequately in the courts and that the administration would be recommending stronger voting rights laws to the Congress within a few days.

Outside the White House some six hundred pickets marched to protest what they believed to be the administration's inaction, while at the Justice Department, where some twenty-five SNCC members had been evicted after a Monday evening sit-in, 150 others staged a similar vigil. Johnson was to write later that these Washington protests, which continued throughout the week, "deeply hurt" him; despite "the deep outrage" he felt upon viewing the television films of Sunday's assault, a feeling he felt "millions of Americans" shared, he believed strongly that any "hasty display of federal force," which was what the protestors called for, could "destroy whatever possibilities existed for the passage of voting rights legislation." But having seen the film of Sunday's attack, Johnson added, he knew also that he must move "at once," before the reaction had melted away.[14]

On Tuesday afternoon, forty-eight hours after the attack, Reedy read the president's first public comment to the White House press.

Ever since the events of Sunday afternoon in Selma, Alabama, the Administration has been in close touch with the situation and has made every effort to prevent a repetition. I am certain Americans everywhere join me in deploring the brutality with which a number of Negro citizens of Alabama were treated when they sought to dramatize their deep and sincere interest in attaining the precious right to vote.

The best legal talent in the federal government is engaged in preparing legislation which will secure that right for every American. I expect to complete work on my recommendations by this weekend and shall dispatch a special message to Congress as soon as the drafting of the legislation is finished.

Federal officials have been sent to Selma and are supplying up-to-the-minute reports on developments there.

The Federal District Court in Alabama has before it a request to enjoin state officials from interfering with the right of Alabama citizens to walk from Selma to Montgomery in order to focus attention on their efforts to secure the right to register and vote. I have directed the Justice Department to enter the case as a "friend of the Court" so that it can present its recommendations and otherwise assist the court in every manner in resolving the legal issues involved in the case.

We will continue our efforts to work with the individuals involved to relieve tensions and to make it possible for every citizen to vote. I urge all who are in positions of leadership and capable of influencing the conduct of others to approach this tense situation with calmness, reasonableness and respect for law and order.[15]

At about the same time that Reedy was reading that statement and announcing a presidential news conference within two or three days, twenty-five of the White House pickets were granted a brief audience with Vice-President Humphrey in the Old Executive Office Building. Humphrey also received a group of local District of Columbia civil rights leaders who had wanted to see the president. Also in Washington on Tuesday Senator Dirksen continued to peruse the administration's bill, and some observers speculated that the Republican leader was not eager to accept the idea of federal registrars. The House Judiciary Committee's ranking Republican, William McCulloch, along with several colleagues, issued a statement decrying the delay in the submission of the administration proposal. Reporters believed that what really was bothering McCulloch, as well as liberals of both parties in both houses, was not so much the delay as the fact that the administration had consulted only the Senate leadership about the forthcoming bill's provisions and that the nature of those provisions remained unknown to almost all members of Congress except Dirksen.

In Selma late Tuesday, Ralph Abernathy announced a march to the courthouse the next day, in which the more than 450 white clergymen who had arrived in town could take part. As darkness fell, three of those visitors emerged from a black diner where they had eaten dinner and took an apparent wrong turn, which brought them by the Silver Moon Cafe, a white racist den and the one Selma restaurant the movement had avoided "testing" under the 1964 act's public accommodations provisions. As the three white clergymen passed the cafe, they were set upon by several local whites armed with clubs. Although after a few seconds the clergymen were able to fend off their attackers, the Selma whites did not flee before one of them had struck a heavy blow to the skull of the Reverend James J. Reeb, a Boston Unitarian. Although Reeb was able to arise, he was dizzy, and his senses, particularly his eyesight, were disoriented. While his two companions quickly realized the seriousness of Reeb's injury and took him to a local physician, it took more than four hours to get Reeb to Birmingham's University Hospital, as the first ambulance broke down just outside Selma.[16]

Wednesday began with both of the major papers, the *Times* and the *Post*, giving headline coverage to the preceding day's events, including sympathy marches that had been staged in Boston, New York, Chicago, Los Angeles, Syracuse, Hartford, and numerous other cities. In Detroit, Michigan's governor, George Romney, and Mayor Jerome Cavanaugh had led a crowd of some ten thousand through the downtown area at midday. On Wednesday morning in Washington the congressional reaction to the Selma crisis and particularly Sunday's attack continued, albeit at a somewhat lesser volume, as seven representatives and five senators delivered floor statements. Several of them directed their comments to the attack on Reeb the previous evening.

At the White House, Jack Valenti received from Jack Rosenthal, the Justice Department's director of public information, a status report on the department's intervention in the SCLC's suit against Alabama, and the march to the courthouse expected later that day in Selma. The report also reviewed possible questions and suggested answers for the president's impending news conference. One called for Johnson to reply that no "deal" had governed Tuesday morning's events, and another called for him to note that he had not spoken personally to either King or Wallace. Johnson himself called Katzenbach at 9:00 A.M. for a status report on Selma, and Lawrence F. O'Brien, congressional liason chief, subsequently reported to the president that Katzenbach would be meeting with the Senate majority leader, Mike Mansfield, at 3:00 P.M. to discuss the voting rights legislation. Mansfield's reported feelings, which Dirksen also shared, were that the administration's draft bill was too

lengthy and complex, and he had his aides working on something simpler. Dirksen also had his staff at work on a far shorter draft, and further
sessions between the two senators and the attorney general were set for
Thursday. Lee White spent part of Wednesday drafting a possible introductory statement for the president to read at a Thursday press conference, but that statement and a subsequent version prepared by
speechwriter Harry McPherson were never used. Press Secretary Reedy
also found it necessary to deny reports that the president had called
Judge Johnson and that he had called steel company executives in an
effort to have them put pressure on Governor Wallace.[17]

In Selma, Abernathy's announced march to the courthouse, led by the
Reverend L.L. Anderson, was blocked on Sylvan Street by Wilson
Baker and Mayor Smitherman, who had decided to ban any marches
outside of the Brown's Chapel area. A number of marchers came forward to lead prayers and make impromptu statements to the large crowd
of onlooking newsmen as state and local officials proceeded to cordon
off the area around Brown's, in which the movement was headquar-
tered. Late that afternoon Baker announced the arrest of three men
alleged to have attacked Reeb, whose wife had arrived in Alabama earlier that day aboard a special government jet. Dr. King himself "stayed
in seclusion" in the rear of Brown's throughout the day because of the
strong feelings against him that had been aroused by Tuesday's turning
back. Wednesday evening, as the blocked marchers began an all-night
vigil in Sylvan Street, King left for Montgomery, where Judge Johnson's
hearing would commence the next morning at nine o'clock. Earlier on
Wednesday, Montgomery had been the scene of a SNCC-sponsored
demonstration in front of the state capitol by seven hundred Tuskegee
Institute students, an event which the SCLC had opposed and which
eventually lasted well into Wednesday night.[18]

Thursday morning's papers gave front-page coverage to the blocked
marchers in Selma, focusing particular photographic attention on the
nuns at the forefront of the group.[19] The papers also reported the continuing national reaction as prominent figures spoke out and as the National Council of Churches called a Thursday afternoon meeting in
Washington to discuss the Selma situation.

As Thursday morning began at the White House, Jack Valenti informed the president: "all quiet on the civil rights front. Mostly waiting
to see what happens to the beaten minister. Trouble will erupt when he
dies." Various ministers and religious leaders, Valenti went on, would
meet in the morning with Bill Moyers and at 2:00 P.M. with Moyers,
Vice-President Humphrey, Lee White, and Katzenbach. White and

Horace Busby were continuing to work on an opening statement for the president's upcoming news conference, and Attorney General Katzenbach would be on hand for a noontime session the president was to have with a group of black newspaper publishers.[20] In the briefing paper for that session, written by Katzenbach and passed on by Valenti, it was suggested that the president deny that any agreement had existed on Tuesday morning. Johnson might also tell them, "strictly off the record," that he had been "so concerned" about Tuesday's march becoming a possible repetition of Sunday's that he had had "armed forces available nearby for possible use." The president was to say further that legislation on voting rights would go to Congress "very very soon" and that criminal prosecution of Clark and other officers for Sunday's attack was planned.

Before that noontime meeting began, however, Johnson was informed at about 11:20 that twelve demonstrators who had entered the White House on one of the regular tours had begun a sit-in in a first-floor hallway. Rufus Youngblood, the Secret Service agent who informed the president of the development, advised arresting them immediately, but Johnson called Lee White and then ordered, as the White House Daily Diary's account reports it, "that if they could be isolated, then let us leave them alone and we'll look into it." After seeking Moyers' and Valenti's views as well, Johnson

> ordered that all traffic be detoured away from the demonstrators. No staff people were allowed near them. They were not to be given the satisfaction of being seen by anyone other than the police and Secret Service men who were surrounding them. They were to be given no attention—by the people who work in the White House. The President gave Rufus certain instructions as to how the demonstrators should be removed from the White House. He suggested that they use plain clothesmen and in combination of both negro and white policemen and they get about 3 to 5 cars and put a couple of the demonstrators in each car and take them out different gates at different intervals, and take them to different police stations.[21]

It is not without reason that many have noted Lyndon Johnson's interest in managing his public image.

Also that morning, Katzenbach was meeting with Senators Mansfield and Dirksen in the latter's Capitol office. Both of the senators had their own draft proposals, and the discussion considered those as well as the administration's version. Senators Kuchel of California and Long of Louisiana also attended. The two basic questions reportedly discussed were, first, what basis should be used for determining the assignment of federal registrars and, second, by whom should such assignments be initiated and overseen. A substantial consensus formed that states or counties whose registration fell below fifty percent should be eligible for such appointments. In regard to the latter issue, Dirksen supported a requirement that some judicial finding be made before federal officials—hopefully under judicial control—were sent in, while Mansfield favored a series of administrative procedures to be performed by the attorney general or the Civil Rights Commission with subsequent court action being possible if a party so desired. By the time that the morning session broke up, however, Katzenbach could say that no "substantial disagreement" existed and that what differences did remain were ones over "method." Such "substantial agreement" had been reached, in fact, that Katzenbach had hopes of sending a draft of the proposed message accompanying the legislation to Johnson on Friday.

Justice Department attorneys met with the two senators and their aides again later that afternoon to work on the remaining differences.[22] Just what those differences were was outlined in a memo prepared within the Justice Department that day. First among those issues to be resolved was whether the legislation should include any congressional "findings," and that if it did, should one of them relate to the southern states' failure to provide blacks with equal educational opportunities. In regard to title I of the basic administration draft, several questions remained. First, should any other "trigger formula" for suspending literacy tests be considered other than a registration or turnout level below a certain percentage? Second, if a state's literacy test had been suspended, should a county or parish within that state be able to resume tests if *it* could show that it had practiced no discrimination? Further, should some simple literacy test, such as the completion of a brief registration form approved by the attorney general, be allowed in areas where state-imposed tests were suspended? Additionally, "Shall the state be permitted to reject those who have not completed six grades (as in the Lindsay bill)?" The fifth question the memo posed was whether a state whose registration or turnout level fell below the minimum specified percentage should be allowed to impose literacy tests under some circumstances, such as after approval from the Civil Rights Commission? Also, should the statistical findings of the Census Bureau be reviewable in any forum? The last item in regard to title I concerned whether the attorney general should be assigned the authority to limit what voting qualifications a jurisdiction could impose after its literacy tests had been suspended.

Concerning title II of the administration draft, the Justice Department memo indicated that agreement had yet to be reached with the two senate leaders on the method of assigning federal registrars. Should they be assigned to all jurisdictions whose tests were suspended? to whichever of such jurisdictions the attorney general chose to assign them? to counties where black registration was below 15 percent of the black voting age population? to counties where the black registration percentage was "significantly" less than the white percentage? or to jurisdictions from which some specific number of complaints of racially discriminatory registration practices had been received and verified? Further, the memo asked, should the draft proposal's requirement that those individuals registered by federal officials have failed in a recent effort to register with local officials, unless some certain number of applicants had been rejected wrongfully, be retained? Also, should federal registrars be empowered to accept local poll tax payments, or should poll taxes be eliminated altogether in areas to which federal registrars were assigned? Additionally, should the decisions of federal registrars be subject to appeal, either by rejected applicants or by state and local officials, to an administrative body or to the courts? Lastly, the memo asked, what means should be adopted for insuring that federal registrations would be honored at the polls? While the present departmental draft specified civil suit remedies and criminal penalties, other possible options contained in the Lindsay and Resnick bills included the use of federal election overseers or the voiding of elections in which federal registrations were not honored.[23]

While that list of questions was most on the minds of those few individuals meeting that Thursday morning to discuss the legislation's particulars, other senators who had not been taken into the administration's confidence—such as liberal Republicans Javits, Case, and Cooper—rose on the Senate floor to make known their intent to introduce voting rights proposals of their own within the next few days. Katzenbach, these senators stated, had urged them to wait until the administration had worked out a final proposal that would carry the endorsements of the two Senate leaders. If they were not admitted to these ongoing consultations, however, these other senators saw no point in simply cooling their heels. All told, six senators and twelve representatives delivered floor remarks concerning Selma and voting rights on Thursday, and aside from that matter of consultations the remarks focused primarily on the need for prompt legislation and the continuing reaction to Selma's violence, in particular the assault on Reeb.

In Montgomery Thursday morning, King appeared at the first day of hearings before Judge Johnson in the SCLC's suit to block state interference with any future attempts to march from Selma to Montgomery. Under questioning from Wallace's and Lingo's attorney, King, who reporters now were saying was being held in "open contempt" by other movement figures who felt that his actions Tuesday had "betrayed" the cause, admitted that he had termed Judge Johnson's Tuesday morning restraining order "unjust," but added later that he had had no intention of marching to Montgomery. King said he had feared what would happen if no march were held, claiming, "I did it to give them an outlet." Under direct questioning from Johnson, King openly admitted that there had been "a tacit agreement" arranged by Collins.[24] Fifty miles away in Selma a quiet day ensued as the confined crowd of would-be marchers, still blocked on Sylvan Street by state troopers, continued their vigil in the rain, waiting for word from Birmingham on the fate of the Reverend Reeb.

At midday on Thursday, President Johnson, accompanied by White, Clifford Alexander, Louis Martin, Moyers and Valenti, met with the black newspaper publishers. In midafternoon the president met twice with White, Moyers, Alexander, Valenti, and Reedy concerning the sit-in demonstrators in the East Wing. When Johnson made a brief trip to Capitol Hill to dedicate a congressional gymnasium, the demonstrators were removed in accordance with the scenario the president had outlined that morning. Back in the Oval Office shortly after 5:00 P.M., Johnson closely watched a televised press conference by Attorney General Katzenbach. Speaking of Sunday's attack, Katzenbach told the newsmen, "The sheriff's men and troopers used a totally unreasonable amount of force under the circumstances, in violation of constitutional rights." Johnson's own news conference, Reedy announced, would be held within a few days, once final agreement had been reached with the Senate leadership on the voting rights proposal.

After monitoring the evening news shows' coverage of the White House sit-in, Johnson proceeded to an East Room reception for some sixty members of Congress at which both he and Attorney General Katzenbach gave the first semipublic briefing on the Selma situation and the general provisions in the voting rights legislation. The president, those present recounted,

> laid heavy emphasis on the need for voting rights legislation and on his determination to get a bill that could be passed, that would be constitutional, and that would be effective in quickly registering all those entitled to vote.
>
> The formal presentation to the members of Congress was made by Attorney General Nicholas deB. Katzenbach, but Mr. Johnson

often took over for him, particularly in answering questions.

It was not enough, he told the group, to be concerned with demonstrations and their possible violent consequences. It was the causes of the demonstrations that had to be met, he said, and the cause of those in Alabama and at the White House was the desire for voting rights and opportunities.

At one point, Mr. Katzenbach told the legislators his department had started drawing up voting rights legislation as far back as November 5, two days after the Presidential election of 1964.

Representative James C. Cleveland, Republican of New Hampshire, broke in with some heat to ask, "Where is your bill then? Why has it taken four months?"

Before Katzenbach could reply, President Johnson stood up, "obviously stung," as one witness described it.

Mr. Johnson replied that many proposals had been considered, all constitutional questions had been weighed, and that Republican voting rights bills—including one introduced by Mr. Cleveland—were being taken into account.

Some sharp questions were also delivered by Mississippi's John Bell Williams and by Alabama representative Glenn Andrews, in whose district Dallas County lay. The president, Tom Wicker wrote in Friday's *New York Times*, "replied forcefully to Mr. Andrews, strongly upholding the right of all citizens to vote freely, and pledging uncompromising action to reach that goal." Some ninety minutes into that session, at about 9:00 P.M. Marvin Watson relayed to Johnson the news that the Reverend Reeb had died in Birmingham an hour earlier. Johnson, accompanied by Lady Bird and Vice-President Humphrey, then called Mrs. Reeb and the slain man's father.[25]

Friday morning's papers highlighted the passing of Reeb and the mounting reaction to the Selma situation among the nation's clergy. A group of national religious leaders announced a rally in Lafayette Park on Sunday to protest President Johnson's "lack of action," and a number of denominational leaders in Washington and New York made it known that they had written letters to their priests, rabbis, and ministers urging that weekend sermons speak to the events in Selma. At the White House two quickly scheduled meetings with the president had been arranged for two groups of religious leaders, each to last forty-five minutes. The first session, with a delegation of Washington area clergy led by Walter Fauntroy and including Bishop Paul Moore, began with "considerable tension" as the clergymen made known their unhappiness with what they believed to be Johnson's lack of action, especially in terms of arranging for federal troops to protect the Selma demonstrators, a call which many around the country, and a few in Congress, had taken up. Johnson himself had been advised by Lee White to detail for the clergymen, as he had for the black publishers on Thursday, those steps that the federal government had taken and his very close monitoring of continuing developments. By the time the meeting eventually ended two hours later, the atmosphere had "gradually eased," but the clergy remained far from happy with Johnson.

The second session, which also lasted over two hours, was with a delegation from the National Council of Churches which included Bishop John Wesley Lord, Dr. Eugene Carson Blake, and Birmingham's Reverend Joseph Ellwanger, who had led the white Alabamians in their Saturday demonstration in Selma. In this meeting, which was more "amicable" than the first one, Johnson stressed not only his commitment to obtaining voting rights legislation but also his more wide-ranging legislative goals. The day's other appointments were kept waiting as this session went on until 2:30 P.M. Later that afternoon Johnson had an hour-long discussion of the civil rights and Selma situations with Katzenbach, Moyers, Harry McPherson, and Douglass Cater, and a presidential press conference was announced for 3:30 P.M. on Saturday.[26]

Also on Friday afternoon, Katzenbach met again with Mansfield and Dirksen to reduce further the number of items in the draft legislation on which differences of opinion remained. Three of the issues noted in Thursday's Justice Department memorandum were the primary topics of discussion. In regard to determining the basis on which tests would be suspended and a locale would become eligible for federal registrars, a substantial consensus was reached that a failure to have at least a 50 percent turnout or registration at either the state or county level at the time of the 1964 presidential election would be the basic "trigger formula." Some disagreement still remained on the details of the federal registration process, for Dirksen continued to articulate his dislike for a program administered by the federal executive branch rather than by the local federal district courts. In regard to how the actual voting of federal registrants should be protected, the three men agreed that federal district judges should be called upon to immediately hear such complaints and could take control of the election and bar certification of its results.

The draft version at the end of that Friday afternoon session stood as follows. The initial declaration of congressional "findings" had been dispensed with, and the trigger formula and the appointment of federal registrars by the Civil Service Commission to locales covered by the trigger at the discretion of the attorney general were detailed in sections

3 and 4. The requirement that federal registrants must have tried and failed to obtain registration through local officials was retained in section 5, though it now could be waived at the attorney general's discretion rather than only after the accumulation of some specific number of verified cases of erroneous rejections by local registrars. Section 6 specified that federal registrars' decisions could be appealed first to a Civil Service Commission hearing examiner and then to a circuit court of appeals. Section 7 retained the criminal and civil penalties for obstructing voting by a federal registrant that had been outlined in the earlier departmental draft, and section 8 of the present version specified that federal registrars could be withdrawn by decision of the attorney general.[27] Neither house of Congress met on Friday, but visiting clergymen met with a number of members, including large groups that saw Robert F. Kennedy and Jacob Javits of New York and Leverett Saltonstall of Massachusetts.

In Alabama on Friday, in the second day of Judge Johnson's hearing, five FBI agents testified about Sunday's attack, and a three-minute CBS film of the violence was shown as well.[28] In Selma the Sylvan Street vigil continued as city officials persisted in their refusal to allow the marchers outside of the Brown's Chapel area. Attempts by the CRS director, Collins, to arrange permission for a rally at the courthouse in Reeb's memory proved unsuccessful. Dr. King, as on Thursday, remained in Montgomery. At the state capitol late Friday afternoon, Wallace advisors Earl Morgan, Seymour Trammell, Bill Jones, Hugh Maddox, and Cecil Jackson went to the governor and recommended that he wire Johnson asking to discuss the Selma situation with him. Wallace did so, though emphasizing in the telegram, "State authorities are completely adequate to cope with the situation." Two hours later Johnson replied that he would be willing to see the governor at any time. Trammell thereupon called OEP Director Buford Ellington and an appointment was arranged for noontime Saturday at the White House.

On Saturday morning as Wallace flew into Washington, the public demonstrations that had gone on all week throughout the country continued in the nation's capital and in other major cities. Also that morning, Deputy Attorney General Ramsey Clark sent to Bill Moyers the latest draft of the voting rights legislation, which had been the subject of another meeting between the two Senate leaders and their staffs and Justice Department representatives at the Capitol earlier in the day. Most of the changes made between Friday's and Saturday's drafts involved only minor alterations in wording; federal registrars, for example, became federal "examiners." In the majority of sections, such as 5 and 6, the wording had been tightened up, but no substantive changes of note had taken place. Section 7, though, had been revised to provide a more detailed explanation of how federal registrants faced with obstructions at the polls could enlist the help of the local U.S. attorney, who immediately would bring the matter before a federal district judge, who would be asked to enjoin the certification of the election results.

After receiving a short briefing from Katzenbach and Burke Marshall, Johnson and the attorney general received Wallace and his aides at the White House a few moments before noon. The two principals, along with Katzenbach, Marshall, and Trammell, went into the Oval Office, and then Johnson and Wallace adjourned for a private session. Johnson later described the meeting as one in which he kept his eyes "directly on the Governor's face the entire time," and he characterized Wallace, who insisted that the demonstrators themselves, and not their grievances, were the problem, as "nervous" and "aggressive."

At 3:10 P.M., with no major decisions or concessions having been made, Johnson, accompanied by Wallace, emerged for the press conference, which at the last moment had been opened to radio and TV coverage and moved outside to the Rose Garden to accommodate the number of newsmen present. As more than one thousand civil rights supporters continued to picket outside the mansion's fences, Johnson began the session by stating, "This March week has brought a very deep and painful challenge to the unending search for American freedom. . . . Last Sunday a group of Negro Americans in Selma, Alabama, attempted peacefully to protest the denial of the most basic political right of all—the right to vote. They were attacked and some were brutally beaten." After briefly reviewing the efforts of the executive branch over the preceding six days, Johnson went on:

> The events of last Sunday cannot and will not be repeated, but the demonstrations in Selma have a much larger meaning. They are a protest against a deep and very unjust flaw in American democracy itself.
>
> Ninety-five years ago our Constitution was amended to require that no American be denied the right to vote because of race or color. Almost a century later, many Americans, are kept from voting simply because they are Negroes.
>
> Therefore, this Monday I will send to the Congress a request for legislation to carry out the amendment of the Constitution.

After describing the administration bill in extremely general terms, Johnson continued.

What happened in Selma was an American tragedy. The blows that were received, the blood that was shed, the life of the good man that was lost, must strengthen the determination of each of us to bring full and equal and exact justice to all of our people.

This is not just the policy of your government or your President. It is in the heart and the purpose and the meaning of America itself.

We all know how complex and how difficult it is to bring about basic social change in a democracy, but this complexity must not obscure the clear and simple moral issues.

It is wrong to do violence to peaceful citizens in the streets of their town. It is wrong to deny Americans the right to vote. It is wrong to deny any person full equality because of the color of his skin.

After continuing on in this vein for another five paragraphs, the president discussed his conversation with Governor Wallace. Johnson reported that he had said to Wallace "that those Negro citizens of Alabama who have systematically been denied the right to register and to participate in the choice of those who govern them should be provided the opportunity of directing national attention to their plight. They feel that they are being denied a very precious right. And I understand their concern." He had added, he said, that he was "firmly convinced . . . that when all of the eligible Negroes of Alabama have been registered, the economic and social injustices they have experienced throughout will be righted, and the demonstrations . . . will stop."

After further relating how he had impressed upon Wallace his belief that the supremacy of law, and law and order, must always be maintained, Johnson went on to say that he had "told the Governor that the brutality in Selma last Sunday just must not be repeated." The president then concluded his prepared remarks by outlining the three steps that he had advised Wallace to take: to declare publicly his support for universal suffrage; to assure the right of peaceful assembly in Alabama; and to hold biracial meetings to strive for greater interracial cooperation.

In response to the questions that followed, Johnson spoke of his support for Selma-related demonstrations elsewhere in the country, of Wallace's expressed desire for the president to take some action to halt the demonstrations in Alabama, and of his response that efforts should be focused on eliminating the cause of the demonstrations rather than the demonstrations themselves. In answer to a later question, Johnson in effect confirmed that federal troops were ready if the president should conclude they were needed in Selma. Johnson also stated that he had seen no purpose in having a press conference before the voting rights legislative proposals were ready, and for that reason this was his first appearance before the press since Sunday's attack. The White House, he said, had received the approved draft of the legislation from Justice just a few hours earlier. After the formal news conference had ended and the recording devices had been turned off, Katzenbach gave a background briefing on the content of the voting rights bill and detailed the areas to which it would apply. After that, Johnson told the press that he hoped the message accompanying the proposal would be ready for them Monday morning, and that the actual bill would go to Congress either on Monday or shortly thereafter. Governor Wallace made no substantive comments before departing for Montgomery.[29]

In Alabama on Saturday Judge Johnson had held a third day of hearings, and the testimony of the main witness, Colonel Lingo, had failed to explicate just who had initiated the Sunday attack. Several blacks also testified in detail about the attacks upon them in Marion on February 18 and in Selma in the aftermath of the March 7 attack on U.S. 80. In Selma on Saturday the faceoff between the would-be marchers and Baker's city police continued as efforts by Collins, and reportedly Baker himself, to persuade Smitherman to allow a march downtown proved unavailing. One group of about 175 clergymen, led by the Reverend C.T. Vivian and former Notre Dame president John J. Cavanaugh, failed in an attempt to evade the surrounding forces and head downtown. An attempt later in the day by seventeen black Selma youths and one white SNCC worker to reach the courthouse by quietly sneaking out of the area around Brown's worked, but Baker had to rescue them from a threatening white mob when Clark's men around the courthouse refused to intervene and protect them.[30] Around the country the Sylvan Street standoff continued to receive front-page coverage in newspapers, and vigils or marches memorializing or protesting the situation, and particularly Reeb's death, were held in a number of major cities—including Boston, Philadelphia, Cincinnati, Toledo, Milwaukee, Los Angeles, and St. Louis—and smaller towns on Saturday.

Sunday's papers gave front-page coverage to the president's news conference and to the continuing national protests. Many also reported the substantial foreign coverage that Selma had received, something a number of congressmen had noted with despair in their earlier floor statements. Photographs of the previous Sunday's assault accompanied the weekly wrap-up stories carried in several major papers, and the theme that unjustified violence had been done to peaceful marchers seeking the franchise thus was reiterated. The *New York Times Magazine* published an article by Martin Luther King, Jr., that emphasized how crucial the movement believed the franchise to be. King's article detailed the several incidents of official violence that had taken place in Selma in February for those readers who might have forgotten them.[31]

At 12:30 P.M. on Sunday, Governor Wallace appeared live from Montgomery on CBS's "Face the Nation," and he devoted most of his remarks to attacking the press coverage of events in Selma. Not only were the television networks and the wire services distorting the news of Selma, Wallace charged, but many northern papers were giving more prominent attention to the continuing stalemate in Selma than they were to what the Alabama governor said were more serious news events in their own states or towns. Following that program Wallace held a news conference, televised live by ABC, at which he repeated his allegations. NBC broadcast a one-hour special report reviewing the previous week's events in Selma, and in Washington more than 15,000 persons gathered in Lafayette Park to participate in an ecumenical protest, sponsored by the National Council of Churches, over alleged federal inaction. In Boston a memorial rally for Reeb drew an estimated 20,000 persons, and other major public marches or rallies were held in Manhattan, Louisville, San Francisco, and New Orleans as well as in countless smaller towns.

While some minor changes in the draft proposal's language still were being discussed on Sunday afternoon, at 5:00 P.M. Johnson met in the Cabinet Room with the congressional leadership to discuss the question of how the voting rights message should be transmitted to the Congress. In attendance, besides Johnson, Humphrey, and Katzenbach, were the House Speaker, John McCormack, the House majority leader, Carl Albert, the House majority whip, Hale Boggs, Republican representative William McCulloch, Senators Mansfield, Dirksen and Kuchel, and Ramsey Clark, Lawrence F. O'Brien, Lee White, Jack Valenti, Harry McPherson, Harold F. Reis, Barefoot Sanders, and Burke Marshall.

Johnson began by reviewing the preparation of the bill, his responses to the Selma crisis, and his fear of any confrontation between federal and state forces in Alabama. Many people who had been criticizing his restraint, Johnson said, "don't understand what we have been doing." Johnson then went on to summarize his meeting with Governor Wallace.

Mansfield then spoke up and suggested that Johnson send up the voting rights bill on Tuesday. Dirksen suggested Tuesday afternoon, so that it could be previewed at a Republican policy meeting scheduled for earlier that day. McCulloch endorsed what Dirksen had suggested. McCormack then spoke up and advocated that Johnson go before a joint session and speak about the bill, and also perhaps about Vietnam. Dirksen disagreed. "Don't panic now. This is a deliberate government. Don't circumvent Congress. Don't let these people say 'we scared him into it'."

"I wouldn't think about that," Johnson replied. "People do not know the facts—that we are doing all we can to solve this. We must tell the people to give us time to work this out."

Humphrey spoke up in support of McCormack's idea, saying, "Emotions are running high. A message of what this government is doing— simply—is what is needed." Humphrey's own civil rights advisors, the vice-president told Johnson, all believed that the president should go on television.

Johnson remained undecided on McCormack's suggestion. "I intend to tell the country what we recommend," he remarked. "Either I do it on TV or through the newspapers—or through the Congress."

Carl Albert interjected, "I don't think you coming before the Congress would be a sign of panic. I think it would help."

"It would show bipartisanship," McCormack added, "and it would show the world."

"Probably I could come down Monday or Tuesday night—about 9:00 P.M.," Johnson mused, "and then send the bill up Wednesday."

Kuchel emphasized how strong the position of the administration and congressional proponents of voting rights legislation was. Johnson recalled his endorsement of a voting bill in the State of the Union message and spoke of his desire that registration requirements be reduced to a minimum. McCulloch endorsed McCormack's and Albert's suggestion that Johnson go before the Congress and the president's suggestion that the bill then go up on Wednesday. Johnson then noted, as he had several times earlier in the week, that the noise of the White House pickets had disturbed his daughters' sleep.

McCormack brought the discussion back on track, asking straight out, "Do you want to address a joint session?"

Katzenbach urged the president to do so. "This would put the problem and the solution before the country."

Johnson acquiesced. "Let's say Tuesday night and send the bill up Wednesday," he said. He turned to the Senate minority leader and added, "Dirksen, you started this arm-twisting label. I don't arm twist anybody."

Humphrey interrupted, asking, "Isn't Tuesday the day for the march?" Katzenbach responded that he did not think King would do anything until the court order had been issued by Judge Johnson, but that King was "unpredictable."

By the time the session ended at 6:30, agreement had been reached on a Monday evening appearance. A statement drafted largely by Johnson was issued, saying that the congressional leadership had invited the president to appear before a joint session.

After the congressmen had departed, Johnson gathered a number of staff members and for five hours the group discussed what the subsequent evening's speech should contain. Johnson later wrote that he had told the aides that he "wanted to use every ounce of moral persuasion the Presidency held. I wanted no hedging, no equivocation. And I wanted to talk from my own heart, from my own experience." Towards the end of the session Johnson paused to call King, who was in Chicago, to invite him to attend the Monday address. He also called Whitney Young and Roy Wilkins. At about midnight speechwriter Richard Goodwin began work on a draft of the address, a draft that Johnson received when he awoke on Monday morning.[32]

Monday, March 15, was a notable day, and not only for the speech that Johnson was to deliver that evening. In Alabama early that morning Wilcox County's first black voter of the twentieth century was registered, as were the first ones in nearby Lowndes—twelve in number. In Selma, LeRoy Collins and Wilson Baker managed to enlist Judge Thomas in their continuing effort to arrange permission for a courthouse rally in Reeb's memory. Thomas called Sheriff Clark, and that afternoon, with Baker's officers between Clark's men and the more than two thousand marchers, the lengthy column moved downtown for a twenty-minute service on the courthouse steps that concluded before the rear of the column arrived.

In his first public appearance in Selma in six days, King himself led the service. With him on the steps were Episcopal Bishop John E. Hines, Greek Orthodox Archbishop Iakovos, United Auto Workers President Walter P. Reuther, and Massachusetts representatives Edward Boland and Silvio Conte. Despite its brevity, Coretta Scott King later was to refer to the memorial gathering as "perhaps the greatest and most inspiring ecumenical service ever held." Later that evening in Selma, the open feud between Baker and Clark escalated to a physical confrontation that ended only when Mayor Smitherman stepped between the two men's raised fists. In Montgomery on Monday Judge Johnson held the fourth day of hearings on the SCLC's request for an order allowing the march to Montgomery, which a number of state troopers testified would be dangerous.[33]

In Washington on Monday further last-minute consideration was given to the precise wording of the proposed bill at a morning meeting in Dirksen's office. Ramsey Clark's assistant Barefoot Sanders sent Representative McCulloch several copies of the most up-to-date draft, noting that it was still being discussed further but that "the basic approach which this draft represents will remain as is." This Monday draft differed from those of Friday and Saturday in only a few respects, but one very important change was the addition to section 8 of a new provision that declared a moratorium on any new voter qualifications after March 15, 1965 by any jurisdiction covered under the basic trigger formula. The Monday draft also dropped a phrase that would have required federal examiners to be legal residents of the state in which they served; it also added new penalties for the destruction of ballots. The Monday version also waived the need for registrants to make timely payments of their poll taxes in counties assigned federal examiners.[34]

On Capitol Hill during the day, eight senators and eight representatives spoke on the need for voting rights legislation, while two Alabama representatives rose to defend their state. In the Senate Paul Douglas of Illinois fulfilled the promise—or threat—from the bipartisan group of liberals to introduce their own voting bill by formally putting forward such a proposal on behalf of himself, Case, Clark, Cooper, Fong, Hart, Javits, McNamara, Proxmire, and Scott. In the House, Alabama representative Dave Martin accused President Johnson of having given in to "these demands of the mob" for voting rights legislation. New Jersey Democrat Frank Thompson responded with a heated attack upon Martin himself, saying that Martin "not only opposes giving the Negro the right to vote but fears that if they do vote he will be defeated."[35]

Throughout the day at the White House work continued on the speech for that evening. While the final speech closely resembled the first draft prepared by Goodwin, Johnson himself added a long section towards the end on his own experiences as a young man in Texas and also inserted several references to his own role in earlier civil rights legislation. Johnson also added to the text several references to the bipartisan authorship and support of this present voting rights proposal, and he continued reworking the text up until less than an hour before its 9:00 P.M. delivery.

Some seventy million Americans viewed on all three television networks the first personally delivered special presidential message on a piece of domestic legislation in nineteen years. Lyndon Johnson, as Tom Wicker wrote in the *Times*, "took the rallying cry of American Negroes into Congress and millions of American homes tonight by pledging that 'we shall overcome' what he called 'a crippling legacy of bigotry and injustice.'" As he had in his remarks on Saturday, the president once again denounced the actions that state and local officials had taken against the Selma protestors. "Many were brutally assaulted," Johnson noted. "One good man—a man of God—was killed." Reviewing the history of black suffrage in the South, Johnson stated, "Every device of which human ingenuity is capable has been used to deny" the right to vote. "It is wrong—deadly wrong," the president continued, "to deny any of your fellow Americans the right to vote in this country." Calling for no delay, no hesitation, and no compromise, Johnson reminded the assembled legislators that "outside this chamber is the outraged conscience of a nation." Dropping from the prepared text a line criticizing the tactics of some demonstrators in northern cities who had blocked traffic, Johnson went on to endorse the Selma demonstrations, saying of the black American, "His actions and protests, his courage to risk safety and even to risk his life, have awakened the conscience of this nation. His demonstrations have been designed to call attention to injustice, designed to provoke change, designed to stir reform. . . . Equality depends," the president stated, "not on the force of arms or tear gas but upon the force of moral right."

In the course of his forty-five minute address Johnson was interrupted forty times by applause and received two standing ovations, the first coming after his call for "no delay, no hesitation, no compromise with our purpose," and the second occurring in response to Johnson's relating near the end of the speech the story of his first personal encounter with poverty and racism as a young teacher in Texas. The president made explicit reference to Selma more than a dozen times, in one instance comparing it to Lexington, Concord, and Appomattox, saying that "at times history and fate meet at a single time in a single place to shape a turning point in man's unending search for freedom. . . . So it was last week in Selma, Alabama."[36]

Observers were seemingly unanimous in their praise of the address. Goldman reported that "veteran congressmen could not recall when the room had been so hushed" as it was during many parts of Johnson's speech. Evans and Novak later were to call the address "by all odds the best, most genuinely moving speech Johnson had made as President." Johnson's handpicked biographer subsequently was to call it "probably the most important speech of the decade," while two civil rights commentators who otherwise were sharply critical of Johnson termed it "the most radical statement ever made by a President on civil rights" and "one of the two or three most important Presidential pronouncements ever on the nature of social change."[37]

In Tuesday morning's newspapers the speech was given banner headlines, and the *Post*'s Carroll Kilpatrick wrote that in official Washington it had received "a reception that has seldom been witnessed before." At the White House Tuesday morning, congratulatory phone calls and telegrams poured in, including a note from Supreme Court Justice William O. Douglas telling the president that the address had been "absolutely superb . . . the best ever."

That afternoon Katzenbach, Mansfield, and Dirksen met once again to work on details, and at a dinnertime meeting with the House Democratic leadership and assistant whips Johnson stressed his strong desire for quick passage. Observers were unanimous in predicting swift passage of the bill with few amendments, noting that many southern senators had not spoken out against Johnson's move and that some—Long, Fulbright, Smathers, and Gore—were privately commenting that they might be able to support the bill. On Capitol Hill Tuesday, several members rose to commend the president on the speech, while two southerners—Alabama's Glenn Andrews and Louisiana's Allen Ellender—rose to attack it.[38]

On Tuesday morning in Selma several attempted marches were blocked by either Baker's men or Clark's. In Montgomery, Judge Johnson's hearing was concluded with the submission by SCLC attorneys of a detailed plan for the actual march. Wednesday's headlines, though, were to concern an incident that occurred later that afternoon in Montgomery. Some six hundred voting rights marchers, mostly young, northern and white, had gathered near the state capitol early in the afternoon. Keeping watch on the group were a number of officers from city, county, and state police forces. Suddenly a handful of mounted officers rode into a small group of demonstrators that was separated by about a block from the main body of the protestors. As Roy Reed's account in the Wednesday *Times* described it,

> One rider began striking the demonstrators with a rope and another beat them with a nightstick.
>
> A posseman dressed in green clothes and a white 10-gallon hat stepped up on foot and, while the horses partly hid him from view, began clubbing the demonstrators. Several still refused to move, and the man's nightstick began falling with great force on their heads.
>
> There was a moment of freakish near-quiet, when the yells all seemed to subside at once, and in that instant the man in green struck hard on the head of a young man. The sound of the nightstick carried up and down the block.
>
> Across Decatur Street, the larger crowd was almost hysterical.
>
> "They're killing them. They're killing them," a voice kept cry-

ing. "There, you photographers, get pictures of them killing them."

When the smaller group was routed, the mounted officers waded into the larger one.

The horsemen routed all the demonstrators after about ten minutes and herded them back toward the South Jackson Street Baptist Church.

Although the impact of the Montgomery attack was not to rival that of Selma's "Bloody Sunday," it was nonetheless quite substantial. In Washington, Manhattan Democrat William F. Ryan, seeing the news of the attack on the wire-service tickers in the Speaker's Lobby, rushed on to the floor and angrily read the wire copy to his colleagues, announcing that he would immediately telegram President Johnson to request that federal troops be sent in. On Wednesday morning both the *Washington Post* and the *New York Times* printed two photos of the attack and its victims on their front pages. One particular picture, portraying the

United Press International Photo

New York Times, March 17, 1965, p. 1—

"Members of civil rights group are hemmed in by mounted possemen and a state trooper during melee in Montgomery."

Washington Post, March 17, 1965, p. 1—

"Sheriff's deputies and a state policeman, wielding canes and sticks, ride into demonstrators in Montgomery, Ala." (UPI)

mounted officers attacking the demonstrators with sticks and canes, was featured by both papers. Many of Wednesday morning's papers also carried editorials praising Johnson's Monday night address.[39]

On Wednesday morning the formal letters from the president to Vice-President Humphrey and Speaker McCormack conveying the actual legislation went to Capitol Hill. The draft as submitted differed only minutely from that which Sanders had sent to McCulloch on Monday, the one notable change being that states and counties subject to the bill's provisions could institute suits in the Federal District Court for the District of Columbia seeking to prove that they had not engaged in any racial discrimination in the electoral field in the previous ten years. If they were able to prove such a contention they would be exempted from the act's provisions. The proposal as submitted, observers noted, failed to stake out any clear position on the question of voting by illiterates, a matter that some had feared would become a bone of contention. While published reports indicated that the maximum possible opposition to the bill numbered eighteen in the Senate and about one hundred in the House, private reports reaching the White House from members of the Louisiana delegation indicated an even rosier situation. White House assistant James R. Jones related to Marvin Watson that Senator Russell Long had spoken strongly in favor of the bill at a private dinner party on Tuesday evening, and that Long had indicated he might be able to persuade half of the South's twenty-two senators to support the bill. Representative Jimmy Morrison himself called Watson and predicted that at least half of Louisiana's eight House members would vote for it, and that no more than seventy-five representatives would vote against it.[40]

On Capitol Hill Wednesday, following a telegram from Wallace to Representative George W. Andrews, those who sought to defend Alabama's recent record and to declare their opposition to any voting rights bill made their first substantial number of speeches. Andrews himself declared that no voter registration problems existed in Dallas County and that King's presence was the source of all the state's current problems. Similar comments were made by Andrews' seven Alabama colleagues and by William M. Tuck of Virginia, John Bell Williams of Mississippi, and Joe D. Waggonner of Louisiana, and in the Senate by Sam Ervin of North Carolina. Williams went so far as to say that the Reverend Reeb had "found the trouble he was looking for."[41]

In Selma, Judge Thomas again arranged permission for a march to the courthouse with Sheriff Clark, while an angry Baker arrested a small group picketing Mayor Smitherman's home in a residential section of town. In Montgomery, King, James Forman of SNCC, and John Doar of the Justice Department met with local Montgomery officials, including the county sheriff, Mac Sim Butler. Following the meeting Butler publicly apologized for the previous day's attack, attributing it to a "misunderstanding." King then led a rally on the steps of the Montgomery County courthouse, remarking, "We are here today to say to the white men that we will no longer let them use their clubs on us in dark corners. We are going to make them do it in the glaring light of television."[42]

A bit later that afternoon, several blocks away Judge Johnson handed down his ruling in the SCLC suit against the state authorities, *Williams v. Wallace*. Johnson began by reviewing the largely unsuccessful efforts of Dallas County blacks to register to vote in any substantial numbers, and the reactions that those efforts had drawn from the local authorities. "The evidence in this case," Johnson wrote, "reflects that . . . an almost continuous pattern of conduct has existed on the part of defendant Sheriff Clark, his deputies, and his auxiliary deputies known as 'possemen' of harassment, intimidation, coercion, threatening conduct, and, sometimes, brutal mistreatment toward these plaintiffs and other members of their class." The judge went on to describe the tactics and weapons utilized on February 10 in the forced march and on February 18 in the Marion assault. "The harassment and and brutal treatment on the part of defendants Lingo and Clark . . . while acting under instructions from Governor Wallace," Johnson continued, "reached a climax on Sunday, March 7." He went on to give a detailed description of Sunday's events, noting that the marchers had observed all traffic regulations in making their way from Brown's Chapel to the spot of the attack. Johnson described the assault and the use of tear gas, and concluded that Cloud, in ordering the troopers forward, had acted "upon specific instructions from his superior officers" and that the "general plan as followed by the State troopers in this instance had been discussed with and was known to Governor Wallace."

"The attempted march alongside U.S. Highway 80 . . . on March 7, 1965," the judge concluded, "involved nothing more than a peaceful effort on the part of Negro citizens to exercise a classic constitutional right; that is, the right to assemble peaceably and to petition one's government for the redress of grievances." The conduct of the defendants, Johnson found, had been aimed not at enforcing any valid laws but merely at "preventing and discouraging Negro citizens from exercising their rights of citizenship, particularly the right to register to vote and the right to demonstrate peaceably for the purpose of protesting discriminatory practices."

Having made these findings of fact, Johnson proceeded to articulate the principle that would govern the granting of the appropriate relief. After outlining both the protestors' right to march and the general public's right to transit on the highways, Johnson wrote that

> there must be in cases like the one now presented, a "constitutional boundary line" drawn between the competing interests of society. This Court has the duty and responsibility in this case of drawing the "constitutional boundary line." In doing so, it seems basic to our constitutional principles that the extent of the right to assemble, demonstrate and march peaceably along the highways and streets in an orderly manner should be commensurate with the enormity of the wrongs that are being protested and petitioned against. In this case, the wrongs are enormous. The extent of the right to demonstrate against these wrongs should be determined accordingly.

After stating that Wallace's March 6 proclamation banning any such march had stepped across that "constitutional boundary line," Johnson went on to outline and approve the march plan submitted by the SCLC's attorneys. It called for approval of an unlimited number of marchers on those sections of Highway 80 which had four lanes, and a three hundred-marcher limit on the portion with only two lanes. Support services and evening camp grounds for the five-day trek were also spelled out. Calling the plan "reasonable," the judge noted that it reached, "under the particular circumstances of this case, to the outer limits of what is constitutionally allowed. However, the wrongs and injustices inflicted upon these plaintiffs and the members of their class . . . have clearly exceeded—and continue to exceed—the outer limits of what is constitutionally permissible. . . The extent of a group's constitutional right to protest peaceably and petition one's government for redress of grievances must be, if our American Constitution is to be a flexible and 'living' document, found and held to be commensurate with the enormity of the wrongs being protested and petitioned against. This is particularly true when the usual, basic and constitutionally-provided means of protesting in our American way—voting—have been deprived."

Johnson then proceeded to deny Wallace's request for an injunction against any march and announced that he would grant the SCLC's request for an injunction against state and Dallas County officials prohibiting interference with the approved march and enjoining them from failing to assist it. The Justice Department, the judge added, had informed him that the federal government stood ready to respond to any request for assistance in protecting the march which Governor Wallace might make. Later that Wednesday evening Hosea Williams told newsmen that the now sanctioned march would begin on Sunday, the twenty-first.[43]

Following Wednesday's formal presentation of the voting legislation, action began in a rush on Thursday morning. In the Senate, after some confusion resulting from Dirksen's surprise that the actual bill did not require that federal examiners be residents of the state in which they served, a provision that was dropped over the weekend but which Dirksen apparently believed had been reinserted early Wednesday, the legislation was referred to the Judiciary Committee with instructions to report it back to the floor no later than April 9. That move was approved on a 67 to 13 vote—66 Senators had joined in sponsoring the bill—with 12 southerners objecting to the limitation and Margaret Chase Smith of Maine protesting its referral to that committee at all.

In the House, Subcommittee No. 5 of the Judiciary Committee began hearings on the bill with the committee chairman, Emanuel Celler, presiding. "Recent events in Alabama, involving murder, savage brutality, and violence by local police, state troopers, and posses," Celler observed in opening the session, "have so aroused the nation as to make action by this Congress necessary and speedy. . . . The climate of public opinion throughout the nation has so changed because of the Alabama outrages, as to make assured passage of this solid bill—a bill that would have been inconceivable a year ago."

The first witness before the subcommittee was Attorney General Katzenbach, whose opening remarks were devoted to emphasizing how important the franchise was in the eyes of the Justice Department. "There is," he said, "no right more central and no right more precious than the right to vote." Citing the very limited registration gains in the hard-core areas of the Deep South between 1957 and 1964, and detailing in particular the Dallas County experience, Katzenbach went on to argue that this record indicated "the inadequacy of the judicial process to deal effectively and expeditiously with a problem so deep-seated and so complex" as racial discrimination in voting. Referring to the Civil Rights Acts of 1957, 1960, and 1964, the attorney general stated that these "three present statutes have had only minimal effect. They have been too slow."

Katzenbach went on to detail the provisions of the new 1965 bill. Most central were the suspension of all literacy tests and devices in areas covered by the trigger formula, the discretionary assignment by the attorney general of federal "examiners" to those electoral jurisdictions, and the moratorium on the imposition of any new voter qualifications by states and localities covered under the trigger. The key feature of the bill, though, was that it gave to the executive branch the responsibility for registering unenrolled black voters, a job that the 1957, 1960, and 1964 acts had assigned to the federal courts. As one evaluation of the bill put it, the proposal represented "a conscious decision that the procedure of the courtroom with its inherent delays was not an adequate answer to the massive problem of Negro disfranchisement." Constitutional scholar Alexander Bickel noted at the time, "The essence of the 1965 act, and the source of its great promise, is that it makes an end run around the judicial process, and confronts recalcitrant Southern officials with the real locus of continuously effective federal power, which is the executive rather than the judiciary."[44]

In Alabama on Thursday, Wallace requested Johnson to stay his order, and without waiting for a reply the governor went before the state legislature at 6:30 P.M. to deliver on statewide television a twenty-minute speech attacking the judge's Wednesday ruling and excoriating Johnson's "mock court." Wallace asserted that Alabama did not have enough state personnel to protect the march and that U.S. marshalls would have to do the job. After the speech Wallace telegraphed a similar statement to President Johnson, requesting that "federal civil authorities" be provided to guard the march. Johnson replied that the federal government did not have sufficient "civilian" personnel and suggested that Wallace call the Alabama National Guard into state service. If Wallace was unable or unwilling to do so, Johnson said, he himself would call the Alabama Guard into federal service.[45]

On Friday the House hearings on the voting rights bill continued, with Republicans John Lindsay and William Cramer criticizing the trigger formula. Its coverage of states and counties that possessed both some form of literacy test and a 1964 registration or turnout level of less than 50 percent, they charged, would exclude some areas in which voting discrimination was known to exist, such as southeastern Arkansas and northern Florida, and would include others where no discrimination was present.

In Selma, while preparations for Sunday's march went forward, Baker arrested three hundred protestors arriving at Smitherman's home, and five hundred others marched uneventfully downtown in front of the city hall. In Montgomery, where sporadic SNCC demonstrations and resulting arrests continued, Governor Wallace, after having his request for a stay rejected by both Judge Johnson and a panel of the Fifth Circuit Court of Appeals, telegraphed President Johnson, who had flown to his Texas ranch the previous evening. Wallace told the president that Alabama did not have sufficient funds for calling up the National Guard to protect the march. After receiving that wire, Johnson, at 1:30 A.M. Saturday morning, signed an executive order and a presidential proclamation calling 1,800 Alabama national guardsmen into federal service. The president then got several hours sleep before appearing at an 11:00

A.M. press conference at which he announced the troop call-up and the assignment of Ramsey Clark to coordinate federal efforts to protect the marchers in Alabama. Several questions concerning the voting rights proposal were asked of the president, but he avoided giving a direct answer concerning the registration of illiterates.[46]

After several days of hectic preparations for the fifty-four-mile trek to Montgomery, early Sunday afternoon a column of some 3,200 people wound its way down Water Street and across the Pettus Bridge, all but surrounded by newsmen and the federalized guardsmen. Local and state officials patrolled the route as well, along with 150 federal officials headed by Clark and Assistant Attorney General John Doar. Singing as they moved along, with King and other personalities at the head of the column, the marchers covered seven miles before arriving at the night's campsite, where they were met by the crews that were handling the camp gear and food. At that point most of the crowd returned to Selma in preparation for the next day's reduction to three hundred marchers when the column reached the two-lane section of U.S. 80. On Monday morning that reduced group resumed the journey and covered sixteen miles before again bedding down for the evening. A similar schedule was followed on Tuesday, as the marchers walked eleven often rain-swept miles before arriving at a muddy campsite. Newspapers across the country reported the marchers' daily progress in front-page stories.[47]

In Washington the hearings on the legislation before the House Judiciary subcommittee continued, with few opponents appearing, and similar sessions began on March 23 before the Senate Judiciary Committee as well. A number of Republicans continued to suggest that the trigger formula would fail to provide coverage of pockets of discrimination in several states, and Roy Wilkins of the NAACP seconded their complaint. As the hearings moved ahead, Senate leader Mansfield announced that there would be no Easter recess for that body if the bill had not been passed by April 15, and House leaders said they were hoping for floor action during the week of April 11.

Within the Justice Department, discussions about desirable changes in the text of the legislation continued. An attorney in the Solicitor General's Office, Louis Claiborne, had written a memo arguing that the present bill was unconstitutional, and Solicitor General Cox himself wrote to Attorney General Katzenbach to express his fear that the two-part trigger formula—the use of tests, and registration or turnout of less than 50 percent of the voting-age population in 1964—bore only "a coincidental relationship" to the presence of racial discrimination in voting. That left open the possibility, Cox warned, that the Supreme Court might find the bill to be "inappropriate" legislation under the language of the Fifteenth Amendment. "One might equally well," Cox explained, "make the Act applicable to any State whose name begins with Vi or Mi or Lo or Al or Ge or So. Indeed, since even this description covers Alaska as well as Alabama, it has exactly the same effect as the determinations now required to be made" in the trigger formula. In a more serious vein, Cox proposed that section 3 of the present bill be revised substantially, and that at a minimum a third requirement—that at least 20 percent of a state's, county's, or parish's voting-age population be nonwhite—be added to the trigger.

Cox also argued that the "escape clause" provision should be eased or weakened. The present requirement that a state or county prove *no* discrimination had been practiced in the preceding ten years, Cox asserted, was excessively difficult, and vindictive. Cox suggested that only the absence of any "significant extent" of discrimination need be proven, and he recommended a full redrafting of section 3(c), which contained the "escape clause" provisions. Cox also objected that the present section 8, which mandated that covered jurisdictions submit changes in their electoral laws and procedures to the Federal District Court for the District of Columbia, was too broadly worded, and he suggested that it be redrafted to cover only voter qualifications and not such things as changes in the location of polling places. He also suggested that instead of having all such changes cleared by that court, that they first be submitted to the attorney general, and that any he adjudged discriminatory in purpose or effect would then be contested before that court. Any changes to which the Justice Department did not object could go into force, though the federal government would retain the right to later challenge changes which it did not oppose initially.[48]

In Alabama, meanwhile, the marchers on Wednesday had covered sixteen miles, bringing them to the outskirts of Montgomery. Their numbers had swelled when U.S. 80 widened to four lanes as it approached Montgomery, and late Wednesday afternoon the column entered the City of St. Jude, a Roman Catholic conference center outside of town where the marchers were to spend the night. Their entry there, Roy Reed wrote in the *Times*, had "a grandeur that was almost biblical." That evening the weary travelers were joined by King, who had departed for a day-long trip to Cleveland for a speaking engagement, and by thousands of colleagues and sympathizers for a rally at which entertainment was provided by a bevy of visiting celebrities.

On Thursday morning, with King once again in the lead, the long column began its triumphal march through the streets of Montgomery towards the state capitol, where a culminating rally would be held. By the time the procession made its way up Dexter Avenue toward the gleaming white statehouse it numbered more than 25,000 individuals. All three television networks covered the event live. The 3:00 P.M. rally in front of the capitol was climaxed by one of Dr. King's most notable orations. Calling the national response to Selma "a shining moment in the conscience of man," King declared, "We are on the move now. . . . We are moving to the land of freedom." Let us march on the ballot boxes, he urged, while reminding his listeners that there would still be "a season of suffering" in many hard-core Deep South areas. But eventually, King said, "a society at peace with itself, a society that can live with its conscience" would be achieved. "How long will it take?" he asked, beginning his peroration. "I come to say to you this afternoon however difficult the moment, however frustrating the hour, it will not be long, because truth pressed to earth will rise again. How long?" he continued. "Not long, because no lie can live forever. How long? Not long, because you still reap what you sow." King closed with several more repetitions of that dialogue, ending with the words of "The Battle Hymn of the Republic." The rally concluded, the great crowd began to disperse to make its way home, and a small group of black Alabamians who had been designated to deliver the marchers' petition to Wallace, who had watched the gathering through his office blinds, were turned away by a staff member at the capitol door.[49]

The SCLC staff had emphasized to the marchers and visitors that they must depart from Montgomery as quickly as possible, so as not to provide targets to racist whites who had been drawn to watch the procession, and who, it was assumed, hoped to vent their hatred upon whatever unwary participants they could later waylay. Part of the movement's transportation plans involved carrying some marchers back to Selma, and on the way back to Montgomery following such a trip one SCLC volunteer driver, a Michigan housewife and mother of five, Mrs. Viola Gregg Liuzzo, was shot to death at about 8:00 P.M. by a carload of pursuing Klansmen who overtook her car on a deserted stretch of Highway 80 in Lowndes County. A young Selma SCLC volunteer, Leroy Moton, who was also in the car, escaped death only by acting dead when the murderers returned to examine their victims. While the frightened Moton was able to flag down another SCLC vehicle and return to Selma, within several hours the Birmingham FBI office had a call from one of its undercover informants in the Klan, Gary Thomas Rowe, Jr., who informed his control agent that he had been one of the four men in the car. Within hours on that early Friday morning Rowe and his three companions were taken into custody, and at 12:40 P.M. Friday, with Attorney General Katzenbach and FBI Director Hoover flanking him, President Johnson went on live nationwide television to announce the suspects' arrests and to vow to eliminate the Ku Klux Klan. Aides described Johnson's mood as one of "sheer wrath," and strong emotional reactions to the killing also were voiced by Michigan Representative Martha Griffiths and House Speaker McCormack. At 8:00 P.M. that evening Governor Wallace, who earlier that day in an appearance on "Today" had belittled the shooting, issued a statement condemning it.[50]

In Selma on Friday evening the SCLC staff met to consider resuming the Alabama demonstrations and to chart what immediate course the movement should take. On Saturday it was announced that an expansion of the Selma effort into Lowndes County would take place and that demonstrations would continue in Dallas County. Although later that day the SCLC's James Orange led several hundred marchers to the courthouse, little further public activity occurred in the Selma area.

On Sunday Dr. King appeared on "Meet the Press" and spoke of the SCLC's intent to keep up the pressure in Alabama, and of the consideration that it was giving to calling for a nationwide economic boycott of Alabama and its products. That idea, and other possible SCLC courses of action, were to be discussed at a board meeting in Baltimore on Thursday and Friday, April 1 and 2.

In Washington as the new week began comment upon the voting rights bill continued. Deep South senators and representatives began to voice their opposition to the proposal, more often than not drawing upon columns unfavorable to the bill written by Arthur Krock of the *Times*, David Lawrence of *U.S. News & World Report*, the editorial writers of the *Wall Street Journal*, and southern segregationist stalwart James J. Kilpatrick. In both houses of Congress a considerable number of proponents of the bill spoke out as well, though in the House the Republican leadership refused to support the administration proposal as had Dirksen, who had chosen to be its coauthor in the Senate. House Republicans, led by William McCulloch and John V. Lindsay, indicated that they were at work on a different trigger formula under which the attorney general, upon receipt of some specified number of complaints from a certain locale alleging racially discriminatory voting practices, could request the Civil Service Commission to investigate the charges. If the commission found them to be valid, it could order the registration of all those who had been discriminated against. Local officials could challenge the commission's decisions in federal court if they so wished. If the court did not rule within a specified amount of time, the proposal said, the commission's decision would stand.

Doubts about the precise language and provisions of the administration proposal persisted in other circles, too, as Cox's memo of a week earlier had indicated. A number of interested parties, such as Joseph Rauh of the Leadership Conference on Civil Rights (LCCR) and Senator Edward M. Kennedy indicated that they were concerned about the outlying pockets of discrimination the administration proposal's trigger formula would not cover, and they suggested several possible alterations that closely resembled those the House Republicans were advocating.

Within the Justice Department, which was aware of what E. W. Kenworthy of the *Times* referred to as the "mounting criticism" of the trigger formula, Louis Claiborne prepared a new draft which, he wrote, made it "appear that there is a quasi-automatic remedy for 'pockets' . . . while, at the same time, preserving the Attorney General's discretion in fact." Under Claiborne's new section 4(a), the attorney general, ten days after having brought a civil action against local voting officials of one of the "pocket" counties, could send in federal examiners to register unenrolled citizens, with the final acceptance of the examiners' registrations depending upon the judicial resolution of the case. Claiborne, like Cox, also continued to argue for a loosening of the escape clause provision in section 3(c). As critical comments continued to increase, Katzenbach and Dirksen announced on Wednesday that the administration bill would be broadened, and after a Thursday meeting the two men reported that changes had been agreed upon and that a new draft would be produced.[51]

Also on Wednesday, the House Un-American Activities Committee, under substantial pressure from the administration, voted to begin an investigation of the Ku Klux Klan. There was also talk, in the wake of the Liuzzo murder, of strengthening the statutory provisions and penalties aimed at those who conspired to violate another person's civil rights. In Alabama on Wednesday, Governor Wallace quietly received the marchers' petition of a week earlier during an eighty-five-minute meeting with a sixteen-member delegation which included James Bevel, Tuskegee Institute President L. H. Foster and Professor C. G. Gomillion, and Birmingham's Reverend Ellwanger.

In New York, King announced that he intended to press ahead with plans for an economic boycott of Alabama, despite the heavily negative public reaction that had greeted the idea, with Whitney Young, Jacob Javits, and the editorial page of the *Times* all attacking it. The next day King and the SCLC staff assembled in Baltimore to consider future plans, with Bevel pressing for an all-out effort behind the boycott plan and Hosea Williams advocating an emphasis upon a large-scale summer registration effort throughout all of the South's 120 Black Belt counties.

King avoided making a choice between one plan or the other, and so both moved forward slowly and with little public attention. In Washington that same day President Johnson avoided any direct comment on the boycott plan, though noting, as had many of its critics, that it would hurt Alabama blacks as well as whites. In Camden, a Thursday march of 120 black teenagers was dispersed with smoke bombs, and subsequent march attempts there were blocked peacefully as well.[52]

On Friday Justice Department attorneys met with Mansfield's and Dirksen's staff aides and drafted into the administration bill a provision that would allow for federal district courts to send in Civil Service Commission examiners to register local voters after having made a finding of discrimination against a "pocket" county in a suit brought by the attorney general. Discussions also continued concerning Cox's suggestion that the constitutionality of the trigger formula would be strengthened if an additional requirement specifying some minimum nonwhite percentage of the population was added. Hearings on the original administration bill ended on April 1 in the House and on Monday, April 5, in the Senate, and over that weekend discussions continued in an effort to devise specific language that would be agreeable to all so that a new draft in the form of a substitute would be ready for the upcoming markup sessions in both the House Judiciary Subcommittee and the full Senate Judiciary Committee. Katzenbach and Dirksen reluctantly agreed to insert into the new version a provision calling for the federal courts to suspend poll tax requirements in areas where such a tax had been used for racial discrimination, a subject the two men had hoped to avoid in this bill because of widespread doubts concerning the constitutionality of any statutory pronouncement concerning state poll taxes. They also added to the trigger formula Cox's suggested requirement that a covered jurisdiction must possess a voting-age population at least 20 percent nonwhite, and they modified the preclearance requirement so that the attorney general could consent to some election law changes in lieu of court approval.

By Tuesday morning, April 6, when Celler's subcommittee began its markup, a new version had been drafted, though further discussions between Katzenbach and the Senate leadership continued. Katzenbach himself sat in on the House subcommittee's Tuesday markup session and tentatively accepted an amendment offered by Louisiana's Edwin Willis which would have barred the use of federal examiners in any jurisdiction with more than 30 percent of its nonwhite voting-age population registered in November 1964 and where more than half of those so registered had actually voted. The amendment subsequently was dropped. Chairman Celler also indicated that he and a majority of his sub-committee colleagues favored inserting an outright ban on the poll tax into the bill in place of the Katzenbach-Dirksen wording, which called for a federal district judge to void the tax where it was being used for discriminatory purposes.

On Thursday, April 8, less than forty-eight hours before the bill had to be reported out, the Senate Judiciary Committee began its markup session by adopting the new administration draft offered by Dirksen. Then, over Dirksen's strong objection, a coalition of nine Democrats and Republicans added five strengthening provisions to the new draft of the bill. These changes added to the bill an outright ban on the poll tax, a requirement that federal examiners automatically be dispatched to any covered jurisdiction where less than 25 percent of the minority voting-age population was registered, and a provision calling for Civil Service Commission poll watchers at future elections in covered jurisdictions. The changes removed from the bill any mention that federal registrants must first have attempted to register with local officials and also increased the criminal penalties for attempts to hinder the voting of those registered by federal examiners.[53]

On Friday, April 9, both the House Judiciary subcommittee and the Senate Judiciary Committee finished their markups. The House bill moved on to the full committee, and the Senate version directly onto the calendar. The Senate markup had ended without the resolution of several issues, as the committee had spent most of Friday deadlocked over a newly proposed amendment offered by Dirksen—and opposed by the administration—which would have allowed any county to apply to the Federal District Court in the District of Columbia for "escape" from the act's provisions whenever the percentage of its voting-age population actually voting exceeded the national average *or* when over 60 percent of the voting-age population was registered. A late-evening compromise allowed for an "escape" when the 60 percent registration level was reached *and* a court decision found no present discrimination. Some observers reasoned that Dirksen had advocated that amendment solely to have something to bargain away later in exchange for the deletion of one or more of the changes pushed through the previous day by the liberals, such as the poll tax ban.

In the House subcommittee a poll tax ban had been inserted, as well as a federal poll watchers provision, both of which now were present in the Senate bill too. The subcommittee also had expanded the bill's definition of "vote" so that elections of political party officers would be covered as well. The House bill did not include the 20 percent nonwhite

population requirement Cox had recommended and which had been inserted into the Senate bill, though both bills now possessed the provision
agreed to a week earlier by the department and the Senate leadership
which called for court appointment of federal examiners in "pocket"
counties against which successful voting suits had been brought. The full
House Judiciary Committee began consideration of the bill on April 13,
with no action expected for two weeks, and on that same day the Senate
moved to consider its version of the bill, with actual debate scheduled to
begin on April 21.[54]

Throughout April, Selma, which had dominated the front pages of
March's newspapers, largely dropped from sight in the national press.
Black registration in Dallas County had increased since the first of the
year by about 250, to 600, though on the opposite side of the ledger was
the fact that local black leaders estimated 150 blacks had lost jobs with
local whites as a result of the movement. On April 7 those local black
leaders began weekly meetings with Mayor Smitherman to discuss jobs
for blacks in city government and in the downtown stores, the paving of
streets in black neighborhoods, and the integration of city recreational
facilities. The meetings produced no progress, as extremist whites who
were displeased with what they believed to be Smitherman's "moderation" pushed for his ouster and provided a potent counterweight to the
demands of the blacks. Within the black community problems developed
concerning the allocation of donations of food and clothing that had been
sent by northern supporters, and in the white community the private
efforts of the moderates to win additional allies produced little support
and much hostility.

In mid-April a county grand jury indicted three men for the assault on
Reeb. Several days later Judge Thomas dissolved Hare's injunction that
dated from the previous summer, and at the same time a three-judge
district court composed of Thomas, Johnson, and Richard T. Rives ordered Sheriff Clark to disband his "posse" and enjoined him from harassing or intimidating those seeking to vote or participating in demonstrations aimed at securing that right. During that same week the
Alabama State Chamber of Commerce and local Chambers in more than
a dozen cities around the state placed a full-page ad urging obedience to
the provisions of the 1964 Civil Rights Act and equal voting rights for all
in the *Wall Street Journal* and in all of Alabama's daily papers. The
absence of the Selma-Dallas County Chamber of Commerce from the list
of those endorsing the ad produced national pressures upon the Hammermill Paper Company and Dan River Mills, both of which had announced their intentions to build major plants near Selma, and their

initiatives in Selma persuaded the Chamber and the City Council to endorse the ad's statement. Dr. King returned to town on Sunday, April 18, for some brief meetings with the SCLC staffers still present and for an evening speech.[55]

On Thursday night, April 22, the Senate's floor debate on the voting rights bill began, one day behind schedule, with senators and observers believing that only the question of a statutory ban on the poll tax and Dirksen's late amendment concerning the "escape" provision would be serious matters of discussion beyond the expected southern opposition.[56] Much attention was focused on what appeared to be the brewing fight over the poll tax question. Mansfield, Dirksen, and the administration all favored avoiding a straight-out statutory ban on the tax because of substantial fears within Justice that such an action was of doubtful constitutionality, especially in light of the fact that a constitutional amendment had been employed to void poll taxes for federal elections. In an attempt to assuage those who desired something stronger than the administration draft, Harold H. Greene of the Civil Rights Division wrote up a new poll tax provision which forbade deprivation of the right to vote for failure to pay any tax and authorized the attorney general to seek injunctive relief in any instances where such deprivation persisted. If such a ban were voided by the courts, a clause of the provision specified that late payments from those who had not paid prior to the striking down of the ban must be accepted. Despite that effort to stimulate something of a compromise, however, a sizable group of liberal senators, under the emerging leadership of Judiciary Committee Democrat Edward M. Kennedy, signaled that they would press for an explicit, no-holds-barred abolition of the poll tax. All concerned realized that such an effort was "less substantial than symbolic," but the liberals' stubbornness largely reflected their resentment over being excluded from the initial drafting process and over the large role that had been played by Dirksen.

As the third day of the Senate debate began on Monday, April 26, Majority Leader Mansfield spoke hopefully of passage of the bill within two weeks, though private administration estimates were that four to six weeks actually would be required. Attorney General Katzenbach continued his efforts to dissuade those who wanted to push for an outright ban on the poll tax, a group that included not only the Leadership Conference on Civil Rights lobbyists but also Dr. King himself, who had dropped broad hints about resuming demonstrations in an effort to stimulate adoption of a statutory ban. Private discussions also sought to reach an accommodation on the other amendments added in committee by the liberals and on the loosened escape provision backed by Dirksen, though the liberals refused to drop their poll tax ban effort in exchange for the removal of Dirksen's added escape hatch provision.

Uneventful floor debate continued throughout the week, mainly on amendments concerning voting fraud which Williams of Delaware and Miller of Iowa sought to add to the bill. By late Thursday, April 29, Katzenbach, Mansfield, and Dirksen had agreed on a new substitute bill to be offered on the floor, a draft that dropped Dirksen's escape hatch amendment and called for a court test of the poll tax's constitutionality. It also reinserted into the bill the suspendable requirement that applicants for federal registration must have tried and failed to register with local officials, and it also specified that federal poll watchers would be assigned by the courts rather than by the attorney general. Mansfield formally introduced the new substitute on Friday and told the Senate that lengthier sessions would begin the following week. Although both of the Senate leaders believed that this new version should be acceptable to the bipartisan liberal bloc, that group of senators kept their own counsel, and a meeting between them and the two leaders was scheduled for Monday, May 3.

On Monday morning at a meeting in Javits's office the liberals decided to continue their effort for a stronger poll tax provision and agreed to support such an amendment to the leadership substitute, an amendment that did not differ greatly from the proposal Harold Greene had drafted a week and a half earlier. Mansfield was informed of the liberals' decision, and after a Tuesday morning meeting between Johnson and the leadership at the White House, Mansfield on the Senate floor moved to obtain unanimous consent to set a time limit on future debate on the bill. The administration's hope was that Senate action, to be delayed somewhat on account of the poll tax dispute, could be completed before the House bill emerged from the Judiciary Committee so that the option of offering the Senate-passed version as a substitute to the House Judiciary Committee's bill on the House floor would be available. Mansfield's request, however, was blocked by Louisiana's Allen Ellender, and the majority leader announced that he thus would file a cloture petition on Monday, May 10. Mansfield subsequently postponed that move. The majority leader was able, though, to obtain agreement that the first of the southerners' amendments would be voted on on Thursday, May 6, and that the liberals' poll tax amendment would be called up early the following week. The southern opponents themselves were divided on the question of how much effort should be exerted to delay what all regarded as certain passage of the measure.

Thursday witnessed the defeat of the first opposition amendment, one offered by Sam Ervin of North Carolina to delete section 3, which contained the trigger formula. The vote was 64 to 25, with 17 Southerners being joined by 7 conservative Republicans and Ohio Democrat Frank Lausche. Reporters described the debate as "desultory" and focused their attention on the upcoming Tuesday vote on the poll tax question, which was termed "the only drama" in the congressional consideration of the voting bill. The liberals rejected an offer that they drop their poll tax effort in exchange for the excision of the two Dirksen-backed provisions requiring previous registration attempts by applicants for federal registration and court control of poll watchers which had been reinserted into the latest substitute, and the administration and the Senate leadership turned their attention to securing votes for the Tuesday roll call. Substantial energy toward that end was exerted by the administration and the leadership over the weekend and on Monday, and their prediction that they had the votes to win was proven accurate when the Kennedy-sponsored amendment was defeated 49 to 45. A last-minute effort by Kennedy, Javits, and Hart, assisted by UAW President Reuther, to arrange a compromise similar to that which they had rejected several days earlier, rather than go down to defeat, was rebuffed by Mansfield, who told them that the scheduled vote could not be canceled on only several hours notice.[57]

As the Senate proceeded to reject another amendment of Ervin's by 62 to 28 on Wednesday afternoon, the House Judiciary Committee, which had been having difficulty in maintaining a quorum at markup sessions and hence had taken few votes on proposed amendments to the subcommittee bill, rebuffed the administration by voting to retain the poll tax ban. The committee then moved to report the bill, which next would go before the Rules Committee. The following morning, May 13, Speaker McCormack spoke out in support of the Judiciary Committee's action, thus breaking with the administration and virtually assuring that the House as a whole would retain the ban on the poll tax.

Later Thursday afternoon in the Senate, as an amendment offered by John Sparkman was being voted down, Mansfield attempted to assuage Javits's and Hart's feelings on the now-approved poll tax provision's language by allowing them to make several minor proposals to alter the wording, but the effort went for naught when Dirksen's aides, unbeknownst to Mansfield, revised the suggested changes in ways that the liberals found unacceptable.

On Friday another in the series of weakening amendments offered by the southern senators was defeated, and on Monday an additional one was rejected as well. Also on Monday, Mansfield put forward yet another newly worded poll tax provision, which stated in marginally stronger terms that the Congress had found that the tax frequently was a tool for racial discrimination. This new wording proved acceptable to both the defeated liberals and Dirksen. Two days later, on Wednesday, with a public letter from Katzenbach endorsing the new wording, Mansfield's poll tax provision was adopted by the Senate 69 to 20, with only the southerners and two conservative Republicans, Carl Curtis and Bourke Hickenlooper, in opposition. After that amendment had won approval, Mansfield proposed a unanimous consent agreement that a vote on the pending substitute, and on the final passage of the bill, come at 4:00 P.M. on May 25. Louisiana's Ellender again voiced opposition, and Mansfield responded by saying that he would file for cloture on Friday, May 21, with the cloture vote to be taken on Tuesday. After that announcement had been made, the Senate approved 56 to 25 an amendment offered by Hawaii's Hiram Fong which revised the poll watchers provision and specified that such federal observers could be sent by the attorney general to any jurisdiction designated to receive federal examiners.

The following day, Thursday, May 20, with no doubt in any observer's mind that the bill's proponents had the necessary votes for cloture, an amendment enfranchising Spanish-speaking citizens who had been educated in "American flag" schools, such as those in Puerto Rico, was adopted, with observers noting that its major impact would come in New York City. On Friday morning Philip Hart, the bill's official floor manager, filed a cloture petition with thirty-eight signatures, and prior to the vote on Tuesday three other amendments, offered by Ervin, John Tower of Texas, and Jack Miller of Iowa, were all defeated. When the cloture vote came, the motion carried 70 to 30. After that tally was recorded, nine amendments proposed by Ervin and John Stennis were called up and quickly voted down. Several minor technical amendments offered by Hart, as well as one proposed by Russell Long that would allow for the "escape" of counties "innocent" of discrimination which were located in "guilty" states, all were agreed to. The next day, Wednesday, May 26, the Senate adopted the Mansfield-Dirksen substitute by 78 to 18 and then passed the Voting Rights Act of 1965 on a vote of 77 to 19. Ten weeks had passed since the original bill had been sent up on March 17.[58]

While that legislative progress was being achieved in Washington, black citizens in Selma were experiencing little improvement in their political situation, though the national press had not lost total interest in them. In the last days of April, Judge Thomas had begun a hearing into whether Sheriff Clark's forced march of the teenagers on February 10 represented a violation of Thomas's order of January 23. True to form, the judge issued no ruling until well into the fall. In the meantime, Montgomery representative William Dickinson, for the second time, publicly accused the actual Highway 80 marchers of having engaged in various sorts of misbehavior during their five-day trek. Dickinson was unable to produce any evidence to support his charges, however, and his accusations were attacked and ridiculed by movement spokesmen and the press.

SNCC organizers, particularly Stokely Carmichael, continued to work quietly in Lowndes County, and on Monday, May 3, 150 blacks appeared at the Hayneville registration office. That same day in Hayneville jury selection began in the trial of Collie Leroy Wilkins, one of the three Klansmen accused of killing Mrs. Liuzzo. After a brief trial noted mainly for the testimony of Rowe, the eyewitness FBI informer, and the virulent racism of defense counsel Matt Murphy, the jury deadlocked ten to two in favor of conviction.

On May 10, two days after that outcome, King himself returned to Selma, met with the SCLC's Alabama staff, and held a press conference at Brown's Chapel at which he admitted that the movement had been "relatively quiet" since late March. The following day King traveled to several of the surrounding towns and counties, and he spoke of the possibility of demonstrating against the Alabama legislature in Montgomery.

In Selma the weekly meetings between the local black leadership and Smitherman had continued to produce nothing but a stalemate, as Smitherman offered the blacks minor concessions which they had not requested while refusing to make any moves on those items the black leadership was interested in. At the May 12 session the Reverend F.D. Reese announced that he saw no purpose in continuing the meetings until Smitherman was willing to make some solid proposals, but the black leadership had little power with which to force the matter, as "mass meetings" no longer filled Brown's Chapel unless King was speaking. The boycott of the downtown stores had collapsed completely, and attempts to picket the stores drew only small numbers of volunteers, most of whom were young people. Voter registration gains continued to be very limited, though movement workers were no longer harassed in the ways that they had been only six months earlier. Sheriff Clark had begun to muse openly about running for governor in 1966, and by late May the SCLC Alabama staff had shifted its primary attention from Selma to Montgomery. A series of moderately well attended rallies in

that city was capped not by demonstrations in front of the capitol but by
the cordial reception of thirty-five black "lobbyists" inside the building
by House Speaker Albert P. Brewer on May 25. In both Alabama and
Mississippi the state legislatures busied themselves with what many
members realized were futile attempts to alter state laws to escape
coverage by the provisions of the soon-to-be-enacted voting rights act.[59]

While the House Judiciary Committee had reported out the voting
rights bill, H.R. 6400, on May 12, it was not until the first day of June
that the committee's formal report was filed. In that document eight
Republicans, led by ranking minority member William McCulloch, dissented from the approval given the committee bill and instead cham-
pioned one advocated by McCulloch himself, which made no use of any
trigger formula designed to concentrate the statute's focus on hard-core
areas. The Rules Committee was expected to take some two weeks in
readying the bill for floor action, and administration officials were hopeful of being able to substitute the Senate bill for the committee version
on the House floor if the House could be persuaded to accept the Senate's poll tax provision. If successful, such an action would obviate the
need for a conference committee on the act, a setting in which House
support for an explicit poll tax ban and Dirksen's immovable opposition
to such a provision might produce either a deadlock or opposition to the
conference report by one side or the other. House Rules Committee
Chairman Howard Smith delayed calling hearings on the Judiciary
Committee bill, however, and it was not until June 24, under substantial
pressure from Celler, that the Rules hearings began.[60] One week later,
on July 1, Smith's committee granted an open rule providing for ten
hours of debate, which was to begin on Tuesday, July 6.

As general debate began the Democratic leadership devoted its ener-
gies to marshaling votes against the Republican bill McCulloch was
planning to propose as a substitute. McCulloch objected to the automatic
suspension of literacy tests on the basis of statistical evidence, as the
administration bill provided, and instead advocated a bill whose key
section allowed the Civil Service Commission to appoint federal examiners for any county or parish from which the attorney general had
received twenty-five or more meritorious complaints of racially discriminatory registration and voting practices. Applicants for federal registration would not have to pass a literacy test if they could provide
evidence of at least a sixth-grade education, but if they could not do so
they would have to demonstrate their literacy to the examiner. Southern
Democrats were expected to support the McCulloch substitute, and administration strategists believed that the expected support of approxi-

mately a dozen liberal Republican representatives would supply the last handful of votes necessary to defeat the McCulloch substitute. That strategy was aided immeasurably when Virginia representative William Tuck, a vocal segregationist and former governor, gave the McCulloch substitute an unintended kiss of death on July 7 by remarking that he hoped "that every member opposed to these so-called voting rights bills will vote for" the Republican proposal. In the aftermath of that statement, the Republican hopes for success, which previously had been characterized as "narrow" at best, "almost vanished" as a dozen or more Republican representatives indicated that they could no longer back the McCulloch version when it was drawing such outspoken southern support. When the vote on the McCulloch substitute came on Friday, July 9, after Illinois's Robert McClory had succeeded in adding a poll tax ban provision to it, the Republican proposal went down to defeat by 215 to 166.

After rejecting a southern amendment to remove the trigger formula from the pending Judiciary Committee bill and approving an amendment offered by Cramer of Florida which provided penalties for the giving of false registration data, the House defeated a move to recommit the committee bill and to substitute the McCulloch bill in its place by a vote of 248 to 171. The House then proceeded to pass H.R. 6400 by 333 to 85, with 21 Democrats from the eleven southern states, plus Florida Republican Cramer, voting for it. That action meant that a conference committee would have to attempt to resolve the differences between the House and the Senate bills, the most notable of which were the House's explicit poll tax ban provision and the Senate's inclusion of what commonly was termed the Puerto Rican amendment. The conferees also would have to consider the third requirement that the Senate had added to the trigger formula, which specified that covered jurisdictions possess a voting-age population at least 20 percent nonwhite.

President Johnson was elated at the House passage of the bill, and he issued a statement praising the House's action. The statement also criticized strongly the efforts of the House Republican leadership to substitute their weaker bill in place of the administration's proposal. Minority Leader Ford and McCulloch responded with an attack upon Johnson's civil rights record of the past, and the voting rights bill moved to conference amidst an atmosphere of growing partisan bitterness.[61]

While in Washington the House had consumed all of June and the first part of July before passing the voting bill, in Selma during those same weeks the black community had been shaken by the arrest of one out-of-town, self-appointed "leader" on obscenity charges and the subsequent arrest of the Voters' League president, F.D. Reese, on charges of having misappropriated contributions the group had received from outside supporters. SCLC leaders Bevel and Abernathy stepped forward immediately to defend Reese, and SCLC Selma staffer Harold Middlebrook persevered in the continuing voter registration campaign, which was beginning to experience increased success. By July 19, black registration in Dallas County had risen to 1,470, or just short of 10 percent of those eligible. Nonetheless, Justice Department figures showed that of 2,693 black applicants processed between February 4 and late July, the board had rejected 1,416, including several dozen individuals with substantial educational experience. More than 1,600 of those approximately 2,700 applications had been processed during June and July, after Judge Thomas began having rejected Dallas County applicants reconsidered by the referee whom he previously had appointed to deal with Perry County, O.S. Burke. Burke and Thomas ordered the enrollment of several hundred previously rejected applicants, though it was clear to Justice Department observers that discriminatory registration practices continued to be employed by the Dallas County registrars throughout July. Meanwhile, no substantial progress for Selma blacks in employment opportunities, housing, or education was being achieved either.[62]

While modest black registration gains in many areas of the South were being reported as local registrars began to see the writing on the wall and sought to avoid the assignment of federal examiners to their counties, the movement itself experienced a quiet summer in the South. In mid-June a series of demonstrations in Jackson, Mississippi, sponsored by the MFDP against the all-white legislature, produced several hundred arrests, several days of national press attention, and half-a-dozen comments on the House floor by members who had received telegrams from SNCC asking them to speak out. That brief event, however, was the only civil rights story that stirred any measurable press interest or congressional comment, aside from a dozen or more speeches in late June that commemorated the first anniversary of the 1964 killings of the three movement workers in Neshoba County, Mississippi. Later in the summer demonstrations in Bogalusa, Louisiana, and Americus, Georgia, were to stir substantial press attention but virtually no congressional comment.[63]

The conferees on the voting rights bill—Dirksen, Hart, Hruska, Eastland, Dodd, and Edward V. Long for the Senate, and Celler, McCulloch, Rodino, Byron Rogers, Harold Donohue, and Cramer for the House—held their first meeting the week of July 19 but failed to resolve their differences. On Tuesday, July 27, Dirksen and Celler met privately to consider a newly worded poll tax provision which Katzenbach had proposed, a provision that included a somewhat stronger "finding" than that presently in the Senate bill but which was not by any means the statutory ban contained in the House version. Both men were willing to accept the new wording, but at a meeting of the full conference committee later that day, four of the House conferees—Rodino, Donohue, McCulloch and Cramer—refused to endorse the new language.

In the wake of that rebuff, a second compromise was proposed under which the Senate would drop the Puerto Rican amendment and the House would give up the poll tax ban in return, an exchange McCulloch and Cramer could be expected to accept. While those two Republicans had refused to approve the newly suggested poll tax compromise in the hope of torpedoing the entire bill, or at least blocking the addition of so many Spanish-speaking voters in New York, Rodino and Donohue had refused to endorse it because of the great—and truly excessive— importance that the civil rights lobby, such as the LCCR organizations, had attached to a complete ban on the poll tax.

Hoping to achieve acceptance of the new poll tax language while also retaining the Puerto Rican amendment, Katzenbach early on July 29 sent to Celler a letter which the attorney general rightfully believed would persuade Rodino and Donohue to accept the compromise provision.

> Late last night I discussed with Martin Luther King the proposed voting rights bill as it now stands in conference, and particularly the new poll tax provision. Dr. King strongly expressed to me his desire that the bill promptly be enacted into law and said that he felt this was an overriding consideration. He expressed his understanding and appreciation of the difficulties in achieving a satisfactory compromise in conference.
>
> With respect to the poll tax provision he expressed his view to me thusly: "While I would have preferred that the bill eliminate the poll tax at this time—once and for all—it does contain an express declaration by Congress that the poll tax abridges and denies the right to vote. In addition, Congress directs the Attorney General 'to institute forthwith' suits which will eliminate and prevent the use of the poll tax in the four States where it is still employed. I am confident that the poll tax provision of the bill—with vigorous action by the Attorney General—will operate finally to bury this iniquitous device.' "
>
> Dr. King further assured me that he would make this statement publicly at an appropriate time.

While you are free to show this letter privately to whomsoever you wish, I would appreciate it if you did not use it publicly without informing me so that I, in turn, may discuss it with Dr. King.

Later that day Rodino and Donohue indicated their approval of the new poll tax provision and the conference committee reached agreement on the entire bill, with the House accepting the Senate's Puerto Rican amendment and Russell Long's escape provision and the Senate dropping the third trigger formula requirement that covered jurisdictions possess a voting-age population at least 20 percent nonwhite.

The conferees' reports were submitted early the following week, and on Tuesday, August 3, the House defeated a motion to recommit it by 284 to 188 and then went on to approve the report and the Voting Rights Act of 1965 by a vote of 328 to 74. Seven southern Representatives who had opposed the bill less than a month before now voted for it. The next day the report was called up in the Senate and it and the bill were approved 79 to 18, with Florida Democrat George Smathers, who had opposed the measure in late May, now voting in favor of it.[64]

Two days later, on Friday, August 6, in a televised noontime ceremony that was the product of substantial White House planning, President Johnson signed the Voting Rights Act of 1965 into law in a room of the Capitol following remarks in the Rotunda. Declaring, "The vote is the most powerful instrument ever devised by man for breaking down injustice and destroying the terrible walls which imprison men because they are different from other men," Johnson told his audience that the Voting Rights Act was "one of the most monumental laws in the entire history of American freedom."[65]

4 Reactions and Responses: Selma, Birmingham, and Civil Rights Legislation

Since 1965 various observers have written that the Voting Rights Act was "produced by" or was "the result of" the events in Selma, particularly the March 7 attack.[1] Scholars have suggested, often without equivocation, that had it not been for Selma, there would have been no Johnson administration initiative on voting rights in 1965.[2] Such an account certainly is not implausible, though when the actual evidence is weighed, it is clearly incorrect.

Much of the debate on the origins of the Voting Rights Act has centered on the civil rights views of Lyndon B. Johnson. Was he, as some have charged, a "mirror politician," whose actions and language were colored by "no independent idealism," but merely reflected current trends, a president whose decisions were based, as had been his actions while Senate majority leader, merely on a desire to support bills that would be successful and oppose ones unlikely to secure passage?[3] Or had Johnson grown beyond a Senate record of little sympathy for the needs of the underprivileged into a president whose "desire to benefit others was ever the prime motive for his quest for power?"[4] No comprehensive answer is offered here; as a noted jurist once wrote, "Certainty is generally illusion." But one fact with a clear bearing upon the discussion can be stated: Lyndon B. Johnson had decided before the last day of 1964, before the Reverend Martin Luther King, Jr., opened the Selma campaign on January 2, that an administration proposal for new voting rights legislation that would provide for federal registration officials would be put forward in 1965.[5] No certain conclusion follows from that fact. Johnson may well have concluded that the record of eight years of federal voting rights litigation indicated clearly that some further step had to be taken, or he merely may have realized that King's upcoming campaign might well generate some of the congressional and public interest that it in fact soon did. All that can be said with certainty is that the relationship between the events of Selma and the birth of the Voting Rights Act of 1965 is much less simple than many people heretofore have thought.

Up through mid-February 1965, the Justice Department's perhaps impractical preference was for a constitutional amendment, and not for a mere statute, concerning the right to vote and particularly the problem of discriminatory application of registration tests in many areas of the South. As late as February 23, the department had not devoted any substantial effort to drafting a statutory proposal concerning the assignment of federal registrars. But by March 5, two days before Bloody Sunday, the basic contents of what was to become the Voting Rights Act of 1965 already had been crafted into a draft bill, albeit one that needed and would receive further thought and refinement.[6] So it was not the vivid attack on Highway 80 that stimulated administration interest in a voting rights bill. That interest, characterized by the hurried drafting efforts of the last week of February and the first week of March, had been stimulated more than enough by the events and the effects of Selma prior to March 7.

The influential stimuli had been not only King's and the SCLC's efforts and communications, but also the active interest in new voting rights legislation the SCLC's well-planned and well-orchestrated campaign had succeeded in arousing among liberals of both parties in both houses of Congress and the more self-interested House Republican leadership. From all three quarters—the representatives who traveled to Selma; Javits, Hart, Case, and Douglas in the upper chamber; and Ford and McCulloch—came the signal that a strong administration voting rights measure, not in the form of a constitutional amendment, had better be proposed or sharp criticism and independent legislative efforts soon would follow. In that atmosphere the administration moved forward quickly and rather secretively, largely ignoring the liberals and spurned by Ford and McCulloch, and eventually drawing in to the actual drafting and decision-making process only two legislators—Dirksen and Mansfield. Despite the hurt feelings and bruised egos in the Congress, hindsight shows the administration's course to have been generally successful.

Although the events of that earlier period are crucially important, it would be a major error to downplay the importance of Bloody Sunday. That day's attack and the week of crisis that followed produced the largest and most intense congressional and public reaction of any of the SCLC's southern campaigns in the 1960s. While the voting rights bill had been drafted prior to that now famous afternoon, there is little doubt that the attack of March 7 and the news coverage it received ensured that the bill would be enacted into law, and with only minimal delay and no weakening amendments. The changes made in the bill between March 7 and its signing into law five months later, in fact, made it not only a better bill but also, in several important respects, a significantly stronger piece of legislation. The events of Selma, both in the first two months of 1965 *and* in March, heavily influenced the production of the Voting Rights Act of 1965.

Many of those who claim the Voting Rights Act was "the result" of Selma also assert that events in Birmingham, Alabama, in April and May of 1963 "produced" the Civil Rights Act of 1964.[7] To such writers, the two series of events appear quite similar. In each case black citizens led by the Reverend Martin Luther King, Jr., demonstrated against discriminatory treatment and were met on one or more occasions by outrageous law-enforcement tactics. Substantial press attention was devoted to the clashes, the federal administration made attempts to mediate the situations, and political leaders cited the events as indicating the need for federal action.

In fact, however, Birmingham and Selma were very different stories which produced noticeably different reactions and responses, especially in the Congress. Why those reactions and responses were so different can best be understood when Birmingham and Selma are compared on each of three important dimensions. Each of the three dimensions exerts an important influence upon the way in which third-party audiences such as the Congress react to a protest event. Furthermore, when combined, these three influences go very far toward determining the quality and quantity of reactions to a protest event.

The first dimension concerns the conduct and appearance of the protestors themselves. In Selma, as we have seen, the demonstrators almost without exception were completely peaceful and ostensibly nonprovocative when confronting law-enforcement officials. In Birmingham at times the case was different.

The second influential dimension concerns the behavior and conduct of the protestors' immediate opponents. In Selma this conduct on a number of occasions was violent and apparently unprovoked, with officers employing a variety of weapons, including whips and cattle prods, against the unarmed and unresisting demonstrators. In Birmingham the conduct was essentially similar, with dogs and high-powered fire hoses being the most prominent weapons.

The third influential dimension concerns the goals of the protestors. Do they have a single clear goal, such as nondiscrimination in the electoral process, or a multiplicity of related aims? In the latter case, as in Birmingham, third-party audiences would have greater difficulty in understanding and appreciating the protestors' cause, than if the movement, as in Selma, explicitly stressed one easily grasped aim.

Birmingham and Selma differ on all three of these dimensions, though less so on the second than on the first and third, and these differences were responsible for the different quality and quantity of reactions to the two events. In one instance all three dimensions worked together to propel third-party audiences toward active support of the movement's cause. In the other, earlier instance, however, the second dimension alone worked to stimulate support for the protestors, while the character of occurrences on the other two hindered the development of backing for the demonstrators.

The SCLC's 1963 campaign in Birmingham officially began on the evening of April 3, when King and Ralph Abernathy flew into town and spoke at an evening rally attended by some three hundred people. The following day the two SCLC leaders held a press conference at which they outlined the goals of the campaign, which was beginning just as Birmingham was shifting to a new form of city government. Several days earlier moderate segregationist Albert Boutwell had defeated strong segregationist and longtime public safety commissioner, Eugene "Bull" Connor, for the new office of mayor. Connor and a fellow commissioner, Arthur Hanes, the acting mayor, were planning to challenge the changeover to the new administration in the state courts. At that press conference on Thursday, April 4, King said that the campaign's goals were sixfold:

1. the desegregation of lunch counters and other facilities in Birmingham's downtown stores;
2. the adoption of fair hiring practices by those stores;
3. the dropping of charges against those who had participated in earlier sit-ins in those stores;
4. the adoption of fair hiring practices by the city government;
5. the reopening on a desegregated basis of the city's closed recreational facilities; and
6. the establishment of a biracial committee to facilitate the desegregation of additional aspects of Birmingham life.

Demonstrations planned for later that same day failed to materialize, but on Friday ten sit-in demonstrators were arrested in the downtown stores' lunch counters, bringing the week's arrests to thirty-five. The expected large demonstrations, though, again failed to materialize, and it was made known that a number of leading blacks in Birmingham opposed the timing of King's direct action campaign, arguing that the new city administration should be given a chance to take office and disclose its intentions. Most of the lunch counters, the initial focal point of the effort, had been closed, and little attention, even locally, was being given to the small number of sit-in participants at the few that had not been closed by the end of the week.

On Saturday the first street demonstration of the campaign, a brief walk by some forty blacks led by the Reverend Fred Shuttlesworth, a local activist, was held, and the participants were arrested after moving three blocks toward city hall on charges of parading without a permit. A repetition of that march was attempted on Sunday, April 7, and as the participants, led by the Reverend A.D. King, were being loaded into police vans, a black male bystander armed with a large knife lunged at one of the police dogs that had been brought to the scene by the officers. As Monday morning's account in the *Times* described it, "The dog immediately attacked and there was a rush of other Negroes toward the spot where the dog had pinned the man to the ground. Policemen with two more dogs and other policemen who were congregated in the area quickly rushed against the crowd, swinging clubs." The black onlookers then dispersed as the marchers were carted away, and the "peaceful prayer march on city hall" ended.

On Monday, with no street demonstrations and the few sit-in participants not arrested, local black leaders, a biracial clergy group, and Justice Department officials all attempted to persuade King and Shuttlesworth to postpone the campaign because of the current changeover of city administrations. They refused to do so, and on Tuesday, with northern reporters describing police conduct in handling spectators as racially "impartial," nineteen demonstrators picketing and sitting in at downtown stores were arrested.

On Wednesday, a number of influential black community leaders decided to support King's campaign rather than divide the black community in the face of King's determination to continue. Pickets at the downtown stores were arrested while black onlookers cheered them, and several sit-in activists who briefly patronized a segregated library were not arrested. Late that evening a county judge issued an injunction, naming King, which barred further public protests conducted without permission from city authorities.

Early Thursday, King, who up until that time merely had spoken at rallies and had not participated personally in any protest, announced that he and the other leaders of the campaign would lead a march in defiance of the injunction on Friday, April 12. That plan was publicized further at two large rallies on Thursday evening following some sporadic picketing activities during the day. On Friday, with the Birmingham story making its initial appearance on the front page of the *Times*, King and Abernathy led some sixty followers toward the downtown area and promptly were arrested by police as some one thousand blacks looked on. A large four-column photo of the two leaders being led off to jail appeared with the accompanying story on the front page of Saturday's *Times*.

On Saturday, as several more pickets were arrested and plans were laid for attempts to desegregate Birmingham churches the next day, President Kennedy, in Florida for the weekend, called Assistant Attorney General Burke Marshall to "express concern" about the Friday arrests. Earlier in the morning Marshall had been called by the SCLC's Wyatt T. Walker, who had complained that the jailed King was being held incommunicado. Marshall reportedly told both of his callers that no legal basis existed for any federal intervention, but in response to Walker's concern he subsequently called Birmingham authorities and found that the situation had been resolved. Also on Saturday a group of Birmingham clergy issued a statement calling the direct action campaign "unwise and untimely," while telegrams to the president and the attorney general from Harry Belafonte of the SCLC's Advisory Committee decried the "brutal use of police dogs against Negro citizens peacefully protesting segregated public facilities." Such a scene, Belafonte said, "shocks the conscience of America and reflects an ugly stain upon the United States throughout the entire world."[8]

On Sunday the day began with mixed results in the attempts to desegregate a number of white churches. In the afternoon, the Reverend A.D. King and thirty others attempted to march to the jail where King's brother and Abernathy remained. The marchers were halted and arrested almost immediately, but police vehicles to take them to jail were slow in arriving and a crowd of several thousand blacks gathered. Angry shouts arose, and after the paddy wagons had arrived and taken the prisoners away, some in the crowd began to hurl rocks at the police following their arrest of a black woman onlooker. The officers responded by clubbing and arresting several members of the crowd, which then gradually dispersed. That clash, and the earlier attempts to attend the white churches, were given prominent play in Monday's national newspapers.

Following calls to King's wife, Coretta, on Sunday by Attorney General Robert F. Kennedy and Press Secretary Pierre Salinger to reassure her of federal interest in her husband's confinement, President Kennedy himself called her on Monday. That same day the new Boutwell administration was sworn into office in Birmingham, and no major demonstrations were held either that day or on Tuesday. Wednesday witnessed only the arrest of some fifteen blacks walking toward the county voter registration office and of some thirty others who picketed and sat in at the downtown stores.

On Thursday there were no arrests, and Mrs. King visited her husband in the jail. Friday was quiet too, and on Saturday, King and Abernathy left jail, with the SCLC president reiterating to newsmen the first three, and the last, of the six goals he had outlined for the campaign some two weeks earlier. Several dozen sit-in participants were arrested on Saturday, though Sunday was uneventful, and the subsequent three days witnessed only the contempt trial of King in county court on charges of having violated the injunction of April 10. Convictions for King and ten others were handed down on Friday, April 26. A number of uneventful days followed in which the Birmingham story disappeared almost completely from the major national newspapers.[9]

The campaign came to life once again on Thursday, May 2, with the arrest of seven hundred teenage blacks who had attempted to march downtown, and the following morning the Birmingham story returned to the front pages of the *Times* and the *Post*, where it was to remain for the next twelve consecutive days. On Friday another protest march was staged, and as the column arrived at the spot where the police sought to halt it, a large crowd of black onlookers once again gathered. As some of those onlookers began to taunt and shout at the officers, Connor ordered six police dogs brought forward to drive the crowd back. Fire hoses also were readied and primed. At the sight of the dogs the onlookers became more aroused, and missiles sailed out of the crowd toward the officers. Connor's response to the bottles and stones was to order the dogs forward. "I want to see the dogs work. Look at those niggers run," Connor was quoted as yelling. The hoses also were brought into play against the now angry crowd, and the results, as shown in Saturday morning's papers, were predictable.

The *Times* headlined its lefthand lead column "Dogs and Hoses Repulse Negroes at Birmingham." In the three columns to the right of that story the *Times* printed two photos under the heading "Violence Explodes at Racial Protests in Alabama." The top photo pictured a police dog, held on a very short leash by a uniformed officer, apparently biting a black male in the stomach, while the officer held him by the shirt collar. Below, a second picture showed demonstrators pinned to a wall by water delivered under high pressure from a fire hose. The lead story in the lefthand column, written by Foster Hailey, began: "Fire hoses and police dogs were used here today to disperse Negro students protesting racial segregation." It went on to report that three blacks had been sent to the hospital for treatment of dog bites, and that brickbats and bottles had been thrown by black bystanders. On page 8 of the *Times* there was an additional photo showing a black man holding a knife being confronted by an officer with a dog. Coupled with this coverage was an additional page-one story reporting on how ten movement 'Free-

United Press International Photo

New York Times, May 4, 1963, p. 1—
"Fireman turns high pressure hose on demonstrators who sought to escape at doorway." (UPI)

dom Walkers' had been greeted at the Alabama state line by highway patrolmen armed with electric cattle prods and a crowd of 1,500 white onlookers. As Claude Sitton described it,

Patrol officers brought up three-foot-long prod poles, usually used for forcing cattle in chutes, and jabbed the demonstrators, giving them repeated electrical shocks.

As one of the Negroes flinched and twisted in the grip of the four troopers, an elderly, toothless white man shouted from a roadside pasture: "Stick him again! Stick him again!"

The Birmingham coverage in Saturday morning's *Washington Post* was very similar to that in the *Times*, even to the extent of printing at the top of page 1 the same wire-service photo that the *Times* had presented in that position. The accompanying story said that five black children had been injured, that a black woman had complained of police kicking her in the stomach, and that a woman and a man had been bitten by the dogs, the man sustaining "four or five deep wounds on his leg." The story also told its readers that blacks had thrown bottles, stones, and chunks of concrete at the police, who had used their nightsticks freely in dispersing the crowd. On an inside page the *Post* ran three additional photos, one depicting the fire hoses being used on blacks, the second picturing a lunging dog, and the third the same one that the *Times* had printed showing a black man armed with a knife facing an officer and dog. Several of these photos were used in many other Saturday morning papers as well.[10]

In some quarters the reaction to Friday's clash was swift. During a thirty-minute meeting Saturday afternoon with a number of leaders of the Americans for Democratic Action, President Kennedy reportedly said that the photo of the leashed dog lunging at the demonstrator had made him "sick." Kennedy also was reported to have "voiced dismay" over the use of fire hoses as well as the dogs. But, the president told the group, the limitations imposed by the Constitution on the use of federal power meant that he could not intervene directly, though he had ordered Assistant Attorney General Burke Marshall and Assistant Deputy Attorney General Joseph Dolan to go to Birmingham and to attempt to negotiate a truce. The same photo "profoundly affected" Attorney General Robert F. Kennedy, and the first public congressional comment came from Texas senator Ralph W. Yarborough, who denounced the use of the dogs in remarks to an audience at a Maryland dinner.[11]

In Birmingham on Saturday another march was attempted, and this time Connor moved to disperse it by using only the hoses, while the dogs remained in their kennel trucks. Once again black onlookers became angry and taunted the officials, challenging them to use the dogs. The SCLC's James Bevel advised the crowd to disperse, and a major conflict was averted, though some rocks were thrown from the crowd. Sunday's morning newspapers featured a photograph of a black woman soaked by the hoses being pursued by a nightstick-wielding officer. Typical of that day's editorials was the *Times'*, which called the use of the dogs and hoses "a national disgrace" and also decried the "welcome" given to the Freedom Walkers by the Alabama highway patrol.[12]

Sunday, May 5, in Birmingham witnessed only an uneventful march, and a similar large gathering the next day ended peacefully as well, with Connor and his men arresting about one thousand participants. Also on Monday came the first comments on the Birmingham campaign on the floor of either house of Congress as Senators Wayne Morse and John Sherman Cooper rose to denounce the use of the dogs and hoses on

Friday. Tuesday morning's papers, like Monday's, had little picturesque to report, though both the *Times* and the *Post* did print on inside pages a photo of a black woman being wrestled to the pavement by five police officers, one of whom had his knee on her neck. Reports said that the woman had failed to move off the sidewalk when ordered to do so. Tuesday's *Post* also carried a report by a foreign correspondent on how the Birmingham story was "front page news in Europe." The headlines and photographs depicting the use of the hoses, the reporter wrote, conveyed to Europeans the impression "that the United States is a land of brutality and repression."[13]

In Birmingham the relative calm of Sunday and Monday did not continue on Tuesday. Another attempted march erupted into violence as black onlookers hurled bricks and bottles at the police forces. "Dr. King and his lieutenants," Claude Sitton wrote, "appeared to have little control of the demonstrations, which were joined by hundreds of bystanders." Wednesday morning headlines read "Rioting Negroes Routed By Police" and were accompanied by photos depicting the hoses once again being used. While the news stories noted that Commissioner Connor had voiced his unhappiness that SCLC aide Fred Shuttlesworth, who had been carried away on a stretcher after being hit by the high-pressured water, had not departed in a hearse, the accounts also spoke of black "rioters" as well as "demonstrators."[14] Later on Tuesday Burke Marshall was able to establish a truce, and no marches occurred on Wednesday as negotiations began with Birmingham merchants in an effort to secure the campaign's major goals.

In Washington on Wednesday a number of members of Congress commented on the Birmingham situation both on the floor and in hearings conducted by a House Judiciary subcommittee. Emanuel Celler termed the police's actions "barbaric," and his comments were echoed by his New York colleague Jacob Gilbert, among others. On the House floor Alabama's George Huddleston termed the use of the dogs "disturbing" but "necessary" and went on to blame "professional agitators" for the situation. At a Wednesday news conference, President Kennedy expressed his hope that the recently instituted negotiations would resolve the Birmingham situation. He avoided any characterizations of either the police's or the blacks' activities, but he did voice his "strong view that there is an important moral issue involved of equality for all our citizens." The president further observed that the Birmingham clashes had hurt both the city's and the nation's reputation.[15]

Birmingham remained quiet on Thursday and Friday as the negotiating efforts continued, and on Friday afternoon an agreement specifying substantial desegregation in the not-too-distant future was announced.[16] Late Saturday evening, May 11, however, two bombs exploded, one destroying the home of the Reverend A.D. King, Martin's brother, and the other demolishing a part of the A.G. Gaston Motel, a building the movement leaders had used as a meeting site which was owned by a prominent Birmingham black man. Although no one was injured in either blast, infuriated blacks took to the streets and substantial "rioting," as the Sunday *Times* characterized it, ensued. City officials called out both the police dogs and an armored car in their effort to disperse the "mob," but peace and quiet were not restored to the nine-block area involved until late Sunday morning. At 9:00 Sunday evening President Kennedy appeared on nationwide television from the Oval Office to announce that Burke Marshall was returning to Birmingham in an effort to insure that the bombings and their aftermath did not wreck the agreement reached on Friday. He also announced that armed forces units trained in riot control had been alerted, and that the preliminary moves for calling the Alabama National Guard into federal service had been taken. The president expressed hope that there would be no need to use either force.

Monday morning's papers gave substantial coverage to the late Saturday and early Sunday disturbances in Birmingham, and an inside page of the *Times* featured a rather ghoulish photo of the bloodied face of a Birmingham police official who had been struck by a rock. Monday's *Washington Post* featured that same photo, along with ones of a burning building and an overturned and burning car, on page 4. The front-page story spoke of the stabbing of a policeman. Both papers also carried small wire-service items noting that rallies had been held in both Boston and Philadelphia on Sunday to show support for Birmingham's blacks. Attendance at each numbered several thousand. Only four congressional comments were made on the floors on Monday, with Senators Javits and Keating of New York and Williams of New Jersey expressing concern over the violence of the weekend. Florida representative Robert L.F. Sikes devoted his remarks to an attack upon Dr. King.[17]

In Birmingham on Monday King and his aides devoted the day to attempts to calm the black population, and Tuesday's papers gave featured coverage to King collecting knives from black men in a poolroom. The situation remained peaceful for the following two days, and on Wednesday the story made its last appearance on the *Times'* front page, having moved off of the *Post's* on Tuesday. A smattering of congressional speeches on the topic continued throughout the week, with a majority coming from Alabama representatives and fellow southerners such as Joe Waggonner and John C. Stennis. On Tuesday morning the

Democratic leadership had their weekly breakfast meeting with the president at the White House, and Senate majority leader Mansfield told newsmen afterward that "much attention was devoted to the Birmingham situation, but none to the possibility of seeking additional civil rights laws." By the end of that week the immediate story of the Birmingham campaign had ended.[18]

Some four weeks later, on June 11, the president again went on nationwide television, this time in regard to federal efforts to assure the admission of two black students to the University of Alabama. He repeated his earlier remark that the nation faced a "moral issue" and a "moral crisis" on the matter of racial discrimination. Eight days later the president sent to the Congress a package of civil rights proposals substantially stronger than those he had proposed in late February. Late in October of 1963 a heavily amended version of the June proposals was approved by the House Judiciary Committee, and more than three months after that, on February 10, 1964, the bill was approved by the entire House of Representatives. Exactly four months after that, cloture was obtained in a historic Senate vote, and on July 2, the Civil Rights Act of 1964 was signed into law. Some fourteen months had passed since the days in which news of the Birmingham campaign had occupied the front pages of the nation's newspapers.[19]

Clearly, Birmingham and Selma were quite different events. In the first case, although the clear weight of available evidence indicates that April's and May's events deeply affected the president, there was no widespread national outcry, no vocal reaction by the nation's clergy, and no immediate move by the administration to propose salutary legislation.[20] Although in time proposals aimed at remedying the ills of segregation were put forward by the Kennedy administration, many relevant events intervened as those proposals made their way slowly forward in the Congress. In the week preceding Kennedy's announcement of them came the face-off at Tuscaloosa. Later in the summer came the triumphal March on Washington, and then in September there was the Sunday morning bombing of a Birmingham church which took the lives of four young black girls.[21] Then came the death of John F. Kennedy and the elevation to the presidency of Lyndon B. Johnson, who told the Congress in his initial address, "No memorial oration or eulogy could more eloquently honor President Kennedy's memory than the earliest possible passage of the civil rights bill for which he fought so long." Johnson then proceeded to throw his own substantial legislative weight behind that bill. It was following that chain of events that the Civil Rights Act of 1964 began to win approval from the Congress, aided inestimably by an extensive and well-organized lobbying effort heavily sponsored by labor and religious groups. That pattern contrasts sharply with the far more speedy legislative approval given to the Voting Rights Act of 1965, which, following Selma, took place during months in which there were virtually no significant civil rights stories. So the quantity, and perhaps the quality, of reactions to Birmingham was far different from those at the time of Selma. But that difference can be appreciated more fully by focusing upon one particular body: the Congress of the United States.

Throughout April and May of 1963, twenty-seven speeches touching in some way upon the Birmingham campaign were delivered in, or inserted into the proceedings of, the Senate and House by some seventeen members. Of those twenty-seven speeches, however, only seventeen, delivered by ten different men, articulated support for the goals and/or the actions of Birmingham's black citizens. The other speeches voiced opposition, often very strongly worded, to the blacks' efforts in Birmingham. In contrast, in February and March of 1965, 267 speeches concerning events in Selma and/or the issue of voting rights appeared in the *Congressional Record*. Of these, 199 were delivered by 122 different speakers who supported the Selma campaign and its goal of additional voting rights legislation. Twenty-six members of Congress delivered a total of 60 addresses attacking the SCLC's effort and opposing new legislation. More than half of those opposition speeches were delivered by Alabama's eight representatives and two senators.[22]

Those statistics show that favorable congressional reactions to the Selma campaign and its goals exceeded by about twelvefold the number of similar statements made during the Birmingham campaign. Some rather clear indications of why that substantial quantitative difference occurred are provided by a close examination of the content of the remarks of the ten congressional supporters of the movement at the time of Birmingham and of the 122 proponents who spoke out in February and March of 1965. Coverage of, and reactions to, both Birmingham and Selma, as our earlier narratives have reflected, often devoted substantial attention to the tactics and weaponry used by the law-enforcement personnel who were confronting the civil rights activists. Not surprisingly, congressional comments concerning both Birmingham and Selma are replete with references to and condemnations of such tactics and weapons. The most common references in the floor remarks regarding Birmingham are to the police dogs and fire hoses used against the marchers and onlookers. While over half of the speeches mentioned those two items, less frequent mention also was made of the armored car city police had standing by and of the use of clubs by officers. During the

Selma campaign the frequency of such references varied greatly. Prior to the March 7 attack, no substantial percentage of the relevant floor remarks made mention of police behavior, though references to nightsticks, arrests, and jailings were by no means absent. In the aftermath of Bloody Sunday, however, far more congressional attention focused upon such official tactics and weaponry. Dozens of speakers decried the troopers' and possemen's "brutality" and characterized their actions as "brutal," "savage," and "disgraceful." Many of those same speakers, as well as other colleagues, also objected to more specific practices. Beatings, clubs, and clubbings were mentioned and denounced by some two dozen congressmen in the first two days after Sunday's attack alone, and in the course of that week—both houses were in session from Monday through Thursday—seventeen speeches made mention of the whips used by Sunday's posse, while twenty-six sets of remarks referred to the use of tear gas against the marchers. One dozen speakers, many of whom lashed out at Governor Wallace as personally responsible for the attack, went so far as to draw parallels between the Alabama action and the official conduct typical of totalitarian regimes such as Nazi Germany. Comparisons of the Alabama governor and his forces to "Hitler" and "storm troopers" were not at all rare in the congressional comments of March 8 and 9.

While the tear gas, clubs, and whips of Selma were as notable to those in Congress who spoke out at that time as the police dogs and fire hoses of Birmingham had been to the lesser number of speakers who had voiced their reactions in 1963, in neither instance were the congressional comments characterized solely by an interest in the behavior and weaponry of the law-enforcement officials. Congressmen also took note, particularly in 1965, of the purpose and goals of the demonstrations. In 1963, a few references were made to the Birmingham protestors' constitutional right to voice their grievances, though hardly a speaker touched upon lunch-counter desegregation or fair hiring practices. Such a lack of references to the Birmingham campaign's articulated goals appears to indicate that the congressional speakers either were unaware of or disinterested in the demonstrators' precise aims, or that to them the importance of the ways in which the movement's actual protest events were handled by local authorities vastly outweighed the significance of the demonstration's concrete purposes.

In 1965, however, a substantial percentage of those congressmen who spoke out made it clear that not only were they aware that voting rights was *the* purpose and goal of the Selma demonstrations, but also that they believed that the Selma protestors had a constitutional right to that which they sought. Many of these same speakers also stressed the crucial role they believed the franchise would play in southern blacks' quest for equality in other areas. Because the ballot was an essential right in the entire democratic process, and was thought to be of assistance in securing other goals, these members often tended to suggest that equal voting rights was a more important and loftier aim than the other ends which the civil rights movement of the 1960s was seeking. As a result, members appeared to find violent efforts against those seeking the ballot more offensive than when such actions were directed against persons seeking more pedestrian and perhaps "material" policy ends. Furthermore, in the wake of March 7, substantial numbers of congressmen also stressed that not only was the protestors' right to vote constitutionally protected, but that the right to petition one's government for redress of grievances—as the marchers intended to do upon arriving in Montgomery—also was guaranteed by the Constitution. In the days immediately after Bloody Sunday, speaker after speaker expressed "shock," as many termed it, that citizens engaging in a constitutionally mandated appeal for rights embodied in that same document had been set upon in such a "brutal" fashion with clubs, whips, and tear gas.

While it seems clear that the one clear goal of the Selma campaign played a much larger role in influencing the congressional reactions to that 1965 effort than had been the case with the more numerous and less well articulated aims of the Birmingham campaign two years earlier, the demonstrators' goals were not the only thing about them to which congressmen often were attuned. In 1963 very few speeches noted that the marchers themselves—as distinct from the onlookers and bystanders—had been peaceful, and that some of those subjected to the local officials' tactics had been "children." During the Selma campaign, however, and especially in the days directly after March 7, dozens of speakers emphasized that the marchers had been entirely peaceful and law-abiding, and that no actions on their part had in any way served to provoke or warrant the reactions of the state and county forces. A substantial number of congressmen stated that "unoffending" citizens who merely were seeking their constitutional rights in a "nonviolent" fashion had been the "innocent" victims of a vicious and completely unjustifiable assault. No such extreme characterizations were offered by those who spoke in response to Birmingham.[23]

The reactions to Selma also included far more mention than had been the case with Birmingham of certain other characteristics of the protestors; many of them had been women or children; they had been praying just prior to the Sunday attack; and, especially in the days after March 9, many in their ranks were members of the clergy. References to the religious nature of the demonstrators soared in the wake of the assault on the Reverend Reeb, and two weeks later a number of statements laid heavy emphasis upon the fact that another victim, Mrs. Liuzzo, had been a woman, a wife, and a mother of five. Throughout such references runs the implicit theme that children, women, and members of the clergy were especially undeserving victims of unjust treatment.[24] Just as many speakers appeared to suggest that violence aimed at those seeking the constitutionally guaranteed right to vote was somehow more wrong than if it were aimed at those who sought some other end, a good number of speakers also seemed to be saying that unjustified violence directed at women, children, and clergymen was somehow even more unjustified than similar action taken in similar circumstances against lay adult males.

Thus, differences in the *quantity* of congressional reactions are not the only important differences between the reactions of 1963 and those of 1965. The great majority of congressional reactions to both Birmingham and Selma devote substantial attention, and strong criticism, to the tactics of the lawmen, and particularly to the weapons they employed: police dogs and fire hoses in Birmingham, and clubs, whips, and tear gas in Selma. Much of the congressional outrage on both occasions hence appears to be somewhat the result of the behavior of the demonstrators' opponents. But that focus clearly is not the sole determinant of the quantities and qualities of the overall congressional reaction.

A secondary but nonetheless extremely influential factor is the perceived conduct of the demonstrators themselves. On that dimension substantial differences clearly exist between Birmingham and Selma, at least in terms of how the behavior of the black activists and their allies was portrayed in the news coverage provided by the two newspapers most widely read on Capitol Hill. Whereas at Selma there was little mention of any aggressive actions taken by marchers or their sympathizers, news accounts of the confrontations at Birmingham were laced with references to how some black onlookers, if not actual marchers, bombarded police with stones, bottles, and other objects. And whereas at the time of Selma a number of congressmen describing the peaceful nature of the demonstrators used the word "unarmed," that word was not used by any representative or senator who spoke out at the time of Birmingham, perhaps because of their familiarity with the photo of the knife-wielding black man confronting the police officer and dog. This difference, while very substantial, is basically one of degree, however, and not of kind. Several mentions of aggressive behavior by the movement forces at Selma was contained in news reports: Mrs. Cooper's punching of Sheriff Clark and a brief spate of rock-throwing as the pursuit of Sunday's marchers ended in the Brown's Chapel area. But in both cases such references virtually were swallowed up by the far greater emphasis put upon the violence of the officials. No such imbalance existed at Birmingham, where each story that described aggressive official action also made prominent mention of belligerent behavior on the part of blacks.

While this very substantial difference may be the major reason why congressional commentary supportive of the civil rights activists at Birmingham was less than 10 percent of that voiced at the time of Selma, a second, though less influential factor, also played a role. That supporting factor is the differing goals of the two campaigns, and the far greater emphasis that news coverage of Selma placed upon voting rights than coverage of Birmingham had placed upon desegregation of lunch counters and fair hiring practices. While some of this difference was related directly to the fact that the "drawing power" of a protest concerning voting rights was greater among those imbued with a strong belief in the importance of the franchise than was that of a protest aimed at the desegregation of private retail businesses, the lesser attention given to the goals of Birmingham as compared to Selma by both the major newspapers and congressional speakers was also partially the result of the fact that the goals of the Birmingham effort were numerous, poorly articulated, and hence somewhat diffuse. While Selma concerned one clearly articulated issue, which was reiterated daily, Birmingham had half a dozen aims, none of which movement leaders stressed to the news media on as regular a basis as they might have. As a result, only twice in two months did the leading national newspaper, the *Times*, give its readers a clear account of the demonstrators' goals.[25] In this light the failure of congressional comments to make mention of the demonstrations' goals is all the more understandable.

Thus, in the case of Selma a sizable percentage of the congressional "audience" was revolted and shocked by the tactics of Clark, Lingo, and their various troops. That strong negative reaction was magnified further when the congressmen took into account the unaggressive conduct and demeanor of the protestors themselves, whose effort also was clothed to some extent in the garb of religious support and conviction. The outrage many congressmen felt from that combination of the two sides' conduct was heightened further for many of them when the factor of the demonstrators' goal—the right to vote—was added into the equation. All together, those three factors produced a mammoth and rather vociferous congressional response.

The case of Birmingham is quite dissimilar. There too a number of congressional observers were very much disturbed by the officials' use of dogs and hoses. While some representatives and senators *did* distinguish the conduct of the actual demonstrators from that of some of the black onlookers, far more apparently did not. While the outrage at law-enforcement tactics at Selma was magnified further by the blacks' own commendable conduct, at Birmingham the perceived conduct of the blacks served to *reduce* the quantity and intensity of the outrage generated by the use of dogs and hoses. Additionally, while congressional shock and anger in 1965 was increased somewhat further on account of what the victims of official violence were seeking, such a multiplier was largely, though not entirely, absent at Birmingham in 1963, as that campaign's goals were both less clear and, while nonetheless noble and moral, somewhat less lofty in many people's minds than was the case at Selma.

While no precisely weighted equation can be suggested, it is thus clear that while at Selma support for the SCLC's campaign was stimulated by Clark's conduct, the demonstrators' own demeanor, and the protests' goal, at Birmingham support for the blacks' effort was aided by Connor's tactics, decreased by the perceptions of the blacks' own often violent belligerence, and essentially unaffected by the nature of the campaign's goals. All in all, however, it is clear that when the conduct of both "sides" at Birmingham was weighed by many members of the national audience, the blacks still came out ahead, though very largely because the officials' actions were judged more detestable than those of some movement supporters.[26]

Thus, the factors involved in shaping the reactions to confrontations such as Selma and Birmingham are clearly detectable but cannot be converted into any precisely weighted quantitative formula whereby pluses can be cumulated and minuses deducted. The sign of each factor—positive or negative—often can be arrived at, but the composite reaction in the end is based on a complex and largely subjective comparison: how much more positively, or negatively, is one "side" and its actions and goals perceived by the "audience" than is the other side, the side attempting to frustrate their opponents' aims. Between Birmingham and Selma the relative differences are great enough to suggest strongly why one confrontation produced some twelve times the quantity of congressional statements supportive of the civil rights movement than did the other. But this result of these examinations merely serves to raise yet a further, and perhaps more basic, query: What is it about the audience of a Birmingham or Selma—the "audience" being those exposed to the news coverage—that leads the majority of them to assign negative values to some items and characteristics (such as tear gas and belligerent taunts) and positive ones to others (such as the right to vote, orderliness, and religiousness)? Why is it that those who are able to portrary themselves as peaceful, religious, and seeking constitutionally protected rights, and whose opponents are perceived to be violent and brutish, gain support, while their opponents receive from the audience only vituperative castigations?

To answer these questions we must enter into the often cloudy contours of what is termed "political culture," in this case American "political culture." "Political culture," Lucian W. Pye has written, "is the set of attitudes, beliefs, and sentiments which give order and meaning to a political process and which provide the underlying assumptions and rules that govern behavior in the political system. It encompasses both the political ideals and the operating norms of a polity." It also includes, Pye adds, the political orientations of both leaders and citizens. Sidney Verba has stated, "The political culture of a society consists of the system of empirical beliefs, expressive symbols, and values which defines the situation in which political action takes place. It provides the subjective orientation to politics." Most important for our purposes, Verba has stated further that "Political culture forms an important link between the events of politics and the behavior of individuals in reaction to those events."[27]

Scholarly inquiries into the political culture of the United States have been few and not often attuned to those items that would have a bearing on both mass and elite reactions to events such as Selma and Birmingham. While in some regards that lack of pertinent data has resulted from a lack of scholarly interest and funds, it is also the result of the fact that the major public opinion polling organizations have made few if any efforts to sample public sentiment on specific news events such as Selma and Birmingham. And even in those few instances where sample surveys have included such "topical" questions, rarely if ever have those questions been so constructed as to probe the reasons for respondents' views.

Writers who have considered the available data on American political culture have chosen to characterize that culture with a variety of sweeping phrases, such as "the American democratic ideology" and "the Lockean liberal tradition." Encompassed within that ideology or tradition, they have added, are a number of principles or concepts, such as majority rule, minority rights, individual liberty and freedom, legal equality, religious toleration, and freedom of speech, thought and the press.[28] Those doctrines, and similar ones, often have been found, however, to hold for many people a meaning or message more symbolic than real. Two scholars who conducted several surveys in the late 1950s reported that "a general consensus was found on the idea of democracy itself and on the broad principles of majority rule and minority rights, but it disappeared when these principles were put in more specific form." Similarly, a parallel inquiry several years later discovered that when both general and more specific formulations of statements embodying a variety of presumably important democratic values were presented to people, "respondents were considerably less likely to endorse the specific valuations than the general valuations."[29]

While those principles thus appear to be endorsed by many people only when they are voiced in general and rather symbolic terms, and not when they are stated as guides to actual conduct, one important though often ill defined group of individuals has been found to be more apt than others to adhere to those doctrines in practice as well as in theory. "People who occupy themselves with public affairs to an unusual degree," Herbert McClosky has stated, "exhibit stronger support for democratic values than does the electorate" as a whole and "are also more consistent in applying the general principle to the specific instance" than is the general public. A similar conclusion had been reached a decade earlier by Samuel Stouffer, whose study concerned itself with "all categories of community leaders."[30] Presumably these findings that America's politically active citizens are more imbued with the ideals of its political culture than is the general populace also would apply to those who sit in the Senate and the House of Representatives.

While these writers and others have concerned themselves with the varying degrees of endorsement that the American public and various subgroups within it will give to various formulations of different principles thought by the researchers to be part of the "democratic creed,"[31] other scholars in more recent years have chosen to approach the matter from a somewhat different direction. Instead of attempting to determine which portions of the Bill of Rights the majority of the American public supports and which it rejects, they have grounded their thinking in Murray Edelman's thought-provoking discussions of the symbolic uses of politics and have focused upon the varying positive and negative "weights" that different "symbols" possess for either the entire American public or certain groups within it.[32] While to date these writings have been more suggestive than informative, they do indicate clearly that many items and characteristics in addition to King George III, the Declaration of Independence, and Abraham Lincoln can be thought of as politically potent "symbols." Various phrases—such as "fair play" or "states' rights," for instance—can be spoken of as "symbols" in this regard, so long as some segment of the population has an "emotive response" to the phrase or item in question. Emotive responses clearly can be either positive or negative and need not be the same throughout an entire society; witness "law and order." The most potent or "weighty" symbols are those that possess or produce the greatest homogeneity of sentiment and the strongest or most intense sentiment —depth as well as breadth, one might say. Particularly important symbols—one writer has suggested the term "metasymbols"—can "overpower" those of less wide and less intense appeal, though here again, while relative weights often can be estimated, no precise quantitative system of weights has yet been suggested or devised.

Although these initial soundings concerning the differential power of symbolic items, characteristics, and phrases give to us no greater precision of measurement than that which characterized our earlier discussion of the "positive and negative signs" of what we termed the three factors or general concerns visible in congressional reactions to Selma and Birmingham, it certainly is possible to draw upon what relevent data there is and suggest what the "symbol weights" of a number of matters salient in the Selma and Birmingham stories were—and perhaps still are— within the context of the American political culture. To begin with the most potent influence upon reactions to Selma and Birmingham, what relevant data there is on Americans' overall attitudes to violence indicate that violence, and presumably items and characteristics strongly associated with it, carrys a very strong negative symbol weight. "The average person, when asked about violence," one scholar concluded, "automatically views it as negative behavior. Violence to most people means illegitimate behavior—behavior that is contrary to the mores or against the law, behavior that exceeds the tolerance limits of the society or community."[33]

A number of research findings, however, indicate that observers' condemnation of violence is both more widespread and stronger when the violence in question is seen as directed at victims who are themselves peaceful rather than at individuals whose own actions are aggressive. As two researchers wrote in reporting the results of an experimental study in which a selection of photographs of civil rights incidents was presented to subjects who then gave their evaluations, "aggression alone did not arouse condemnation; observers also had to perceive the attacker as *unjustly* aggressive."[34] Much of what is involved in determining whether or not an action is justified, research findings indicate, is the impression that the observer has of the person or group against whom that action is directed. That impression in turn is the result not solely of the conduct of the recipient, but also of other perceived characteristics of those who are the targets of physical aggression. A long line of works support the position that the sight of physical aggression directed against those who are peaceful and nonresisting produces within observers both sympathy for the victim and the conclusion that the aggressor's acts are unjust.[35] That feeling of sympathy and the concomitant anger at the unjustified aggressor are both further heightened if the victim possesses what the observer regards as other "positive attributes" beyond his or her nonviolence.[36]

While no survey data concerning detailed public impressions of the actions of either side at Birmingham or Selma was gathered, these research findings indicate clearly that the actions of the county posse and the state troopers at Selma carried weights that were strongly negative. While the symbol of "police brutality" was in that instance clearly a powerful one, coupled with it, as we have seen, were the additional negative though lower-order symbols of tear gas, nightsticks, and the other weaponry involved. Also, as we noted earlier, the perceived illegitimacy of those actions and tactics was increased further by the perception that the marchers had in no way done anything to deserve the treatment they received and by the gender and religious nature of some of the victims. At Birmingham, however, the actions of not only the officials but also the demonstrators possessed some negatively potent symbols, and the aggressive and riotous actions of the latter group increased the chances that observers would see the police's actions as at least somewhat justified. While it appears that the negative symbols of police dogs and fire hoses proved to be somewhat more weighty than those of an occasional knife and various thrown debris in the eyes of a plurality of observers, there are also indications that to some not necessarily racist onlookers the negative weights of the demonstrators' own conduct at least wholly counterbalanced or more than exceeded those associated with Connor and his men.[37]

While at Selma the combination of positively perceived symbols associated with the movement and the negatively weighted symbols associated with its opponents combined to produce a public reaction greater than that of any other civil rights effort of the 1960s, and while Birmingham on balance produced responses favorable to the movement for racial equality, in both of those campaigns as well as in every other direct action effort, the civil rights movement began with one strike against it: Any act of public protest, no matter how peaceful and orderly, was and is seen by some Americans as illegitimate per se, with some respondents refusing to draw any distinction between protest and violence.[38] The right to protest is apt to be endorsed by more respondents when stated in the most general of terms, while substantially smaller percentages of interviewees endorse any specific form of demonstration, no matter how restrained. Thus, while a Harris poll conducted in midsummer 1964 received 61 percent positive and 32 percent negative responses to the question "Do people have a right to demonstrate for civil rights?" only 31 percent of those who knew of the Mississippi Freedom Summer were willing to voice approval of it, even though it did not feature direct action methods. While one might think that 31 percent figure low, earlier polls had found that the Freedom Riders' effort could draw a positive response from only 24 percent of those individuals interviewed, while the planned March on Washington obtained only 22 percent support. Although after its actual occurrence that march was able to obtain a supportive response from a plurality of the respondents to one Harris survey, pollster Harris summarized the results of similar questions in the same survey as follows:

> When asked in detail about the methods of the Negro revolution, whites went on record as 2 to 1 in opposition to the lunch-counter sit-ins, 4 to 3 against Negro willingness to go to jail voluntarily for their cause, 5 to 3 against picketing of stores and over 10 to 1 against "lie-downs" in front of trucks at construction sites. However, by slim margins, whites do accept the general idea of demonstrating.[39]

Survey data directly relevant to an effort to examine the public attitude towards civil rights activity at the time of Birmingham and Selma is not plentiful, though some hints can be obtained. One question used on a number of occasions by several polling organizations asked respondents whether they believed blacks' demonstrations had "hurt" or "helped" the civil rights cause. Due to the vagaries of survey research, often traceable to variations in the wording of queries, essentially the same question asked by two different organizations at about the same time could produce noticeably different results. Thus, in the wake of Birmingham a Harris survey reported an almost exact 50-50 split on "hurt" or "helped," while a Gallup poll result reported at the same time showed that 60 percent had chosen "hurt" and only 27 percent "helped." Such numbers may well be thought to raise more questions than they answer.[40]

In the period of interest concerning Selma, the most important surveys were periodic inquiries about the pace of the civil rights effort. Both

Gallup and Harris, as well as other public opinion research organizations, would ask if the respondent felt that black rights were being "pushed" too fast or too slow. Here again different wordings of the actual queries resulted in quite disparate results. The Gallup organization asked whether the Johnson administration was "pushing integration too fast," and among white nonsoutherners in both early February 1964 and mid-March 1965 it found 28 percent responding Yes. An early April 1965 survey asking that same question found 41 percent responding affirmatively. Seventy percent of white southerners anwered Yes, up from 49 and 67 percent, respectively, in the two earlier surveys. Affirmative answers from 36 percent of white northerners and 69 percent of white southerners were received in another subsequent survey conducted in mid-July 1965. Slightly different wordings of that same question, however, produced markedly different figures during that same period. While Gallup had phrased the query in terms of the Johnson administration's pace, a Survey Research Center poll in the fall of 1964 found that 62 percent of respondents answered affirmatively when asked if "civil rights leaders" were going too fast. A Gallup poll several weeks later gave respondents a choice between one statement saying that blacks should continue to demonstrate for their rights and another stating that they should stop now that they had made their point. Nineteen percent chose the former and 73 percent the latter. Lastly, a Harris query that asked the "too fast or too slow" question without mentioning any particular actor found that 32 percent chose "too fast" in November 1964, while in May 1965 it had risen to 41 percent.[41]

While those results can be read to suggest that the events of Selma contributed in some ways to the moderate rise in the percentage of respondents choosing "too fast" to describe the pace of black progress, the only certain interpretation is that regardless of specific times or events, 30 percent or more of Americans regarded any public direct action efforts of civil rights proponents "negatively." Although each and every campaign in the movement for racial equality confronted that initial public opinion barrier, observers at the time were quick to note that "the goals of the civil rights movement enjoy considerably more social legitimacy than do many of the actions being utilized by protest groups."[42] As one writer phrased it, blacks' aims in the early years of the 1960s possessed an initial legitimacy because the movement sought "to achieve goals and effectuate values that are already acknowledged to be inherent in a political democracy and which are firmly established in our national culture." They had been denied to black citizens solely because they were black.[43]

That did not mean, however, that great majorities of American whites were willing to endorse, even in a conversation with a polling organization's interviewer, blacks' demands for equal treatment. While a lengthy 1966 survey established that 87 percent of those questioned would endorse legislation to assure fair jury trials in which blacks were represented fully in the venire, and that 72 percent favored legislation to insure integrated education, a majority of that same sample voiced opposition to the elimination of racial discrimination in housing practices. Furthermore, although no 1963 data is available, between 20 and 30 percent of whites in 1966 admitted to interviewers that they would object to sitting next to a black person in a restaurant or a theater, to using an integrated rest room, and to patronizing the same clothing store if the same garments were tried on by members of both races.[44]

While those results reflect that the goals of the Birmingham campaign, to the extent that they were well articulated and publicized, enjoyed less widespread legitimacy than some might presume in light of America's oft-quoted ideals, similar statistics regarding equal voting rights indicate that the goal of the Selma effort was in the eyes of the American public the most legitimate of the civil rights movement.[45] In a July 1963 Harris poll, 93 percent of all respondents, and 88 percent of those in the South, voiced approval of voting by blacks. A National Opinion Research Center poll conducted in December 1963 found that 79 percent of a sample of white citizens nationwide agreed with the statement "It should be made easier than it is now for Negroes to vote in the South." A number of other late 1963 queries similarly produced support percentages ranging from the low 80s to the mid 90s.[46] Survey results dating from 1965 reiterate this general theme concerning the Voting Rights Act itself in particular. "A law has been proposed," the Gallup organization asked respondents to a survey conducted between March 18 and 23, "that would allow the federal government to send officials into areas where the turnout of eligible adults in the last presidential election was so low that it suggested that some persons were denied the right to vote. These officials would make sure Negroes and whites are given an equal opportunity to register and to vote. Would you favor or oppose such a law?" Nationally, 76 percent favored and 16 percent opposed, with the breakdown among southern whites being 49 and 37, respectively. Eighty percent of Democrats, 72 percent of Republicans, and 70 percent of Independents endorsed such a statute.

Somewhat different results were obtained by a Harris poll conducted a month later, however. That query, though, invoked a second symbolic phrase that counterbalanced "equal opportunity to register and to vote" when it told respondents that opponents of the bill "feel it's an invasion of states' rights to conduct their own elections." With that countervailing position suggested, support for the voting rights bill dropped to 53 percent. Although a Harris poll using a differently worded question a year later found 95 percent support for the Voting Rights Act, these contrasting figures once again show that a question's construction and the symbolic appeals it contains can produce substantial—and predictable—shifts in the ostensible levels of public sentiment.[47]

Two survey research questions concerning no single one of the three aspects of reactions to Selma which we have highlighted but instead touching upon overall perceptions were put to two different groups of respondents in the wake of the campaign. In April 1965, a poll restricted to residents of Minnesota found that 46 percent of respondents believed that "the Selma march" would "help" the cause of civil rights, while 36 percent felt it would "hurt."[48] A Harris poll completed in mid-May asked a national sample, "In the recent showdown in Selma, Alabama, over Negro voting rights, have you tended to side more with the civil rights groups or more with the state of Alabama?" Forty-eight percent of the entire sample indicated "civil rights groups," 21 percent chose the state of Alabama, and 31 percent responded that they were uncertain. The results for certain subgroups within that national sample are displayed in table 4-1. While the relative levels of support of "civil rights groups" and "Alabama" are perhaps not surprising, the substantial percentage of respondents unwilling or unable to choose either side may be the result of any number or combination of factors. While no certain explanation can be given, two reasons may be the pre-eminent causes of that substantial percentage of "undecideds." Foremost would be that the exposure to and interest in news coverage of many respondents was slight or nonexistent. A second cause would be those individuals who had had substantially equal negative reactions to both the conduct of the law-enforcement forces and the direct action tactics of the movement. As we suggested earlier, the continuing presence of this substantial body of opposition to any public protest tactics was, and is, of real importance in affecting the overall public reaction to each and every direct action campaign for equal rights.

While this data on those aspects of American public opinion presumed to have had relevant bearing upon how the "symbols" of Birmingham and Selma were interpreted and reacted to across the country may paint a far from complete picture, this information has served to reinforce further the earlier conclusions about the relative "potency" and "signs" of the three factors with which most congressional reactions to the two

TABLE 4-1

Reactions to Selma

	Percentage of Respondents Favoring Civil Rights Groups	Percentage of Respondents Favoring State of Alabama	Percentage of Respondents Uncertain
National	48	21	31
East	61	9	30
Midwest	51	14	35
West	48	18	34
South	19	54	27
Cities	60	14	26
Suburbs	48	19	33
Towns	44	27	29
Rural	33	26	41
Democrats	54	20	26
Republicans	43	20	37
Independents	39	23	38

Source: Hazel Erskine, "The Polls: Demonstrations and Race Riots," *Public Opinion Quarterly* 31 (Winter 1967-1968): 655-77, at 658.

campaigns were concerned. It is unfortunate that none of the pollsters who inquired about which "side" the respondent favored, or about what actions or goals a respondent supported and which he opposed, ever followed up those queries by asking the interviewee why he believed he felt as he did, but the outlines of the overall picture are clear. The key to the SCLC's great success at Selma and the contrasting, more limited success at Birmingham was that "the illegitimacy of the movement's methods was greatly outweighed by that of the opposition's." Behind the common observation that "the movement owed no little of its success to the Jim Clarks and "Bull" Connors"[49] lay the fact that the tactics and weapons used by those two officers and their associates created such a substantial negative reaction among the mass of the American people that whatever inherent distaste there was for the movement's direct action methods was greatly outweighed by the more abhorrent nature of the segregationists' behavior. Coupled with goals that the American political culture largely held to be laudable and quite legitimate, the movement, and especially the SCLC, was able to obtain widespread support throughout the nation and especially in Washington because the press coverage of Selma, and to a lesser extent Birmingham, showed the movement's opponents to be unjustifiably aggressive. Violence by a political actor was, within the context of the American political culture, certain to rebound to that actor's disadvantage to the extent that the polity was made aware of it and perceived that actor to be the initiator of it. Throughout the early 1960s the movement was more often than not successful in assuring—by means of methods and strategies we shall consider in detail in chapter 7—that the blame for violent incidents would be placed upon the shoulders of southern law-enforcement officials by the majority of the American people and their representatives in Washington. Violence by segregationists, combined with what was portrayed and perceived as the movement's generally nonviolent nature and its highly legitimate goals, had the effect both of making the movement appear "extremely virtuous" in comparsion to its opponents and of depicting racial segregation as far more brutal than the great majority of white Americans previously had realized.[50] Needless to say, a very major role in creating those all-important perceptions and reactions among both the society at large and political actors in Washington was played by the news media, particularly certain segments of it. It is to that subject that we now turn.

It has been rightly observed, that "a comprehensive analysis of the total range of communications which play a role in forming and influencing nationwide public opinion is probably impossible and certainly beyond the capabilities of any single research effort."[1] However, it is possible to analyze in large part the different and varied sources of news information that provided members of Congress with knowledge of one specific event, the confrontation at Selma.

Throughout the two months of the Selma campaign, February and March 1965, there appear in the texts of the congressional comments whose substantive themes we discussed in the previous chapter approximately six dozen explicit references to sources of information concerning the Selma campaign and public reactions to it. A majority of these references are to newspapers, either generally or to particular papers. Twenty are to television, and one dozen more make general reference to photographic coverage without specifying the method of transmission. A half dozen speakers mentioned radio, though most often in describing the overall coverage of Selma rather than as a source of their own news information. Five congressmen referred to the wire-service reports that came in on the news tickers located just off the floor of each house. The great majority of all these references to news sources came in the four days immediately following March 7. In that period twelve speakers made explicit mention of the television coverage of Selma which they themselves had witnessed, and several, such as Oregon senator Wayne Morse, took the time to describe in detail on the floor their perceptions and reactions.[2]

Many members of Congress, however, first learned of Sunday's attack by seeing a newspaper, in most instances the *Washington Post*. Some members, such as Senator Mondale, read or inserted into the *Record* the vivid UPI description of Sunday's events in Monday morning's *Post*. Running a clear but close second to the *Post* was the *New York Times*, which not surprisingly was most often referred to by members from the New York City metropolitan area. Other members indicated that they had first read of Sunday's attack in a variety of other papers: Wyoming

Senator McGee in the *Washington Daily News*, California Representative Hawkins in Monday's *Washington Evening Star*, and several New York members in the *Herald Tribune* or the *New York Post*. A good number of members also mentioned the newspaper editorials that denounced Sunday's violence and generally appeared in the Monday evening and Tuesday morning papers. Once again the favorite source was the *Post*, whose Tuesday morning editorial was mentioned or inserted into the *Congressional Record* by five members: Democratic representatives Scheuer, Conyers, and Fraser and Senators Ribicoff and Tydings. Three of those legislators also referred to the *Times*'s Tuesday morning editorial, which also was cited by California Democrat Jeffrey Cohelan. Editorials from the *New York Herald Tribune* and the *Baltimore Sun* each were cited by two members, and New York representative John Murphy inserted that of the *New York Daily News*.

These references make it clear that two papers in particular had a wide congressional readership: the *Times* and the *Post*. As we move into the second week following March 7, however, references to newspapers located in a particular member's district or state, which were virtually nil in the first week aside from the New York and Washington areas, begin to appear in moderate numbers. A smattering of nonsouthern members indicated that they had learned of sympathy protests in their home states from such sources as the *Louisville Courier-Journal* and the *Madison Capital Times*, but the notable increase in references to papers other than the *Post* and *Times* came mostly from those southern members who rose to express opposition to President Johnson's legislative initiative of March 15 and who sought to bolster their position by citing editorial criticism of the proposed bill. While several Alabama members, as in February, cited items from the *Montgomery Advertiser* and the *Birmingham Post Herald* in their defenses of Alabama officials' conduct, most references to local southern papers were to their editorial views. Senators Thurmond and Ervin in particular made an effort to emphasize editorials from papers throughout the Southeast which criticized the administration's voting bill. In this same effort toward the end of March the two senators and other southerners began to make regular reference to critical editorials in the *Wall Street Journal*, the *Washington Evening Star*, and *U.S. News & World Report*.

Aside from this effort by a small minority to find editorial material supporting their own positions, however, most media references by nonsouthern supporters of the voting rights proposal were to a relatively limited number of news sources. These same members also made well over a dozen references to the overseas coverage of Selma. While most of these references were to how the member believed such scenes would affect foreigners' views of the United States, and not to actual coverage abroad, several members did exhibit to their colleagues specific examples of foreign coverage. Such a sensitivity also had been voiced some half dozen times in the far fewer congressional remarks made two years earlier concerning Birmingham, remarks which, in contrast to those regarding Selma, made only a few references to any specific domestic news sources.

What is most impressive about the congressional references to the news coverage of Selma, and in particular that of Bloody Sunday, is that speaker after speaker who mentioned the news coverage devoted particular attention to the photographic coverage, as opposed to the verbal reporting. Although a number of members specifically referred to newspaper photographs, and others simply spoke of "pictures" in a general fashion, a larger number of comments dwelt upon the television films of Sunday's attack. Those members seemed to be saying that televised film coverage of Selma had had a more intense impact upon them than had still photographs or written reports. In that regard, many writers have commented upon what they believe to be the apparently substantial impact that television coverage of civil rights confrontations in the South had upon many who viewed it.[3] Such coverage is believed to have been extremely influential in bringing large numbers of Americans to a new level of awareness concerning racism in the South, an awareness that stimulated the application of the culturally based valuations discussed in the preceding chapter.

Such comments on the relationship between television and the civil rights revolution have two different but nonetheless closely related themes. The first often includes a reference to how "the rise of demonstrations to the status of a prominent and daily instrument of political expression dates . . . from the age of television."[4] The implicit, at times even explicit, suggestion is that the civil rights movement, with its heavy reliance upon direct action methods, would not have been possible without television. Although there is a basic and important truth in that suggestion, not all writers have focused clearly upon why that is so. The peculiar power of television is its ability to publicize a struggle, to "socialize" a conflict, to a far wider, a far more immediate degree than can any other news medium. As James Reston put it very well at the time, "It is the almost instantaneous television reporting of the struggle in the streets of Selma, Ala., that has transformed what would have been mainly a local event a generation ago into a national issue overnight." Russell Baker enlarged upon that theme several years later. "The difference between barbarity now and in other times," he wrote, "is that now everybody sees it on television." While such things as racially motivated violence against blacks "used to be conducted in comparative privacy," now "television sits in the living room corner ready to show us the absolute worst at the touch of a switch."[5]

Many members of news organizations were quite conscious of their role and of how that role had altered appreciably the context of what previously had been merely "local" problems.[6] Pondering whether the civil rights efforts of the 1950s and 1960s would have made such gains without television, one CBS correspondent observed, "I guess you could say we were partly responsible for the civil rights revolution. Certainly the conditions were already there, but no one knew it until fifty million Americans began seeing it on their television screens." NBC's David Brinkley expressed much the same view, noting that "these same things had been happening for years" although "until the last few years there wasn't any national television news of any importance."[7]

While essentially accurate, these observations should not obscure several other important points: that news organizations regard as news that which is unusual, and that open violence was regarded by those men and organizations at that time as unusual, as well as frequently dramatic and picturesque, and hence deserving of coverage. Just as important is that the "unusual" in news terms is very often something the culture as a whole finds shocking and illegitimate.[8] Perhaps the movement's greatest advantage was that it came to understand the dynamics of these processes earlier and better than did many of its direct opponents.

There can be no doubt that the burgeoning television news industry and the civil rights movement found each quite deserving of the other's attention, and out of that situation grew coverage that served the movement well in the central years when its goals and tactics most often were seen as considerably more legitimate than those of the southern lawmen and other racists who opposed it. As television journalist Robert Mac-Neil wrote in looking back at that coverage, "The tone of network programming has been emphatically liberal, identifying the advancement of the American Negro toward equality as unquestionably linked to the health of this nation." Up through 1965, MacNeil reported, "television presented a sympathetic picture of the Negro struggle. It was a sympathy dictated by events. In each of the major episodes of those years, the Negro demonstrators were on the defensive. They were taking the initiative in provoking confrontations but they were under physical attack."[9]

But the knife of television can cut both ways. By providing a forum in which protest causes and their repression could be emotionally and dramatically portrayed, television assisted the demonstrators as long as their actions were perceived by audience members as being more justified, or less illegitimate, than those of their opponents. Once that measure of "relative justification," as determined by the audience's values and beliefs, swung against the protestors, as in those instances in which protestors themselves turned violent, television coverage of confrontations (or "riots") began to work at cross-purposes with those of the demonstrators. As one student of the process concluded, "Television thus aided passage of civil rights legislation, but also permitted the rapid mobilization of adverse white reaction to Negro violence in the wake of the Watts riots" in mid-August of 1965.[10] Noting how the creation of simplistic "good guy" versus "bad guy" roles was difficult to avoid in some television newscasting, and responding to criticism by blacks of such coverage during the urban riot years, Mississippi newspaperman Hodding Carter III reminded the critics, "It was this same kind of simplistic coverage just three and four years ago of the Deep South situation—the Birmingham bombings, the Selma marches and attacks—that in large part impressed the national community, prodded its collective conscience and led to the passing of the civil rights bills of 1964 and 1965."[11] Carter was correct. It was not the media coverage that had changed, but instead the roles to which the audience now assigned each of the groups of combatants. While peaceful southern marchers had been "good guys" and brutal southern lawmen "bad guys," angry urban blacks burning and looting became "bad guys" just as much as harassed northern policemen were seen as "good guys."

The extensive and effective coverage the movement received from television news through the mid-1960s is only the first of the two interconnected themes that permeate the comments of those who have spoken of the powerful assistance television news gave the civil rights effort. The second concerns what accurately has been termed "the much discussed and little proven . . . emotional impact of video."[12] Said NBC's William B. Monroe, in discussing the medium's coverage of civil rights events in the early 1960s,

> Television conveyed the emotional values of a basically emotional contest with a richness and fidelity never before achieved in mass communications. When you *see* and *hear* a wildly angry man talking, whether he is a segregationist or integrationist, you can understand the man's anger, you can feel it—the depth of it, the power of it, the suffering in it. But if you *read* a description of what the

man said, you find that, by comparison, the words are dried-up little symbols through which only a fraction of the story comes."[13]

Monroe's opinion has been echoed by others, such as English journalist
Henry Fairlie, who wrote, "The impact of violence . . . is much greater
in a moving picture than in a still picture or descriptive prose. Violence
is movement—the raising of an arm, the smashing of it on someone's
head—and movement is what television cannot help emphasizing."[14]

The reactions to Selma which have made their way into print make it
clear that the television films of Sunday's attack had a powerful impact
upon many of those who viewed them, both congressmen and others.
Many in Washington, including President Johnson, and many who
traveled to Selma after Sunday's clash, including the Reverend Reeb,
reported reactions similar to those of a Washington pastor, George
Docherty, who said that when on "Sunday evening my wife and I
watched TV and saw those ghastly scenes, our stomachs turned."[15] One
well-known law professor later was to write, instructively though not
wholly accurately, "The television views of Selma produced at long last
an effective voting rights statute."[16]

Neither Selma nor Birmingham, however, had been the first occasion
on which the American public had had racial confrontations and virulent
white racism depicted in their own homes. It had happened in 1957 at
Little Rock, in 1960 at New Orleans, where white women had cursed
and spat upon black children entering a newly desegregated school, and
in 1961 and 1962 at Anniston, Montgomery, and Oxford.[17] The networks' failure to retain transcripts or tapes of any pre-1968 news broadcasts makes it impossible to reconstruct or analyze the actual coverage
given those stories and others, such as the March on Washington.[18] The
cumulative impact of this earlier coverage on viewers can only be sur-
mised.

While it appears clear that photographic coverage of Selma, Birmingham, and similar events was a greater stimulus to audience reaction
than was written coverage, it would be an error to assume that television
alone conveyed these apparently powerful visual portrayals. News
photos appearing in newspapers and magazines often did the same, and
what is perhaps the best remembered and most commented upon visual
image of the movement's efforts in the first half of the 1960s is indeed a
single news photo which appeared in many newspapers on May 4, 1963
and in a number of prominent newsmagazines later in the month. Coming out of Friday's clash between marchers, onlookers, and the police in
Birmingham, it portrayed a police dog lunging at the stomach of a black

Wide World Photo

New York Times, May 4, 1963, p. 1—
   "Police dog lunges at demonstrator during the protest against segregation in Birmingham."

Washington Post, May 4, 1963, p. 1—
   "A police dog lunges at a Negro during yesterday's racial demonstrations in Birmingham, Ala. At extreme right, another dog stands ready." (AP)

man while the officer handling the dog grasped the collar of the victim's shirt.[19] One historian has gone so far as to trace much of the success of the Birmingham campaign to the appearance of that one picture.[20] Reaction to the photo can best be conveyed by two letters to the editor that appeared in the *Washington Post* of Thursday, May 16, 1963. The first, written by Ruth R. Hemphill of Forest Heights, Maryland, read:

> Now I've seen everything. The news photographer who took the picture of a police dog lunging at a human being has shown us in unmistakable terms how low we have sunk and will surely have awakened a feeling of shame in all who have seen that picture, who have any notion of human dignity.
>
> The man being lunged at was not a criminal being tracked down to prevent his murdering other men; he was, and is, a man. If he can have a beast deliberately urged to lunge at him, then so can any man, woman or child in the United States. I don't wish to have beasts deliberately urged to lunge at me or my children and therefore I don't wish to have beasts lunging at the citizens of Birmingham or any other place.
>
> If the United States doesn't stand for some average decent level of human dignity, what does it stand for?

The statements in this letter are quite interesting in light of the points made in the preceding chapter, for while Ms. Hemphill was undoubtedly most exercised about the use of a dog on a man being an unjustified tactic (or weapon), she also clearly took into account in forming her opinion the status of the victim. If the victim were a "criminal," she implied, her attitude about a dog being instructed to lunge at him would be somewhat different.

The second letter came from Denise A. Goode of Washington. It read:

> I am 12 years old. I am writing to let you know how I feel about the Birmingham incidents. I was very displeased to see the front page picture of a police dog lunging at a Negro who was marching for civil rights and human dignity. It is a disgrace that here in the United States where we speak of liberty and justice for all that human beings should be attacked by dogs without committing a crime.
>
> For Judge Ellis [a Birmingham figure] and others who criticized the teachers and Negro leaders who let the children take part in the protest marches it would not be necessary for this to happen if they would not practice segregation. For America to be a great world leader she must first rid herself of segregation.[21]

While the young girl may well have had a little assistance in drafting her first paragraph, the point about dogs, and the one about "criminals," appears to be just as applicable here as it was to Ms. Hemphill's letter. Note also Miss Goode's favorable reference to the marchers' goal, which she speaks of as "civil rights and human dignity."

One other reference to that same photo was made by New Jersey Democratic representative Peter W. Rodino in a statement read to a House Judiciary subcommittee in mid-July 1963, in testimony supporting the Kennedy administration's civil rights proposals. Rodino related an experience he had had while abroad in early May.

> I was attending a conference at Geneva . . . and the incident of the police dog attacking the Negro in Birmingham was printed all over the world. One of the delegates from one of the nations represented at the conference there showed me the front page of the European edition of the *Times* and he was a little more frank than some of the others, and he asked me, "Is this the way you practice democracy?" And I had no answer.[22]

Rodino's story serves to highlight a sensitivity shared by a number of congressmen who spoke out concerning Birmingham and Selma. More than half a dozen in 1963, and well over a dozen in 1965, expressed their concern about how American racial problems were being portrayed abroad, and about how the actions of Connor, Clark, and other racists could greatly harm the United States image abroad and particularly in those nations whose citizens were not Caucasian. To many who heard Rodino's story, it must have seemed symptomatic of what they believed to be one of the ill effects of American racism, and another reason for them to heighten their efforts to eliminate or at least mitigate it and its effects.

The apparent impact of the incident upon Representative Rodino raises two interrelated and not completely answerable questions concerning the sources of certain influences that might have affected the reactions that congressmen voiced to Selma and to the news coverage that they had seen of events there. One is What interaction took place between members of Congress and their constituents concerning events in Selma and voting rights during February and March, and particularly in the wake of March 7? The second and more intriguing question is To what extent did congressmen's perceptions of their constituents' reactions to events in Selma shape the reactions that they themselves voiced publicly? Did those members who spoke out voice sentiments they personally felt because they were affected strongly by the news coverage of

Selma, or did they say what they did because they perceived that certain groups of voters in their district or state expected them to react in that way, and that their reaction would affect those constituents when they entered the voting booth a year-and-a-half later?[23] Recently it has been suggested that congressmen are largely if not wholly "single-minded seekers of reelection," in the pursuit of which one of their favorite devices is "position-taking."[24] Were those members of Congress who voiced outrage at the time of Selma merely taking positions that would sit favorably with certain voters whose support they believed they needed, or were they reacting largely in terms of their own personal feelings, and without any such calculated forethought?

While an extensive program of interviews might produce some success in answering these queries, both in terms of individual members and the entire group of "Selma speakers" as a whole, other methods less susceptible to the vagaries induced by the passage of ten years' time can provide suggestive results as well. First, however, we should take note of previous efforts. The connections between a representative's *voting* position on civil rights issues and the attitudes of a majority of his constituents on those same issues has been explored thoroughly in two articles, one by Miller and Stokes,[25] and another, a follow-up on that first one, by Cnudde and McCrone.[26] Miller and Stokes found that a high correlation existed between a representative's roll call behavior and the attitude of his constituents on civil rights questions. In further refining that analysis, Cnudde and McCrone came to several important conclusions. Instead of finding a high correlation between the representative's attitude and that of his constituents, the second study demonstrated that the primary link between a representative's roll call behavior and the attitudes of his district ran through what his perception of his constituents' attitudes was. This two-step process accounted for 60 percent of the total correlation between the two variables, Cnudde and McCrone stated. An additional 28 percent was accounted for by a similar path, which ran from district attitude to the representative's perception of that attitude to the representative's *own attitudes* and then on to his roll call behavior. Hence, a representative might well shift his own attitudes as he moved to bring his voting performance into closer agreement with what he perceived to be the wishes of his constituents on civil rights issues. While a correlation of .721 was found between the representative's own personal attitude on civil rights and his votes on bills embodying those issues, a higher correlation of .823 was found to exist between his perception of what his constituents' attitude was and his roll call behavior.

Cnudde and McCrone concluded, "Constituencies do not influence civil rights roll calls in the House of Repesentatives by selecting congressmen whose attitudes mirror their own. Instead, congressmen vote their constituencies' attitudes (as they perceive them) with a mind to the next election."[27] They go on to say that those representatives who either fail to perceive that their attitudes do not correspond with those of their constituency, or those who, knowing that, do not change their roll call behavior, are not likely to remain long in the House if those civil rights votes have a high visibility.

This general conclusion that most members of Congress act largely as "instructed delegates" on issues involving civil rights has long been regarded as true for those representatives and senators from the South. It likewise is true that many members from nonsouthern constituencies might well find themselves in electoral difficulty if their voting record indicated anything less than solid support of civil rights legislation. It might well be assumed that the same "law of anticipated reactions" would influence their public utterances just as it appears to have influenced their roll call behavior. However, while such electorally minded rationality may govern much congressional action, the reader of the early 1965 congressional comments supporting the SCLC's Selma campaign and urging further legislative action on voting rights soon realizes that the subjective indications are that the great majority of the sentiments contained in those remarks are not the dutiful utterances of an electorally conscious politician but instead are the personal feelings of that man or woman. In an effort to provide a test of that impression and hypothesis, a null hypothesis was fashioned from the presumption that those constituents who would be most interested in congressional action and comment supportive of the Selma effort and its goals would be black citizens themselves.

Admittedly, blacks clearly were not the only portion of any member's constituency who had an interest in demands for federal action supportive of the Selma campaign. Many "liberal" whites no doubt had similar feelings and interests. But although no measures of the percentage of racially liberal whites in each state and congressional district exist, statistics on the number of black citizens who are constituents of any given member of Congress are readily available. So the null hypothesis that "the larger the percentage of black residents in a constituency, the more vocal that constituency's representative should have been in calling for federal action and legislation in response to Selma" was fashioned. Excluded from this were the eight southern states from which no member of Congress indicated support of the movement. If it was true that much of the congressional reaction to Selma was expressed for electoral reasons, it would be likely that those members whose distircts and states had disproportionately high numbers of black citizens for the nonsouthern United States would be the most outspoken members concerning Selma and voting rights. If, on the other hand, members' reactions to the news coverage of Selma were largely "personal" rather than electorally motivated, no substantial tendency for heavily black constituencies to be overrepresented among those whose members spoke out should appear.

An empirical examination of the statements made in the House and Senate in response to Selma indicates clearly that those members who were most vocal in their support of the movement and its goals did not come from districts and states which were disproportionately black. All in all, 128 members of the 435 person House (or 29.4 percent) and 27 of the 100 senators made at least one public statement concerning Selma and voting rights in February and March of 1965 which was supportive of the movement and which found its way into the *Congressional Record*. This group ranged from New York representative William F. Ryan on the one hand, who made eight floor statements on the subject and personally traveled to Selma, to several dozen representatives and one senator on the other, who only affixed their names to one or more of the several group telegrams and statements concerning Selma which were sent to the president.

To make the analysis of the racial composition of the constituencies of these senators and representatives both more detailed and more enlightening, within each house those members who did speak out have been subdivided into three groups on the basis of the number and form of their remarks concerning Selma. Group One in each body is composed of those members who made at least two major statements in the *Congressional Record* concerning Selma and voting rights over the course of those two months. Twenty-nine representatives and 13 senators met or exceeded this requirement. Group Two, composed of those senators and representatives who made one major statement in the *Record*, consisted of 13 members from the upper body and 67 from the lower. In Group Three were placed those members who issued no major personal statement but who did sign one or more of the group telegrams. Thirty-two representatives and one senator, Republican Gordon Allott of Colorado, qualified for Group Three.

To consider the figures on the racial composition of the representatives' constituencies first, we can begin by noting that the average percentage of black residents in those 128 districts was 9.2 percent, which is somewhat higher than the average for all nonsouthern districts, 7.6 percent.[28] However, figures more interesting than that composite one are revealed when each of our three groups and certain subgroups are examined individually. For the 29 representatives in Group One, in 1965 their districts had an average of 11.8 percent black residents. Two of those 29, however, were themselves black—Hawkins of California and Conyers of Michigan—and represented districts 62.9 and 52.3 percent black, respectively. Of the remaining 27 white representatives, only 8 came from districts more than 10 percent black, while fourteen of these most vocal white congressmen represented districts less than 5 percent black. In fact, the average percentage black for those twenty-seven districts represented by white congressmen was only 8.4, just .8 percent above the national, nonsouthern average of 7.6 and actually less than the average for nonsouthern districts represented by *white* congressmen.

For Group Two, the average percentage black for all 67 districts was 9.2. However, when one removes from the calculations the districts of the two black representatives in Group Two, Philadelphia's Robert N. C. Nix and Detroit's Charles C. Diggs, whose districts were at that time 58.4 and 54.9 percent black, the average for the remaining 65 white representatives' districts is only 7.8 percent, just barely higher than the nonsouthern average of 7.6. Of those 65, 18 representatives' districts were more than 10 percent black, while 39 had constituencies less than 5 percent black. The average percentage black for Group Three's 32 members was 6.7. When black representative Adam Clayton Powell and his 66.9 percent black district are removed from the calculations, however, the average for the remaining 31 white representatives, only 2 of whom had districts more than 10 percent black, falls to 4.8 percent, substantially below the national nonsouthern average of 7.6. Twenty-one of those 31 had districts 5 percent black or less. A similar computation for the group of 15 representatives who made the February trip to Selma reveals the average percentage black for their districts was 17.2. However, when figures for the heavily black districts of black representatives Conyers, Hawkins, and Diggs are removed, the average for the remaining 12 white congressmen falls to 7.4, below the nonsouthern average.

A similar analysis of Senate Groups One and Two also can be made. For the 13 in Group One, the average percentage black in their states was 6.4, and for the like number in Group Two it was 5.7. The only senators to speak out who came from states whose populations were more than 10 percent black were Douglas of Illinois and Yarborough of Texas in Group One, and Dirksen of Illinois and Tydings of Maryland in Group Two. Five members of the former group and 6 of the latter had constituencies less than 5 percent black. As noted previously, the only member of the Senate who qualified for Group Three was Allott of Colorado, a state then 2.3 percent black. The overall average percentage for all 27 senators' states was 5.9, considerably below the national non-southern average of 7.6.

These statistics concerning the racial compositions of the constituencies of all 155 members of Congress who spoke out in support of the movement and voting rights at the time of Selma provide a convincing indication, though not by any means conclusive proof, that the great majority of senators and representatives who rose to speak out did so because of their personal reactions to the news of Selma and not because they felt it desirable to "play to" those constituents whose own viewing of that coverage would most likely stimulate them to want federal action and to respond to any calls for such from their own representative and senators. No doubt some members who did speak out, such as white representatives not known for their civil rights initiatives but who had a substantial number of black constituents, were motivated largely by the knowledge that taking such a position would likely increase their standing among the electorate at home. But the fact that 74 of those 155 members, or 47.7 percent, had constituencies less than 5 percent black, while only 32 white members came from districts or states with at least a 10 percent black population, lends substantial credence to the hypothesis that the majority of outspoken congressmen did not make the statements they did simply out of a desire to appeal to any substantial number of black constituents. Whether some members might have made their remarks simply to appeal to white voters whose reactions might well have been expected to be similar to those of blacks cannot be answered, but it is likely to have been true in some instances. Overall, however, this statistical exercise has provided some limited empirical support for the subjective impression that congressional comments came more from the feelings and emotions of the members themselves than from any electorally calculated stratagems.

Before examining in detail just what constituency contacts and communications concerning Selma and voting rights may have influenced or affected certain members, two other characteristics of our overall group of the 155 members who spoke out warrant some discussion. First is party affiliations. In both the House and the Senate, Democrats were represented more heavily among the speakers than they were in the body itself. While the House, with 295 Democrats and 140 Republicans, had a GOP contingent that represented 32.2 percent of the body, only 38 of the 128 Representatives who made or endorsed some public statement, or 29.7 percent, were Republicans. Furthermore, 16 of those 38 were Group Three members who merely affixed their names to one or more of the group telegrams. When one restricts the analysis to the 96 members of Groups One and Two, the Republican contingent falls to 22, or 22.9 percent. Republicans also were underrepresented slightly among the group of vocal senators, for while 32 percent of the 100 member Senate belonged to the GOP, only 8 of the 27 Senators who spoke out on Selma and voting rights, or 29.6 percent, were Republicans. When restricted to Groups One and Two, that percentage dips a bit more to 26.9, with the exclusion of Republican Allott of Colorado, the only member of Group Three.

The second dimension on which we can examine the 155 members who spoke out is seniority. Several writers have argued unconvincingly that the well-known influx of many new members following the 1964 elections "may have been the key" to congressional action on civil rights matters and other issues in the Eighty-ninth Congress.[29] While that may well be true for other issues, it certainly does not appear to have been the case with congressional interest in Selma and voting rights. In the House of Representatives, 86 members were freshmen, or 19.8 percent of the entire House. Among the 128 representatives who spoke out in some fashion concerning Selma and voting rights, twenty-nine, or 22.7 percent, were first-termers. While those figures indicate that freshmen were overrepresented slightly in that vocal group, they certainly do not show that such new members, who, it must be recalled, were then still subject to the long-held norm that freshmen were to be seen and not heard, had a disproportionate influence on the issue of voting rights.

That new members did not exert a disproportionate influence is even more clear on the Senate side, where there was considerably more drafting activity in the weeks prior to March 7 than there was in the House. None of the 7 new first-term senators was involved at all in either the administration's consultations with the bipartisan leadership or the Javits-Case-Douglas-Hart group which tried to exert an influence of their own. In fact, only two of the freshman senators, Joseph Tydings and Fred Harris, spoke out at all on voting rights during February and March. While freshmen represented 7 percent of the Senate, they thus composed 2 of 27 speakers, or 7.4 percent. It is perhaps also relevant that of the 155 members who spoke out at the time of Selma, 122 were in the Congress at the time of Birmingham.[30] Only 8 of them made any public utterance at that time, and only one member who spoke out on Birmingham, New Jersey's Cornelius Gallagher, remained publicly silent during Selma. When fully examined, then, these figures would tend to indicate that it was the activation of members who had already spent some time in the Congress, and not the actions or views of the newly arrived freshmen, that characterized the congressional reaction to Selma and voting rights in February and March of 1965.

While these analyses of the outspoken members' black constituencies, party affiliations, and terms of service have not detected any apparent major influences upon congressional behavior in addition to those discussed in the previous chapter, our earlier conclusion that the majority of members were voicing personal sentiments rather than consciously "playing to the galleries" for political effect should not be taken to mean that congressional reactions to Selma were uninfluenced by communications from constituents. Evidence indicates rather clearly that a number of members were affected by a variety of forms of contact by people in their state or district. Twenty-six of the 122 members who made major statements in the *Congressional Record* during February and March included in those remarks an explicit reference to their constituents' feelings or to specific communications from them. Virtually all of these references came in the wake of the March 7 attack, and the majority of them were about the volume of telegrams and letters the member was receiving from people "back home" who had seen the news coverage of Sunday's assault. Representatives Conyers, O'Neill, McCarthy, Dyal and Minish all commented on how their desks were piled high with such written communications, while other members, such as Senators Cooper and Gruening, made mention on the floor of petitions which had arrived in the mail from hundreds of constituents calling for federal action. Some representatives and senators rose to insert into the *Record* particular telegrams they had received from NAACP branches or local labor organizations, while others indicated their special sensitivity to communications from church leaders in their state or district. In a number of instances the receiving member, such as Philadelphia representative William Barrett, made it clear in his accompanying comments that he was aware of the direct or indirect political power possessed by the group sending the message.

The most telling constituency contacts, however, appear to have been those in which the member of Congress was either personally acquainted with the constituent in question or in which the elected representative was personally impressed or touched by what his constituent had experienced or how a constituent expressed himself. Indicative of the former circumstance were the comments of Illinois representative Barratt O'Hara, who recalled the experiences that a friend and constituent of his had had in a civil rights effort in Mississippi. Speaking on Tuesday, March 9, Rhode Island senator John Pastore indicated what he was hearing from people in his state. "Telegrams from horrified citizens— neighbors of mine—pour into me," the senator said. "They reveal the deepfelt dismay—the heartfelt resentment that helpless Americans anywhere in America could be subjected to such savagery."[31] Several other members, such as the very outspoken Don Edwards, whose California district was only 1.2 percent black but whose son Len had worked with COFO in Mississippi in 1964 where Edwards had visited him, were no doubt influenced by their own experiences or those of close friends and relatives.[32]

In regard to communications from constituents with whom the member is not personally acquainted, the most important thing in determining how a letter or telegram is evaluated by the congressman and his staff is, as Bauer, Pool and Dexter say, "the degree of spontaneity, sincerity, and urgency" of the communication.[33] Perhaps the best example of a communication that possessed those values to a high degree and was taken very much to heart by a member of Congress at the time of Selma was a telegram sent by a Wisconsin newspaper publisher to Senator William Proxmire. Proxmire's introductory comments on the floor before reading the message to his colleagues are instructive as well.

> I am sure that Senators from virtually all states have received telegrams relating to the situation in Selma, Alabama, and to the protests by Negroes, whites and others because of the inability of Negroes to register to vote in Alabama and the terrible brutality visited upon them because they peacefully attempted to protest this abridgement of their rights.
>
> Several of the telegrams I have received from prominent and thoughtful people in Wisconsin have been highly eloquent. I should like to put them in the *Record*. I shall read only one of them. That telegram was received from the publisher of the *Chippewa Herald Telegram*. Chippewa Falls is a city in northwestern Wisconsin. Incidentally, it is the hometown of former Senator Wiley. It is a town in which people are careful and stable in their attitudes. It is a town that is certainly not characterized by emotional reaction. This telegram from Mr. Lavine, who publishes the paper—the only daily newspaper in the city, and a newspaper which has been, by and large, conservative, careful, and thoughtful in its remarks—reads as follows:

March 9, 1965

Dear Senator Proxmire:
Never in our experience have [we] received such reaction from normally political, nonemotional leaders of our community and "workingman" alike as we have as a result of the brutality in Alabama. Isn't it possible that this bloody disregard of Americans' constitutional rights can be protected by the intervention of Federal marshalls and/or law enforcement officers? Please understand, we and the many citizens who have contacted us, are generally not advocates of this type of intervention, but we see no other recourse in this situation. It is not a time for words; it is a time for action.

Cordially,
John M. Lavine[34]

These individual incidents, coupled with the earlier analysis of the racial composition of the constituencies of those members of Congress who spoke out at the time of Selma, indicate that the balance of the "objective" evidence supports the subjective impression that the great majority of congressional remarks concerning Selma and voting rights represented not conscious political calculation but instead the personal feelings and reactions of individual members to the news coverage of Selma and the reactions to that coverage voiced to them by certain of their constituents. In the majority of cases the comments made and the feelings expressed on the floor of the House and Senate appear to have been those of individuals who first and foremost were voicing their own personal sentiments and not those of politicians acting to meet what they perceived to be their constituents' expectations of how their elected representatives should respond. Bauer and his colleagues wrote that the effect upon a member of Congress of heightened public interest and communication concerning an issue is that "he reacts more, but reacts in terms of his own accumulated predispositions, not in terms of the content of the communication. Messages serve more as triggers than persuaders." Those same writers have said "The demands that seem compelling to congressmen are apt to be those which fit their own psychic needs and their images of the world. Things interior to the congressman's mind largely determine what events he will perceive as external pressures on him. He unconsciously chooses what pressures to recognize."[35]

6 Enforcement and Effects: The Voting Rights Act and Black Political Participation in the South, 1965–1976

In the dozen years since the Voting Rights Act of 1965 became law, the literature on its effects on southern politics slowly has mushroomed. Less attention has been given the continuing criticism of the Justice Department's enforcement of the act's provisions, criticism that began only weeks after President Johnson signed the bill into law on August 6, 1965. But the story of the enforcement of the Voting Rights Act and the effects of its provisions begins prior to August 6, for by that time the Justice Department and the Civil Service Commission had been working for over two months on plans for the act's initial implementation.

On June 2, while the House version of the voting rights bill remained before the Rules Committee, representatives of the Justice Department and the Civil Service Commission met to discuss preparations for the implementation of those provisions of the forthcoming act which dealt with the appointment of federal examiners for southern counties and parishes which would be covered under section 4(b)'s trigger formula. The officials' main concern was the speed with which examiners would be sent South after the bill became law, and to how many counties and parishes examiners would be sent at the outset. The Civil Service Commission representatives believed that it would take from two to three months for their personnel to begin actual operation, and they also were interested in whether those examiners would require protection and whether any effort should be made to recruit black examiners. Within Justice, which inclined toward a more widespread initial assignment of examiners than the commission preferred, no need for either protection or a special effort to recruit black personnel was seen. Justice also was beginning to discuss the formal procedures implementing the trigger with the Census Bureau, which would have to determine exactly which jurisdictions had had less than 50 percent of their voting-age population registered or turning out to vote in the 1964 presidential election.[1] Following several more meetings in mid-June, Assistant Attorney General John Doar on July 6 gave to Wilson Matthews of the Civil Service

Commission the Justice Department's initial list of those counties and parishes that were likely candidates for the assignment of examiners by the attorney general when the voting rights bill became law.

Doar's list specified two groups of four counties each for each of three states: Alabama, Louisiana, and Mississippi. The Civil Service Commission was to be ready to send examiners to those twelve Group A subdivisions, plus two Group A counties in Georgia, within three days after the signing of the act, while the twelve counties in Group B, along with two more Georgia counties, should be readied for the assignment of examiners within ten to fifteen days of signing. In addition to those twenty-eight subdivisions, Doar also instructed Matthews that the commission should prepare for the early assignment of examiners to two urban counties in each of the three major target states: Jefferson and Mobile in Alabama, Caddo and Orleans parishes in Louisiana, and Hinds and Lauderdale counties in Mississippi.

Ten days later Doar's assistant, Stephen Pollak, got in touch with Matthews again to specify additional counties targeted for examiners. Pollak added three counties in Mississippi, two in Alabama, two in South Carolina, and two Louisiana parishes to the Group A list, while naming three additional Mississippi counties, three Louisiana parishes, four Georgia counties, and three in Alabama, and two in South Carolina to the Group B list. One Louisiana parish initially targeted for Group B by Doar—West Carroll—was dropped. Pollak also specified three South Carolina counties as a Group C, which should be readied for the assignment of examiners at some point in the future, but not in the first weeks after the act's signing. Group A then totalled twenty-three subdivisions and B twenty-eight, and discussions within the department about adding several others, such as Plaquemines Parish, to one group or the other continued into late July.[2] At that same time Pollak, Ramsey Clark, and Barefoot Sanders also were speaking with the OEP director, Buford Ellington, about the possibility that Ellington, a former Tennessee governor, could have some informal and private conversations with the governors of the five states to which examiners likely would be sent, conversations aimed at minimizing any antagonism that might result from the federal intervention.[3]

By the first week of August, when it was clear that President Johnson would be signing the bill into law within a few days, the administration's preparations for implementation were all but complete. Civil Service Commission Chairman John Macy reported that some six dozen commission personnel would undergo a three-day training session in preparation for serving as examiners, and Attorney General Katzenbach informed the White House that Justice was ready to complete the formalities for suspending all "tests and devices" in covered jurisdictions and for beginning the assignment of examiners as soon as the Voting Rights Act was signed into law.[4] Justice also was ready to file suits challenging the poll taxes of Alabama, Mississippi, Texas, and Virginia, as called for by section 10. While some movement leaders apparently were expecting that dozens of southern counties would be assigned examiners,[5] Justice Department officials made it clear to the press that their goal would be to achieve as much voluntary compliance with the act's commands by local registrars as possible in an effort to minimize the number of examiners sent South. Registration of illiterate blacks by local registrars, something implicitly mandated by the suspension of all literacy tests and devices in covered jurisdictions, was expected to produce the greatest problems of compliance, but Justice made it clear that "as long as a county makes progress in registering applicants, . . . it should not be necessary to send in an examiner," and initial assignments of examiners would be made only to those counties where Justice expected no substantial compliance by local registrars.[6]

Following President Johnson's signing of the Voting Rights Act on Friday, August 6, the federal implementation effort quickly sprang into action. Some four dozen Civil Service personnel headed South after completing their training session that day, and early Saturday afternoon the first of the suits challenging the four states' poll taxes was filed in Jackson, Mississippi. Also on Saturday the Justice Department and the Census Bureau issued their official determinations concerning the trigger, and Katzenbach's office began notifying state and local officials in Alabama, Georgia, Louisiana, Mississippi, South Carolina, Virginia, and more than two dozen North Carolina counties that all "tests and devices" related to voter registration were thereby suspended. On Monday Justice announced that examiners would begin work the next morning, August 10, in nine southern counties and parishes: Dallas, Hale, Lowndes, and Marengo in Alabama; East Carroll, East Feliciana, and Plaquemines in Louisiana; and Leflore and Madison in Mississippi.[7]

By Tuesday evening it was clear that the first day's effort in those nine counties had produced impressive results; 1,144 black applicants had been "listed" by the examiners. Madison County lead the list with 209, and in Dallas County, 107 new black voters were added. Applicants had been turned away at the end of the day in several counties, and the Civil Service Commission announced that additional personnel would be sent immediately to eight of the nine counties. A Justice Department spokesman admitted, "The turnout far exceeded expectations."[8] On the second day, Wednesday, an even higher total of 1,733 new registrants was added by the examiners, and by the close of business Friday, Civil Service Commission Chairman Macy reported to Johnson that the examiners in the nine counties had registered 6,998 new black voters. Statistics showed that prior to August 10 those same nine counties combined had had only 1,764 registered black voters.[9]

Some voices within civil rights circles, such as the NAACP, issued a call for the assignment of examiners to additional counties, such as Jones, Hinds, and Coahoma in Mississippi, and as the heavy turnout at examiners' offices continued during the second week of federal listing activity, the Justice Department on Wednesday, August 18, designated five more counties—Jones and Jefferson Davis in Mississippi, Wilcox and Perry in Alabama, and Ouachita Parish in Louisiana—for examiners. On Friday morning examiners began work in four of those five; no federal property existed in Jefferson Davis, and no local property owner would rent facilities for the examiners to the government. That evening Macy reported that a total of 19,178 new black registrants had been listed by the federal officials operating in the thirteen counties.[10] In only one, Plaquemines Parish, was the black registration not substantial, and that was the result of local white leader Leander Perez's effort to have unregistered white citizens compete with unregistered blacks for the examiners' time.[11]

The following week examiners were able to begin work in Jefferson Davis County as well, following a federal court order directing a motel owner to rent facilities to the federal registrars, and by the end of August, Civil Service Commission figures indicated that the examiners had processed 27,463 new black registrants. At the same time a Justice Department survey indicated that an additional 32,000 new black voters had been registered by local officials in Alabama, Georgia, Louisiana, and Mississippi since August 6, for a total increase in black registration of at least 60,000 in those four states alone in less than one month.[12]

As the first few weeks of September passed, however, it slowly became clear that the number of new registrants was declining noticeably from the levels experienced in August. Although figures from early September revealed that some 41,500 new black registrants had been listed by the examiners in their first thirty days of operations, by mid-September the daily average of new registrants, which had been about 2,000 in late August, had dropped to less than 400.[13] Some observers attributed the falloff to the winding down of movement-sponsored registration drives as college students returned to the campuses for the fall semester, but others noted that many unregistered blacks had yet to see what possible benefits could be derived from their registration, while those who were interested had responded quickly to the new registration opportunity.

At the same time that the number of new registrants was beginning to decline, the examiner program also came under attack by local officials in state courts. On August 31 a state district judge in Plaquemines Parish, acting on a complaint by District Attorney Leander Perez, Jr., issued a restraining order against the federal examiners in the parish, who then closed their office. Three days later, following the issuance of a federal court order, the office reopened.[14] Within the following two weeks similar efforts to hinder and harass the examiner program were made and effectively blocked, though with some delay, in East Carroll and Ouachita parishes, where local judges had moved to enjoin county registrars from placing upon the parishes' voting rolls the names of those citizens listed by the federal examiners. Similar efforts were mounted in Mississippi by the state attorney general, Joe Patterson, and in Alabama by Governor Wallace. In the latter state the county probate judges, who were caught between state court commands to not enter the "listees' " names and federal demands that such action be taken, sought a federal court order to remove the conflict and confusion. An order dissolving the state court injunctions, which had not halted the examiners' actual work but merely the processing of the names they gathered, soon was entered by a three-judge federal district court.[15]

As the pace of new registrations slowed, movement interest in having examiners sent to additional counties increased, and civil rights leaders stepped up their efforts to encourage Justice to send additional federal officers South. The department, however, generally was pleased with the voluntary compliance by the great majority of local registrars in Alabama, Louisiana, and Mississippi and insisted that its policy of sending examiners only to counties where compliance had not been forthcoming would continue despite the movement's growing anger.[16]

By the last week of September many of the initial examiners' offices, which once had been open six days a week, had reduced their schedules to Saturday openings only as the number of black applicants declined further. Six more counties, five in Mississippi and Montgomery County, Alabama, were designated for examiners, but still the overall average of new registrants continued to drop. Despite that decline, however, very substantial gains had been registered, in both examiner and nonexaminer counties, in the first two months of the act's existence. A late October survey indicated that the number of individuals registered by the federal examiners had topped 56,000, while 110,000 more had been registered by local officials in the six states and several dozen North Carolina counties covered by the act in the days since August 6.[17] Those gains increased even further in the aftermath of the assignment of examiners to twelve additional counties on October 29, a move that brought the number of designated counties to thirty-two. In several of the newly added counties, such as Walthall in Mississippi, over a thousand new black voters were listed in the first two weeks of the examiners' presence, but as in the counties designated earlier, the rate of increase steadily declined.[18] By November most offices which had reduced their schedule from six days a week to one had cut back further to one Saturday a month.

As August's and September's amazement at the early gains slowly turned into a realization that black voter registration gains would not continue at that pace, criticism of Justice's reluctance to send examiners into a substantially larger number of counties increased even further. That attack by movement leaders on the administration's strategy, an attack not lessened by several meetings between Katzenbach and black representatives,[19] was fueled further in early December when the Civil Rights Commission issued a report on the Voting Rights Act's first months which criticized the Justice Department's restraint in assigning examiners to counties covered by section 4(b)'s trigger formula.

On December 4, Katzenbach replied to what press reports called the commission's "biting criticism" in a letter to the commission's staff director, William L. Taylor. The attorney general noted that the commission had studied only some thirty-two counties, while Justice recently had surveyed more than five hundred, and that the report's specific allegations concerning the need for examiners in some two dozen particular counties were dated—examiners recently had been sent to six of them—and in some cases inaccurate. Up-to-date figures on those counties the commission said needed examiners, Katzenbach stated, indicated that local registrars in those locales were not rejecting any substantial number of black applicants. Furthermore, while the commission's report alleged that Katzenbach was sending examiners "only where there were flagrant violations of the Act but not where there were delays arising out of the limited number of registration days provided by state law," Justice records, and even some press reports, indicated that the department had sent examiners to several counties —Clarendon and Dorchester in South Carolina, West Feliciana in Louisiana, and Autauga and Greene in Alabama—because of the delays to which blacks were being subjected by those counties' local registrars.[20]

Criticism of the administration's enforcement of the examiners provision of the act continued into 1966. Although figures for calendar 1965 indicated that the examiners had listed 79,593 new black voters, they also showed that only about 3,000 had been added in December, despite the assignment of examiners to four more Mississippi counties in the middle of the month. Indications were that the pace of new registrations by local officials in the covered jurisdictions, which had totaled some 150,000 in mid-December, also had slowed greatly. Katzenbach early in January wrote to a number of local registrars, principally in South Carolina, to warn them that examiners would be appointed if Justice found that any discriminatory practices currently were being employed. Furthermore, the attorney general warned, "If it is necessary to hold extra days in order to correct the effects of past discrimination, Federal law requires that this be done."[21]

Despite this action, however, the dominant voting rights issue in January became the reluctance of the department to send examiners to Jefferson County, Alabama, which encompasses the city of Birmingham. Black leaders there believed that the failure of local registrars to open their office more than two days a month, the schedule called for by state law, was hindering their efforts to increase black registration, even though some 17,000 new black voters had been registered by local officials since August 1965. After a number of protest marches were held to draw attention to the allegedly dilatory conduct, on January 20 Justice gave in to the spreading pressure from the movement and examiners were sent in. In less than four weeks they added some 14,000 new black voters to the Jefferson County voting rolls.[22]

At the end of February 1966, Katzenbach himself went to Atlanta to address a meeting of the Southern Regional Council, the VEP's parent organization, and to deliver a further defense of the department's enforcement of the examiners provision of the act. He told his audience of his early January letter to local officials urging affirmative efforts to eliminate the effects of past discrimination in the registration process and reported that Justice had tried to persuade the Jefferson County officials to liberalize their office hours so as to accommodate all black applicants before the registration books were closed for the upcoming state Democratic primary in early May. When they did not, and with that upcoming election in mind, the decision to send in some twenty examiners was made.

Katzenbach attempted to play down the importance of examiners to black registration gains. While federal registrants now numbered over 100,000, he noted, over 200,000 new black voters had been added by local officials in covered subdivisions. "It is not the presence or absence of federal examiners that makes the difference,'' the attorney general asserted, and neither was it the compliance or lack of it by local officials. The most important factor in producing black registration gains, he argued, was the presence and degree of "local organization" within the black community, organization to sponsor and staff a productive voter registration drive. "Counties which have seen extensive Negro registration, whether by local officials or by federal examiners," Katzenbach stated, "are counties in which registration campaigns have been conducted. In counties without such campaigns even the presence of examiners has been of limited gain."[23]

While the attorney general's assertions were received politely by that Atlanta audience, movement leaders continued to disagree with his views on the use of examiners. Not many weeks after Katzenbach's appearance, the Southern Regional Council itself issued a report that argued that the presence or absence of examiners was by far the most crucial determinant of a county's present black registration level. The council's statistical findings showed that Alabama counties with both federal examiners and a local registration drive had an average of 69.5 percent of their voting-age black citizens presently registered, while those with a local drive but without examiners had a level of 57.6 percent. Alabama counties with examiners but lacking a local registration effort had an average of 63.7, while locales with neither examiners nor a registration drive had an average of only 45.4 percent of their black citizens registered. The corresponding percentages for Mississippi, where five more counties had received examiners in mid-April, were 51.7, 34.9, 41.2, and 24.2. For South Carolina, the third state that the SRC surveyed, the levels were 67.0, 51.6, 71.4, and 48.8.[24] Given statistics such as these, the council argued, the importance of examiners certainly could not be minimized as Katzenbach and the administration were attempting to do. While by late April 1966 forty-two counties had been designated for examiners, developments also began to occur on two other fronts.

The first of these was in the courts, where the efforts to test the constitutionality of the Voting Rights Act, and particularly the constitutionality of section 4's trigger formula, had made their way to the docket of the Supreme Court in a very short time. In late September 1965 the Supreme Court had received a request from the state of South Carolina that it accept original jurisdiction of a challenge to the Voting Rights Act's constitutionality, and the court granted the request in early November. Oral arguments by South Carolina on the one hand and the Justice Department on the other were heard by the Court in mid-January

1966, and on March 7 the High Court affirmed the constitutionality of the trigger formula, the suspension of "tests and devices," the use of federal examiners, and the preclearance provisions of section 5 in an opinion written by Chief Justice Warren.[25] Three weeks later, in a case brought by private parties prior to the passage of the Voting Rights Act, the Supreme Court struck down any and all uses of a poll tax, a decision that brought to a successful conclusion the four suits the Justice Department had brought against individual states as called for by section 10 of the act.[26] Several weeks later, in early June, the High Court rejected a challenge to the constitutionality of section 4(e), the so-called Puerto Rican amendment, instigated by private parties in New York.[27]

The most notable development of the late spring and early summer of 1966, however, was the Alabama Democratic primary in early May, the first notable election held in the South since the passage of the Voting Rights Act nine months earlier. In that period 122,000 black voters had been added to the Alabama voting rolls, and the statewide black registration total of 235,000 now represented one-fourth of the state's electorate. In Dallas County alone, where a year earlier black registration had been well under 1,000, the federal examiners had listed over 8,500 new black registrants, and total black registration had reached 10,300, compared to the 12,500 level of whites.

Both in Selma and across the state these gains produced changes in the climate of Alabama politics unlike any seen before. In the statewide gubernatorial race, Attorney General Richmond Flowers, who had won a name for himself in an unsuccessful effort to obtain convictions in Lowndes County of the men accused of Mrs. Liuzzo's murder and of a local white man accused of gunning down a white seminarian, challenged the husband-and-wife team of George and Lurleen Wallace with a campaign that openly appealed for blacks' votes, a first for a white politician in Alabama. In what press accounts termed "a major revolution in the tone of Alabama political campaigning," no open race-baiting marked the gubernatorial race, and local contests featured appeals to black voters by a variety of candidates. In Birmingham former state public safety director Al Lingo, now running for Jefferson County sheriff in what would prove a futile race, allowed himself to be photographed contributing money to a collection plate at an SCLC gathering, after having promised earlier that he would hire black deputies and clerks. In Selma, where the city's public safety director, Wilson Baker, had resigned to run against Jim Clark for the county sheriff's post, the incumbent threw a barbeque for black voters, but only several dozen chose to attend. Baker had the solid backing of Selma blacks, and as election day approached the contest between the two longtime rivals became increasingly bitter.[28]

In preparation for the actual voting on May 3, the Justice Department made plans to send some three hundred federal observers to polling places in seven Alabama counties, as the Voting Rights Act had provided. When the polls were closed at the end of the voting day and the tallies begun it soon became clear that the Wallaces had won a surprisingly strong victory and that Attorney General Flowers second-place performance had been weaker than expected. In local races none of the fifty-four black candidates won a clear victory, though several who had obtained pluralities but not majorities qualified for runoffs scheduled four weeks later. While black voters had united in support of Flowers in the gubernatorial race, local observers concluded, they had shown less unity when it came to local races involving black candidates. In Selma, however, black voters had registered a heavy turnout, apparently prompted by the opportunity to vote against Clark by voting for Baker. A very close tally was the result, and within forty-eight hours after the polls closed Clark's forces made an attempt to have the ballots cast in six largely black boxes thrown out on the grounds that certain irregularities had occurred at those polling places. The county Democratic Executive Committee voted to accept Clark's claims and to disqualify the challenged black ballots. The Justice Department then stepped in and obtained a temporary restraining order in federal court. A hearing on the county committee's decision was held some two weeks later before Judge Thomas, and after two days of testimony Thomas concluded that Clark's and the committee's claims of irregularities concerning the six black boxes lacked any validity. He ordered the committee to include the ballots from those boxes in the final tally, and those results supplied Baker with the votes necessary to defeat Clark.[29]

While Baker's victory over Clark was perhaps the only race in which a moderate actually won, nevertheless, despite the defeats of Flowers and the black candidates, "the 1966 Democratic primary in Alabama began a new era in that state's electoral politics" because of the new racial tone which had been adopted.[30] Across the South a similar trend was seen in many of the subsequent 1966 elections, and particularly in the general elections of November, by which time black registration throughout the South had climbed to more than 2.5 million.

The most notable victories for moderation in November occurred in Arkansas, where strong black support propelled Republican Winthrop Rockefeller into the governor's chair, and in South Carolina, where black voters supplied the margins for Senator Ernest F. Hollings and

TABLE 6-1

Black Voter Registration in the Southern States, 1966–1968

	Estimated Percentage of Voting-Age Blacks Registered			Estimated Number of Black Registrants		
	1966	*1967*	*1968*	*1966*	*1967*	*1968*
Alabama	51.2	53.1	56.7	246,396	255,000	273,000
Arkansas	59.7	62.8	67.5	115,000	121,000	130,000
Florida	60.9	64.6	62.1	286,446	304,000	292,000
Georgia	47.2	54.5	56.1	289,545	334,000	344,000
Louisiana	47.1	53.2	59.3	242,130	273,000	305,000
Mississippi	32.9	45.1	59.4	139,099	199,000	251,000
North Carolina	51.0	50.3	55.3	281,134	277,000	305,000
South Carolina	51.4	50.8	50.8	190,609	189,000	189,000
Tennessee	71.7	71.7	72.8	225,000	225,000	228,000
Texas	61.6	61.6	83.1	400,000	400,000	540,000
Virginia	46.9	55.6	58.4	205,000	243,000	255,000
All Southern States	52.2	56.2	62.0	2,620,359	2,820,000	3,112,000

Sources: *1966*: Southern Regional Council, *Voter Registration in the South, Summer 1966* (Atlanta: SRC, 1966), as quoted in Congressional Quarterly, *Revolution in Civil Rights,* 3rd ed. (Washington: Congressional Quarterly Service, 1967), p. 74. *1967*: *VEP News* 1 (September 1967): 1. *1968*: *VEP News* 2 (September 1968): 1. As with the pre-1965 years, it should be emphasized that the majority of these figures represent observers' best—and often somewhat imaginative—estimates, and not precise tabulations.

Governor Robert B. McNair. Blacks themselves also began to register some notable election victories, as Lucius Amerson won election as Macon County, Alabama sheriff and as blacks gained five seats in the Tennessee legislature, bringing their total in the eleven southern legislatures to twenty. Those twenty, however, served in only three states— eleven in Georgia, six in Tennessee, and three in Texas—leaving black southerners in the eight other states without even one member of their race in the state legislatures. Furthermore, while some moderate victories—including a second defeat of Clark by Baker—and a continued decline of explicit racism marked the November races, the darker side of southern politics by no means had disappeared. As one reporter noted, with the South Carolina contests in mind, even though open references to the race issue had all but disappeared, "it is the underlying and motivating issue in all contests."[31]

Although most observers chose to concentrate on the positive electoral gains registered by blacks, such as the increase in black elected officials throughout the South from about 72 to 159 as a result of the 1966 elections, far less attention was devoted to a trend whose effect was to reinforce the racial conservatism of white southern politicians: the unprecedented increases in white voter registration across the South which all but outstripped the widely heralded black gains. As two southern political historians recognized a number of years later in commenting upon the numerous 1966 victories of racially conservative whites, "The Maddoxes and Wallaces rode the vote of an expanded white electorate to victory."[32] While it has been suggested that at least some of this white registration increase was a "countermobilization" produced by the initial, heavily publicized black gains, increasing partisan competition, education levels, affluence, and migration in the South may well have affected the growth as well. While no precise explanation for the growth of the white electorate has been offered, those who have devoted the most thought to the matter suspect that racial concerns were the main determinant.[33]

In 1967 the number of southern counties designated for federal examiners continued to grow slowly, as additional examiners went into Mississippi and as the first examiners were sent to counties in Georgia. By the end of the year sixty-two counties had been designated for examiners, and the total of federal black registrants had grown to just over 150,000, an increase of about 20,000 from the total in the early fall of 1966. The major highlight of 1967, however, was the Mississippi elections of August and November. In the initial August Democratic primary fifteen black candidates scored outright victories, while twenty-two others emerged with pluralities. In the late August runoffs, however, all twenty-two went down to defeat amidst charges by blacks of widespread irregularities and intimidation. Although in the November general election the first black member of the Mississippi legislature, Robert Clark of Holmes County, was elected, and twenty-one other blacks won county or local posts, most observers sympathetic to black efforts were disappointed. While the general election had witnessed a turnout of about 100,000 of Mississippi's 200,000 registered black voters, a vast increase from the 1965 registration figure of 28,500, and the same moderation of racial rhetoric which had characterized the 1966 races in other southern states,[34] black political influence in the Deep South, and especially in rural areas, remained only a small shadow of what it might be. Exactly why black political participation, especially in registration and turnout levels, was not greater became a matter of some debate. In a number of locales, such as rural counties in the Mississippi delta, fear of economic—and perhaps physical—intimidation and retaliation by local whites remained the major roadblock to black political gains at the ballot box. As the Voter Education Project observed in the wake of the Mississippi runoff primary, "As ever, fear continues to keep Negroes away from the polls in Mississippi. Many Negroes fear loss of their jobs. And the possibility of violence is always present in election situations."[35]

Some writers suggested, however, that it was not simply fear but apathy, produced by the socioeconomic conditions in which many black southerners found their lives mired, which was tempering any further gains in black registration and turnout. As the two leading students of southern black political participation wrote at the time, in an observation whose truth was accepted by many others, "Most southern Negroes have low social status, relatively small incomes, and limited education received in inferior schools. These attributes are associated with low voter turnout among all populations."[36] This view received additional support when another scholar concluded that at any given socioeconomic level blacks are more active organizational participants than whites, and that hence the gap between black and white levels of political participation was the result of an even larger gap between white and black socioeconomic conditions.[37] The problem for southern black political gains which this analysis highlighted was that certain "social and economic deprivations—lower levels of education, lower status occupations, inadequate income—that political participation is supposed to be used to overcome" themselves impede the political participation that can assist in their mitigation.[38]

While such explanations often were cited to explain the failure of black registration and turnout levels to continue their steady upward rise once the notable gains of the fall of 1965 had been registered, many observers close to the black political effort in the South argued, as the VEP noted in the aftermath of the 1967 Mississippi elections, that black fear of white retaliation was the main factor impeding the growth of black political participation. The most convincing demonstration of the validity of this position was put forward several years thereafter by two political scientists who focused their inquiry on black voter turnout in black majority Mississippi counties in the 1967 and 1968 general elections. Using 1960 census data for those counties, and attempting to estimate the actual black turnout from the vote totals received by candidates who presumably appealed to most black and very few white voters, the two scholars employed statistical tests which led them to the conclusion that "fear is the cause of low turnout among black voters in

Mississippi."[39] Fear in the rural South, they reasoned, was the result of black economic vulnerability, and that economic vulnerability was the result of black economic dependence upon local whites. Increased black political participation would follow only from increased black economic independence. While their general model and their conclusions proved statistically convincing when employed in regard to Mississippi statistics through 1971 and to South Carolina data from 1970, more recent applications of their constructs have raised serious questions about their actual validity.[40]

Although both fear and apathy, in precisely indeterminate proportions, clearly were hindrances to black political gains, they were not the only barriers to an increase in black political power in the South. Other influential, though often seemingly minor, impediments were created by local whites through changes in electoral procedures which were aimed at diluting the power of black voters or hindering black candidates, changes that section 5 of the 1965 act had been intended to block. As one of the most informed observers characterized the changing tactics of whites who sought to restrict black political influence, "the shift was from preventing blacks from voting to preventing blacks from winning or deciding elections."[41] A variety of such changes were attempted throughout the Deep South states. In Mississippi the legislature moved to require that all members of the five-person county boards of supervisors be elected at-large rather than in one of five separate "beats" as previously had been the rule. Blacks would have a more difficult time in electing a member of their race in a countywide contest, it was believed, than if all a black candidate needed was majority support in a smaller geographic area where blacks might constitute a majority even if they were outnumbered at the county level. Other changes proposed with a discriminatory intent included making previously elective offices—such as county school superintendents—appointive, requiring "full slate" voting in multipost races so as to deny blacks the opportunity of maximizing their support for one minority candidate by "bullet voting," and increasing the number of petition signatures required of an independent candidate seeking a place on the ballot. Black voters and candidates were also hindered by the location of polling place facilities, the denial of accurate information to prospective black candidates, filing deadlines, the certification of nominating petitions, and the bonding of elected black officials.[42] Some of these changes, of which the Justice Department often was not notified, in violation of section 5, were contested by the department, as in the 1966 case of *U.S.* v. *Crook*, where an Alabama effort to extend the terms of incumbent white officials was blocked. Up through 1968, however, the provisions of section 5 were ignored almost completely both in the South and in Washington.[43]

As the numerous electoral contests of 1968 were conducted, the number of black elected officials in the South, which had stood at 248 in early February, climbed steadily but slowly. Early in the year Mississippi civil rights leader Charles Evers made a run for the congressional seat vacated by the state's newly elected governor, John Bell Williams. His effort, though far from successful, did mark something of an end to a feud within black political ranks which had developed between Evers and Lawrence Guyot of the Mississippi Freedom Democratic party.

By midyear figures from across the South indicated that some 62 percent of voting-age blacks were registered as the primary season began. Record numbers of black candidates ran for offices in ten of the southern states. Record numbers also won posts, and by early 1969 VEP totals indicated that the number of black elected officials throughout the eleven southern states had risen to 389, a jump of approximately 140 in less than a year's time. By late spring a revised tally that took into account the results of local municipal elections in Louisiana, Mississippi, and North Carolina had raised that total to 473.[44] While the great majority of those elected officials held local offices that most outside observers regarded as minor, Marvin Rich was very correct when he wrote that spring, "While most offices won by Negroes are minor ones, the local impact of their success is anything but minor."[45]

While journalists were wont to focus upon particularly notable instances of black political success—such as the late July 1969 sweep of Greene County, Alabama offices by a slate of black candidates, and the victory of Charles Evers in a race for mayor of the small Mississippi town of Fayette—[46]less "popular" attention was devoted to more limited black gains elsewhere and to just what actual benefits black voters derived from the election to public office of either sympathetic, black-supported white candidates or black officials themselves.[47] The first scholarly inquiry to concentrate upon this latter topic concluded in 1968, after a study of two very different southern cities, that black citizens did not begin to get material rewards from local officeholders, in the forms of paved streets, recreational facilities, and other such governmental services, until blacks themselves were elected to office.[48] The intimation was that white candidates often failed to follow through on their campaign promises to blacks. While such concrete gains came only after blacks themselves had been elected,[49] a number of studies indicated that substantial black voting even in the absence of black elected officials did produce some improvements for black citizens. In the wake of black voting, a political scientist who studied one Mississippi county concluded, perhaps "the most basic change the Negro could see was the curbing of official violence."[50] Wrote two other scholars, "Police brutality tends to decline and, to a lesser extent, the entire administration of justice tends to improve after southern Negroes become active members of the electorate."[51]

While improvements such as these were being registered in many parts of the Deep South as the 1960s closed, the advent of the Nixon administration early in 1969 posed a serious threat to the maintenance of even the most easygoing enforcement of the Voting Rights Act's key provisions. As some backers of the 1965 act had come to realize even during the tenures of Katzenbach and Ramsey Clark, the enforcement provisions of the act granted a very large amount of discretionary authority to the attorney general. That this need not always work to blacks' advantage was brought home clearly when John N. Mitchell took charge at Justice in 1969.[52]

Mitchell's first visible action in the voting rights field took place on June 26, 1969 when he testified at the fourth day of hearings that House Judiciary Subcommittee No. 5 was conducting on the extension of the Voting Rights Act. Lacking reenactment, sections 4 and 5—the heart of the act—would expire in August 1970, five years after their initial passage. Mitchell proposed that the attorney general be granted the power to use examiners and observers anywhere in the country and that literacy "tests and devices" be suspended throughout the nation so that the "regional" character of the act, heretofore aimed only at the South, would be removed. Mitchell also recommended the dropping of section 5's requirement that covered jurisdictions submit all election and voting regulation changes either to Justice or the federal district court in Washington, and that local—i.e., southern—federal district courts be allowed to handle voting rights cases over which the 1965 act had given the District of Columbia federal courts exclusive jurisdiction.

Mitchell's proposals received a hostile reaction from both the subcommittee and civil rights proponents, and when he returned to continue his testimony on July 1 the subcommittee gave him a very rough time. As *Congressional Quarterly* noted, "The major opposition to the substance of the Mitchell proposals centered on the proposed changes in Section 5." Those who favored a simple extension of the provisions of the 1965 act focused their arguments on the real importance of section 5 and the other provisions of the 1965 act for black southerners. They also devoted substantial time to arguing that Mitchell's Justice Department was not properly enforcing section 5 as it now stood. Not only had the department objected to only ten of the 345 changes submitted to it by states and localities; it also had failed to inquire about hundreds of apparent changes that had not been submitted for preclearance prior to their implementation. In addition, critics charged (as they had during the

Johnson administration) that examiners and observers were not being used as widely as they should be. Those who opposed any weakening of the act argued further that the original section 5 had been correct in placing the burden of proof upon the submitting jurisdiction, which was required to show to the satisfaction of Justice or the D.C. court that the proposed change would not have a discriminatory effect upon black voters or candidates. Mitchell's suggestion that section 5 be reduced to a provision allowing Justice to bring a civil action against any change whose actual effect the department judged to be discriminatory, the act's proponents stated, would return the entire voting rights enforcement effort to the slow, costly, and ineffective judicial route of case-by-case litigation which had stymied the achievement of equal political rights for southern blacks in the eight years prior to 1965.[53]

Those who testified in favor of a simple extension, such as the Civil Rights Commission staff director, Howard Glickstein, also placed emphasis upon the hindrances that continued to face black voters in the South, hindrances recently revealed once again in the mid-May municipal primaries in Mississippi.[54] By the time that the House hearings were concluded in early July, with ranking Republican William McCulloch and Senate minority leader Hugh Scott voicing their opposition to the Nixon administration effort to gut section 5, it appeared that the proponents of simple extension had both the factual evidence and a majority of congressional sentiment on their side. On July 10 the House subcommittee voted for and reported to the full Judiciary Committee a five-year simple extension of the 1965 act's provisions, and seven days later the entire committee gave its approval to the same bill. Civil rights lobbyist Clarence Mitchell was quoted as saying, "We have the votes" to obtain approval of a simple extension in both the House and the Senate, and *Congressional Quarterly* reported, "Many observers predict that the Nixon proposals stand little chance for serious consideration by Congress." In mid-July hearings on extension began before a Senate Judiciary subcommittee, where action was not expected until after House approval had been given to a simple extension bill.[55]

By early September, however, it was clear that House floor action on the voting rights extension measure approved by the Judiciary Committee would be delayed greatly because the Rules Committee chairman, William Colmer of Mississippi, was refusing to heed leadership requests that the extension bill be cleared for consideration by the entire House. Such a delay, in turn, made it likely that no Senate action would be possible until Congress reconvened in early 1970. It was not until November 18 that Rules approved the bill, H.R. 4249, for floor consideration, and the Nixon administration moved to pressure GOP representatives to support the administration-proposed substitute in a floor vote. That roll call came on December 11, and by a somewhat surprising vote of 208 to 203, with only 49 Republicans supporting a simple extension, the House substituted the administration proposals for the simple extension that had been approved by the Judiciary Committee. Later that same day the House gave final approval to that very watered down extension on a vote of 234 to 179. Civil rights supporters were described as "stunned" by the setback, and five days later the Senate sent the House-passed bill to the Judiciary Committee with instructions to report it back by March 1, 1970.[56]

In mid-February the Senate committee resumed its hearings on the extension measure, with Assistant Attorney General for Civil Rights David L. Norman claiming that the potential effectiveness of section 5 had been "overstated." Maryland's Joseph Tydings voiced the opposite viewpoint and noted, "Any enforcement of a voting rights law which depends solely on court suits," as the administration's newly proposed version of section 5 would, "is too slow and too easily circumvented to provide an effective remedy" to discriminatory voting and election practices.

The House-passed substitute extension came to the Senate floor on March 2, and minority leader Scott promptly introduced a substitute for the House version which called for a simple five-year extension of the 1965 act's provisions plus a five-year suspension of all literacy tests throughout the United States. Majority leader Mansfield decreed that a vote on the voting rights extension measure would come before floor consideration of the pending Supreme Court nomination of G. Harrold Carswell, and with opposition to that nominee growing daily, southern supporters of the Florida judge reduced their delaying tactics on the voting rights measure to a minimum. A move to table Scott's substitute failed by 47 to 32, and other weakening amendments failed by even more decisive margins. A well-publicized amendment to add a provision lowering the voting age to eighteen was approved on a vote of 64 to 17. After approving by 50 to 37 an amendment by John Sherman Cooper of Kentucky to include under the act's provisions those areas, mainly New York City and a handful of New England towns, which had failed to meet the 50 percent turnout or trigger figure in the 1968 elections, the Senate adopted the Scott substitute on March 13 by a vote of 51 to 22, and later that same day it approved the extension as amended by the Scott substitute 64 to 12.

Civil rights proponents thus had rewon much of the ground they had lost three months earlier. As one observer wrote, "A measure that had gone into the Senate weakened severely by House reverses emerged dramatically as a more powerful bill than anyone had expected." In large part this was because the "tactical need of the conservatives to gain an early vote on Carswell" had forced those opponents of civil rights to drop filibuster plans and avoid delaying tactics. The House then was faced with a choice of accepting the Senate version or taking the differences to conference. Despite strong White House pressure against the eighteen-year-old vote provision added in the Senate, and despite initial fears that the House Judiciary Committee chairman, Emanuel Celler, would oppose that provision as well, Celler announced that he would back the Senate bill, and Republican efforts to rally opposition to the strengthened version proved unsuccessful. On June 17, following a 224-to-183 victory for civil rights proponents on a key procedural tally, the House approved the Senate-passed bill on a vote of 272 to 132. Five days later President Nixon signed the five-year extension into law.[57]

While advocates of a strong voting rights enforcement effort were able to defeat that attempt by the Nixon administration to gut the 1965 act in the halls of Congress, they were far less able to block what many oberv-ers believed was a notable weakening of administrative enforcement of the act by the Justice Department's Civil Rights Division. One group of observers wrote early in 1971, "The Department of Justice has revoked through executive policy what the Administration did not succeed in eliminating through legislation," and many other commentators echoed their views.[58]

As had been the case at the House extension hearings in mid-1969, the controversy two and three years later continued to center on the Nixon Justice Department's enforcement of section 5's preclearance pro-visions, provisions the administration had wanted to eliminate from the act. The section 5 enforcement controversy had been fueled by an im-portant 1969 Supreme Court decision concerning the scope of the pre-clearance requirement and the standing of private parties to challenge the implementation of unsubmitted changes. In that case, *Allen* v. *State Board of Elections*, which represented a combination of three cases from Mississippi and one from Virginia, the High Court ruled that private parties could challenge unsubmitted changes and that local federal dis-trict courts could consider whether section 5's requirements were perti-nent to the changes at issue, but that only the D.C. district court or the attorney general could rule that a "covered" change did not have a discriminatory effect upon black people.[59] In the wake of that ruling, which served to call attention to the important role that section 5 could play, a role which prior to 1969 had been largely invisible, politically active southern blacks and attorneys sympathetic to their strivings for greater political power began to devote far more attention to blocking subtly discriminatory changes that whites were using to dilute black voting power and which ostensibly were subject to the requirements of section 5.

In the wake of *Allen* an increasing number of changes were submitted for review and approval as southern officials became more aware of the statutory requirements imposed upon them by section 5. Hardly without exception, however, every submitted change was sent to the Justice Department rather than to the Federal District Court in Washington. While this imbalance was thought by many to be contrary to what the drafters of the 1965 act had intended, it was considerably easier—and less costly—for states and subdivisions to conduct correspondence with Justice than to engage in legal proceedings before a somewhat distant court. At Justice, section 5 called upon the attorney general to object within sixty days of receipt to any change whose effect could not be shown to be nondiscriminatory. In practice, however, it soon became clear that Justice was objecting only to those submitted changes whose clear effect would be discriminatory, a very different standard than that called for by the 1965 act. Whereas the statutory language placed the burden of proof upon the submitting jurisdiction, which was required to show that a change would not harm black citizens, the department's actual practices removed that burden by requiring that either the department or interested private parties develop evidence that the proposed change would be iniquitous to blacks. The effects of this policy were reflected most clearly by the fact that through the end of 1970 the department had entered objections to only about twenty of the more than seven hundred submitted changes.[60]

Criticism of this perhaps intentional misreading of the statute and of congressional intent jelled in May and June of 1971 when Representative Don Edwards's Civil Rights Oversight Subcommittee of the House Judiciary Committee began hearings on the enforcement of the Voting Rights Act by the Department of Justice. Edwards himself began the sessions by noting that reregistration of all voters was underway in several dozen Mississippi counties, and that the department had displayed almost no interest in considering whether any of these reregistrations could work to dilute black voting strength. Furthermore, a number of the counties conducting reregistrations had not even submitted their plans for doing so to Justice, and the department, lacking any system for detecting the illegal implementation of unsubmitted changes, had failed to take any action to insure compliance with section 5 by those subdivisions prior to the implementation of the reregistration plans.

Replying for the Justice Department, in the absence of Attorney General Mitchell, who refused to appear personally, were Civil Rights Division officials David L. Norman, James P. Turner, and Gerald W. Jones. They attempted to defend the department's enforcement effort and stressed that Justice presently was adopting a new series of guidelines to govern the enforcement of section 5's provisions. When these regulations officially were promulgated in mid-September 1971, they indicated that the department had switched its position and in the future would correctly place the burden of proof on the submitting jurisdiction as specified by section 5.[61] Nevertheless, Edwards's subcommittee, in a report on the hearings issued in early 1972, urged that Justice develop a policy of searching out unsubmitted changes and seeking to enjoin their enforcement, rather than leaving such protective oversight to those victimized by such electoral alterations, victims who often lacked the legal knowledge and resources necessary for challenging such illegally implemented changes. As the subcommittee put it, "Present enforcement policies of the Department have placed the burden on the people Congress sought to protect rather than on the covered jurisdictions," as the Eighty-ninth and Ninety-first Congresses had intended.[62]

While controversy over the Nixon administration's enforcement of the Voting Rights Act brewed, political gains for and by black people continued in the South. By mid-1970 black registration in the eleven states had topped 3.3 million, an increase of more than 200,000 since the 1968 elections and a notable rise when contrasted with the approximately 2 million black registrants at the time that the 1965 act was passed. White registration had increased even more substantially, as we noted earlier, but the election results of 1970 indicated that both black gains and a stronger trend toward racial moderation were occurring in most states of the South. Some 370 black candidates ran for a large variety of offices, and 110 won election, including the first black members of the Alabama and South Carolina legislatures. Those victories brought the number of elected black public officials throughout the South to 711 at the end of 1970, a figure nearly ten times that of 1965.

The growing tendency for southern states to choose as governors moderate white politicians with a liberal position on racial matters, a tendency first signaled by the elections of Winthrop Rockefeller in Arkansas and Linwood Holton in Virginia, blossomed into a major trend in 1970 as Reubin Askew, Dale Bumpers, Jimmy Carter, and John West won the gubernatorial races in Florida, Arkansas, Georgia, and South

TABLE 6-2

Black Voter Registration in the Southern States, 1969–1971

	Estimated Percentage of Voting-Age Blacks Registered			Estimated Number of Black Registrants		
	1969	1970	1971	1969	1970	1971
Alabama	61.3	64.0	54.7	295,000	308,000	290,057
Arkansas	77.9	71.6	80.9	150,000	138,000	165,000
Florida	67.0	67.0	52.9	315,000	315,000	320,640
Georgia	60.4	63.6	64.2	370,000	390,000	450,000
Louisiana	60.8	61.8	56.6	313,000	318,000	354,607
Mississippi	66.5	67.5	59.4	281,000	285,000	268,440
North Carolina	53.7	54.8	44.4	296,000	302,000	298,427
South Carolina	54.6	57.3	45.9	203,000	213,000	206,394
Tennessee	92.1	76.5	65.6	289,000	240,000	245,000
Texas	73.1	84.7	68.2	475,000	550,000	575,000
Virginia	59.4	60.7	52.0	261,000	265,000	275,000
All Southern States	64.8	66.3	58.6	3,248,000	3,324,000	3,448,565

Sources: *1969*: *VEP News* 3 (November 1969): 2. *1970*: William C. Havard, ed., *The Changing Politics of the South* (Baton Rouge: Louisiana State University Press, 1972), p. 21; and Congressional Quarterly, *Civil Rights Progress Report 1970* (Washington: Congressional Quarterly Service, 1971), p. 74, who both cite the VEP as their source. *1971*: Charles V. Hamilton, *The Bench and The Ballot: Southern Federal Judges and Black Voters* (New York: Oxford University Press, 1973), p. 239, who cites the VEP as his source. Also see Penn Kimball, *The Disconnected* (New York: Columbia University Press, 1972), p. 263. The noticeable drop in percentages from 1970 to 1971 is the wholly artificial result of the fact that the 1971 percentages were calculated on the basis of 1970 Census data, which indicated that the southern black voting-age population—those eighteen and over—was 5,997,664, while the percentages for 1970 and previous years were calculated on the basis of the 1960 Census's population figures, which gave a total of 5,016,100 southern black citizens twenty-one years of age or over. As in preceding years, once again these figures represent estimates, and often rather hopeful ones, whose accuracy is by no means certain. As of the mid-1970s only three southern states—Louisiana, North Carolina, and South Carolina—kept official tabulations of registered voters by race, and unofficial estimates by various observers had declined greatly in frequency.

Carolina, respectively.[63] While much attention was focused upon these "New South" governors, the leading representative of Southern racism, George Wallace, prevailed again in Alabama after trailing the incumbent, Albert Brewer, who had succeeded to the governorship upon the death of Lurleen Wallace, in the first primary. The Wallace comeback over Brewer in the runoff was accomplished only after the former third-party presidential candidate explicitly attacked Brewer on the race issue, alleging that the incumbent was the candidate of the black "bloc vote."[64] While the overall pattern of the 1970 races in the South suggested that visible political racism was on the wane, Wallace's successful effort, and another race waged in Tennessee by William Brock, indicated that adept white politicians still could profitably use race as an explicit campaign issue.

In off-year gubernatorial elections in Louisiana and Mississippi in 1971, the number of racially moderate southern governors increased by two as Edwin Edwards won in Louisiana and William Waller in Mississippi.[65] The year's major story lay in the Mississippi contest, where Waller emerged triumphant in the Democratic runoff after trailing another racial moderate, Lieutenant Governor Charles L. Sullivan, in the first primary.[66] In the general election, however, the black mayor of Fayette, Charles Evers, waged a dogged independent campaign against Waller and succeeded in capturing 22 percent, or approximately 173,000, of the more than 750,000 ballots cast. Observers stated that "voting was largely along racial lines" as 74 percent of registered whites and 63 percent of the approximately 300,000 registered blacks turned out. Some commentators suggested that the most notable effect of the highly visible Evers challenge had been its stimulation of white turnout to the great detriment of local black candidates. Some 309 black citizens ran for legislative, county, or local offices in about half of the state's eighty-two counties, but only fifty-one won their races. Forty-eight blacks sought seats in the Mississippi legislature, but only one, incumbent Robert Clark, won election.[67]

While those associated with the Evers campaign and a number of more independent observers reported instances of harassment, intimidation, and polling place irregularities,[68] academic observers within the state said that there were really "few such charges" and argued that "white opposition to Negro voting was not necessarily a significant deterrent to Negro turnout."[69] Despite such differing views on the degree to which intimidation and fear continued to hinder black political efforts, all observers agreed that the 1971 campaign was a memorable event in Mississippi history because of the numerous "explicit white efforts to court black votes."[70] In spite of that heartening development, however, participants and observers sympathetic to the black cause were unable to regard the election returns as even a moral victory, largely because so few of the black candidates won at the local level.[71]

To explain why the Evers race, which had been undertaken in the hope of stimulating black voter turnout and the election of local black candidates, had not succeeded to the degree expected, some attention was focused upon the federal oversight effort. In the belief that the conduct of the election at many polling places had reduced the number of black voters casting votes for black candidates, Evers supporters and others criticized the federal observers program. In what was now the most visible part of the Voting Rights Act enforcement effort, Justice and the Civil Service Commission, under the provisions of section 8, often sent substantial numbers of commission personnel to potential problem counties on election day to watch what went on at polling places both as votes were cast and as they subsequently were counted. While almost 1,000 such personnel were employed in Mississippi in 1971—down about 100 from the number used for the similar elections in 1967—civil rights proponents believed them to be of very limited assistance. An impressive 1975 Civil Rights Commission study summed up the pluses and minuses of the federal observers program very well.

> Black residents of jurisdictions that have had observers view the program with mixed reactions. Most believe that the presence of observers deters local officials from preventing blacks from voting and, to a lesser extent, from treating black voters discourteously. Most also believe that the presence of observers, if known in advance, encourages blacks to vote because the Federal presence can help to alleviate the widespread distrust of local election officials. Department of Justice staff attorneys who have served with observers expressed similar views.
>
> Nevertheless, black residents of observer jurisdictions visited by the Commission staff expressed some dissatisfaction with the program. They complain that most observers are white Southerners from nearby states and often indistinguishable from the local election officials.

The commission staff also reported:

> Black residents of observer jurisdictions also complain that the practice of last-minute assignment of observers tends to diminish the effectiveness of the program. One attorney noted that the observers arrive just before the election and are not well informed about local conditions. Their last minute assignment precludes widespread publicity about their presence, so the reassuring effect of their presence for minority voters may well be lost.

But the most notable complaint, the commission reported, was that observers never took corrective action, although many blacks felt that they should. The federal observers, the report noted, "merely observe and report the conduct of the election in the polling place they are assigned to; they do not participate in managing the poll in any way."[72]

Despite the fact that many felt it to be of limited value, throughout the first half of the 1970s the observers program continued to be the most visible federal voting rights enforcement effort. That higher visibility was the indirect result of the fact that the examiners program had been all but terminated; in the eight years from 1968 through 1975 examiners actually were sent to only two new counties, Pearl River and Tallahatchie in Mississippi, where they listed a total of some 450 black citizens.[73] Also, the processes of section 5 review and preclearance were not particularly newsworthy.

Although section 5 approvals and objections rarely received any journalistic attention, in the wake of the 1970 Census and the attendant redistrictings, a substantial number of important submissions—and some resulting court cases—suggested that racial gerrymandering was becoming the leading weapon of those southern white officials who sought to limit and dilute the influence of black voters. Specialists in the reapportionment field believed that the "one man, one vote" doctrine provided racist white officials with a substantial opportunity to create congressional, legislative, county, and municipal districts in which blacks would be disadvantaged.[74] Most of the controversy developed in 1971 as a number of Deep South states began legislative redistricting. In some states, such as Louisiana, the charge was that reapportionment plans for the lower house of the state legislature sought to crowd as many black voters as possible into one district that certainly would choose a black representative while minimizing the number of black voters in surrounding districts so as to limit the number of black legislators. A less racially motivated set of boundary lines, observers suggested, could have opened the way for the election of additional black legislators through the creation of several districts with moderate black majorities.[75] Similar charges of racial gerrymandering were made in regard to legislative districting in Georgia, where a contiguous group of black majority counties in the east-central portion of the state had been divided and placed in several different white-majority districts rather than being combined to form one district capable of electing a black legislator.[76]

While the manipulation of district boundaries has been termed "ad hoc gerrymandering," a subtler, more widespread, and more pernicious form of racial gerrymandering has proven to be the use of multimember legislative, councilmanic, or supervisory districts in which a concentration of black voters that could form a majority in one or more single-member districts is submerged under a larger number of white voters. This has been termed an "institutional gerrymander" and allows the white majority to block the election of even one black official if it is so disposed. A number of civil rights attorneys sought to convince federal courts that any multimember district scheme in which a potential black majority is submerged is unfairly discriminatory against black citizens. While Justice blocked a Mississippi attempt to switch the election of county supervisory boards from five single-member "beats" to at-large, and while the Supreme Court indicated in an early 1971 Mississippi legislative redistricting case that its preference was for single-member districts,[77] in an important decision handed down late in 1971, the High Court refused to find that such submersion was inherently discriminatory and reversed a district court finding which had held against the use of a multimember district in Marion County, Indiana.[78] Voting rights attorneys predicted that future challenges to multimember districting plans that appeared to be limiting—or preventing—the election of blacks would have less chance of success in the wake of that ruling.

Early in 1972, however, Judge Frank M. Johnson, Jr., in Alabama ruled that that state must adopt single-member legislative districts and distinguished his ruling from that of the Supreme Court in the Indiana case on the grounds that racial discrimination and racially motivated political prejudice had a much longer and more virulent history in Alabama than in Indiana. While in the earlier case the High Court had held that Indianapolis blacks lacked representation in Marion County's large multimember legislative delegation because of "losing elections" rather than as a result of racial discrimination, Johnson held that Alabama's situation was distinguishably different.[79] Not long after that order for single-member districts was entered in Alabama, a similar opinion was issued by a federal district court in Texas. A series of subsequent Supreme Court holdings continued to reflect a marked preference on the part of the High Court for single-member rather than multimember districts, and as time passed the damage of the decision in the Indiana case appeared less extensive than originally had been feared.[80]

While various gerrymanders and the multimember district issue were the focus of much attention, litigation in the early years of the 1970s also challenged other procedures that blacks believed were being used to restrain their political power. Often the most prevalent of these weapons, such as numbered-place laws and full-slate requirements, were used hand in hand with the multimember district tactic. In a number of instances, such as in the Carolinas, such election law changes were challenged in the courts and struck down.[81]

Lengthy and complex litigation also developed concerning efforts by a number of southern cities, such as Richmond and Petersburg, Virginia, to annex largely white outlying areas just as the city's population was about to become majority black. In the Petersburg case the Justice Department objected to the annexation of white areas by a city that conducted municipal elections at-large, and following litigation a solution was agreed upon which allowed for the annexation but required that the city shift to ward-level elections for council members. A similar solution was subsequently arrived at in the Richmond case, and the first ward-level elections, held early in 1977, resulted in the selection of a black-majority city council which chose Henry L. Marsh III as Richmond's first black mayor.[82] Despite the essentially favorable outcomes in these two cases, however, racial gerrymandering and the additional procedures often appended to it remained far subtler acts of voting discrimination than those that had gone before. Voting rights attorneys bemoaned the difficulties they faced in proving their cases and decried what they called "a general pattern of unresponsiveness by the courts to claims of racial gerrymandering." Judges, they argued, needed to become "more sensitive to the intricacies of racial gerrymandering,"[83] but the case law record on the whole reflected more successes than failures in the litigation to prevent the dilution of black voting strength.

While this series of judicial actions continued in the courts throughout the early 1970s, blacks continued to make gains at the ballot box. As of early 1972, following the Mississippi elections of 1971, the number of black elected officials throughout the South had reached 872, including forty-one state representatives in ten of the eleven states but only six state senators.[84] In municipal elections in August a black man was elected mayor of Alabama's seventh largest city, Prichard, a municipality of 40,000 near Mobile.[85] At the same time a major breakthrough occurred in Selma as five blacks, including Mrs. Amelia Boynton and the Reverend F.D. Reese, won election to the ten-member city council in the first election held under a ward system rather than at-large. White journalists revisiting the town five or more years after the events of 1965 reported that they saw visible progress in such matters as hiring, education, and law enforcement, and quoted black leaders as saying, "By and large, things have improved," although "a fairly hardy racism still thrives beneath the surface."[86]

In the fall 1972 general elections throughout the South the two most notable stories were the victories of Andrew Young in Atlanta and state senator Barbara Jordan in Houston in races for seats in the U.S. House of Representatives. In Georgia black voters also played a crucial role in defeating conservative Republican Fletcher Thompson, the previous occupant of Young's new seat, in his race for the Senate against Sam Nunn. Blacks also entered the last of the southern legislatures to which they long had been denied entry as four were elected in Arkansas, and the overall total of black elected officials throughout the South rose to 1,144 as 1973 began. In August of that year 194 black candidates ran in Mississippi's municipal elections and fifty-eight won, including black mayoral candidates in seven small towns.[87] That brought the number of southern black mayors to forty-six at the beginning of 1974, and the overall number of elected black officials in the South reached 1,314 as a result of 1973 local elections throughout the region. Southern black registration levels continued to inch forward and to approach more closely those of whites as the 1974 political season began, though observers noted that despite the steadily growing number of black elected officials, the majority of black majority counties continued to be run by governing bodies that were all or largely white.[88]

In the fall 1974 elections the success of moderate, racially liberal statewide leaders continued in Georgia and Arkansas as George Busbee and David Pryor were elected to succeed Carter and Bumpers.[89] While a very racially conservative Republican squeaked through to victory as a result of unusual circumstances in South Carolina, in Alabama the reelection of Governor Wallace was marked by a series of highly touted endorsements of him by elected black officials who had benefited from gubernatorial assistance in obtaining state public works funds.[90] Although well-known racial conservatives such as John C. Stennis, James O. Eastland, and James B. Allen continued to represent southern states in the Senate, the number of racially moderate southern senators grew as Dale Bumpers, Richard Stone, and Robert Morgan won election to that body. Other old-line senators, such as Herman Talmadge and Strom Thurmond, moved to adopt ostensibly more moderate racial views, with the latter adding a black man to his staff and recommending a well-known civil rights attorney for an important federal appointment.[91]

By far the most important result of the 1974 elections in the South, however, was the remarkable increase in the number of black state legislators elected, an increase that in many states followed on the heals of new legislative reapportionments which had been subjected to close scrutiny by civil rights attorneys, the Justice Department, and the federal courts. Black candidates gained some four dozen legislative seats to raise the southern total to ninety-four. Blacks scored notable gains in

Birmingham as Alabama's black legislative delegation rose to fifteen, trailed closely by Georgia's fourteen and South Carolina's thirteen. A third black member of Congress from the South also was elected as Democrat Harold Ford nosed out incumbent Republican Dan Kuykendall in a Memphis area district. All in all, an early 1975 accounting reported that the number of southern black elected officials had risen to a new high of 1,588.[92]

In 1975, as in 1971, statewide contests were held in Louisiana and Mississippi, and local races took place in a number of southern states. By far the most notable story of the year was the Mississippi gubernatorial contest, where for the first time in history race was not a visible issue. Both of the major Democratic contenders, William Winter and Cliff Finch, the latter of whom won in a runoff primary, and the Republican candidate, Gil Carmichael, who lost to Finch in November, openly sought black votes. While journalists reported that politicians did not believe "that white Mississippians had changed their racial attitudes to the extent of welcoming black participation," it also was noted that Finch was the first Mississippi governor to be somewhat beholden to black people, whose support of his candidacy in the general election was described as "pivotal."

The 1975 Mississippi contests also resulted in the election of three black legislators from the Jackson area, who joined their one black predecessor, Holmes County's Robert Clark. Despite that gain, however, those four represented less than 2 percent of a 225 member legislature in a state whose population was 37 percent black. Another important byproduct of the 1975 political season, and the impending 1976 delegate-selection process, was the formal reunification of the Democratic party's two long-split factions, the Loyalists and the Regulars.[93]

The most important voting rights development in 1975, though, was the congressional consideration of a further extension of the Voting Rights Act's key provisions, sections 4 and 5, which were due to expire in August, five years after their 1970 renewal. A House Judiciary subcommittee began hearings on the subject in late February, with the committee chairman, Peter W. Rodino, and the subcommittee chairman, Don Edwards, sponsoring a bill which would provide for a ten-year extension of sections 4 and 5 and a permanent nationwide ban on all literacy tests. While the Civil Rights Commission endorsed those proposals and also favored expanding the protection offered linguistic minorities, the Ford administration countered with a measure calling for a five-year extension of sections 4 and 5 and a five-year extension of the nationwide literacy test ban.[94] Southern opposition to an extension was far less widespread and vociferous than in 1970, and when Assistant Attorney General J. Stanley Pottinger testified that section 5 enforcement was now "the highest priority" of the Civil Rights Division's voting section, he was not greeted by the harsh criticism to which Norman had been subjected in 1971, when the section 5 enforcement effort was far less vigorous.[95] In mid-April similarly cordial hearings began in the Senate, while the House subcommittee prepared to begin its markup of the extension bill. In both bodies suggestions were made that additional provisions expanding the act's coverage to language minorities throughout the country be added, and some proponents of extension whose prime concern was with southern blacks voiced fears that differences over such expansion suggestions might serve to delay a simple extension until after the August expiration deadline.[96]

On April 23 the House subcommittee, after defeating Republican attempts to limit extension to five years, reported to the full committee a clean bill providing for a ten-year extension and a permanent ban on all literacy tests. The bill also contained two new titles. The first extended the act's protection to language minorities who comprised at least 5 percent of the citizenry in jurisdictions in which election materials had been provided only in English in 1972 *and* where the 1972 presidential election turnout had been less than 50 percent of the voting-age citizens. The second new title prohibited the use of English-only election materials in any jurisdiction where more than 5 percent of the citizenry were members of one single-language minority *and* where the English illiteracy rate of that minority was greater than the national English illiteracy rate. The provisions of those two new titles would apply to portions of some twenty-seven states.[97]

On May 1, as the Senate hearings concluded, the full House Judiciary Committee approved the subcommittee's bill without making any changes, after defeating Republican attempts to delete the language minority provisions and reduce the extension of the other provisions to five years. The House Judiciary Committee bill was granted an open rule by the Rules Committee on May 14 after weakening amendments offered by California Republican Charles Wiggins had been rejected, and House floor consideration began on June 3.[98] A number of weakening amendments offered by Wiggins and Virginia Republican Caldwell Butler were beaten back on June 3, and the following day the House approved the Judiciary Committee's bill by a vote of 341 to 70 without notable amendment. Noteworthy was that only 25 of those 70 opponents of the bill were southern Democrats, while the 45 others were Republicans, 17 of whom were from the South. Fifty-two southern Democrats and 10 southern Republicans were among the representatives who voted for passage and extension of the Voting Rights Act.[99]

Following that House approval, on June 11 the Senate Judiciary Committee's Constitutional Rights Subcommittee approved a ten-year extension measure very similar to the House bill by a vote of 8 to 2. Consideration of the bill by the full Judiciary Committee was delayed by the committee chairman, James O. Eastland, however, and it was not until July 17, with the expiration deadline fast approaching, that the hospitalized Eastland allowed the acting chairman, Philip Hart, to begin action on the measure. The full committee, divided 10 to 4 in favor of approving the subcommittee's bill, defeated weakening amendments offered by the bill's opponents, but was unable to give final approval to the measure that day because of delaying tactics employed by Virginia Republican William L. Scott. With Scott's antics thus holding up the Senate bill, Democratic leaders Mansfield and Byrd called up the House bill, which had been held at the desk, as the Senate convened on July 18. Later that same day, a Friday, the Judiciary Committee completed action on the Senate version.

On Monday morning, following some adept parliamentary maneuvering by Byrd, the majority whip, who prevented Alabama's James B. Allen from beginning a filibuster, the Senate voted cloture on a motion to move to consider the House-passed bill by 72 to 19. Subsequently the Senate voted to consider the House bill, and a vote to invoke cloture upon debate on the bill itself succeeded on Wednesday by 76 to 20 after several weakening amendments had been narrowly defeated. Later that day, however, matters were complicated when the White House announced that President Ford wanted to expand the act's coverage to the entire nation, a desire reporters termed a "surprise request" and which closely resembled the Nixon administration's strategy and rhetoric in the 1970 extension fight. Such a move, formally proposed in the aftermath of the Ford request by Mississippi's John Stennis, was defeated by the Senate 58 to 38. West Virginia's Byrd, who thus far had guided the House bill safely through the Senate's parliamentary shoals, then rose to suggest that the extension be reduced from ten to five years. California's John Tunney, who had led the proponents of a strong extension measure, objected to Byrd's request and noted that such a move would terminate section 5 just as the redistrictings following the 1980 Census began. Byrd accepted Tunney's point and amended his request to call for a reduction in the extension to seven years. When a vote was taken on that proposal, Byrd's amendment carried by 52 to 42.

The following morning, Thursday, July 24, Rodino and Edwards announced that they reluctantly would approve a seven-year rather than a
ten-year extension so that a time-consuming conference, which could
well delay approval until after the expiration deadline, could be avoided.
Later that evening the Senate gave its final approval to the extension
measure as amended on a vote of 77 to 12, and on July 28, without any
debate, the House approved the bill as amended by the Senate on a vote
of 346 to 56. On August 6, exactly ten years to the day after the original
act had been signed into law by Lyndon B. Johnson, President Ford
signed the bill extending the Voting Rights Act to 1982 in a ceremony in
the White House Rose Garden.[100]

While the proponents of an effective federal voting rights enforcement
effort thus had won their third battle in the space of ten years, as the
United States prepared to celebrate its bicentennial the political gains
actually registered by blacks in the South remained far short of what
they might—and should—have been. Although in the spring of 1976 the
VEP announced that the number of black elected officials in the eleven
states had increased by some 356 in the preceding twelve months to
reach a new high of 1,944, even that figure, though very impressive in
light of the fact that a decade earlier the total had been well under 100,
indicated that blacks continued to be greatly underrepresented throughout the South. Although blacks made up 20.4 percent of the South's
population, the 1,944 total represented only 2.5 percent of the South's
elected officials.[101]

While popular writing regularly made much of the vast growth of black
political influence in the South, a growth often seen as personified by
Georgia representative Andrew Young,[102] who eleven years before had
been one of the main strategists at Selma, those writings most often
examined only the bright side of the coin. As longtime Mississippi activist Aaron Henry told the House extension hearings in 1975, the "reports of tremendous progress in black participation" in his state since
1965 were "greatly exaggerated. . . . Fair and effective representation of
blacks at the most significant levels of government," Henry told the
subcommittee, "is still far from a reality," as the fact that only four of
Mississippi's 225 legislators were black made clear. "Little progress has
been made," he noted, "in electing blacks to positions of real power and
responsibilities in which we can affect state policy or exercise real political power on the county level."[103] Statistics collected in early 1976
reflected that 67 of the South's 103 counties with black population
majorities were without an elected black official, and that blacks controlled the governing boards in only 6 of those counties. Additionally, at

least 362 black majority municipalities of more than 1,000 persons were without a single black elected official.[104]

But even in those towns and counties where blacks had won elective office or actually had taken control of local government, serious problems remained. While some of those problems were largely "political," more often than not they were "economic." Black mayors in the South, who with some half-dozen exceptions served small, rural communities with limited resources and few public services, commonly found themselves unable to stimulate any progress. The poverty of their communities supplied a multitude of pressing problems but no taxable resources, and lack of staff support and governmental experience made it almost impossible to penetrate the federal bureaucracy in search of assistance and grants. A wide-ranging study of the mayors' challenges found inadequate housing to be the most pressing need in such black-governed communities, with such basic necessities as sewer and water service often lacking as well.[105]

In these locales and others, the major problem facing black citizens was their very limited supply of economic resources. In Alabama's Lowndes County, where a sustained independent black political effort had produced the election of a black sheriff and several other county officials, the lack of employment opportunities outside of agriculture and the declining number of agricultural jobs seemed to leave the county's black population without any realistic hopes of improving their poverty-stricken situation.[106] While in some places across the South black officials had had success in obtaining "distributive" benefits from white officials at the state or federal level, it was clear to all that any further growth in black political power would have to go hand in hand with increasing economic might and economic independence from local whites.[107] As the Voting Rights Act approached the thirteenth anniversary of its enactment, it continued to be clear that "the economically depressed and dependent position of blacks in the South remains the greatest barrier to their achieving equal political rights," proportional political representation and proportional political power.[108]

7 The Strategy of Protest and the SCLC at Selma

Within the past decade a substantial body of academic literature has focused upon the ways in which various social and political groups who believe their interests to be unrepresented in the major political institutions of their community or country can seek to obtain some influence upon policy-making processes by engaging in public demonstrations or other forms of "protest." In large part this literature is an outgrowth of the events of the 1960s, which a number of scholars say convinced them that the accepted notions of how political change is wrought in the United States were inaccurate and inadequate. The major target of these writers has been what commonly is termed the pluralist view of American politics.

"Pluralism" in political science is far from monolithic, though a majority of commentators have agreed that pluralism's emphasis on interaction and bargaining between established political groups has saddled it with the preconception that what political change does occur in the United States will take place slowly and incrementally.[1] The emergence in the 1960s of groups that previously had been largely unrepresented in the arenas of pluralist bargaining, coupled with political changes that were far from incremental in nature, these critical writers often suggested, indicated that dynamics of change unmentioned in pluralist accounts of American politics had played a large role in making established political institutions and agencies far more sensitive and responsive to the interests and needs of these newly vocal citizens.[2] Protest activities, a number of these writers stated, constituted a new and valuable political resource for those citizens whose supply of the common resources of politics had been and continued to be minimal or nonexistent.[3] These scholars often set forth a view of protest's own arena in which three parties were present: the protestors or petitioners themselves, their immediate opponents, and those initially uninvolved or neutral third parties who constituted the potential audience for the conflict between the first two parties. Playing an extremely influential role in alerting that audience to the initial conflict and to the characteristics and goals of the two sides were the news media, the "fourth estate." Several writers have employed this quadripartite model with differing variations in examining the American civil rights movement of the 1960s, and the format lends itself very well to an examination of the events of Selma and their repercussions.

Perhaps the initial acknowledgment of the importance of "audience" reactions in determining the outcome of a conflict between protestors and their opponents was made early in the 1920s by a pioneering sociologist.[4] In the current generation of social science literature, the dynamics governing the interactions of those three major parties received their first implicit examination in a brief monograph by James S. Coleman in 1957. Each side in a political conflict, Coleman wrote, attempts to "win new adherents from, the still uncommitted neutrals." Such appeals, he observed, are based upon the invocation of "certain basic values and dispositions" with the intent of associating positive and widely supported values with one's own efforts and negatively regarded and unpopular values with one's opponents and their cause. The important strategic concern here, of course, is to invoke successfully the more powerful of such values in such a way as to increase the support for one's own side while decreasing one's opponent's support. The strategic question then is to determine "the relative strengths of different values," so that one's appeal is based upon a value or values to which the relevant audience gives more credence than to those upon which one's opponents may be basing their appeal. "If we knew the relative strength of certain social values among various segments of the population," Coleman observed, "we would be far better able" to predict which appeals would be most successful when directed at some audience than is presently the case.[5] Imperfect knowledge about the relative strengths of such values appears unavoidable, however.

By recognizing the substantial importance that value appeals could have in lining up audience support of and opposition to political contestants, Coleman's discussion of community politics foreshadowed in some respects the later observations of Merelman and of Cobb and Elder, to which we have made reference earlier. Not until several years after the publication of Coleman's monograph, however, did a political scientist choose to emphasize the crucially important role that audiences to political conflicts could and usually did play in determining the outcome of such conflicts. "To understand any conflict," the late E.E. Schattschneider wrote in 1960, "it is necessary . . . to keep constantly in mind the relations between the combatants and the audience because the audience is likely to do the kinds of things that determine the outcome of the fight." The moral, Schattschneider said, was: "If a fight starts, watch the crowd, because the crowd plays the decisive role." Because the audience's or the potential audience's strength almost always would far exceed the initial strength of either of the original parties or combatants, each original competitor should be interested in influencing the audience's sentiments in his favor. If one of the original contestants held a clear superiority of strength over his opponent initially, however, it quite likely would be in his favor to seek to minimize the audience's attention to the struggle and to hinder its entrance into the conflict so that his original advantage would not be in danger of being overturned. Such an effort to restrict audience interest and intervention and to limit the "scope" of the conflict was termed by Schattschneider the "privatization" of conflict. Opposite to that was the effort of one or both of the original combatants to increase audience attention and intervention in an attempt to secure greater additional strength than could one's opponent. Such efforts to widen the scope of a conflict Schattschneider called the "socialization" of conflict.

Each of these strategies, privatization and socialization, Schattschneider noted, could employ on their behalf certain widely held American values. "A long list of ideas concerning individualism, free private enterprise, localism, privacy and economy in government seems to be designed to privatize conflict or to restrict its scope or to limit the use of public authority to enlarge the scope of conflict," Schattschneider wrote. On the other hand, though, there also was "another battery of ideas contributing to the socialization of conflict. . . . Ideas concerning equality, consistency, equal protection of the laws, justice, liberty, freedom of movement, freedom of speech and association and civil rights tend to" assist in the socializations of conflicts, Schattschneider stated. "These concepts," he wrote, "tend to make conflict contagious; they invite outside intervention in conflict and form the basis of appeals" for such intervention."[6]

In the wake of Schattschneider's observations, an increasing number of scholars began to discuss the dynamics of political conflict, especially conflict centering around protest actions, in what was largely a tripartite format focusing upon the two original contestants and the initially uninvolved audience. Political scientist James Q. Wilson wrote an influential article on the subject in 1961. Where blacks lack the political resources necessary for successful involvement in intergroup bargaining, Wilson said, they must be able to offer "negative inducements" to those from whom they seek benefits if they are to realize any material or symbolic gains. A negative inducement would probably involve some form of protest. For such a protest to attract "the support of the many," Wilson wrote, "general reasons of an ethical character must be offered" by the protestors.[7]

Four years later, in a volume that received far less attention, Harvey Seifert devoted far more consideration to the tripartite format and its dynamics than had prevous writers on nonviolent action.[8] Seifert outlined the three groups involved: the resisters or protestors themselves, their opponents, and "spectators or third parties, those who are not directly engaged in the dispute, but who are sufficiently involved to be aware of events and who may come to throw their support to one side or the other." Seifert gave far more attention than previous writers to the considerations that most likely would determine the audience's interest in throwing the bulk of its support behind one or the other of the two initial contestants. To obtain the audience's attention, Seifert recognized, the protestors themselves would have to engage in some demonstrative activity that would be thought unusual enough to receive attention. In the great majority of cases, he recognized, protestors would have to obtain the attention of the press and television news if the wider public audience was to be made aware of the pending conflict. For the protestors, however, the greatest danger lay in the fact that the tactics or actions necessary to obtain public attention might be such as to offend the bulk of an American audience that commonly considered all public demonstrations of dubious legitimacy. As Seifert noted, "A problem of the resister is to keep to a minimum the defection of [possible] support due to his nonconformity." While he must avoid "utterly proscribed behavior," he could never be certain whether any particular form of protest action either would fail to spark public interest or whether it would not only do that but would also "turn off" some substantial portion of the audience whose support he was seeking.

> Leaders of nonviolent movements, of course, may not know in which area a particular act will prove to lie until they have tried it. The conduct might be too novel to have been attempted before. Besides, societies do not publish lists of all possible actions with the degrees of intensity of opposition that will be applied. Insofar as practical considerations of strategy are taken seriously, occasional probing operations and continuous adaptability are called for.

Much of the struggle between protestors and their opponents, Seifert realized, revolves around the fact that the public without fail becomes estranged from the party it blames for the occurrence of violence. As Seifert expressed it, "When anyone goes beyond the bounds of tolerated behavior, society tends to be alienated from his cause." Protestors should be warned, Seifert noted, that their opponents might well attempt to incite them to violence so as to deflect whatever potential support the protestors might have. In protestors' own search for attention-getting tactics, Seifert warned, "If nonconformity goes too far, then opponents and bystanders feel that there is justification for sternly repressive violence" against the protestors. While that would be the worst of all possible situations for the protestors, alienating most of the audience from their cause, the best of all possible situations for a protest group, Seifert emphasized, came when protestors' opponents employed violence against them and the audience perceived that officially sponsored violence to be unjustifiable. The suffering of undeserving victims, Seifert argued, attracted widespread public support and sympathy. "Every additional brutality" committed by nonviolent protestors' opponents, Seifert wrote, "helps to convince those on the fence" that the protestors' complaints against their opponents are substantially valid. "As enemies of the resisters become more violent," Seifert added, the protestors' friends "become more numerous and outspoken."

While apparently unprovoked violence visited upon them by their opponents was, in practical terms, the most profitable occurrence for protestors, in the absence of such conduct by their adversaries, protestors' hopes for achieving some success in attracting new support from previously uncommitted and uninvolved audience members depended almost exclusively upon their ability to convey their goals to that audience repeatedly and in such a way that the audience would believe those goals to be deserving of their support. Concerning the latter point, Seifert used words reminiscent of Coleman's: "The issue," he instructed protestors, "should be defined in such a way as to attach maximum support to the campaign and to detach maximum support from the opposition." While such a strategic choice based upon the audience's value preferences often could be made without substantial difficulty, maintaining constant public attention often would prove to be more difficult, Seifert accurately noted. Any initially newsworthy protest tactic becomes increasingly less newsworthy with continued repetition, Seifert stated, as publicity often depends upon novelty. Excessive search for novelty could well lead the protestors into behavior that the audience would reject, and "it is doubtful whether any major use of nonviolent resistance could succeed without such third party help." The outcome of a resistance campaign, Seifert emphasized, almost echoing Schattschneider, "depends largely on the direction in which third parties swing their support."[9]

Some four years after Seifert wrote, political scientist Michael Lipsky put forward a model of protest activity and its repercussions which is widely regarded as the most important statement to date on the factors that determine how much effect protest will have on public opinion and governmental decision making.[10] While the apparent intellectual debt of Lipsky and more recent writers on protest to Coleman and especially Schattschneider often is not fully acknowledged, Lipsky's work is important not solely because it represented the first attempt to systematically map out the factors present in any protest's environment, but also because it devoted a greater amount of attention to the importance of news media coverage of protest actions. "If protest tactics are not considered significant by the media," Lipsky wrote, "or if newspapers and television reporters or editors decide to overlook protest tactics, protest organizations will not succeed. Like the tree falling unheard in the forest, there is no protest unless protest is perceived and projected." Like Seifert and others, Lipsky emphasized that media attention would be forthcoming only so long as the protestors pursued novel actions. "Protest leaders," Lipsky wrote, "must continually develop new, dramatic techniques in order to receive their lifeblood of publicity." It is vital that a protest leader "know what the media consider newsworthy."[11]

In its essence, however, Lipsky's generally well developed model was largely similar to the perspectives put forward by Schattschneider and Seifert. "The essence of political protest," Lipsky wrote, "consists of activating third parties to participate in controversy in ways favorable to protest goals." Lipsky's explication of a model of protest activity, however, did introduce into the literature two important distinctions that previous writers had not drawn with any clarity. In the process of doing so, however, the accuracy of the model declined in other important ways. Lipsky's outline focused upon four parties: the protestors, the media, the target group or institution from which the protestors sought some benefit, and what he termed the "reference publics" of that target. At the same time, Lipsky noted that a protest leader had four separate and different constituencies: his own followers, the media, the target institution, and the third-party "reference publics" or audience, each of which could require different and perhaps incompatible statements or actions from the protest leader.

Lipsky concentrated his model upon efforts by protestors to activate interest and support for the protest's goals among the reference publics or constituencies of those public officials from whom the protestors sought that goal. Lipsky also attempted to draw a distinction between this activation of initially uninvolved third parties and the formation of alliances between the protestors and other organized groups with similar or at least not incompatible objectives. The key link in the major chain of publicity and activation, however, was that between the reference public and that audience's presumably elected representatives. As Lipsky spoke of it, "protest is a highly indirect process in which communications media and reference publics of protest targets play critical roles. . . . The success of protest activity seems directly related to the amount of publicity it receives outside of the immediate arena in which protest takes place." That publicity, however, must be such as to activate support for the protestors' goals among an influential segment of the audience. "Successful protest must operate in the zone bounded by community hostility on one side, and community disinterest on the other."

Therefore, the "sympathies and support of third parties are essential to the success of protesters," and "protest will be successful to the extent that the protesters can get third parties to put pressure on the targets." Lipsky went on, "To the extent that the influence of reference publics is supportive of protest goals, target groups will dispense symbolic or material rewards" to either the protestors and the reference public or perhaps simply to the reference public to quiet their support of the protestors' goals. Target groups need not meet the demands of the protestors, Lipsky emphasized, when their reference public's interest and concern can be deflected and assuaged by largely symbolic reassurances.[12]

Lipsky devoted somewhat less attention to the value bases of the protestors' appeals and the importance of how those invoked values were viewed by the audience or reference public. He did note, as had Seifert and others, that undeserving victims generated sympathy for their cause among the audience, but he exhibited less awareness of the power that specific tactics or weapons could have in the realm of public opinion. While he too, like so many popular writers, made reference at one point to the public reactions to the use of police dogs and cattle prods in the South in the 1960s, in his own major study of rent strikes in New York City, Lipsky failed to emphasize adequately that the protestors had captured and caged a number of rats—one of the major housing ills that they wanted alleviated—and had displayed them for the media so that the rats came to symbolize for the audience the plight of the New York protestors in much the same way that police dogs, high-pressure fire hoses, cattle prods, and tear gas had symbolized the victimization of black southerners at Birmingham and Selma.[13]

More important shortcomings in Professor Lipsky's model are the clear result of his exclusive focus upon protest aimed at a single city's local government and its housing policies. Because of this focus, Lipsky is unable to accommodate within his model's outlines the fact that the protestors might have actual, physically active opponents who are not the protestors' "target group." By concentrating exclusively upon one level of government—the local level—Lipsky's model loses applicability to a situation in which the protestors seek to appeal beyond local government, which seeks to "privatize" the grievances, to a higher level of government.

Most important, however, Professor Lipsky's model envisions that the protestors' target will move towards meeting the protestors' demands only when the protestors succeed in activating support for themselves among the reference public of those targeted officials. Lipsky's model fails to recognize the possibility that in going over the heads of their immediate opponents, protestors' appeals can well meet with a positive response from their more distant target because of the reactions of those targeted officials themselves, and not solely because those officials are reacting to the activation of their own constituents. As the examination of presidential and especially congressional actions and statements on voting rights in late 1964 and early 1965 makes clear, reactions in those branches to southern blacks' voting rights grievances were grounded mainly in those officials' own personal perceptions and feelings and were not to any substantial degree solely an effort to appease or act in concert with the aroused sentiments of their constituents. While the Lipsky model appears to include all that is necessary for an accurate and complete conceptualization of protest activities by urban neighborhood groups aimed at city agencies or administrations, its purview is too narrow and limited to accommodate or appreciate fully the processes and ramifications of protest activities that take place within a wider scope of conflict. Those more wide-ranging dynamics of protest activities were grasped more completely and more accurately by Schattschneider and Seifert.

In the last several years a number of writers have retraced the steps taken by Coleman, Schattschneider, Seifert, and Lipsky without introducing any notable conceptual innovations into those earlier accounts and discussions. Some, such as James Q. Wilson, Ronald J. Terchek, and Paul D. Schumaker, largely have concerned themselves with reiterating and commenting upon Lipsky's work without suggesting any substantial alterations in it.[14] All emphasized the importance of third parties' roles and protestors' appeals to that audience, and each of the three also noted to some extent the importance of the audience's perceiving the protestors' goals as acceptable or "legitimate" if support for the protestors is to develop in that crucial sector. Other recent writings have been more in the tradition of either Schattschneider[15] or Seifert[16] and have not concerned themselves with models of protest activity to the extent that Lipsky and those who have commented upon his writings have. They too, however, have introduced no particularly new insights or concepts.

The applicability of the writings of this group of scholars, dating from Coleman and Schattschneider to the present, to the successes of the civil rights movement in the 1960s should be clear. In Schattschneiderian terms it is obvious that the white officials in the South who attempted to maintain the barriers of racial segregation sought to "privatize" a developing conflict in which they correctly expected that the majority of nonsoutherners and the federal government would side with the aspirations and goals of black citizens if the local and regional struggles in the South were portrayed to the national audience.[17] The value bases of the blacks' appeals, and the news media's inherent interest in public protest activities at which racist violence was always a possibility, assured that the blacks' appeals would be conveyed to a national audience and that the general reactions of that audience to those appeals would be positive and supportive.

Perhaps the most important point to be made in noting the applicability of these somewhat theoretical writings on protest activity to the events of Selma is that no group of individuals understood the dynamics and processes involved any better than Martin Luther King, Jr., and the SCLC leadership circle. King had been a vocal advocate of nonviolent resistance to evil since his first published writings in the wake of the Montgomery bus boycott campaign in the mid-1950's, but by 1965 his actual views had changed from those that he had articulated in earlier years. While that shift was not apparent to many observers, because King's own writings largely obscured both it and its significance, the change is of the utmost importance to any understanding of the story of Selma and the SCLC's effort to build support for new and stronger federal voting rights legislation.

King's views on the utility of nonviolent protest, views that he ostensibly held until his death, were first set forth early in 1957. "Nonviolent resistance," King wrote at that time, "does not seek to defeat or humiliate the opponent, but to win his friendship and understanding." It is "constantly seeking to persuade the opponent that he is mistaken," King said, and seeks "to awaken a sense of moral shame in the opponent." The oppressor, he wrote, should never be personified. The person of the oppressor must be loved at the same time that his evil deeds are hated.[18] That view of nonviolence that King articulated in his early writings of the mid and late 1950s is what one writer has termed "conscientious nonviolence."[19] Another has labeled it as a "philosophy" of nonviolence, which is to be distinguished from a "technique" of nonviolence.[20] In Gandhian terms it is an allegiance to nonviolence that is spoken of as *satyagraha*, a term that can be defined as "a moral commitment to nonviolence." Separate from satyagraha, and characterizable as more a technique of nonviolence, is what is termed *duragraha*. "Duragraha," one writer has explained, "is an approach to social and political change having a purely tactical commitment to nonviolent action as the most effective means to certain ends."[21]

What King believed in and advocated in the late 1950s and the very first years of the 1960s was nonviolent *persuasion*. This was resistance that employed moral suasion upon one's opponents, and it was basically not coercive. This was what King articulated in *Stride Toward Freedom*, and it was given its first real trial in the Albany campaign of 1961 and 1962.[22] Albany was not a success for King and the SCLC. Much of the reason for the movement's failure there was the conduct of the Albany police chief, Laurie Pritchett, who peacefully arrested all of the SCLC's numerous groups of marchers. The Albany campaign indicated that a strategy of nonviolent persuasion would not necessarily move the SCLC's opponents towards reforms and a lessening of racial injustice, and Pritchett's quiet conduct aroused neither the interest of the news media nor the anger of the movement's potential allies.[23]

Approximately eight months passed between the end of the Albany effort and the SCLC's active intervention in Birmingham, and the conduct of the Birmingham effort was to show that King and his colleagues definitely had learned some lessons from the Albany campaign and its failure. The most prominent of these lessons was that a strategy of nonviolent persuasion which focused on changing the hearts and minds of one's opponents was unrealistic and ineffective.[24] No substantive or symbolic gains had resulted from its use in Albany, and it appeared unlikely that its implementation elsewhere would result in progress towards a more just society and a weakening of white racism. Only in the wake of Albany did King begin to realize that *coercive* nonviolence would be necessary if progress was to be achieved.[25] While progress could not be achieved through efforts to convince the movement's white opponents that they were mistaken, progress could be achieved if the movement, and its external allies, could *force* southern localities to implement progressive changes. Federal legislation, King increasingly realized, was one route by which effective change could be brought about. The path to such legislation, in turn, lay through the national news media and the audiences to which they could convey the move-ment's pleas for assistance and reforms.

If nonviolent coercion, rather than nonviolent persuasion, was to be the SCLC's strategy for bringing about change in the South, Chief Pritchett was not the best type of opponent. National news attention was essential to any campaign aimed more at acquiring and activating allies outside of the campaign's own locale than at converting its immediate opponents, and the news media's interest in a campaign quickly waned when no violent or unusually dramatic confrontations were occurring. Peaceful opponents such as Chief Pritchett would be of no help in con-veying to the entire nation the brutality that southern blacks could and often did suffer in a society dominated by racial segregation and dis-crimination. Not many viewers or readers watching or being told of Pritchett's peaceful arrests would find racism to be profoundly revolting because of what they saw or read, and no great additional number of Americans would be sensitized to the plight of southern blacks. For the movement to obtain the national news coverage and national public sup-port necessary for obtaining federal legislation and real gains in the South, less circumspect opponents would be needed.

One year later the SCLC chose to concentrate its efforts upon Birming-ham, where law enforcement was under the direction of the well-known public safety commissioner, Eugene "Bull" Connor. That choice itself is probably the best available evidence of the lesson the SCLC leadership had learned at Albany. Eighteen months after Birmingham, the SCLC's choice was Selma, where Sheriff Clark's conduct already had earned him a reputation within movement circles. While by late 1964 there may well still have been a "philosophy" of nonviolence within the SCLC leadership, the choice of Clark and Selma, and the SCLC's tactical decisions once there, both served to indicate that it was a philosophy based not upon a moral commitment to nonviolence or upon a desire to reform the hearts and minds of the likes of Jim Clark, but upon the pragmatic knowledge that nonviolence, coupled with violent opponents, would best serve the movement in its effort to gain active support from the American populace. As one sociologist has written, "The 'techni-cian' of nonviolence does not attempt to convert his opponent by chang-ing his heart, though he might agree that this would be a good side-effect. He is concerned predominantly with changing the situation—that is, winning for his side."[26] By the time that the SCLC and King arrived in Selma in January of 1965, "winning" was clearly their foremost goal, and nonviolence had become more the "technique" of duragraha than the "moral commitment" of satyagraha.[27]

The evolution in King's thought concerning nonviolent action has gone largely unacknowledged by those who have written about him.[28] This shift from nonviolent persuasion to a more aggressive nonviolent coercion was based upon a very shrewd and wholly accurate understanding of the dynamics of protest and of what would most aid the movement in its attempt to secure the enactment of a new federal voting rights law. King accurately believed that nothing could be more effective in activating support among the national audience for the movement and its goal of equal suffrage than scenes of peaceful demonstrators, seeking their birthright as American citizens, being violently attacked by southern whites. Not only would such attacks draw substantial news coverage, but the perceptions of rank injustice stemming from such scenes would be the most effective stimulus of all in appealing to the values and norms of the American people and their political leaders in Washington.

It was such a strategy that called for the choice of Selma as the focal point of the SCLC's efforts to win from the federal government a new voting rights statute that would provide more effective enforcement of black southerners' equal right to vote than had the judicial enforcement route. The choice, however, was not really so much one of Selma as of Dallas County's sheriff, Jim Clark, whose conduct in response to the SNCC efforts of 1963 and 1964 indicated to the SCLC that he was the Connor type of opponent whom they needed.

King had voiced his desire for a new law providing for federal registrars and observers to journalists in early November of 1964 and had mentioned at that time how the movement would have to bring "moral pressure" to bear on the federal government if such a new statute was to be generated.[29] By early January of 1965, King publicly was emphasizing that the SCLC's goal in the Selma effort was new federal voting rights legislation, and that an appeal to "the conscience of the Congress" would be a necessary precondition for achieving that goal.[30]

Such was the SCLC's desire when it first began the active pursuit of the Selma campaign on January 18. From that day on, the organization's strategic concerns and tactical goals were geared toward the "socialization" of the conflict between it and the local white officials. Central to those plans was the hope—and expectation—that Sheriff Clark would respond to the movement's public demonstrations with conduct that national viewers would find far less acceptable than the SCLC's sidewalk marches.

Following the initial march downtown on January 18, during which Clark remained restrained, the SCLC staff expressed its disappointment that no exhibition of the sheriff's true feelings and temper had taken place. As one SCLC staffer later was to write, "The press could not be expected to stay around and give the movement the national exposure it must have unless there was some action to photograph and write about." Without a notable incident soon, another Albany might well be in the offing. A decision to try again the following day was arrived at, with the proviso that if no newsworthy occurrence could be produced, then the campaign would shift its focus to another town to see if "some action" could be found there. On January 19, though, Clark "came through" and provided the desired "action" when he roughed up Mrs. Boynton without any visible provocation. The SCLC staff was pleased that this reflection of southern racism had been brought to the surface in the presence of the national media, and it then proceeded to step up the campaign's activities in Selma itself.[31]

Although such instances provide an important insight into the SCLC's strategy at Selma, a strategy that operated with a very deft understanding and application of the principles of conflict socialization outlined by Schattschneider and Seifert, the SCLC's motives and tactics also are reflected to a limited extent in Dr. King's own writings.[32] Implicit in a number of his statements is the declaration that action by the protestors' opponents that would offend the national audience was a necessity if the movement was to succeed in its quest for federal legislation. Although the movement could try to elicit such behavior from the likes of Jim Clark, it was important that the movement not be seen widely as provoking or "asking for" such treatment. Such a perception would deflate much if not all of the public support that the movement sought to achieve, and King was never one to downplay the importance of that audience to the realization of the goals that the SCLC sought. Writing in late February 1965, before the events of Bloody Sunday had propelled Selma to the status of a daily, front-page story, King stated, "Demonstrations, experience has shown, are part of the process of stimulating legislation and law enforcement. The federal government," he went on, without saying just how such "stimulation" took place, "reacts to events more quickly when a situation cries out for its intervention."[33]

King's other references to protest activity and its beneficial effects were very similar; they left unsaid more than they stated, and what insights they did convey were likely to come from between the lines of King's often euphemistic or symbol-laden prose. Typical of such language was a passage from a 1964 volume. Speaking of what the southern black must do, King wrote:

> Instead of submitting to surreptitious cruelty in thousands of dark
> jail cells and on countless shadowed street corners, he would force

his oppressor to commit his brutality openly—in the light of day—
with the rest of the world looking on.[34]

Although such statements were suggestive, though not explicit, on
occasion King did allow himself to be a bit more revealing. In one
volume published several years after the events of Selma, King observed, "The organized strength of Negroes alone would have been
insufficient to move Congress and the administration without the weight
of the aroused conscience of white America." Referring to the 1964 and
1965 acts, King went on to detail further of just what sort of process that
audience's "aroused conscience" had been a part.

> It was not necessary to build a widespread organization in order to
> win legislative victories. Sound effort in a single city such as Bir-
> mingham or Selma produced situations that symbolized the evil
> everywhere and inflamed public opinion against it. Where the spot-
> light illuminated the evil, a legislative remedy was soon obtained
> that applied everywhere.[35]

King's clearest and most forthright account of the process that direct
action methods were used to trigger appeared in an early April 1965
article written primarily to repudiate the charges made concerning
King's role in prearranging the termination of the short march of Tuesday, March 9. King set forth something of an outline of the ostensible
strategy that the SCLC had followed at Selma. "The goal of the demonstrations in Selma, as elsewhere," he remarked, "is to dramatize the
existence of injustice and to bring about the presence of justice by
methods of nonviolence. Long years of experience indicate to us that
Negroes can achieve this goal when four things occur." First, "nonviolent demonstrators go into the streets to exercise their constitutional
rights." Second, "racists resist by unleashing violence against them."
Third, "Americans of conscience in the name of decency demand federal intervention and legislation." Fourth, and last, "the administration,
under mass pressure, initiates measures of immediate intervention and
remedial legislation."[36]

That four-item list is revealing for several reasons. First, it makes two
major admissions: racist violence is crucial to the movement's progress;
and viewing of it by the national audience is necessary if any substantive, government-induced progress is to result from the confrontation.
King's choice of words in the last two of his four points indicates an
apparent belief that the power of scenes of racist violence lies not in the
direct perceptions of them that will be registered in Washington, but
instead in the communications and reactions aimed at Washington from

those throughout the country who witness such confrontations. Hence, the SCLC leader may have underestimated the direct effect that such occurrences can have on members of Congress or presidents themselves, and overestimated somewhat the extent to which those actors' reactions in such situations are responses to popular sentiment rather than to their own personal perceptions and feelings.

King's list is also important because of one striking omission: the news media. In an otherwise largely accurate description of the process of the socialization of a conflict through public protest activity, King fails to make any reference to the crucial role that the news media must play if the second item—racist violence against nonviolent demonstrators—is to result in the third—outrage and anger among the American populace. Such an omission, it is reasonable to suggest, was not unconscious. King certainly was not unaware of the importance of newspaper and television coverage to the movement in transmitting its appeals to the nation, as the preplanned "Letter From A Selma Jail" advertisement used in the *New York Times* in early February of 1965 clearly demonstrates. But at no point in any of his writings or public statements did King fully admit just how important news coverage was to the movement. Describing the process of protest, appeal, and national reaction, King and his associates would avoid explicit references to the news media. Instead, there was, on occasion, a euphemistic allusion to the role that the news media played. More often than not such allusions employed a word or phrase connoting visibility or light, as when King spoke of the "light of day" or the "spotlight" that illuminated the evil of racist brutality. Typical of his phraseology was his statement in his last volume that when the movement's opponents chose to employ their "clubs, dogs, and guns, they found the world was watching, and then the power of nonviolent protest became manifest. It dramatized the essential meaning of the conflict and in magnified strokes made clear who was the evildoer and who was the undeserving victim. The nation and the world were sickened." Thus, King noted that "the world was watching," and that they had been "sickened," but he consistently avoided mentioning just how they were able to "watch" and be sickened.[37]

Although such elliptical references are not rare in King's writings, it is clear that the absence of any more forthright acknowledgment of publicity's role was due to a fear that any such admission would leave King and the SCLC open to the charge that they were seeking to "manipulate" the media, and would leave the press and the networks themselves more vulnerable to southern charges that they consciously or unconsciously were assisting in the propogation of one political cause over another simply because of the news coverage that they gave the movement's activities. Any such admission likely would have made the movement, and Dr. King, appear considerably more "calculating" than they wanted to seem and also would have appeared somewhat inconsistent with the religious and moral themes in which the movement commonly wrapped itself. Hence, the SCLC leadership quite likely presumed that any such acknowledgment would lend a somewhat negative hue to the movement's image, and they quite wisely avoided any such self-inflicted wounds.

The omission of any acknowledgment of the news media's role in taking the movement's appeal to the country is minor, however, in comparison with a far more delicate matter of SCLC strategy that the organization's leaders also avoided commenting on in public. We already have noted that by the time the SCLC arrived in Selma its employment of nonviolence had become more pragmatic than moral, and that King himself had acknowledged that the SCLC realized how much their efforts were aided by violence aimed at the peaceful demonstrators by white opponents. In the spring of 1964, two very observant viewers of the civil rights scene had commented upon this. "It is sometimes implied," Tom Kahn and August Meier suggested, "that it may be necessary to precipitate police violence and brutality in order to focus national and international public attention on and obtain federal intervention in the South." Noting the SCLC campaigns in Albany, Birmingham, and Danville, they further observed, "Although perhaps not consciously, this is the way SCLC has operated."[38]

Kahn's and Meier's insight was accurate and, by the time of Selma, no longer in need of any qualification or equivocation. Even with the limited amount of knowledge publicly available then and now about the SCLC's strategic concerns and deliberations, it is clear that by January 1965 King and the SCLC consciously had decided to attempt to elicit violent behavior from their immediate opponents. Such an intent governed the choice of Selma and Jim Clark, and such an intent governed all of the tactical choices that the SCLC leadership made throughout the campaign, such as the choice to go into Marion, to adopt night marches there, and to try to adopt night marches in Selma. The attempted trek to Montgomery along U.S. 80 was merely another in a continuing series of efforts to evoke from Clark and his men, as well as from Lingo and the troopers, the behavior of which the SCLC knew those men capable. The attempted march to Montgomery is memorable largely because it succeeded in evoking that violent police conduct to a far more visible extent than had the SCLC's previous tactics.

That such a strategy of nonviolent provocation governed their actions was something that the SCLC leadership could not admit then and cannot admit even now.[39] In the eyes of many onlookers, such a strategy, if admitted, would have lessened substantially the legitimacy of the movement, a legitimacy that had been built not on religious and moral themes alone, but to an even greater extent upon an image of being the undeserving victims of racial hatred, victims who responded not in kind but simply by turning the other cheek. If the movement suddenly was pictured in a far more pragmatic light, the benefits that accrued to it from racist violence and the public opinion support that it enjoyed might well both have plummeted dramatically. In all likelihood the SCLC leadership was well aware of the likely public reaction if it were openly demonstrated that the movement intentionally was engaging in actions aimed at bringing down violence upon itself and its followers, and they wisely sought to avoid any such controversy. If the tenets of such a strategy had become public, the SCLC leadership no doubt realized, to many onlookers the moral judgments involved would have seemed far simpler than in fact they actually were. Most people, it was believed, would feel that the provocation of violence was wrong, and that any who engaged in such provocation, even if nonviolent, deserved what they got in return.

To the SCLC leadership, however, the moral questions no doubt were not so simple: black southerners had been subjected to frequent, often seemingly casual racist violence for some three centuries, and such acts were almost always committed in circumstances where they would not receive widespread attention.[40] Such violence and acts of intimidation and harassment were still far from uncommon in the mid-1960s, as the events of the 1964 Freedom Summer had demonstrated, but the SCLC leadership was plagued by the problem of how to convey those conditions and crimes, the almost palpable fear of white violence and the even more tangible racial hatred and contempt, to the millions of Americans who would react with shock and contempt if they could only be made truly aware of just what such victimization looked and felt like.[41] The SCLC leadership's apparent answer by the time that it arrived in Selma was that it was the movement's rightful duty to assure that the reality of such scenes would be portrayed "in the light of day—with the rest of the world looking on" and not simply in the dark of night in largely deserted rural areas.[42]

Aside from the suggestive observations made by Kahn and Meier early in 1964, it was not until early 1966 that a writer interested in the movement suggested that the SCLC's actual strategy was one of nonviolently provoking violence against itself. Quoting the four-point description of the process employed by the SCLC at Selma that King had set forth in his April 1965 article, Jan Howard suggested that the movement was "relying on violence to achieve" its ends and that it was adopting goals that it believed could be achieved only through the violent actions of its opponents. While admitting that such a contention "is difficult to prove," Howard wrote that King's article "clearly suggests that the movement in Selma . . . was relying on violence." Speaking as a movement activist, Howard went on to say, "We are consciously and unconsciously drawn toward violence because violence pays dividends for the movement." Police violence was something that the movement could capitalize upon and served as "a powerful catalyst to arouse public opinion. . . . When bigotry erupts into violence," Howard noted, "this dramatizes the everyday plight of the Negro and shows the righteousness of the movement's cause. . . . Violence is dramatic, and Americans like the dramatic. Mass media will give extensive coverage to violence and threats of violence while they ignore more subtle injustices against the Negro and more subtle attempts to remedy injustice. And the federal government can be forced to intervene in situations of violence while it turns its back on less inflammatory brutality."[43]

Although it received little apparent attention at the time of its publication, the Howard article is important because of the initial articulation it gives of an unadulterated but nevertheless sympathetic view of the movement's strategy. Implicit is the suggestion that the movement had come to seek violence against itself by its opponents because that was just the sort of action that appealed to the news values of the American media and that would produce a reaction favorable to the movement among the American people. Such a process had come to be the most effective—perhaps the only—way of winning the new federal civil rights legislation that the SCLC leadership desired, and the perhaps reluctant adoption of that strategy is not difficult to understand. Howard straightforwardly wrote what even the most outspoken, such as August Meier, were voicing only with some hesitation.[44] Although noting that the character, and often the race, of the victim, as well as the unusualness of given types of brutality, both played major roles in determining the level of media attention and the degree of public outrage and interest, Howard raised the basic question, did the movement "inherently need violence to sustain it? The evidence," Howard wrote, "suggests that it does. . . . The philosophy of nonviolent struggle," Howard concluded, "seems in part to be predicated on the idea that there will be violence against the movement."[45]

Howard's words echoed almost exactly those of the SCLC's Andrew Young late in March 1965. In one of the most revealing public utterances of the SCLC leadership, Young remarked to a newsman that the South was becoming somewhat less hostile towards the civil rights movement. "In the past," Young went on, "the movement has been sustained more or less by violence. But when you go into a place like Wilcox County [Alabama] and get a cordial welcome from the sheriff, it may be time to spend more time on organizing and educating than on marching."[46] The implication was that marches were worth pursuing only when local whites could be expected to vent their hostility upon the marchers. Without such harassment or attacks, marches per se were of rather limited value to the movement's cause.

Some two years later, the Howard article was followed by another piece that developed a very similar theme. Howard Hubbard wrote that "despite their nonviolent label, the demonstrations had to provoke a violent response in order to succeed."[47] King's skill, Hubbard said, "consisted mainly in his ability to *contrive*—in the best Machiavellian tradition—a situation in which he was the injured party." Being such a seemingly innocent victim, Hubbard noted, commonly leads to an outpouring of sympathetic support from onlookers.[48] The important requirement, however, was to avoid any appearance of having brought that violence down upon oneself. "To arrange to have violence visited upon oneself reflexively for the benefit of an influential audience is an exercise in public relations,—but, to be effective, must not appear as such."[49] All of this that Hubbard articulated so well had no doubt been understood just as clearly by the SCLC leadership in early 1965. Only on very rare occasions did media coverage of the movement ever suggest that the movement consciously was attempting to manipulate the ways in which it was being portrayed to the national audience.[50]

The efforts of King and the SCLC at Selma thus reflected an extremely sophisticated understanding of how a conflict could be "socialized" and how that socialization could serve to increase and arouse support for the SCLC's voting rights goals both throughout the nation and especially in Washington. The most important and most difficult matter to understand and predict was just what values, symbols, and themes would have such an appeal to the American people as to develop the most support for the SCLC. Helpful indeed was a single, simple aim that had widespread popular endorsement—equal voting rights—and helpful too were the strong religious overtones of the movement, which assisted further in lending legitimacy to its cause.[51] But, as we have noted earlier, the crux of the movement's struggle at Selma, as well as at Birmingham, concerned its efforts to convey to the national audience certain perceptions of its conduct and certain perceptions of its opponents' conduct. Therein lay the heart of the SCLC's strategy of protest, and therein lies the explanation for why that strategy proved so effective in February and March of 1965.

As we detailed in chapter 4, that strategy was significantly more successful at Selma than had been the case at Birmingham, although both campaigns benefited greatly from white violence. First, the Selma effort benefited from its clear articulation of a single easily grasped goal: equal voting rights. At Birmingham the national audience did not receive so clear a picture of just what it was that the movement sought, for the campaign's goals there were less well articulated. Not only were they numerous and thus somewhat diffuse, but they were clearly stressed by the SCLC leadership and the news media on only a few occasions. Second, the Birmingham campaign, unlike the Selma effort, was substantially hindered in its effort to gain "audience support" by the fact that violent and "illegitimate" black behavior counterbalanced the outrages of Connor's men on several important occasions. That harmful black response, however, did not fully negate the audience impact of white violence, and so, on balance, Birmingham as well as Selma proved to be a notable victory for the SCLC and its strategy of protest.

King and his associates within the SCLC leadership proved more adept at employing the strategy of protest as a means for socializing a conflict than any other political actors in recent American history. That aspect of King's remarkable career has gone almost wholly unappreciated, though a full account of his thoughts on that topic will remain unwritten until the SCLC's papers are opened and his surviving associates become willing to talk frankly of the events of the 1960s. Selma, though, represented not only the culmination but also, in effect, the end of the movement's successful employment of direct action tactics. While in part owing to the growing conflicts within the movement itself, conflicts that erupted briefly in the wake of March 9, the ending of the direct action phase of the movement was perhaps more the result of changes in the movement's policy agenda.[52] While King and the SCLC in particular had become very successful at employing protest to win national popular support and political support in Washington for the movement's mid-1960s legislative goals, the strategy of protest was not, and is not, a political resource that can be employed successfully in pursuit of *any* policy goal. While a national audience stood ready to be activated in support of appeals concerning the equal right to vote, subsequent SCLC efforts to employ socialization of conflict tactics to win open-housing progress in the North generated no such widespread "audience" or Washington support. As Lipsky has written, "Only if the relationship between protest objectives and the probable response of the reference publics of target groups is positive" will such a strategy of protest and conflict socialization prove beneficial to the protestors.[53]

In recent years an increasing number of groups and organizations have attempted to employ a strategy of protest in an effort to win additional support for their cause or policy goals. Most often their efforts have encountered one or both of two sometimes insurmountable barriers. The first is that of media attention. One of the best examples of a group that has tried to socialize a conflict by means reminiscent of those of the civil rights movement of the early 1960s has been the United Farm Workers Union in California, which has sought to win union representation and higher wages for the farmhands who harvest various fruits and vegetables. While on occasion their struggle against both the growers and the rival Teamsters Union, which was charged with maintaining "sweetheart" contracts with the growers, received national news coverage, that coverage was not widespread or continuous enough for the UFW to develop the strong national support that would assist in its organizing campaign against the growers. Although UFW President Cesar Chavez has appeared well attuned to the political dynamics that King and the SCLC understood so well, and although in a number of incidents UFW organizers or members were subject to physical harassment and violence, the UFW effort in the early 1970s was unable to stimulate enough newsworthy events so that continuing coverage would be given to the UFW's organizing campaigns by the national media.[54]

While the UFW's efforts have been hampered by spotty news coverage, another protest effort aimed at socializing a conflict made clear the important difference between what one recent writer has termed "publicity," or news coverage, and "persuasion," or the generation of audience support. In this instance, the protestors received all the news coverage that they might have desired, only to have public support of their cause *decrease* because of that extensive coverage. Indeed, this occurred even though the protestors in question—those at the Democratic National Convention in Chicago on August 28, 1968—were attacked by Chicago law-enforcement officials in what investigating authorities later termed a "police riot." While television commentators and press observers were quick to call the police action "excessive," given the demonstrators' own conduct, public opinion research quickly established that the vast majority of Americans regarded the police attack as justified and sided with the law-enforcement officials and not their victims. A telephone poll conducted the following day by the Sindlinger organization found that only 20 percent of those called condemned the police's behavior, and a Survey Research Center poll conducted two months later found that of the 88 percent of the respondents who recalled the clash, only 19 percent believed that the police had used too much force. Some 32 percent of the informed respondents characterized the police action as employing "the right amount" of force, while 25 percent said that "not enough force" had been used by the officials.[55] While no clear-cut explanation for this reaction has yet been put forward, it is apparent that the majority of audience members regarded the demonstrators themselves so negatively—on the basis of life-style, political views, and personal conduct—that the police action against them produced no sympathy for the victims of it and no condemnation of the officials themselves. The moral here for protestors is that they can expect no audience support, even in the wake of violence against them, if the audience regards them and their cause as being wholly or largely illegitimate to begin with.

While some political groups seeking an expanded scope of conflict, such as Chavez and the UFW, encounter problems in securing news media and audience attention, the Chicago story highlights the second major barrier faced by many groups that seek to employ a strategy of protest. That problem revolves around what values concerning the protestors' goals and tactics are conveyed to the audience. In the case of the Chicago protestors, as we noted, their "value appeal" was to a very small minority of the audience to which their conflict was socialized. Other groups employing a strategy of protest will be well advised to fashion their goals and conduct in a manner that they believe will win at least grudging approval and passing marks of legitimacy from their desired audience. Most often the protestors' appeal will be aimed at what many writers have termed "the simple democratic creed which nearly every citizen believes in," a creed "which itself gives legitimacy to an appeal to the populace." Appeals to that "creed," or to what more precisely might be labeled the core beliefs of the American political culture, are often spoken of as "moral" appeals and involve attempts by the protestors to convince the national audience and its political leaders of the legitimacy of their goals and the justifiability of their tactics.[56] Such appeals, and the conflicts of which they are a part, consist basically, as we noted earlier, of efforts to associate certain positive values with the appeal and with those making it, and certain negative values with those who are opposing both it and its sponsors. As Richard Merelman wrote more than a decade ago, "Most major political conflicts within any policy area may be seen as the attempt by partisans to attach the available legitimacy symbols to the policies they advocate and to sever the relationship between these symbols and the policies of their opponents.''

Merelman also correctly emphasized that in the struggle to achieve new policy ends through the attraction of additional support from those who initially were uncommitted, progress was heavily dependent upon the degree of ''success with which already established legitimacy symbols can be associated with'' those desired new ends.[57] Different ''symbols'' can have different ''weights,'' and much of the success or lack of success of a protest group is a result of its ability or inability to perceive correctly what symbols and values the audience responds to positively and which it responds to negatively. When one's opponents act to eliminate the legitimacy of their own position, as was true at Selma, the cause of the protestors should advance with greater, perhaps substantial, ease. Success in a conflict that is being socialized to an audience of increasingly wide scope almost always lies with the side that is more perceptive and adept at picturing itself in such a way that the initially uninvolved audience will be drawn into the conflict on its side on the basis of the audience's own values and beliefs.

While the successful employment of protest appeals is limited to those causes that can be portrayed in some fashion that will invoke in a positive way values held by the requisite audience,[58] the socialization of conflict perspective that Schattschneider first articulated nearly two decades ago can be applied profitably to many political actions and contests that do not come under any of the several definitions offered for ''protest'' and ''protest activities.''[59] While the academic study of politics presently stands in severe need of further inquiries concerning the values and symbols with which appeals to audiences can be made, a number of recent works reflect the growing academic realization that Schattschneider's format represents a conceptual approach to many political events that has not yet has been fully explored. Several scholars and journalists have written of how public hearings, pushed or sponsored by one political interest, have increased public interest in and attention to matters such as pollution standards, consumer protection statutes, and reform of fiscal corruption and inadequate care in many of New York state's nursing homes.[60] All of these stories convey the message that publicity in the form of news coverage is essential to the socialization of a conflict, and that the prime result of such a socialization process is the stimulation of governmental action. While, on occasion, such news coverage and public interest leads to action on a topic with which the government previously had not concerned itself, more often such a widening of the scope of conflict serves to activate a higher agency of government to oversee or supercede the apparently inadequate action of some subordinate agency of government.[61] In a somewhat different fashion, bureaucratic action that involves the "leaking" of some information to the news media is, at base, an effort to socialize a conflict which up until that time had been privatized within a narrower range of awareness.[62] Thus, a more wide-ranging application of Schattschneider's conceptualization of conflict can be productive indeed.

It was just such a process of widening the scope of a long-standing conflict that played such an influential role in the emergence of the legislative proposal which was to become the Voting Rights Act of 1965. While the federal courts played a vanguard role in expanding the rights of black people, black southerners were unable to experience truly substantial gains in voting rights until, through their own actions, they were able to activate the federal executive and Congress.[63] During the last days of 1964 and the first three months of 1965 Lyndon B. Johnson, a number of particularly sensitive members of Congress, and the leadership of the Southern Christian Leadership Conference all acted to bring forward and speed to enactment a voting rights measure that in a matter of months produced far greater black registration gains than had eight years worth of federal litigation. Although the initial decision that there would be a Voting Rights Act of 1965 appears to have been that of Lyndon Johnson himself, despite contrary counsel from a number of aides, and although the emergence of that proposal from the administration was influenced substantially by members of Congress of both parties, the national consensus in favor of that bill, a consensus expressed in the words of more than ten dozen members of Congress, was primarily the result of the very skillful actions of the SCLC in Selma.

Although some might choose to criticize the SCLC's true strategy as provocative and markedly at odds with its own public image, the political sagacity of Martin Luther King, Jr., and his aides, a sagacity not yet fully appreciated by King's admirers, was demonstrated by their very deft creation in Selma of events that spurred support both in Washington and across the country for more stringent voting rights safeguards to be enforced not by the federal courts but by the federal executive branch. In creating those events, King and his aides evinced a remarkably complete understanding of how the attention of the American people could be gained, and they correctly realized that it was not so much their own clearly articulated goal nor their own aggressively passive conduct that would gain them that attention and support, as it was the often irrationally violent conduct of their immediate opponents that would work to obtain news coverage for them and rally the support of much of the American populace to their cause. With that realization in hand, they proceeded to pursue a wise and pragmatic tactical course which on occasion brought them physical injury but which at the same time served to advance a truly noble cause. From their efforts in those early months of 1965, as well as from the efforts of Johnson, his men at Justice, and certain members of Congress, sprang a legislative enactment that was to stimulate as great a change in American politics as any one law ever has. Within twelve years of its passage, all of America was to witness just how great an effect the Voting Rights Act of 1965 had had.

Notes

Preface

1. Gene Roberts, *New York Times*, 7 August 1965, p. 1.
2. See U.S. Congress, Senate, Committee on the Judiciary, *Extension of the Voting Rights Act of 1965—Hearings Before the Subcommittee on Constitutional Rights*, 94th Congress, 1st session, 1975, p. 121, for the April 10 testimony of Nicholas deB. Katzenbach; and U.S. Congress, House, Committee on the Judiciary, *Extension of the Voting Rights Act—Hearings Before the Subcommittee on Civil and Constitutional Rights*, 94th Congress, 1st session, 1975, p. 319, for the March 6 testimony of the Reverend Theodore M. Hesburgh. Also see the words of Senator John Tunney on page 1 of the Senate hearings, and those of Lisle C. Carter, Jr., in the *New York Times*, 28 March 1975, p. 27.
3. See James Reston, *New York Times*, 7 November 1976, p. E17, who wrote, "This election was won primarily by the black voters of the South."
4. Roy Reed, *New York Times*, 6 November 1976, p. 1; Paul Delaney, *New York Times*, 7 November 1976, p. 39; and Thomas A. Johnson, *New York Times*, 6 November 1976, p. 8.
5. See B. D. Ayres, Jr., *New York Times*, 8 November 1976, p. 19, for the words of Julian Bond; and Jerry Allegood, *Raleigh News and Observer*, 12 November 1976, p. 35, for the comments of Coretta Scott King.
6. Thomas A. Johnson, *New York Times*, 2 November 1976, p. 18; and 5 November 1976, p. A17. Also see Tom Wicker, *New York Times*, 16 August 1977, p. 35, who relates some 1975 irregularities in Terrell County, Georgia; and U.S. Commission on Civil Rights, *The Unfinished Business, Twenty Years Later* . . . (Washington: USGPO, 1977), p. 8, which describes some 1976 problems in Covington County, Alabama.
7. See Warren Brown's story on Terrell County, Georgia, *Washington Post*, 3 September 1977, pp. A1 and A12.
8. On Williamsburg County's Theodore McFarlin, see Mary Whittle, *The State*, 4 November 1976, p. B1.
9. See Martin Donsky, *Raleigh News and Observer*, 15 September 1976, p. 1; and Bill Gilkeson, *Durham Morning Herald*, 19 September 1976, p. 1. Lee subsequently was appointed to the cabinet of North Carolina governor James B. Hunt, Jr. In Florida, Joseph W. Hatchett, appointed to the state supreme court a year earlier, defeated a white opponent in a statewide race for a full term on the court.
10. As one recent journalistic overview of the situation concluded, "The full potential of black political power in Dixie remains unrealized" (B.D. Ayres, Jr., *New York Times*, 6 November 1977, p. E3).

Introduction

1. Throughout all of the voting rights struggle both black leaders and their white allies believed that the vote was perhaps the most important right for southern blacks to obtain. With the vote, blacks could obtain important gains in other areas such as education, employment, and municipal services. No black leader articulated this belief in the instrumental importance of the ballot as strongly as did Martin King. See the excerpts from his speech of May 17, 1957, which are presented in Charles V. Hamilton, *The Bench and The Ballot: Southern Federal Judges and Black Voters* (New York: Oxford University Press, 1973), pp. 42–43, and his comments in an article that appeared at the height of the Selma struggle: "Civil Right No. 1—The Right to Vote," *New York Times Magazine*, 14 March 1965, pp. 26–27 and 94–95:

> Voting is the foundation stone for political action. With it the Negro can eventually vote out of office public officials who bar the doorway to decent housing, public safety, jobs and decent integrated education. It is now obvious that the basic elements so vital to Negro advancement can only be achieved by seeking redress from government at local, state and Federal levels. To do this the vote is essential.

King was not the only southern black leader to assign such an importance to the franchise. See also the statement by Mississippi's Aaron Henry, which appears in Pat Watters and Reese Cleghorn, *Climbing Jacob's Ladder: The Arrival of Negroes in Southern Politics* (New York: Harcourt, Brace & World, 1967), p. 181; and Henry's subsequent testimony before the U.S. Commission on Civil Rights in *Hearings on Voting in Jackson, Miss., February 16–20, 1965* (Washington: USGPO, 1965), p. 159. Henry told the commission, "My feeling is that all of the problems can be resolved once the right to vote is gained."

Important white officials often allied with the civil rights movement shared this belief. See the comments by three successive attorneys general, Herbert Brownell, William P. Rogers, and Robert F. Kennedy, in U.S. Congress, Senate, Committee on the Judiciary, *Civil Rights—1957—Hearings Before the Subcommittee on Constitutional Rights*, 85th Congress, 1st session, 1957, p. 2; Daniel M. Berman, *A Bill Becomes A Law: The Civil Rights Act of 1960* (New York: Macmillan, 1962), pp. 69–70; and U.S. Congress, House, Committee on the Judiciary, *Civil Rights—Hearings Before Subcommittee No. 5*, 88th Congress, 1st session, 1963, p. 1378. Also see the remarks by Assistant Attorney General Burke Marshall in *Federalism and Civil Rights* (New York: Columbia University Press, 1964), pp. 10–12; and the testimony of the AFL-CIO's Andrew J. Biemiller, in U.S. Congress, House, Committee on the Judiciary, *Civil Rights—Hearings Before Subcommittee No. 5*, 85th Congress, 1st session, 1957, p. 649.

Articulations of that same view by others are quite numerous. See, for instance, editorials from the nation's two most influential newspapers: *New York Times*, 28 January 1965, p. 28; and *Washington Post*, 6 February 1965, p. A12. For congressional expressions, see the remarks of William F. Ryan, 12 January

1965, *Congressional Record* 111 (pt. 1), p. 596; Joseph Y. Resnick, 11 March 1965, *Congressional Record* 111 (pt. 4), pp. 4780–81; and William McCulloch and James C. Corman, U.S. Congress, House, Committee on the Judiciary, *Voting Rights Act Extension—Hearings Before Subcommittee No. 5*, 91st Congress, 1st session, 1969, pp. 4 and 6.

Lyndon Johnson too shared this belief and gave it strong articulation in his famous speech of March 15, 1965, *New York Times*, 16 March 1965, p. 30. Also see Carroll Kilpatrick, *Washington Post*, 5 February 1965, p. 1; and John D. Morris, *New York Times*, 5 February 1965, p. 17, for earlier statements by the president on that same point, and Johnson's own *The Vantage Point— Perspectives of the Presidency* (New York: Holt, Rinehart & Winston, 1971), p. 161.

In addition to this repeated stress on the instrumental importance of the franchise, a smaller group of political figures and commentators active during the voting rights struggle also pointed to what they saw as the more immediate, consummative value of the ballot for the individual who casts it. Registering and voting, these writers believed, gave previously disenfranchised blacks a new sense of "self-worth" and increased self-esteem. By far the best articulation of this important perspective is Stokely Carmichael and Charles V. Hamilton, *Black Power—The Politics of Liberation in America* (New York: Random House, 1967), pp. 103–5. The act of registering to vote, they write,

> gives one a sense of being. The black man who goes to register is saying to the white man, "No." He is saying: "You have said that I cannot vote. You have said that this is my place. This is where I should remain. You have contained me and I am saying 'No' to your containment. I am stepping out of bounds. I am saying 'No' to you and thereby I am creating a better life for myself. I am resisting someone who has contained me." That is what the first act does. The black person begins to live. He begins to create his *own* existence when he says "No" to someone who contains him.

Other less eloquent descriptions of this effect of the ballot appear in Anthony Lewis, *Portrait of a Decade—The Second American Revolution* (New York: Random House, 1965), p. 152; Frederick M. Wirt, *Politics of Southern Equality* (Chicago: Aldine, 1970), p. 78; and Donald R. Matthews and James W. Prothro, *Negroes and the New Southern Politics* (New York: Harcourt, Brace & World, 1966), p. 481.

In the aftermath of this persistent emphasis upon the importance of the ballot, at least one scholar has suggested that the most vocal proponents of that view may well have overstated the real benefits that would result from widespread black enfranchisement in the South; see Hanes Walton, Jr., *Black Politics* (Philadelphia: J.B. Lippincott, 1972), pp. 2–11. His point is well taken, but the actions of these many proponents of the importance of the franchise were shaped by that belief, even if, in retrospect, their assumptions appear somewhat exaggerated. Hence, the *effects* of those beliefs in the value of the ballot should not be slighted. Throughout the heyday of the civil rights movement the majority of the leading figures believed that the ballot should be their most important goal and first priority. See Allan P. Sindler, "Protest Against the Political Status of the Negro," *Annals of the American Academy of Political and Social Science* 357 (January 1965): 48–54.

2. See Martin Luther King, Jr., *Stride Toward Freedom: The Montgomery Story* (New York: Harper & Brothers, 1958), pp. 80–81 and 84–85; and "Nonviolence and Racial Justice," *Christian Century* 74 (6 February 1957): 165–67.

3. "Conflicts," Schattschneider wrote, "are frequently won or lost by the success that the contestants have in getting the audience involved in the fight or ,in excluding it, as the case may be," depending upon which side seeks additional strength to alter the initial balance of forces and which seeks to maintain its initial advantage by restricting the scope of the conflict. "The spectators," Schattschneider emphasized, "are as much a part of the over-all situation as are the overt combatants. The spectators are an integral part of the situation, for, as likely as not, the audience determines the outcome of the fight." *The Semisovereign People* (New York: Holt, Rinehart & Winston, 1960), pp. 4 and 2.

4. Hamilton, *The Bench and The Ballot*, pp. 222–23.

Chapter 1

1. 347 U.S. 483.

2. For example, see Harrell R. Rodgers, Jr. and Charles S. Bullock III, *Law and Social Change: Civil Rights Laws and Their Consequences* (New York: McGraw-Hill, 1972), p. 3; Anthony Oberschall, *Social Conflict and Social Movements* (Englewood Cliffs, N.J.: Prentice-Hall, 1973), p. 138; and August Meier, "New Currents in the Civil Rights Movement," *New Politics* 2 (Summer 1963): 7–32, at 13.

3. 321 U.S. 649, esp. at 664. The earlier white primary cases were *Nixon* v. *Herndon*, 273 U.S. 536 (1927); *Nixon* v. *Condon*, 286 U.S. 73 (1932); and *Grovey* v. *Townsend*, 295 U.S. 45 (1935). The overruling of *Grovey*'s sanctioning of the Texas Democratic party's whites-only primary in *Smith* was presaged by the 1941 decision in *U.S.* v. *Classic*, 313 U.S. 299, which signaled a major reinterpretation of the "state action" doctrine as it related to party primaries. For commentary on the white primary cases, see Robert W. Hainsworth, "The Negro and the Texas Primaries," *Journal of Negro History* 18 (October 1933): 426–50; Robert E. Cushman, "The Texas 'White Primary' Case—*Smith* v. *Allwright*," *Cornell Law Quarterly* 30 (September 1944): 66–76; William H. Hastie, "Appraisal of *Smith* v. *Allwright*," *Law Guild Review* 5 (March–April 1945): 65–72; V.O. Key, *Southern Politics in State and Nation* (New York: Alfred A. Knopf, 1949), chapter 29; Thurgood Marshall, "The Rise and Collapse of the 'White Democratic Primary,' " *Journal of Negro Education* 26 (Summer 1957): 249–54; Richard Claude, *The Supreme Court and the Electoral Process* (Baltimore: Johns Hopkins Press, 1970), pp. 68–71; Clement E. Vose, *Constitutional Change: Amendment Politics and Supreme Court Litigation Since 1900* (Lexington, Mass.: D.C. Heath, 1972), chapter 12; Steven F. Lawson, *Black*

Ballots: Voting Rights in the South, 1944–1969 (New York: Columbia University Press, 1976), pp. 23–54; and Darlene Clark Hine, "Blacks and the Destruction of the Democratic White Primary 1935–1944," *Journal of Negro History* 62 (January 1977): 43–59. Even prior to the series of white primary cases, the Supreme Court already had struck down another well-known, but less effective tool used to bar blacks from the polls: the so-called grandfather clause. See *Guinn* v. *U.S.*, 238 U.S. 347 (1915), and *Lane* v. *Wilson*, 307 U.S. 268 (1939). Also see Vose, *Constitutional Change*, chapter 2; and Lawson, *Black Ballots*, pp. 17–19.

4. Harry Holloway, *The Politics of the Southern Negro* (New York: Random House, 1969), p. 331. For similar expressions of the same opinion, see Francis M. Wilhoit, *The Politics of Massive Resistance* (New York: George Braziller, 1973), p. 226; Richard E. Yates, "Arkansas: Independent and Unpredictable," in William C. Havard, ed., *The Changing Politics of the South* (Baton Rouge: Louisiana State University Press, 1972), p. 226; and Pat Watters and Reese Cleghorn, *Climbing Jacob's Ladder: The Arrival of Negroes in Southern Politics* (New York: Harcourt, Brace & World, 1967), p. 12. Watters and Cleghorn call the *Smith* decision "the most important step since Reconstruction toward restoration of Negro political liberty in the South."

5. For verification, see Hugh Douglas Price, *The Negro and Southern Politics—A Chapter of Florida History* (New York: New York University Press, 1957), p. 21. On the disfranchisement of blacks in the post Reconstruction South, see J. Morgan Kousser, *The Shaping of Southern Politics: Suffrage Restriction and the Establishment of the One-Party South, 1880–1910* (New Haven: Yale University Press, 1974); Paul Lewinson, *Race, Class and Party* (New York: Oxford University Press, 1932); C. Vann Woodward, *Origins of the New South, 1877–1913* (Baton Rouge: Louisiana State University Press, 1951); Sheldon Hackney, "*Origins of the New South* in Retrospect," *Journal of Southern History* 38 (May 1972): 191–216; C. Vann Woodward, "The Political Legacy of Reconstruction," *Journal of Negro Education* 26 (Summer 1957): 231–40; and John Hope Franklin, " 'Legal' Disfranchisement of the Negro," *Journal of Negro Education* 26 (Summer 1957): 241–48. Also relevant to the period before 1940 are George B. Tindall, *The Emergence of the New South, 1913–1945* (Baton Rouge: Louisiana State University Press, 1967); Dewey W. Grantham, *The Democratic South* (Athens: University of Georgia Press, 1963); Leo Alilunas, "Legal Restrictions on the Negro in Politics," *Journal of Negro History* 25 (April 1940): 153–202; John G. Van Deusen, "The Negro in Politics," *Journal of Negro History* 21 (July 1936): 256–74; Brainerd Dyer, "One Hundred Years of Negro Suffrage," *Pacific Historical Review* 37 (February 1968): 1–20; and the oft-cited classic by W.J. Cash, *The Mind of the South* (New York: Alfred A. Knopf, 1941).

6. Luther P. Jackson, "Race and Suffrage in the South Since 1940," *New South* 3 (June–July 1948): 1–26, at 3–4. While other writers have adopted registration totals for 1940 of either 200,000 or 250,000, Jackson's estimates subsequently were evaluated as the most reliable. See Alexander Heard, *A Two-*

Party South? (Chapel Hill: University of North Carolina Press, 1952), p. 181. The higher figures appear in Ralphe J. Bunche's 1940 research manuscript for Gunnar Myrdal, which recently has been published as *The Political Status of the Negro in the Age of FDR* (Chicago: University of Chicago Press, 1973); and in two secondary works, Donald R. Matthews and James W. Prothro, *Negroes and the New Southern Politics* (New York: Harcourt, Brace & World, 1966), p. 18; and Gerald M. Pomper, *Elections in America: Control and Influence in Democratic Politics* (New York: Dodd, Mead, 1968), p. 229. Also see Chuck Stone, *Black Political Power in America*, rev. ed. (New York: Dell, 1970), pp. 234–35; and George C. Stoney, "Suffrage in the South, Part I," *Survey Graphic* 29 (January 1940): 5–9 and 41–43.

7.   Five examples of works that use the exact phrase are Henry Lee Moon, "Counted Out—and In," *Survey Graphic* 36 (January 1947): 78–81, at 78; Moon, "The Negro Vote in the South, 1952," *Nation* 175 (27 September 1952): 245–48, at 245; Donald S. Strong, *Registration of Voters in Alabama* (University: Bureau of Public Administration, University of Alabama, 1956), pp. 21–22; U.S. Commission on Civil Rights, *1959 Report* (Washington: USGPO, 1959), p. 34; and Armand Derfner, "Racial Discrimination and the Right to Vote," *Vanderbilt Law Review* 26 (April 1973): 523–84, at 542. Luther Jackson was another exponent of this view. See "Race and Suffrage in the South," p. 13.

8.   Matthews and Prothro, *Negroes and the New Southern Politics*, p. 17. A similar observation is expressed by Key in *Southern Politics*, p. 518. Several writers have dissented from this position, however. See Donald S. Strong, "The Rise of Negro Voting in Texas," *American Political Science Review* 42 (June 1948): 510–22; and Hanes Walton, Jr., *Black Politics* (Philadelphia: J.B. Lippincott, 1972), p. 42.

9.   See Key, *Southern Politics*, pp. 126, 518, and 636; and Jackson, "Race and Suffrage in the South," p. 5. For the federal court decisions that eliminated the white primary in Georgia, see *King* v. *Chapman*, 62 F. Supp. 639 (1945), and *Chapman* v. *King*, 154 F.2d 460 (1946).

10.   See Heard, *A Two-Party South?*, p. 181, who estimates the total black turnout in 1946 as being one-sixteenth of the potential black vote; and Key, *Southern Politics*, p. 521.

11.   Key, *Southern Politics*, p. 619.

12.   The major decisions were *Elmore* v. *Rice*, 72 F. Supp. 516 (1947); *Rice* v. *Elmore*, 165 F.2d 387 (1947); *Brown* v. *Baskin*, 78 F. Supp. 933 (1948); and *Baskin* v. *Brown*, 174 F.2d 391 (1949), all pertaining to South Carolina, and *Terry* v. *Adams*, 345 U.S. 461 (1953), regarding Texas. Accounts of these attempts to resuscitate the white primary are contained in Key, *Southern Politics*, pp. 626–32; O. Douglas Weeks, "The White Primary: 1944–1948," *American Political Science Review* 42 (June 1948): 500–10; Loren P. Beth, "The White Primary and the Judicial Function in the United States," *Political Quarterly* 29 (October–December 1958): 366–77; Robert L. Gill, "*Smith* v. *Allwright* and Reactions in Some of the Southern States," *Quarterly Review of Higher Education Among Negroes* 35 (July 1967): 154–69; and Clay P. Malick, "*Terry* v. *Adams*: Gov-

ernmental Responsibility for the Protection of Civil Rights," *Western Political Quarterly* 7 (March 1954): 51–64.

13. Key, *Southern Politics*, p. 563. Also see Jackson, "Race and Suffrage in the South," p. 8, who uses the same phrase, and Herbert Hill, "Southern Negroes at the Ballot Box," *The Crisis* 61 (May 1954): 261–66, at 263. Another barrier to black voting, whose impact has been overrated in the public mind, was the poll tax, which by the late 1940s was a serious obstacle only in the three states where its assessment was cumulative: Alabama, Mississippi, and Virginia. In December 1953 that feature was reduced markedly in Alabama, and a substantial number of new registrants, not all of whom were black, soon appeared. See Key, *Southern Politics*, pp. 598 and 612; Frederic D. Ogden, *The Poll Tax in the South* (University: University of Alabama Press, 1958); Lawson, *Black Ballots*, pp. 55–85; Jackson, "Race and Suffrage in the South," pp. 6–8; "Race and Suffrage Today," *New South* 8 (January 1953): 3; and Strong, *Registration of Voters in Alabama*, pp. 30 and 54.

14. See *Davis v. Schnell*, 81 F. Supp. 872 (1949), and 336 U.S. 933 (1949); Lawson, *Black Ballots*, pp. 89–97; Vera C. Foster, " 'Boswellianism': A Technique in the Restriction of Negro Voting," *Phylon* 10 (First Quarter 1949): 26–37; Strong, *Registration of Voters in Alabama*, pp. 22–25; and Francis W. Collopy's brief piece in *Notre Dame Lawyer* 24 (Summer 1949): 571–74. Also see Richard T. Rives, "An Argument Against the Adoption of the Boswell Amendment," *Alabama Lawyer* 7 (July 1946): 291–97; and a virulent racist rebuttal, Horace C. Wilkinson, "Argument For Adoption of Boswell Amendment," *Alabama Lawyer* 7 (October 1946): 375–82.

15. On the registration situation throughout the South as of 1947, see Jackson, "Race and Suffrage in the South," pp. 8–23, who provides some details on just about every state. On the 1947–1952 period, see Moon, "The Negro Vote in the South, 1952," pp. 245–48; "Around the South," *Nation* 175 (27 September 1952): 257–60; "Race and Suffrage Today," *New South* 8 (January 1953): 1–5 and 8; and Lawson, *Black Ballots*, pp. 124–32, all of which provide some details on a number of states. A lengthier account of Alabama's successful 1951 attempt to enact some registration requirements similar to the 1947 Boswell Amendment is contained in Strong, *Registration of Voters in Alabama*, pp. 25–33. Incidents of voter intimidation and harassment from the late 1940s and early 1950s are chronicled in "The Battle for the Ballot," *Nation* 175 (27 September 1952): 250–51.

16. This point is particularly well made in Earl Black, *Southern Governors and Civil Rights* (Cambridge: Harvard University Press, 1976), pp. 7 and 45 and passim. Other relevant works on the post-*Brown* period are Numan V. Bartley, *The Rise of Massive Resistance* (Baton Rouge: Louisiana State University Press, 1969), which possesses a particularly notable bibliography; Neil R. McMillen, *The Citizens' Council* (Urbana: University of Illinois Press, 1971); Wilhoit, *The Politics of Massive Resistance*, and John Bartlow Martin, *The Deep South Says Never* (New York: Ballantine, 1957).

17. See Earl M. Lewis, "The Negro Voter in Mississippi," *Journal of Negro*

Education 26 (Summer 1957): 343–46; and Margaret Price, *The Negro Voter in the South* (Atlanta: Southern Regional Council, 1957), pp. 20–21 and 42.

18. On the Louisiana registration situation in the late.1950s and the purges, see Margaret Price, *The Negro and the Ballot in the South* (Atlanta: Southern Regional Council, 1959), pp. 15–18; Kenneth N. Vines, "A Louisiana Parish: Wholesale Purge," in Price, *The Negro and the Ballot*, pp. 34–46; U.S. Department of Justice, *Annual Report of the Attorney General, 1957* (Washington: USGPO, 1957), pp. 107–9; Robert F. Collins, Nils R. Douglas, and Lolis E. Elie, "Clinton, Louisiana," in Leon Friedman, ed., *Southern Justice* (New York: Random House, 1965), pp. 112–26; Edward Gamarekian, "A Report from the South on the Negro Voter," *Reporter* 16 (27 June 1957): 9–12; John H. Fenton, "The Negro Voter in Louisiana," *Journal of Negro Education* 26 (Summer 1957): 319–28; Daniel C. Thompson, *The Negro Leadership Class* (Englewood Cliffs, N.J.: Prentice-Hall, 1963), pp. 86–96 and 108–9; and John H. Fenton and Kenneth N. Vines, "Negro Registration in Louisiana," *American Political Science Review* 51 (September 1957): 704–13. A particularly accurate accounting of black registration totals is provided in Riley F. Baker, "Negro Voter Registration in Louisiana, 1879–1964," *Louisiana Studies* 4 (Winter 1965): 332–50. The standard political history of the state is Perry H. Howard, *Political Tendencies in Louisiana*, rev. ed. (Baton Rouge: Louisiana State University Press, 1971).

19. The importance of the percentage black of the population and the inverse relationship scholars found between it and the percentage of voting-age blacks registered in the years prior to 1965 has been stressed in a number of works. Key in particular pointed out the relationship and the importance of the 30 percent threshold of black population. See *Southern Politics*, pp. 115 and 132–33. Matthews and Prothro found a similar relationship more than a decade after Key; see *Negroes and the New Southern Politics*, p. 116. That large and inclusive volume paints a very complete picture of southern blacks' political situation, behavior, and views as of the early 1960s. The same authors wrote two earlier articles: "Social and Economic Factors and Negro Voter Registration in the South," *American Political Science Review* 57 (March 1963): 24–44; and "Political Factors and Negro Voter Registration in the South," *American Political Science Review* 57 (June 1963): 355–67. Two other germane volumes are Allan P. Sindler, ed., *Change in the Contemporary South* (Durham, N.C.: Duke University Press, 1963); and Everett Carll Ladd, Jr., *Negro Political Leadership in the South* (Ithaca, N.Y.: Cornell University Press, 1966), which focuses upon Greenville, South Carolina, and Winston-Salem, North Carolina. The continued validity of the Black Belt hypothesis has been the theme of a number of articles, including William J. Keefe, "Southern Politics Revisited," *Public Opinion Quarterly* 20 (Summer 1956): 405–12; Earl Black, "The Militant Segregationist Vote in the Post-*Brown* South: A Comparative Analysis," *Social Science Quarterly* 54 (June 1973): 66–84; and David Knoke and Natalie Kyriazis, "The Persistence of the Black-Belt Vote: A Test of Key's Hypothesis," *Social Science Quarterly* 57 (March 1977): 899–906. A more inclusive overview of Key's work is Gary C.

Ness, "The *Southern Politics* Project and the Writing of Recent Southern History," *South Atlantic Quarterly* 76 (Winter 1977): 58–72.

20. Price, *The Negro and the Ballot*, pp. 15 and 6. Various accounts of the situations in the different states as of the late 1950s, in addition to works cited earlier, include Gamarekian, "A Report from the South," which details the situation in Mississippi; C. G. Gomillion, "The Negro Voter in Alabama," *Journal of Negro Education* 26 (Summer 1957): 281–86; Joseph M. Brittain, "The Return of the Negro to Alabama Politics, 1930–1954," *Negro History Bulletin* 22 (May 1959): 196–99, and "Some Reflections on Negro Suffrage and Politics in Alabama—Past and Present," *Journal of Negro History* 47 (April 1962): 127–38; Strong, *Registration of Voters in Alabama*, chapter 4 of which is as good an account as exists of the difficulties involved in completing Alabama's registration questionnaire; James T. McCain, "The Negro Voter in South Carolina," *Journal of Negro Education* 26 (Summer 1957): 359–61; Joseph L. Bernd and Lynwood M. Holland, "Recent Restrictions Upon Negro Suffrage: The Case of Georgia," *Journal of Politics* 21 (August 1959): 487–513; Clarence A. Bacote, "The Negro Voter in Georgia Politics, Today," *Journal of Negro Education* 26 (Summer 1957): 307–18; H.D. Price, *The Negro and Southern Politics—A Chapter of Florida History*; Charles D. Farris, "The Re-enfranchisement of Negroes in Florida," *Journal of Negro History* 39 (October 1954): 259–83; Hugh Douglas Price, "The Negro and Florida Politics, 1944–1954," *Journal of Politics* 17 (May 1955): 198–220; William G. Carleton and Hugh Douglas Price, "America's Newest Voter: A Florida Case Study," *Antioch Review* 14 (December 1954): 441–57; and Elston E. Roady, "The Expansion of Negro Suffrage in Florida," *Journal of Negro Education* 26 (Summer 1957): 297–306. As this list indicates, some states, such as Florida, are more than well covered in the literature, while others, such as South Carolina, have received very little attention. A competent statistical overview is Virgil C. Stroud, "The Negro Voter in the South," *Quarterly Review of Higher Education Among Negroes* 29 (January 1961): 9–39. Two excellent state studies that are informative on the period are Andrew Buni, *The Negro in Virginia Politics* (Charlottesville: University Press of Virginia, 1967); and Numan V. Bartley, *From Thurmond to Wallace: Political Tendencies in Georgia, 1948–1968* (Baltimore: Johns Hopkins University Press, 1970).

21. On the early efforts of the federal executive branch in the civil rights field during the Roosevelt and Truman administrations, see Robert K. Carr, *Federal Protection of Civil Rights: Quest for a Sword* (Ithaca, N.Y.: Cornell University Press, 1947), which is a history of the Justice Department's Civil Rights Section for the years 1939–1945; John T. Elliff, "Aspects of Federal Civil Rights Enforcement: The Justice Department and the FBI, 1939–1964," *Perspectives in American History* 5 (1971): 603–73, at 605–40; Ruth P. Morgan, *The President and Civil Rights—Policy Making by Executive Order* (New York: St. Martin's Press, 1970); Richard P. Longaker, *The Presidency and Individual Liberties* (Ithaca, N.Y.: Cornell University Press, 1962); and Lawson, *Black Ballots*, pp. 116–23.

On Truman's activity in particular, see William C. Berman, *The Politics of*

Civil Rights in Truman Administration (Columbus: Ohio State University Press, 1970); Donald R. McCoy and Richard T. Ruetten, *Quest and Response—Minority Rights and the Truman Administration* (Lawrence: University Press of Kansas, 1973); Barton J. Bernstein, "The Ambiguous Legacy: Civil Rights," in Bernstein, ed., *Politics and Policies of the Truman Administration* (New York: Quadrangle, 1970); Harvard Sitkoff, "Harry Truman and the Election of 1948: The Coming of Age of Civil Rights in American Politics," *Journal of Southern History* 37 (November 1971): 597–616; Richard Kirkendall, "Truman and Domestic Politics: The Election of 1948," in Robert D. Marcus and David Burner, eds., *America Since 1945* (New York: St. Martin's Press, 1972), pp. 33–54; Monroe Billington, "Civil Rights, President Truman and the South," *Journal of Negro History* 58 (April 1973); 127–39; and the report issued by his special committee, *To Secure These Rights—The Report of the President's Committee on Civil Rights* (New York: Simon & Schuster, 1947), which proposed, among other recommendations, the abolition of the poll tax. Bills intended to accomplish just that had won House approval five times during the 1940s, but had never succeeded in clearing the parliamentary hurdles erected in the Senate by segregationists. The best review of the fate of civil rights legislation in the Congress in the 1940s, including that proposed by Truman in early 1948 as an offshoot of the committee's recommendations, is contained in Congressional Quarterly's *Revolution in Civil Rights*, 3rd ed. (Washington: Congressional Quarterly Service, 1967). There exists within the Truman literature an interesting debate over whether or not the president's sudden activity concerning civil rights in 1947 was largely a personal reaction to a series of well-publicized incidents in which southern blacks had suffered violence at the hands of whites. While ultimately unanswerable, it bears some similarity to questions we shall confront in subsequent chapters.

22.   On the limited civil rights activity in the first few years of the Eisenhower administration, see Congressional Quarterly, *Revolution in Civil Rights*, 3rd ed., p. 36; Morgan, *The President and Civil Rights*, pp. 25–26, 43–46, 57–58, 63–64, and 79; and Lawson, *Black Ballots*, pp. 140–47. Also see Stuart G. Brown, "Civil Rights and National Leadership: Eisenhower and Stevenson in the 1950s," *Ethics* 70 (January 1960): 118–34; and Allan Wolk, *The Presidency and Black Civil Rights—Eisenhower to Nixon* (Rutherford, N.J.: Fairleigh Dickinson University Press, 1971), pp. 219, 224, 228, and 242, both of which criticize Eisenhower's timidity on civil rights issues.

23.   The standard account is J.W. Anderson, *Eisenhower, Brownell, and the Congress: The Tangled Origins of the Civil Rights Bill of 1956–1957* (University: University of Alabama Press, 1964). A more recent and complete account appears in Lawson, *Black Ballots*, pp. 149–202. Other accounts include Carl A. Auerbach, "Jury Trials and Civil Rights," *New Leader* 40 (29 April 1957): 16–18; Telford Taylor, "Crux of the Civil Rights Debate," *New York Times Magazine*, 16 June 1957, p. 11; Walter F. Murphy, "Some Strange New Converts To the Cause of Civil Rights," *Reporter* 16 (27 June 1957): 13–14; Douglass Cater, "The Senate Debate on Civil Rights," *Reporter* 17 (8 August 1957): 37–40; Richard H.

Rovere, "Letter From Washington," *New Yorker* 33 (31 August 1957): 72–82; Carl A. Auerbach, "Is It Strong Enough To Do the Job?," *Reporter* 17 (5 September 1957): 13–15; Douglass Cater, "How the Senate Passed the Civil Rights Bill," *Reporter* 17 (5 September 1957): 9–13; C. Vann Woodward, "The Great Civil Rights Debate," *Commentary* 24 (October 1957): 283–91; Howard E. Shuman, "Senate Rules and the Civil Rights Bill: A Case Study," *American Political Science Review* 51 (December 1957): 955–75; Hubert H. Humphrey, *Beyond Civil Rights: A New Day of Equality* (New York: Random House, 1968), p. 73; and Paul H. Douglas, *In the Fullness of Time* (New York: Harcourt Brace Jovanovich, 1972), pp. 281–91. A good account of the events in July and August, drawn from the *New York Times* coverage at the time, is in Charles V. Hamilton, *The Bench and The Ballot: Southern Federal Judges and Black Voters* (New York: Oxford University Press, 1973), pp. 46–53 and 73. On the impact of black voters in the 1956 elections, see Henry Lee Moon, "The Negro Vote in the Presidential Election of 1956," *Journal of Negro Education* 26 (Summer 1957): 219–30. Moon's well-known argument stressing, and perhaps overemphasizing, the role that could be played by the northern black electorate, is set forth in *Balance of Power: The Negro Vote* (Garden City, N.Y.: Doubleday, 1948).

24. For a more detailed description of the 1957 act's provisions, see Dorsey E. Lane, "The Civil Rights Act of 1957," *Howard Law Journal* 4 (January 1958): 36–49. Armand Derfner, among others, has noted that the 1957 act "was essentially a codification of the major recommendations in the 1947 President's Committee report" ("Racial Discrimination and the Right to Vote," p. 545). On the early years of the Civil Rights Commission, see Foster Rhea Dulles, *The Civil Rights Commission: 1957–1965* (East Lansing: Michigan State University Press, 1968); Lawson, *Black Ballots*, pp. 213–20 and 227–32; Barbara Carter, "The Role of the Civil Rights Commission," *Reporter* 29 (4 July 1963): 10–14; and George T. Sulzner III, "The United States Commission on Civil Rights: A Study of Incrementalism in Policy-Making," Ph.D. dissertation, University of Michigan, 1967.

25. See Shuman, "Senate Rules," p. 975; and Bernard Schwartz, ed., *Statutory History of the United States, Civil Rights* (New York: Chelsea House, 1970), pp. 838–39. Hamilton has written, "The chief significance of the act lay in the fact that it was passed at all" (*The Bench and The Ballot*, p. 59).

26. Hamilton, *The Bench and The Ballot*, pp. 54–55.

27. 172 F. Supp. 552 (1959).

28. 171 F. Supp. 720 (1959), affirmed 267 F.2d 808.

29. 177 F. Supp. 355; 180 F. Supp. 10.

30. Decided *sub nominee U.S. v. Thomas*, 362 U.S. 58; 362 U.S. 17.

31. Accounts of the early litigation under the 1957 act can be found in the *Annual Reports of the Attorney General* for 1958, 1959, and 1960, and also in Ira M. Heyman, "Federal Remedies for Voteless Negroes," *California Law Review* 48 (May 1960): 190–215; and Lawson, *Black Ballots*, pp. 207–12.

32. Allan Lichtman, "The Federal Assault Against Voting Discrimination in the Deep South, 1957–1967," *Journal of Negro History* 54 (October 1969): 346–

67, at 347–48. Lichtman states, "Wilson White's confining directives and the temerity of the President and Attorney General drained all potential from the" 1957 act (p. 366). This excellent article is in fact a history of the Civil Rights Division. For further criticism of the Civil Rights Division in its early years, see Alexander Bickel, *Politics and the Warren Court* (New York: Harper & Row, 1965), p. 50; Elliff, "Aspects of Federal Civil Rights Enforcement," pp. 652–58; Lawson, *Black Ballots*, pp. 203–6; and Anthony Lewis, *Portrait of A Decade— The Second American Revolution* (New York: Random House, 1965), p. 113, who calls White "one of the most feeble initiators in history." The statistics on the number of complaints appear in the *Annual Report of the Attorney General, 1958*, p. 183, and on p. 195 of the 1959 *Annual Report*. At the end of fiscal 1959 only twenty-three complaints had been received since the establishment of the division, and only ten were being investigated. On the lack of lawyers in the South willing to take voting rights cases in the late 1950s and early 1960s, see Frank E. Schwelb, "From Illusion to Reality: Relief in Civil Rights Cases," *Notre Dame Lawyer* 48 (October 1972): 49–79, at 51–52.

33.   Barry E. Hawk and John J. Kirby, Jr., "Federal Protection of Negro Voting Rights," *Virginia Law Review* 51 (October 1965): 1051–1213, at 1060. Also see Comment, "Voting Rights: A Case Study of Madison Parish, Louisiana," *University of Chicago Law Review* 38 (Summer 1971): 726–87, at 738; and Donald S. Strong, *Negroes, Ballots and Judges* (University: University of Alabama Press, 1968), p. 5.

34.   Heyman, "Federal Remedies for Voteless Negroes," p. 204. Other law journal writers whose criticisms were similar to Heyman's included Charles A. Horsky, "The Supreme Court, Congress, and the Right to Vote," *Ohio State Law Journal* 20 (Summer 1959): 549–56, at 553; Alfred de Grazia, "A New Way Towards Equal Suffrage," *New York University Law Review* 34 (April 1959): 716–24, at 716; and John C. McDonald, "Judicial Protection of Minority Voting Rights: The Case for Constitutional Reform," *Ohio State Law Journal* 22 (Spring 1961): 390–420, at 410 and 418.

35.   See the *Annual Report of the Attorney General, 1958*, p. 182, and p. 194 of the 1959 *Annual Report*.

36.   U.S. Commission on Civil Rights, *1959 Report* (Washington: USGPO, 1959). Also see *Voting: 1961 Commission on Civil Rights Report* (Washington: USGPO, 1961).

37.   The standard account is Daniel M. Berman, *A Bill Becomes A Law: The Civil Rights Act of 1960* (New York: Macmillan, 1962). A revised edition was issued in 1966. Also see Lawson, *Black Ballots*, pp. 222–26 and 232–46; Anthony Lewis, "The Professionals Win Out Over Civil Rights," *Reporter* 22 (26 May 1960): 27 and 30; Paul H. Douglas, "The 1960 Voting Rights Bill: the Struggle, the Final Results, and the Reasons," *Journal of Intergroup Relations* 1 (Summer 1960): 82–86; and the brief comments made by Representative Clem Miller in *Member of the House—Letters of a Congressman* (New York: Charles Scribner's Sons, 1962), pp. 127–31.

38.   See Berman, *A Bill Becomes A Law*, pp. 107 and 117; Douglas, "The

1960 Voting Rights Bill," p. 82; Schwartz, *Statutory History*, p. 938; and Lawson, *Black Ballots*, pp. 246–48.

39. For a review of the provisions of the 1960 act, see Charles W. Havens III, "Federal Legislation to Safeguard Voting Rights: The Civil Rights Act of 1960," *Virginia Law Review* 46 (June 1960): 945–75. Also see Heyman, "Federal Remedies for Voteless Negroes," pp. 205–7. On the details of the referee provision, see Strong, *Negroes, Ballots and Judges*, p. 51. The rulings in the Macon County case appear at 362 U.S. 602 and 188 F. Supp. 759.

40. See Heyman, "Federal Remedies for Voteless Negroes," p. 213; J.W. Peltason, *Fifty-Eight Lonely Men*, rev. ed. (Urbana: University of Illinois Press, 1971), p. 252; and Charles V. Hamilton, "It Will Be Token Registration," *Southern Patriot* 18 (May 1960): 1, who correctly predicted, "The voting provisions of the new civil rights bill passed by Congress are cumbersome and complex and, probably, will have little meaning for most of the 3,735,000 potential Negro voters in the South."

41. The purge case was *U.S.* v. *Association of Citizens' Councils*, 196 F. Supp. 908. The district judge, Benjamin Dawkins, ordered the names of 570 purged black voters restored to the rolls and entered a "pattern or practice" finding in regard to the parish, although he declined to appoint a referee. Also see *Annual Report of the Attorney General, 1960*, pp. 193–95. The economic intimidation cases will be discussed shortly.

42. The Kennedy administration's decision to concentrate on court suits, while eschewing any effort to promote additional civil rights legislation in Congress during 1961 and 1962, has been commented on by a large number of writers. See, for instance, Alexander M. Bickel, "Civil Rights: The Kennedy Record," *New Republic* 147 (15 December 1962): 11–16; and two Southern Regional Council pamphlets: *The Federal Executive and Civil Rights* (Atlanta: SRC, 1961), and *Executive Support of Civil Rights* (Atlanta: SRC, 1962).

43. As Burke Marshall wrote in mid 1961, "The resistance encountered and the subsequent court actions have delayed compliance for months" (*Annual Report of the Attorney General, 1961*, p. 165). Also see pp. 181–83 of the 1963 *Annual Report* and p. 172 of the 1964 one, and U.S. Congress, House, Committee on Appropriations, *Hearings on Department of Justice Appropriations for 1966*, 89th Congress, 1st session, 1965, p. 171.

44. Those cases included *Kennedy* v. *Lynd*, in regard to Forrest County, Mississippi; *Kennedy* v. *Bryce* (Bossier Parish, La.); *Kennedy* v. *Clement* (Webster Parish, La.); *Kennedy* v. *Platt* (DeSoto Parish, La.); and *Kennedy* v. *Mitchell* (Caddo Parish, La.). The case that necessitated a ruling by the Fifth Circuit Court of Appeals was *Kennedy* v. *Bruce*, 298 F.2d 860, in which District Judge Daniel H. Thomas initially had rejected the department's request for an order instructing the Wilcox County, Alabama, registrar to hand over his records.

45. 230 F. Supp. 873.

46. *Crum Dinkins* v. *Attorney General*, 285 F.2d 430, cert. denied 366 U.S. 913. Also see *Annual Report of the Attorney General, 1961*, p. 175; and *Coleman*

v. *Kennedy*, *Campbell* v. *Kennedy*, and *Ashford* v. *Kennedy*, all at 373 U.S. 950.

47.   For Atlas's testimony, see U.S. Commission on Civil Rights, *Hearings—New Orleans, Louisiana, 1960 and 1961* (Washington: USGPO, 1961). Hamilton provides a detailed account of the story in *The Bench and The Ballot*, pp. 193–205. Also see Strong, *Negroes, Ballots and Judges*, p. 11; and 6 *Race Relations Law Reporter* 474 (1961). In regard to the voting discrimination in East Carroll Parish, see *U.S.* v. *Manning*, 205 F. Supp. 172. No black had been registered there since 1922.

48.   *U.S.* v. *Beaty* and *U.S.* v. *Barcroft* dealt with Haywood County, while *U.S.* v. *Atkeison* was in regard to Fayette. See 288 F.2d 653 (1961); 6 *Race Relations Law Reporter* 201 (1961); and 7 *Race Relations Law Reporter* 484 (1962). Hamilton provides an account of the cases in *The Bench and The Ballot*, pp. 182–92.

49.   The number of articles on the southwest Tennessee situation and its development over the years since 1959 is substantial. The *Southern Patriot* has provided consistent, though often opinionated, coverage. The June, September, and December 1960 issues cover the first part of the story, while later developments are reported in the February 1961, February 1962, September 1962, August 1966, November 1967, and November 1969 issues. An oral history account is provided in Robert Hamburger, *Our Portion of Hell: Fayette County, Tennessee* (New York: Links, 1973). An earlier account, focusing on the summer of 1964, is Fayette County Project Volunteers, *Step By Step* (New York: W.W. Norton, 1965). Also see John Doar and Dorothy Landsberg, "The Performance of the FBI in Investigating Violations of Federal Laws Protecting the Right to Vote—1960–1967," in U.S. Congress, Senate, Select Committee to Study Governmental Operations with Respect to Intelligence Activities, *Hearings on Intelligence Activities, Federal Bureau of Investigation*, 94th Congress, 1st session, 1975, pp. 888–991, at 912–21; Douglas F. Dowd, "The Campaign in Fayette County," *Monthly Review* 15 (April 1964): 675–79; R. V. Denenberg, "Students Get the Vote Out," *Nation* 199 (10 August 1964): 45–49; Dwayne Walls, *Fayette County, Tennessee: Tragedy and Confrontation* (Atlanta: Southern Regional Council, 1969); James Forman, *The Making of Black Revolutionaries* (New York: Macmillan, 1972), pp. 116–45; and Robert Coles and Tom Davey, "Saving Remnant," *New Republic* 175 (26 September 1976): 20–24.

50.   *U.S.* v. *Board of Education of Greene County*, 332 F.2d 40. Also see Hamilton *The Bench and The Ballot*, pp. 206–17.

51.   Note, "Private Economic Coercion and the Civil Rights Act of 1957," *Yale Law Journal* 71 (January 1962): 536–50, at 550.

52.   Those who noted the difficulties involved in prosecuting subtle acts of economic retaliation included Heyman, "Federal Remedies for Voteless Negroes," p. 210; Richard A. Givens, "Federal Protection of Voting Rights Against Economic Interference," *Rutgers Law Review* 20 (Summer 1966): 696–709, at 698–99; and John Doar, in Doar and Landsberg, "The Performance of the FBI," pp. 910–11. While this problem was severe in *economic* intimidation cases brought under section 1971(b), it was somewhat less of a problem in pursuing

instances of *physical* intimidation, as was done in *U.S.* v. *Wood*, 295 F.2d 772, in regard to the Walthall County, Mississippi sheriff; *U.S.* v. *Mathews*, in regard to the Terrell County, Georgia sheriff; *U.S.* v. *Holmes County*; and *U.S.* v. *City of Greenwood*. The Walthall County story, involving an attack upon civil rights worker John Hardy, has been retold in numerous histories of the movement. One of the original reports is Donald C. Bacon, *Wall Street Journal*, 6 November 1961, p. 1. Also see Hamilton's account in *The Bench and The Ballot*, pp. 178–82. The best journalistic coverage of the movement in the South in the early 1960s was Claude Sitton's in the *New York Times*. A number of his stories concerned Terrell County and its sheriff, Z.T. Mathews, including a particularly vivid one on page 1 of the 27 July 1962 *Times*. Others are excerpted in Lewis, *Portrait of A Decade*, which also includes an account of the Holmes County incident (pp. 290–93).

53. On the voucher system, see Strong, *Negroes, Ballots and Judges*, p. 29.

54. *Annual Report of the Attorney General, 1961*, p. 8. Also see p. 192. See as well the 1962 *Annual Report*, p. 161, and the 1963 *Annual Report*, p. 180. Note also Burke Marshall, *Federalism and Civil Rights* (New York: Columbia University Press, 1964), p. 23; and an earlier article by Marshall, "Federal Protection of Negro Voting Rights," *Law and Contemporary Problems* 27 (Summer 1962): 455–67. A related piece in the same volume of that journal by the Civil Rights Commission's staff director is Berl I. Bernhard, "The Federal Fact-Finding Experience—A Guide to Negro Enfranchisement," pp. 468–80. One locale in which such tactics proved successful was Baker County, Georgia. See Claude Sitton, *New York Times*, 10 July 1963, p. 10.

55. See Victor S. Navasky, *Kennedy Justice* (New York: Atheneum, 1971), pp. 117–19 and 207. Also see Lawson, *Black Ballots*, pp. 265–66; Carl M. Brauer, *John F. Kennedy and the Second Reconstruction* (New York: Columbia University Press, 1977), pp. 112–16; Reese Cleghorn, "The Angels Are White," *New Republic* 149 (17 August 1963): 12–14; Louis E. Lomax, *The Negro Revolt* (New York: Harper & Brothers, 1962), pp. 229–40; and Howell Raines, *My Soul Is Rested* (New York: G.P. Putnam's Sons, 1977), pp. 227–31.

56. Watters and Cleghorn, *Climbing Jacob's Ladder*, pp. 114–15.

57. Perhaps the brightest achievements of the Louisiana drives were the measurable increase registered in Iberville Parish and, in the fall of 1963, the registration of the first black voter in West Feliciana Parish in sixty years. On the Louisiana drives, see August Meier and Elliott Rudwick, *CORE: A Study in the Civil Rights Movement, 1942–1968* (New York: Oxford University Press, 1973), pp. 265–67; Watters and Cleghorn, *Climbing Jacob's Ladder*, pp. 121–28; and two pieces in Friedman, *Southern Justice*: Collins, Douglas, and Elie, "Clinton, Louisiana," and Peter R. Teachout, "Louisiana Underlaw," pp. 57–79.

58. Locales where VEP associated projects were successful included Tallahassee, Jacksonville, Miami, Savannah, Raleigh, Petersburg, Richmond, Charlotte, Birmingham, Nashville, Portsmouth, and Rome, Georgia—all cities. On the VEP pullout from Mississippi, see Wiley A. Branton, "To Register to Vote in Mississippi," *New South* 20 (February 1965): 10–15. Also see Holloway, *The*

Politics of the Southern Negro, p. 70. Invaluable accounts of movement activity in Mississippi in the early 1960s are Howard Zinn, *SNCC: The New Abolitionists* (Boston: Beacon Press, 1965), pp. 62–78; Anne Moody, *Coming of Age in Mississippi* (New York: Dial Press, 1968); and Jack Newfield, *A Prophetic Minority* (New York: New American Library, 1966), pp. 69–96. Also see Neil R. McMillen's excellent recent article, "Black Enfranchisement in Mississippi: Federal Enforcement and Black Protest in the 1960s," *Journal of Southern History* 43 (August 1977): 351–72, at 360–66; Doar and Landsberg, "The Performance of the FBI," pp. 921–28; Jack Minnis, "Courage and Terror in Mississippi," *Dissent* 10 (Summer 1963): 228–31; John Fischer, "A Small Band of Practical Heroes," *Harper's* 227 (October 1963): 16–28; Howard Zinn, "The Battle-Scarred Youngsters," *Nation* 197 (5 October 1963): 193–97; and Carleton Mabee, "Voting in the Black Belt," *Negro History Bulletin* 27 (December 1963): 50–56. A good account of the late 1963 Freedom Election appears in Jeannine Herron, "Underground Election," *Nation* 197 (7 December 1963): 387–89.

59.   Watters and Cleghorn, *Climbing Jacob's Ladder*, p. 121. Also see pp. 127–28. "Much energy of the movement was consumed in all areas in instructions on how to fill out the test forms, the straightforward ones as well as the tricky." Group meetings were recognized as lending a sense of strength and support to individuals who were contemplating making an attempt to register. See the remarks of Charles Sherrod that Watters and Cleghorn quote on p. 172.

60.   Holloway estimates that all in all, COFO registered fewer than 1,000 new black voters over the course of the 1964 summer. See *The Politics of the Southern Negro*, p. 70. Two other sources that also speak of the limited impact that the Summer Project had upon black registration levels in the twenty counties and twenty-five towns in other counties in which it worked are U.S. Commission on Civil Rights, *Hearings on Voting in Jackson, Miss., February 16–20, 1965* (Washington: USGPO, 1965); and U.S. Commission on Civil Rights, *Voting in Mississippi* (Washington: USGPO, 1965). Both of these publications also offer extensive accounts of the harassment and intimidation that pervaded the 1964 summer. For some first-rate analysis of the probable public opinion benefits of the 1964 summer, see McMillen, "Black Enfranchisement in Mississippi," pp. 364–67.

61.   *Climbing Jacob's Ladder*, p. 139. Many participant-observer accounts of the Freedom Summer have been published. Perhaps the best and most complete is Len Holt, *The Summer That Didn't End* (New York: William Morrow, 1965). Others include William McCord, *Mississippi: The Long Hot Summer* (New York: W.W. Norton, 1965); Sally Belfrage, *Freedom Summer* (New York: Viking Press, 1965); Tracy Sugarman, *Stranger at the Gates* (New York: Hill and Wang, 1966); Nicholas von Hoffman, *Mississippi Notebook* (New York: David White, 1964); Elizabeth Sutherland, ed., *Letters From Mississippi* (New York: McGraw-Hill, 1965); William M. Kunstler, *Deep In My Heart* (New York: William Morrow, 1966), pp. 307–23; and Paul Good, *The Trouble I've Seen* (Washington: Howard University Press, 1975), pp. 107–53. The racist view of the Mississippi summer can be seen in Medford Evans, "Mississippi: The Long Hot Summer," *American Opinion* 7 (November 1964): 7–18.

Don Whitehead's *Attack on Terror: The FBI Against the Ku Klux Klan in Mississippi* (New York: Funk & Wagnalls, 1970) and William Bradford Huie's *Three Lives For Mississippi* (New York: WCC Books, 1965) both focus on the killing of Chaney, Schwerner, and Goodman. Also see Huie's earlier article, "The Untold Story of the Mississippi Murders," *Saturday Evening Post* 237 (5 September 1964): 11–15; Jack Mendelsohn, *The Martyrs* (New York: Harper & Row, 1966), pp. 109–32; Doar and Landsberg, "The Performance of the FBI," pp. 933–39; and a special 1964 issue of *Ramparts* entitled "Mississippi Eyewitness," which features several excellent articles. For details on efforts by blacks to run as candidates for electoral offices in Mississippi in the early 1960s, see Leslie B. McLemore, "The Effect of Political Participation Upon A Closed Society—A State in Transition: The Changing Political Climate in Mississippi," *Negro Educational Review* 23 (January 1972): 3–12; and Jerry DeMuth, " 'Tired of Being Sick and Tired,' " *Nation* 198 (1 June 1964): 548–51. Estimates are that there were fewer than twenty-five elected black public officials throughout the South as of the early 1960s. See Neal R. Peirce, *The Deep South States of America* (New York: W.W. Norton, 1974), p. 21. The standard history of Mississippi in the early 1960s is James W. Silver, *Mississippi: The Closed Society* (New York: Harcourt, Brace & World, 1964). Other accounts worth noting are Barbara Carter, "The Fifteenth Amendment Comes to Mississippi," *Reporter* 28 (17 January 1963): 20–24; Claude Sitton, *New York Times*, 2 March 1964, p. 20; James Atwater, " 'If We Can Crack Mississippi. . . ,' " *Saturday Evening Post* 237 (25 July 1964): 15–19; Calvin Trillin, "Letter From Jackson," *New Yorker* 40 (29 August 1964): 80–105; Jerry DeMuth, "Freedom Moves in to Stay," *Nation* 199 (14 September 1964): 104–5 and 108–10; Elizabeth Sutherland, "The Cat and Mouse Game," *Nation* 199 (14 September 1964): 105–8; Bardwell L. Smith, "Meanwhile, in Mississippi," *Commonweal* 82 (2 April 1965): 39–42; and two articles in Friedman, *Southern Justice*: Paul G. Chevigny, "A Busy Spring in the Magnolia State," pp. 13–34, and Marvin Braiterman, "Harold and the Highwaymen," pp. 88–102. See also U.S. Commission on Civil Rights, *Law Enforcement—A Report on Equal Protection in the South* (Washington: USGPO, 1965).

62.   The basic details of the MFDP challenge appear in the brief it submitted to the Convention's Credentials Committee. It is most easily accessible in U.S. Congress, House, Committee on the Judiciary, *The Enforcement of the Voting Rights Act—Hearings Before the Civil Rights Oversight Subcommittee*, 92nd Congress, 1st session, 1971, pp. 124–202. Narrative accounts of the challenge appear in Holt, *The Summer That Didn't End*; Watters and Cleghorn, *Climbing Jacob's Ladder*, pp. 281–89; Lawson, *Black Ballots*, pp. 300–6; and Humphrey, *Beyond Civil Rights*, pp. 110–12. A long list of articles in movement periodicals related to both the Convention challenge and the subsequent 1965 challenge of Mississippi's congressmen is contained in Jennifer McDowell and Milton Loventhal, *Black Politics: A Study and Annotated Bibliography of the Mississippi Freedom Democratic Party* (San Jose, Calif.: Bibliographic Information Center for the Study of Political Science, 1971).

63.   The two other instances were in Greenwood on March 31, 1963, and in

Itta Bena on June 26, 1964. See Strong, *Negroes, Ballots and Judges*, p. 16, in regard to *U.S.* v. *City of Greenwood*; and Watters and Cleghorn, *Climbing Jacob's Ladder*, pp. 59 and 228. Also see Doar and Landsberg, "The Performance of the FBI," p. 940; and Lawson, *Black Ballots*, pp. 275–77. Although the FBI did not intervene actively in the great majority of situations where it might have, some believed that the mere presence of agents in the state "held white terrorists in check." See John Herbers, *New York Times*, 20 August 1964, p. 1.

64. Marshall, *Federalism and Civil Rights*, p. 30. Also see Simon Lazarus III, "Theories of Federalism and Civil Rights," *Yale Law Journal* 75 (May 1966): 1007–52.

65. Navasky, *Kennedy Justice*, pp. 176 and 185. Also see pp. 132 and 207. Typical of the movement's view was the statement made by Meier and Rudwick in *CORE*, p. 180: "CORE's work in the South—like that of other civil rights organizations—was stymied by the ambivalence of President Kennedy's policy, which encouraged the voter registration drive but, faced with southern power and negative attitudes of FBI investigators, failed to protect civil rights activists and blacks attempting to register." Also see Haywood Burns, "The Rule of Law in the South," *Commentary* 40 (September 1965): 80–90; and Richard A. Wasserstrom, "Federalism and Civil Rights," *University of Chicago Law Review* 33 (Winter 1966): 406–13. Navasky has argued persuasively that perhaps the prime explanation for the administration's inability to provide protection lay in the FBI's unwillingness to investigate alleged civil rights violations by local law enforcement personnel with whom the bureau often worked on other types of cases, and that the Kennedys were either unable or unwilling to order FBI Director Hoover, whose own prejudices were well-known, to take a more aggressive stance in regard to civil rights violations. See *Kennedy Justice*, pp. 109, 125, 128, and 134. Far less valuable is John T. Elliff, *Crime, Dissent, and the Attorney General: The Justice Department in the 1960s* (Beverly Hills, Calif.: Sage Publications, 1971). John Doar, however, has avoided making any harsh criticisms of the bureau's performance in the South, though he has termed it "lackluster." See Doar and Landsberg, "The Performance of the FBI," passim, esp. p. 949. For a more critical view, see Arlie Schardt, "Civil Rights: Too Much, Too Late," in Pat Watters and Stephen Gillers, eds., *Investigating the FBI* (Garden City, N.Y.: Doubleday, 1973), pp. 167–205, esp. pp. 167–83.

66. *Annual Report of the Attorney General, 1962*, p. 161; Note, "Judicial Performance in the Fifth Circuit," *Yale Law Journal* 73 (November 1963): 90–133. Also see the 1964 *Annual Report*, p. 181, where Marshall admits that "the law's delays" have "seriously inhibited the effectiveness" of the 1957 and 1960 acts; and the 1965 *Annual Report*, p. 173, where his successor, John Doar, spoke of the "lengthy delays" experienced in "some judicial districts."

67. Strong, *Negroes, Ballots and Judges*, p. 68. General overviews of the southern federal judges include J.W. Peltason, *Fifty-Eight Lonely Men*; Kenneth N. Vines, "Federal District Judges and Race Relations Cases in the South," *Journal of Politics* 26 (May 1964): 337–57; Robert J. Steamer, "The Role of the Federal District Courts in the Segregation Controversy," *Journal of Politics* 22

(August 1960): 417–37; Reed Sarratt, *The Ordeal of Desegregation* (New York: Harper & Row, 1966), chapter 8; George W. Spicer, "The Federal Judiciary and Political Change in the South," *Journal of Politics* 26 (February 1964): 154–76; Kenneth N. Vines, "Courts and Political Change in the South," *Journal of Social Issues* 22 (January 1966): 59–72; and Michael W. Giles and Thomas G. Walker, "Judicial Policy-Making and Southern School Segregation," *Journal of Politics* 37 (November 1975): 917–36. Two interesting pieces written by judges on the Fifth Circuit Court of Appeals exhibit sympathy toward the local peer pressures with which judges, especially those on the district courts, must deal when a controversial ruling is handed down. See John Minor Wisdom, "The Frictionmaking, Exacerbating Political Role of Federal Courts," *Southwestern Law Journal* 21 (Summer 1967): 411–28, at 424 and 426; and John R. Brown, "Hail to the Chief: Hutcheson, the Judge," *Texas Law Review* 38 (December 1959): 140–46, at 145. On the higher state courts, see Michael Meltsner, "Southern Appellate Courts: A Dead End," in Friedman, *Southern Justice*, pp. 136–54.

68.   On Cox, see Strong, *Negroes, Ballots and Judges*, pp. 63 and 75; Hawk and Kirby, "Federal Protection of Negro Voting Rights," pp. 1113–17; and Gerald Stern, "Judge William Harold Cox and the Right to Vote in Clarke County, Mississippi," in Friedman, *Southern Justice*, pp. 165–86. In addition to *Lynd*, Cox's well-known cases included *U.S.* v. *Warner*; *U.S.* v. *Wood*; *U.S.* v. *Holmes County*; *Kennedy* v. *Owen*; *U.S.* v. *Daniel*; *U.S.* v. *Green*; *U.S.* v. *Mississippi*; and *U.S.* v. *Ramsey*, the latter of which was the Clarke County case. In the great majority of these Cox was overruled by the appellate court. See 339 F.2d 679 and 331 F.2d 824. On Cox's conduct in *Kennedy* v. *Owen*, see "More on Kennedy's Judges," *New Republic* 149 (26 October 1963): 5. A subsequent incident is related in Alexander M. Bickel, "Impeach Judge Cox," *New Republic* 153 (4 September 1965): 13.

69.   Fortunately for the department, and for blacks residing in Forrest County, within several weeks the Fifth Circuit Court of Appeals overturned Cox's ruling and issued an injunction against Lynd which specified that in the future he must give to black applicants for registration the same assistance that he previously had given only to whites. It further mandated that he choose sections of the Constitution for interpretation tests more fairly, that he no longer reject applications on the basis of minor errors or omissions, and that he not impose a requirement that rejected applicants wait six months before applying once again. In addition, the appeals court administered a strong verbal tongue-lashing to Cox for his handling of the case. At the time, this ruling represented the Justice Department's first successful prosecution of a voting case in Mississippi, and its issuance evoked a typical response from the Mississippi legislature: passage of four bills requiring (1) that all blanks on an application form be filled in, (2) that registrars not inform rejected applicants of the reason for their failure, (3) that the names of all applicants be printed in the local newspaper, and (4) that applicants prove their "good moral character" to the registrar's satisfaction.

Even after that court order, however, Forrest County's resistance did not cease, for within two months the appeals court had cited Lynd for civil and criminal contempt of its injunction. After a hearing in September 1962, the court in July 1963 found Lynd guilty of civil contempt and ordered the registration of forty-three specific blacks and the cessation of discriminatory registration practices. Despite that ruling, in April 1964 the Justice Department was back in court charging that Lynd was continuing to employ racially discriminatory registration practices. Finally, on June 15, 1965, the appeals court again found Lynd in civil contempt and entered a "pattern or practice" finding against Forrest County, ordering that the actual standards employed in the registration of white applicants in the past be applied to future black applicants as well. Only then, in the summer of 1965, with the threat of federal registrars hanging in the air, did Forrest County begin approving the applications of qualified blacks, some one thousand of whom registered in less than two months.

As Burke Marshall indicated in his last annual report as assistant attorney general for civil rights, the *Lynd* case sharply revealed the effort and lengths to which the department was forced to go in instances where both the defendant and the district judge were extremely recalcitrant. Only the unusually active role the appellate court took in the case produced the eventual, though long-delayed, registration of Forrest County's first black voters. See 301 F.2d 818, cert. denied 371 U.S. 952; 321 F.2d 26; 349 F.2d 785; and the *Annual Reports of the Attorney General* for 1963, 1964, and 1965, at pp. 183; 175 and 181; and 172, respectively. Also see U.S. Congress, House, Committee on Appropriations, *Hearings on Department of Justice Appropriations for 1966*, pp. 172–73.

70.   On Thomas, see three cases in which the Court of Appeals reversed him: *Kennedy* v. *Bruce*, 298 F.2d 860; *U.S.* v. *Bruce*, 353 F.2d 474; and *U.S.* v. *Logue*, 344 F.2d 290. Thomas delayed one Wilcox County case sixteen months, and the Choctaw County case of *U.S.* v. *Ford*, twenty-two months. Thomas's most infamous case was *U.S.* v. *Mayton*, in which he entered a "pattern or practice" finding against Perry County but subsequently failed to appoint a referee or to take any action himself on the requests for consideration sent to him by rejected applicants who claimed that they possessed all the necessary qualifications. Finally the Justice Department moved against Thomas himself in the court of appeals, and that body ordered him to process the letters he had received (335 F.2d 153). Thomas then did appoint a referee, O.S. Burke, who found 33 of the 257 rejected applicants who presented themselves to be qualified. Thomas was also the subject of a mandamus action in regard to a Dallas County case which we shall discuss in the following chapter. On Thomas's rulings, see Strong, *Negroes, Ballots and Judges*, pp. 43, 52–54, and 84.

71.   Clayton was best known for taking twenty-eight months to order Bolivar County's registrar to hand over his records to the Justice Department in *Kennedy* v. *Lewis*. The appropriate order was entered eventually by the court of appeals. Two voting discrimination cases in which Clayton was overruled by the appeals court were *U.S.* v. *Dogan*, 314 F.2d 767, pertaining to Tallahatchie County, and *U.S.* v. *Duke*, in regard to Panola County, in which the appeals court entered an important order commanding that the previous real standards applied to whites be applied to future black applicants as well. Clayton had

waited eighteen months before bringing the *Duke* case to trial, and it was not until fourteen months after that the appeals court reversed him and entered a remedy. See Strong, *Negroes, Ballots and Judges*, p. 82; and, in regard to Panola County, Frederick M. Wirt, *Politics of Southern Equality* (Chicago: Aldine, 1970).

72.   West was best known for his outspoken criticism of the Supreme Court and its decision in *Brown*. See *Davis* v. *East Baton Rouge School Board*, 214 F. Supp. 624. Two voting cases in which his actions were open to criticism were *U.S.* v. *Palmer* and *U.S.* v. *Harvey*. See Strong, *Negroes, Ballots and Judges*, p. 73.

73.   Some observers felt Dawkins to be less obstructive than his colleagues cited above. See Charles V. Hamilton, "Southern Judges and Negro Voting Rights: The Judicial Approach to the Solution of Controversial Social Problems," *Wisconsin Law Review* 1965 (Fall): 72–102, at 88–91, who terms Dawkins a "gradualist." Peltason, however, spoke of him in 1961 as being "among the more ardent segregationists serving on the federal bench" (*Fifty-Eight Lonely Men*, p. 113). A detailed discussion of Dawkin's handling of repeated litigation concerning voting discrimination in Madison Parish is contained in Comment, "Voting Rights: A Case Study of Madison Parish," esp. pp. 742–43.

74.   Derfner, "Racial Discrimination and the Right to Vote," p. 548. A definitive account of the Fifth Circuit Court of Appeals in the 1960s remains to be written. As Watters and Cleghorn have observed, "The history of the civil rights revolution in the South might have been very different but for this force within the Fifth Circuit" (*Climbing Jacob's Ladder*, p. 223). Two relevant articles on the court are Shirley Fingerhood, "The Fifth Circuit Court of Appeals," in Friedman, *Southern Justice*, pp. 214–27; and Burton M. Atkins and William Zavoina, "Judicial Leadership on the Court of Appeals: A Probability Analysis of Panel Assignment in Race Relations Cases on the Fifth Circuit," *American Journal of Political Science* 18 (November 1974): 701–11. For a commentary on "the four" civil rights supporters by their most outspoken critic on the court, ultraconservative Ben F. Cameron, see Cameron's dissent in *Armstrong* v. *Board of Education of Birmingham*, 323 F.2d 337. Also see Note, "Judicial Performance in the Fifth Circuit," pp. 120–21.

75.   All told, the Kennedy administration made twenty appointments within the Fifth Circuit, eighteen at the district court level and two (Griffin B. Bell and Walter Gewin) to the appeals court when it was expanded from seven to nine members in 1961. Gewin, plus five of the district court nominees, Cox, West, J. Robert Elliott of Georgia, Clarence Allgood of Alabama, and Frank Ellis of Louisiana, in their eventual decisions often took positions on civil rights matters that were directly opposed to those of the Justice Department. Prior to his appointment, Cox apparently had given personal assurances to Robert F. Kennedy that he would do his constitutional duty in civil rights cases. See Arthur M. Schlesinger, Jr., *A Thousand Days—John F. Kennedy in the White House* (Boston: Houghton Mifflin, 1965), p. 698; Navasky, *Kennedy Justice*, p. 250; and Wolk, *The Presidency and Black Civil Rights*, pp. 102–4. Also see Louis Lusky,

"Justice With A Southern Accent," *Harper's* 228 (March 1964): 69–77. For later commentary on the Kennedy appointments, see Navasky, *Kennedy Justice*, pp. 255 and 269; Harold W. Chase, *Federal Judges: The Appointing Process* (Minneapolis: University of Minnesota Press, 1972), pp. 81–82 and 118; Brauer, *John F. Kennedy*, pp. 122–24; Mary H. Curzan, "A Case Study in the Selection of Federal Judges in the Fifth Circuit, 1953–63," Ph.D. dissertation, Yale University, 1968; Watters and Cleghorn, *Climbing Jacob's Ladder*, pp. 223, 226, and 240; Leon Friedman, "Judge Bryan Simpson and His Reluctant Brethren," in Friedman, ed., *Southern Justice*, pp. 187–213; Thomas E. Cronin, *The State of the Presidency* (Boston: Little, Brown, 1975), p. 57; Bickel, "Civil Rights: The Kennedy Record," pp. 11 and 16; Note, "Judicial Performance in the Fifth Circuit," pp. 106 and 133; and McMillen, "Black Enfranchisement in Mississippi," pp. 357–58.

76.   For a more detailed account, see Lawson, *Black Ballots*, pp. 290–93; and Brauer, *John F. Kennedy*, pp. 131–37.

77.   See John and E.W. Kenworthy, "The 'Under Standing Neorger' And His Right to Vote," *Reporter* 30 (26 March 1964): 32–34; U.S. Congress, Senate, *Congressional Record* 109 (pt. 5), p. 5952, where a letter of 2 April 1963 from Robert F. Kennedy to Lyndon B. Johnson appears; Brauer, *John F. Kennedy*, pp. 212–14 and 221–24; and Alexander M. Bickel, "The Civil Rights Act of 1964," *Commentary* 38 (August 1964): 33–39, at 36. The Kennedy proposals bore a close resemblance to the recommendations made by the Civil Rights Commission in its *1959 Report*.

78.   Derfner, "Racial Discrimination and the Right to Vote," p. 547. A good account of the voting provisions of the then pending 1964 act is contained in Donald P. Kommers, "The Right to Vote and Its Implementation," *Notre Dame Lawyer* 39 (June 1964): 365–410, at 404–10. Prior to those final pages the article also contains an excellent summary discussion of voting rights developments in the previous quarter-century. Implicit criticism of the 1964 act's provisions occurs on p. 415 of Monroe Lee Billington, *The American South* (New York: Charles Scribner's Sons, 1971), and on p. 118 of his subsequent *The Political South in the Twentieth Century* (New York: Charles Scribner's Sons, 1975). Also see Hawk and Kirby, "Federal Protection of Negro Voting Rights," p. 1190; and Dulles, *The Civil Rights Commission*, p. 241. On the limited impact of the 1964 act's voting provisions, see *Congressional Quarterly Weekly Report*, 9 April 1965, p. 617.

79.   No effort will be made here to survey the remarkable series of important rulings Johnson has handed down over the last two decades. A full-length scholarly evaluation of his career remains to be written. In the meantime, see Robert F. Kennedy, Jr., *Judge Frank M. Johnson, Jr.* (New York: G. P. Putnam's Sons, 1978), and the following journalistic profiles: the cover story in the 12 May 1967 issue of *Time*; Ray Jenkins, *New York Times*, 21 April 1975, p. 20; Neil Maxwell, *Wall Street Journal*, 15 April 1976, p. 1; Steven Brill, "The Real Governor of Alabama," *New York* 9 (26 April 1976): 37–41; Ray Jenkins, *New York Times*, 18 August 1977, pp. 1 and 28; and Lawrence Wright's well-done but

poorly timed "Atticus Finch Goes to Washington," *New Times* 9 (9 December 1977): 30–49. For a no-holds-barred exposition of Johnson's views, see the text of his remarks at the University of Alabama on 4 November 1975, entitled "The Alabama Punting Syndrome" (copy in author's possession).

80. *U.S.* v. *Alabama*, 192 F. Supp. 677 (1961). Within Macon County lay the city of Tuskegee, whose boundaries the Alabama legislature had gerrymandered in the late 1950s in what proved to be a vain attempt to exclude black voters from the city and its elections. See Lewis Jones and Stanley Smith, *Tuskegee, Alabama: Voting Rights and Economic Pressure* (New York: Anti-Defamation League of B'nai B'rith, 1958); Charles V. Hamilton, *Minority Politics in Black Belt Alabama* (New York: McGraw-Hill, 1962); C.G. Gomillion, "The Tuskegee Voting Story," *Freedomways* 2 (Summer 1962): 231–36; Charles V. Hamilton, "The Voteless Seek A Voice," *Southern Patriot* 17 (December 1959): 1; and Bernard Taper, *Gomillion versus Lightfoot* (New York: McGraw-Hill, 1962). The best account of the Macon County case, as well as of those pertaining to Bullock and Montgomery, is chapter 5 of Hamilton, *The Bench and The Ballot*. Also see his earlier article, "Southern Judges and Negro Voting Rights," pp. 83 and 88. An instructive comment by John Doar appears on p. 38 of Brill, "The Real Governor of Alabama." A good account of the changes in Macon County that resulted from Johnson's actions, and the resulting increase in black registration, is Bernard Taper, "A Break With Tradition," *New Yorker* 41 (24 July 1965): 58–86. Also see Paul Good, "Tuskegee's Negro Majority," *Reporter* 33 (1 July 1965): 18–21; and C.G. Gomillion, "Civic Democracy in Tuskegee," *Freedomways* 5 (Summer 1965): 412–16.

81. *Annual Report of the Attorney General, 1962*, p. 162.

82. 212 F. Supp. 913 (1962). Johnson also ordered the immediate registration of 1,076 specific blacks. Also see Johnson's opinion in a subsequent Montgomery County case, *U.S.* v. *Parker*, 236 F. Supp. 511 (1964), and the comments about *Penton* in U.S. Congress, House, Committee on Appropriations, *Hearings on Department of Justice Appropriations for 1964*, 88th Congress, 1st session, 1963, pp. 117–18.

83. See the Court of Appeals' rulings in *U.S.* v. *Duke*, 332 F.2d 759, in regard to Panola County, Mississippi; and *U.S.* v. *Ward*, 349 F.2d 795, in regard to Madison Parish, Louisiana. Also see Judge Rives's dissent in *U.S.* v. *Ramsey*, 331 F.2d 824, 833. As Derfner reports, the idea of "freezing" was present in both the 1960 and 1964 acts. See "Racial Discrimination and the Right to Vote," pp. 546–47. The 1960 act, in effect, directed the district courts to use the registrar's own standards if those had been less stringent than what was specified in state statutes. See Note, "The Federal Voting Referee Plan and the Alteration of State Voting Standards," *Yale Law Journal* 72 (March 1963): 770–87, which also devotes some attention to the *Penton* ruling. Also see Michael Dowling, "The Freezing Concept and Voter Qualifications," *Hastings Law Journal* 16 (February 1965): 440–45; Note, "Freezing Voter Qualifications to Aid Negro Registration," *Michigan Law Review* 63 (March 1965): 932–38; Owen M. Fiss, "*Gaston County* v. *United States*: Fruition of the Freezing Principle," *Supreme Court*

Review 1969, pp. 379–445; Schwelb, "From Illusion to Reality;" and Hawk and Kirby, "Federal Protection of Negro Voting Rights," p. 1138.

84. See Hawk and Kirby, "Federal Protection of Negro Voting Rights," p. 1189.

85. *U.S.* v. *Louisiana*, 225 F. Supp. 353, and *Louisiana* v. *U.S.*, 380 U.S. 145. Also see 265 F. Supp. 703, and 386 U.S. 270. Freezing was involved in this case as well. See 380 U.S. 154. On *U.S.* v. *Mississippi*, the citations are 229 F. Supp. 925; reversed and remanded, 380 U.S. 128. Also see 256 F. Supp. 344. The four new qualifications added in 1962 are detailed in n. 69 above. In response to the Louisiana legislature's new enactment, the Justice Department filed a similar challenge in December 1963. Another such suit, *U.S.* v. *Baggett*, was filed in January 1965 challenging Alabama's new and difficult literacy-comprehension test, but it was mooted by the Voting Rights Act and dismissed. See the *Annual Report of the Attorney General* for 1962 through 1965. Also see Derfner, "Racial Discrimination and the Right to Vote," p. 550; Note, "Civil Rights—Supreme Court Hears Challenge to Southern Voter Registration Systems," *University of Pennsylvania Law Review* 113 (February 1965): 587–606; Hawk and Kirby, "Federal Protection of Negro Voting Rights," p. 1175; and Strong, *Negroes, Ballots and Judges*, pp. 55–59.

86. *Annual Report of the Attorney General, 1965*, p. 173.

87. Marshall indicated an apparent sympathy with this position when he stressed that the only counties that had shown any marked improvement in black registration after suits were brought were those that received "constant, close federal judicial supervision of the registrars' conduct of their office," such as that given by Johnson in the Macon and Bullock cases. See *Federalism and Civil Rights*, pp. 25–26 and 30.

88. See Comment, "Voting Rights: A Case Study of Madison Parish," pp. 742, 745–47, and 751; and Alexander M. Bickel, "Registering Negro Voters in the South," *New Republic* 152 (20 February 1965): 9–10.

89. See Alexander M. Bickel, "The Voting Rights Bill is Tough," *New Republic* 152 (3 April 1965): 16–18, at 18.

90. Elbert P. Tuttle, "Equality and the Vote," *New York University Law Review* 41 (April 1966): 245–66, at 257 and 264. Also see Bernhard, "The Federal Fact-Finding Experience," p. 477. For evidence on the time delays, see Lichtman, "The Federal Assault Against Voting Discrimination," p. 364; and U.S. Commission on Civil Rights, *Voting in Mississippi*, p. 53. For additional criticism of the judicial approach in the voting rights field, see Watters and Cleghorn, *Climbing Jacob's Ladder*, pp. 213–14, 231, and 240; U.S. Commission on Civil Rights, *Civil Rights '63—The 1963 Report of the United States Commission on Civil Rights* (Washington: USGPO, 1963), p. 13, and *Voting in Mississippi*, p. 57; and Kenneth N. Vines, "Epilogue: 1970," in Peltason, *Fifty-Eight Lonely Men*, pp. 257, 262, and 264.

91. See Hamilton, *The Bench and The Ballot*, pp. 222–27, especially at 222–23. Also see Hawk and Kirby, "Federal Protection of Negro Voting Rights," pp. 1054 and 1212; and Hamilton, "Southern Judges and Negro Voting Rights," pp. 73, 91, and 99.

92. Hamilton, "Southern Judges and Negro Voting Rights," p. 72; *The Bench and The Ballot*, p. 218. This defense was cited subsequently by some with a more personal interest in the question. See Wisdom, "The Frictionmaking, Exacerbating Political Role of Federal Courts," p. 424. Hamilton in 1973 did remark, however, "The Selma protests made it clear that no large number of black people would be registered quickly as long as the Southern federal courts were relied on to implement the process," a statement that partially counterbalances his emphasis upon the positive aspects of judicial enforcement. In earlier years, it might be noted, Hamilton had advocated an executive branch enforcement mechanism in place of judicial enforcement. See "It Will Be Token Registration," p. 4.

93. Simpson attempted to restrain white rowdies from repeatedly attacking civil rights demonstrators in St. Augustine, Florida, in June 1964, while Christenberry angrily criticized Bogalusa, Louisiana, officials who had failed to protect demonstrators from similar violence in the summer of 1965. On Simpson, see Friedman's piece on him in *Southern Justice*; Larry Goodwyn, "Anarchy in St. Augustine," *Harper's* 230 (January 1965: 74–81; and Kunstler, *Deep In My Heart*, pp. 273–74, 276–82, and 289–303.

94. See "Southern Judges and Negro Voting Rights," p. 99, where Hamilton considers several weaknesses in or objections to the judicial approach. This is not one of them.

95. See n. 82 above. Other instances came in the *Lynd* case at the behest of the appeals court (n. 69 above) and in *U.S.* v. *Manning*, when on July 24, 1962, District Judge Edwin F. Hunter ordered some two dozen black citizens added to the voting rolls of East Carroll Parish. See James C. Harvey, *Civil Rights During the Kennedy Administration* (Hattiesburg: University & College Press of Mississippi, 1971), p. 37. Also see Congressional Quarterly, "Votes For Negroes," *Weekly Report*, 5 July 1963, pp. 1086–97.

96. See n. 70 above in regard to O.S. Burke of Perry County, Alabama, whose responsibilities were later briefly extended to include Dallas County as well.

97. See Hawk and Kirby, "Federal Protection of Negro Voting Rights," p. 1162.

98. Hamilton, "Southern Judges and Negro Voting Rights," p. 98. On the gains in Macon and Bullock, see the text at n. 81 above.

99. Hawk and Kirby, "Federal Protection of Negro Voting Rights," pp. 1195–96; and Comment, "Voting Rights: A Case Study of Madison Parish," p. 749. Also see the county-level percentages supplied by Marshall in *Federalism and Civil Rights*, pp. 25–27. The only counties that showed increases of greater than 5 percent were three overseen by Johnson—Macon, Bullock, and Montgomery—two in which a substantial number of purge victims were restored to the rolls—Washington and Bienville parishes—and one where the operation of a white primary was halted—Fayette in Tennessee. See also Lichtman, "The Federal Assault Against Voting Discrimination," p. 364. In Terrell County, Georgia, the target of the first voting suit filed, black registration more than five years later had not yet reached 5 percent.

100. *South Carolina* v. *Katzenbach*, 383 U.S. 301, 313 (1966). Also see Derfner, "Racial Discrimination and the Right to Vote," p. 549, who adopts these percentages as well.

101. The phrase is from Stuart A. Scheingold, *The Politics of Rights* (New Haven: Yale University Press, 1974), p. 8. Also see pp. 117–19. The issue of to what degree and in what circumstances the federal courts *can* bring about successful compliance with unpopular constitutional principles by state and local officials is clearly a larger topic whose further consideration must be left for another time.

102. Comment, "Voting Rights: A Case Study of Madison Parish," p. 748. Also see Derfner, "Racial Discrimination and the Right to Vote," p. 548; and Thelton Henderson, "The Law and Civil Rights: The Justice Department in the South," *New University Thought* 3 (1963): 36–45, at 43.

103. Hawk and Kirby, "Federal Protection of Negro Voting Rights," p. 1196.

Chapter 2

1. *U.S.* v. *Majors*, 7 *Race Relations Law Reporter* 463 (1962); *U.S.* v. *Atkins*, 210 F. Supp. 441 (1962). On the history of the city, see Walter M. Jackson, *The Story of Selma* (Birmingham: Birmingham Printing Co., 1954), and Milton Mayer, "The Last Time I Saw Selma," *Progressive* 29 (May 1965): 18–21.

2. SNCC had been invited to send a representative to Selma early in 1962. See "The Selma Story," *Southern Patriot* 23 (February 1965): 1, and Guy and Candie Carawan, *Freedom Is a Constant Struggle* (New York: Oak Publications, 1968), pp. 146–47.

3. On the events in 1963, see James Forman, *The Making of Black Revolutionaries* (New York: Macmillan, 1972), pp. 316–53. Also see Thelton Henderson, "The Law and Civil Rights: The Justice Department in the South," *New University Thought* 3 (1963): 36–45, at 37–38; Ronnie Dugger, "Dead End in the Deep South," *Correspondent* 29 (November–December 1963): 43–48; Howard Zinn, *SNCC: The New Abolitionists* (Boston: Beacon Press, 1965), pp. 147–66; and two earlier articles by Zinn, "Registration in Alabama," *New Republic* 149 (26 October 1963): 11–12; and "A Question of Action," *Correspondent* 29 (November–December 1963): 49–53. Burke Marshall responded to the first Zinn article in a letter entitled "Enforcing Civil Rights," *New Republic* 149 (16 November 1963): 29–30. Federal concern about the campaign apparently led to an October 3 reconnaisance of Selma by officers of the 101st Airborne Division, an action that was not revealed publicly until some eighteen months later. For a partial explanation of the mission, see U.S. Congress, House, *Congressional Record* 111 (27 April 1965), p. 8594. Also see James G. Clark, Jr., *The Jim Clark Story—"I Saw Selma Raped"* (Birmingham: Selma Enterprises, 1966), pp. 62, 64, and 74–78.

4. *U.S.* v. *Atkins*, 323 F.2d 733 (1963); and 10 *Race Relations Law Reporter* 210. Freezing relief was denied, however. Solicitor General Cox later reported that a Justice Department investigation in late 1963 showed that "blatant dis-

crimination" was still being practiced by the Dallas County registrars. Approximately 175 black high-school graduates had been rejected. See Archibald Cox, "Constitutionality of the Proposed Voting Rights Act of 1965," *Houston Law Review* 3 (Spring–Summer 1965): 1–10, at 9.

5.   *U.S. v. Dallas County*, 229 F. Supp. 1014 (1964).

6.   *U.S. v. McLeod*, 229 F. Supp. 383 (1964). While the appellate court denied an injunction prior to the appeal, in October 1967, when the ultimate ruling was issued, Judge John Minor Wisdom wrote that both the June 1964 arrests and those in September and October 1963 as well had been clearly for the purpose of intimidation and nothing else. Wisdom stated that Thomas "was clearly in error in failing to" perceive that, and in failing to realize the real purpose of the local grand jury's pursuit of the federal attorneys, which was not resumed after the temporary restraining order was dissolved. Wisdom, while noting that the four-year-old record was "stale," ordered that the records of the arrest be expunged and that the victims of them be reimbursed for both fines and defense costs. 385 F.2d 734 (1967). For the details of the controversy concerning King's ride in a government-rented car, see Henderson, "The Law and Civil Rights," pp. 36–37. Also see Clark, *The Jim Clark Story*, pp. 64–69.

7.   10 *Race Relations Law Reporter* 210. The eventual ruling, handed down in early February 1965, will be discussed shortly.

8.   On the events in Selma in July, 1964, see *New York Times*, 5 July 1964, p. 37; 6 July 1964, p. 19; 7 July 1964, p. 20; and 8 July 1964, p. 19. On that month as well as on events later in the fall, also see *Dallas County* v. *SNCC* and *State* v. *Allen*, 10 *Race Relations Law Reporter* 234; and the opinion eventually filed in *U.S.* v. *Clark*, 249 F. Supp. 720 (1965); as well as Carol Stevens, "Selma: A Lonely Outpost," *Southern Patriot* 22 (October 1964): 1 and 3; and *New York Times*, 3 September 1964, p. 18. The Justice Department also moved in *U.S.* v. *The Warren Company, Inc.* to have five Selma restaurants enjoined from barring black customers. The suit was successful. See U.S. Department of Justice, *Annual Report of the Attorney General, 1965* (Washington: USGPO, 1965), p. 181.

9.   John Doar to Joseph A. Califano, Jr., 9 August 1965, LBJ Library, White House Central Files, Executive HU 2-7, Box 55. See the Dallas County "justification memo" attached. Also see similar evaluations in Frank E. Schwelb, "From Illusion to Reality: Relief in Civil Rights Cases," *Notre Dame Lawyer* 48 (October 1972): 49–79, at 59; Cox, "Constitutionality of the Proposed Voting Rights Act," p. 10; and *South Carolina* v. *Katzenbach*, 383 U.S. 301, 314.

10.   Fred Powledge, *New York Times*, 5 November 1964, pp. 1 and 33. The best account of the 1964 effort in St. Augustine is Robert W. Hartley, "A Long, Hot Summer: The St. Augustine Racial Disorders of 1964," M.A. thesis, Stetson University, 1972. Also see Paul Good, *The Trouble I've Seen* (Washington: Howard University Press, 1975), pp. 75–103, and the following items: Robert K. Massie, "Don't Tread on Grandmother Peabody," *Saturday Evening Post* 237 (16 May 1964): 74 and 76; George McMillan, "The Klan Scourges Old St. Augustine," *Life* 56 (26 June 1964): 21; Pat Watters, "The Worst Yet," *New Republic* 150 (27 June 1964): 6, and "St. Augustine," *New South* 19 (September 1964):

3–20; Martin Waldron, "After Dark in St. Augustine," *Nation* 198 (29 June 1964): 648–51; John Herbers, "Critical Test for the Nonviolent Way," *New York Times Magazine*, 5 July 1964, pp. 5 and 30–31; Trevor Armbrister, "Portrait of an Extremist," *Saturday Evening Post* 237 (22 August–29 August 1964): 80–83; Larry Goodwyn, "Anarchy in St. Augustine," *Harper's* 230 (January 1965): 74–81; and William M. Kunstler, *Deep In My Heart* (New York: William Morrow, 1966), pp. 271–304. A blatantly inaccurate racist account is presented in A.G. Heinsohn, Jr., "St. Augustine: Rape of the Ancient City," *American Opinion* 7 (October 1964): 1–10.

11.   Until the SCLC's own tightly held papers become available, the details of the planning efforts will remain very cloudy. Charles Fager, himself an SCLC staffer, gives some details on the period, but relies heavily on Wilson Baker's recollections, which may not have been fully accurate. For instance, Baker recalled Robert F. Kennedy's presence at the time that Baker met with Burke Marshall; by mid-November the former attorney general was senator-elect from New York. Baker is now deceased. See *Selma 1965* (New York: Charles Scribner's Sons, 1974), pp. 6–7.

12.   See Robert Alden, *New York Times*, 18 December 1964, p. 37; *New York Times*, 19 December 1964, p. 32; and *Washington Post*, 19 December 1964, p. A2. Also see Martin Luther King, Jr., "Playboy Interview," *Playboy* 12 (January 1965): 65–78, at 70.

13.   See Phillip Sam Hughes of the Bureau of the Budget's Legislative Reference Section to Lee C. White, 11 June 1964, LBJ Library, White Papers, Box 6. On the role of southern black voters in the 1964 presidential election, see Paul Duke, "Southern Politics and the Negroes," *Reporter* 31 (17 December 1964): 18–21.

14.   For Johnson's assertion, see his 6 August 1965 remarks as they appear in *Public Papers of the Presidents, Lyndon B. Johnson, 1965* (Washington: USGPO, 1966), pp. 840–43, and his sanitized account of his years in the White House, *The Vantage Point—Perspectives of the Presidency* (New York: Holt, Rinehart & Winston, 1971), p. 161. Also see Eric F. Goldman, *The Tragedy of Lyndon Johnson* (New York: Alfred A. Knopf, 1969), p. 318; and Doris Kearns, *Lyndon Johnson and the American Dream* (New York: Harper & Row, 1976), p. 228.

15.   The document in question—whose wording in sections bears striking resemblance to that used by Goldman and Kearns—is both undated and unsigned. Apparently written in late 1964 in preparation for the drafting of one or both of those two major addresses, it argued,

> In view of the enactment of the Civil Rights Act of 1964, there is no apparent reason or need to advance an Administration Civil Rights Legislative Program in 1965. A tremendous job of digestion faces the Executive Branch. Although no new program is offered Congress, there should, of course, be reference to the Administration's aims and plans for implementing the [1964] Act in the Inaugural and the State of the Union addresses.

It can be expected that in the coming months errors, omissions, and refinements in the [1964] Act may present themselves, and thus the question of civil rights legislation could well be considered at the end of the next year [1965].

The brief document goes on to note that the 1964 act's voting title was regarded as weak by some, who also advocated federal registrars. After making an implicit reference to the decisions being awaited from the Supreme Court in the *Louisiana* and *Mississippi* cases, and the possibility that those decisions could improve judicial enforcement of voting rights, the unknown author concluded his or her consideration of the voting situation by saying, "In any event, this should be followed carefully through 1965, and any changes considered for proposal in time for the 1966 elections." This writer believes Lee White to have been the likely author. Entitled "Civil Rights," with the notation "Filed 2/5/65," the document can be found in the LBJ Library, WHCF, Ex HU 2, Box 3.

16.   Nicholas deB. Katzenbach to Lyndon B. Johnson, 28 December 1964, LBJ Library, Justice Department Administrative History, Volume 7, Part Xa. The 1963 proposal was the interim referee provision mentioned in the preceding chapter.

17.   Johnson himself apparently shared this estimation of the prospects for success as of early 1965. Describing that period in *The Vantage Point*, he spoke of the prospect then for congressional passage as "unpromising" (p. 161). One subsequent journalistic piece was to assert that certain Senate staffers had discussed voting rights possibilities with administration officials "shortly after Christmas" (Rowland Evans and Robert Novak, "From Selma to Capitol Hill," *Washington Post*, 15 February 1965, p. A15).

18.   Lee C. White to Bill D. Moyers, 30 December 1964, LBJ Library, White Papers, Box 3. The views expressed in this memo bear such close resemblance to those expressed in the unsigned and undated document discussed in n. 15 above as to suggest strongly that White was the author of that earlier memo.

19.   *New York Times*, 29 December 1964, p. 14; 2 January 1965, p. 16; and Paul Good, *Washington Post*, 2 January 1965, p. A2.

20.   John Herbers, *New York Times*, 3 January 1965, pp. 1 and 20; Paul Good, *Washington Post*, 3 January 1965, p. A9. Also see John Herbers, *The Lost Priority* (New York: Funk & Wagnalls, 1970), pp. 3–4 and 15–16. On the unfruitful MFDP effort, see George Slaff, "Five Seats in Congress: The Mississippi Challenge," *Nation* 200 (17 May 1965): 526–29; and Richard H. Rovere, "Letter From Washington," *New Yorker* 41 (16 October 1965): 233–44.

21.   John Herbers, *New York Times*, 4 January 1965, p. 58. On Smeltzer's unique role, see Fager, *Selma 1965*, pp. 214–18.

22.   U.S. Congress, House, *Congressional Record* 111 (pt. 1, 4 January 1965), pp. 29–30.

23.   Robert E. Baker, *Washington Post*, 6 January 1965, p. 1. Both legislative ideas, he noted, had been recommended in the 1959 Civil Rights Commission report and had been advocated by a number of congressmen in the years since then.

24. "Constitutional Amendment, Draft 1/8/65," LBJ Library, Justice Department Administrative History, Volume 7, Part Xa.

25. Reports on Legislation, 11 January 1965, Justice Department, LBJ Library. The most recent previous such report, from September 1964, had contained no mention of voting legislation.

26. *New York Times*, 15 January 1965, p. 14; 16 January 1965, pp. 1 and 17; Paul Good, *Washington Post*, 18 January 1965, p. A3. On the Alabama registration test, see James E. Clayton, *Washington Post*, 24 January 1965, p. E3; and John Herbers, *New York Times*, 31 January 1965, p. 55.

27. John Herbers, *New York Times*, 19 January 1965, p. 1; Paul Good, *Washington Post*, 19 January 1965, p. 1; Fager, *Selma 1965*, p. 31; and Howell Raines, *My Soul Is Rested* (New York: G.P. Putnam's Sons, 1977), pp. 198–200. Governor Wallace was reportedly so pleased with the handling of the demonstration without an incident that he called Smitherman to congratulate him.

28. Reports on Legislation, 18 January 1965, Justice Department, LBJ Library.

29. John Herbers, *New York Times*, 20 January 1965, p. 1; Paul Good, *Washington Post*, 20 January 1965, p. 1.

30. John Herbers, *New York Times*, 21 January 1965, p. 1; John Lynch, *Washington Post*, 21 January 1965, p. B8.

31. Paul Good, *Washington Post*, 22 January 1965, p. A10; John Herbers, *New York Times*, 22 January 1965, p. 16.

32. John Herbers, *New York Times*, 23 January 1965, p. 18; *Washington Post*, 23 January 1965, p. A7.

33. See *Boynton* v. *Clark*, 10 *Race Relations Law Reporter* 215; and *New York Times*, 24 January 1965, p. 40.

34. John Herbers, *New York Times*, 26 January 1965, p. 1; Rex Thomas, *Washington Post*, 26 January 1965, p. A2. Also see Clark, *The Jim Clark Story*, p. 94.

35. Reports on Legislation, 25 January 1965, Justice Department, LBJ Library. Also see E.W. Kenworthy, *New York Times*, 25 April 1965, p. E5.

36. *Washington Post*, 27 January 1965, p. A2; *New York Times*, 27 January 1965, p. 16. Most of the force departed the next day.

37. At about this time a Birmingham reporter somehow acquired a rather pedestrian SCLC planning document for the Alabama Project, which after its subsequent publication on February 2 came to be regarded by segregationists as the SCLC's "master plan." It appears to be something less than that. Consisting mainly of an outline of necessary staff positions and responsibilities, the document called for a "statewide nonviolent campaign" to be organized around the "issues" of "taxation without representation, . . . mass nonviolent education," and "the conducting of freedom registration and mock elections to send men to the House of Representatives and Senate of Alabama to represent the Negro people." It also called for "the execution of a mass direct action program that will dramatize these issues." Although envisioning an eventual statewide campaign for which Selma would be the spark, and thus providing little insight into

the SCLC's strategic concerns at Selma, the document did recommend, as segregationists loudly emphasized, that Dr. King intentionally be arrested in Selma and that a "Letter from the Selma Jail" and other publicity go out in the wake of that event. The document planned that the ultimate culmination of the Alabama effort would come on May 4 with the convening of the Alabama legislature, at which black candidates who had been "nominated" by black conventions and "voted for" in freedom elections would appear with their supporters and protest the exclusion of black citizens from the state's electoral politics. Following the expected rebuff from state officials, the campaign would then begin large-scale demonstrations and issue a call for an economic boycott of Alabama. The similarities between this plan and the 1964 Mississippi Freedom Summer are readily visible. The document makes no reference, however, to the interest in federal action and legislation that the late 1964 and early 1965 comments of King and Young reflected. The entire document appears in Robert M. Mikell, *Selma* (Charlotte: Citadel Press, 1965), pp. 28–38. Apart from this document and several other testimonial statements, the book is virulent racist trash and strewn with factual errors. Like Representative Dickinson's later charges, the volume is notable only because it reflects so well the white racist's fixation with the subject of interracial sex. Other Selma-related examples of this genre are Clark, *The Jim Clark Story*, pp. 29–58; and Albert C. Persons, *The True Selma Story: Sex and Civil Rights* (Birmingham: Esco Publishers, 1965), pp. 2, 4–12, and 28–32, both of which are very similar to portions of the Mikell book, and Scott Stanley, Jr., "Revolution: The Assault on Selma," *American Opinion* 8 (May 1965): 1–10, at 7 and 9–10. On this topic in general, see Calvin C. Hernton, *Sex and Racism in America* (Garden City, N.Y.: Doubleday, 1965), and *Coming Together: Black Power, White Hatred and Sexual Hang-ups* (New York: Random House, 1971); and James P. Comer, "White Racism: Its Root, Form, and Function," *American Journal of Psychiatry* 126 (December 1969): 802–6.

38. *New York Times*, 28 January 1965, p. 15; *Washington Post*, 28 January 1965, p. A15; John Herbers, *New York Times*, 29 January 1965, p. 9; *New York Times*, 30 January 1965, p. 10; *New York Times*, 31 January 1965, pp. 49 and 55; Jim Bishop, *The Days of Martin Luther King, Jr.* (New York: G.P. Putnam's Sons, 1971), p. 373; Robert E. Baker, *Washington Post*, 1 February 1965, p. A3.

39. Eugene Rostow to Bill D. Moyers, 29 January 1965, LBJ Library, WHCF, Ex HU 2/ST 1.

40. *New York Times*, 1 February 1965, p. 16; Paul Good, *Washington Post*, 2 February 1965, pp. A1 and A6; John Herbers, *New York Times*, 2 February 1965, p. 1.

41. John Herbers, *New York Times*, 3 February 1965, p. 1; Paul Good, *Washington Post*, 3 February 1965, p. A3.

42. John Herbers, *New York Times*, 4 February 1965, p. 1; Paul Good, *Washington Post*, 4 February 1965, p. 1; U.S. Congress, Senate, *Congressional Record* 111 (pt. 2, 3 February 1965), p. 1913. Javits inserted into the *Record* a *New York Post* editorial from the previous day's paper that made the same points that he himself articulated.

43. Lee C. White to Lyndon B. Johnson, 3 February 1965, LBJ Library, WHCF, Ex HU 2/ST 1, Box 24.

44. John Herbers, *New York Times*, 5 February 1965; p. 1; 10 *Race Relations Law Reporter* 210; Peter Goldman, *The Death and Life of Malcolm X* (New York: Harper & Row, 1973), pp. 230–31. While the Justice Department had been in touch with Thomas concerning the order, in Selma some thought that Sheriff Clark himself had had a hand in drafting it. See Fager, *Selma 1965*, p. 58.

45. See *Congressional Record* 111, pp. 2031–33, 2052, and 2066; for Johnson's remarks, see *Public Papers of the Presidents, Lyndon B. Johnson, 1965*, pp. 130–31.

46. Roy Reed, *New York Times*, 6 February 1965, p. 1; Clifford Alexander to Lee C. White, 5 February 1965, LBJ Library, White Papers, Box 6. For a very detailed account of the jail conditions, see Ralph Featherstone, "The Stench of Freedom," *Negro History Bulletin* 28 (March 1965): 130. The northern congressmen making the visit were Don Edwards (D-Cal.), whose son Len had worked for COFO in Sunflower County, Mississippi, the previous summer, Jeffrey Cohelan (D-Cal.), Ken W. Dyal (D-Cal.), Weston E. Vivian (D-Mich.), Augustus F. Hawkins (D-Cal.), William F. Ryan (D-N.Y.), James H. Scheuer (D-N.Y.), Charles C. Diggs, Jr. (D-Mich.), Jonathan B. Bingham (D-N.Y.), John Conyers, Jr. (D-Mich.), John G. Dow (D-N.Y.), Joseph Y. Resnick (D-N.Y.), Charles McC. Mathias, Jr. (R-Md.), Bradford Morse (R-Mass.), and Ogden R. Reid (R-N.Y.). Also see Lee C. White to Joseph T. Smitherman, 5 February 1965, LBJ Library, WHCF, Ex HU 2/ST 1; *New York Times*, 6 February 1965, p. 10; and Edward Ranzal, *New York Times*, 6 February 1965, p. 1.

47. John Herbers, "Negro Goals in Selma," *New York Times*, 6 February 1965, p. 10. For a further indication that Clark may not have been so much unable to realize the public relations damage his actions could do as he was unable to restrain himself in tense situations despite his realization of the consequences, see a late April 1965 letter that he wrote that is reprinted in Mikell, *Selma*, pp. 245–50.

48. John D. Morris, *New York Times*, 7 February 1965, p. 1. Also see Congressional Quarterly, "Negro Voting Rights," *Weekly Report*, 19 February 1965, p. 269; and *Washington Post*, 7 February 1965, p. 1. Earlier in the week Johnson had met with Senate minority leader Everett Dirksen to discuss the idea of a new voting rights bill, but no firm commitments were made. Neil MacNeil, *Dirksen: Portrait of a Public Man* (New York: World Publishing Co., 1970), p. 252.

49. Roy Reed, *New York Times*, 7 February 1965, p. 44. Also see p. 45. See as well *New York Times*, 8 February 1965, p. 17.

50. Roy Reed, *New York Times*, 9 February 1965, p. 17; *Congressional Record* 111 (8 February 1965), p. 2508.

51. John D. Morris, *New York Times*, 10 February 1965, p. 1; and Alan F. Westin and Barry Mahoney, *The Trial of Martin Luther King* (New York: Thomas Y. Crowell, 1974), pp. 167–68. Also see Martin Luther King, Jr., "Selma—The Shame and the Promise," *IUD Agenda* 1 (March 1965): 18–21, at 21.

52. Roy Reed, *New York Times*, 11 February 1965, pp. 1 and 19; *Congressional Record* 111 (10 February 1965), p. 2509.

53. Rowland Evans and Robert Novak, "From Selma to Capitol Hill," *Washington Post*, 15 February 1965, p. A15. Katzenbach reportedly also had a considerably more frank discussion that same day with Senate leaders Mansfield and Dirksen. The three men are said to have agreed that a stringent new bill was necessary. See MacNeil, *Dirksen*, pp. 252–53. MacNeil's grasp of the Selma chronology, however, appears to be rather weak, and hence his account may be somewhat inaccurate.

54. John Herbers, *New York Times*, 12 February 1965, p. 58; and LBJ Library, Justice Department Administrative History, Volume 7, Part Xa.

55. John Herbers, "Voting is Crux of Civil Rights Hopes," *New York Times*, 14 February 1965, p. E5.

56. Reports on Legislation, 15 February 1965, Justice Department, LBJ Library. Also see James L. Morrison to Norbert A. Schlei, 15 February 1965, Justice Department Administrative History, Volume 7, Part Xa.

57. See John Herbers, *New York Times*, 17 February 1965, p. 35; and Fager, *Selma 1965*, p. 70. Also see Clark, *The Jim Clark Story*, pp. 105–6. In regard to the press coverage of this incident, see the remarks of Alabama representative James D. Martin, *Congressional Record* 111 (17 February 1965), p. 2928.

58. John Herbers, *New York Times*, 18 February 1965, p. 26.

59. John Lynch, *Washington Post*, 19 February 1965, p. 1; John Herbers, *New York Times*, 19 February 1965, p. 1; and Fager, *Selma 1965*, p. 75. Also see Raines, *My Soul Is Rested*, pp. 191–93 and 371–72. On Jackson, see Jack Mendelsohn, *The Martyrs* (New York: Harper & Row, 1966), pp. 133–52, especially 139–47, where the Thursday evening shooting is described; and Liz Krohne, "The Quiet Martyr," *Southern Patriot* 23 (March 1965): 3.

60. See 10 *Race Relations Law Reporter* 217.

61. *Washington Post*, 22 February 1965, p. A4; on the MFDP memo, see the copy attached to Harold F. Reis to Lee C. White, 5 March 1965, LBJ Library, WHCF, Gen LE/HU 2-7, Box 72.

62. John Herbers, *New York Times*, 23 February 1965, p. 16; also see "The White Citizens' Council," *Student Voice* 6 (26 March 1965): 3.

63. E.W. Kenworthy, *New York Times*, 24 February 1965, p. 1. The governors were Volpe of Massachusetts, Chafee of Rhode Island, Romney of Michigan, Scranton of Pennsylvania, and Smylie of Idaho. The senators were Kuchel of California, Javits of New York, Scott of Pennsylvania, and Allott of Colorado. The representatives, of whom the *Times* listed only twenty, were Lindsay, Halpern, Horton, and Reid of New York; Dwyer and Frelinghuysen of New Jersey; MacGregor and Quie of Minnesota; Harvey and Broomfield of Michigan; Conte and Morse of Massachusetts; McDade, Schweiker, and Fulton of Pennsylvania; Ellsworth of Kansas; Mathias of Maryland; Stanton of Ohio; Maillard of California; and Rumsfeld of Illinois.

64. Archibald Cox to Nicholas deB. Katzenbach, 23 February 1965, LBJ Library, Justice Department Administrative History, Volume 7, Part Xa. Cox

sent copies to Ramsey Clark, John Doar, Harold F. Reis, and Harold H. Greene as well.

65. Roy Reed, *New York Times*, 24 February 1965, pp. 1 and 28.

66. *New York Times*, 26 February 1965, p. 15; Louis Martin to Lee C. White, 24 February 1965, LBJ Library, WHCF, Ex LE/HU 2, Box 66.

67. *New York Times*, 26 February 1965, pp. 14–16.

68. Joseph A. Loftus, *New York Times*, 27 February 1965, p. 11; and Roy Reed, *New York Times*, 27 February 1965, p. 1. Also see Raines, *My Soul Is Rested*, pp. 193–94. The Republican senators were Case, Javits, Kuchel, Fong, Allott, and Cooper. Liberal Democrats such as Paul Douglas were now speaking out against the constitutional amendment idea as well.

69. *Washington Post*, 28 February 1965, p. A2; Horace Busby to Bill D. Moyers and Lee C. White, "The Voting Rights Message," 27 February 1965, LBJ Library, Busby Papers, Box 3. An AP wire story on Ford's statement was printed in many papers.

70. Roy Reed, *New York Times*, 1 March 1965, p. 17; Roy Reed, *New York Times*, 2 March 1965, pp. 1 and 19; Reports on Legislation, 1 March 1965, Justice Department, LBJ Library.

71. Lee C. White to Jack Valenti, 1 March 1965, LBJ Library, WHCF, Ex LE/HU 2, Box 66; Nicholas deB. Katzenbach to Bill D. Moyers and Lee C. White, 1 March 1965, LBJ Library, Busby Papers, Box 3.

72. The Rules hearings did not directly concern voting rights. *New York Times*, 2 March 1965, p. 19; White House Daily Diary, LBJ Library; Roy Reed, *New York Times*, 3 March 1965, p. 24, and 4 March 1965, p. 23. Subsequent statistics showed that despite the many courthouse marches and Thomas's orders, only 112 black applicants were processed by the Dallas County registrars in January and only 95 more were handled in February. Of January's group, 100 were rejected, and in February 59 were turned down.

73. Bill Jones, *The Wallace Story* (Northport: American Southern Publishing Co., 1966), pp. 355–56.

74. M.S. Handler, *New York Times*, 5 March 1965, p. 29; Lee C. White to Lyndon B. Johnson, 4 March 1965, LBJ Library, WHCF, Ex HU 2, Box 3.

75. White House Daily Diary, LBJ Library; Charles Mohr, *New York Times*, 6 March 1965, p. 9.

76. *Washington Post*, 6 March 1965, p. A4.

77. Jones, *The Wallace Story*, pp. 356–58; James Forman, *Sammy Younge, Jr.* (New York: Grove Press, 1968), p. 75; Cleveland Sellers, *The River of No Return* (New York: William Morrow, 1973), pp. 118–21; Roy Reed, *New York Times*, 6 March 1965, p. 10.

78. "An Act," 5 March 1965, LBJ Library, Justice Department Administrative History, Volume 7, Part Xa. The ten-year mandate was later reduced to five without any discernible commentary from any sector. On the strategy behind the choice of the trigger formula, see *New York Times*, 11 April 1965, p. 48; and E.W. Kenworthy, *New York Times*, 25 April 1965, p. E5.

79. Harold F. Reis to Lee C. White, 5 March 1965, LBJ Library, WHCF, Gen LE/HU 2-7, Box 72.

80. Jones, *The Wallace Story*, pp. 357–58.
81. Roy Reed, *New York Times*, 7 March 1965, p. 1; and Fager, *Selma 1965*, pp. 89–90. Also see Raines, *My Soul Is Rested*, pp. 201–3. Copies of Ellwanger's statement were subsequently mailed to a large number of public figures and organizations. On the Ellwanger group, see "More than Moderation," *Southern Patriot* 23 (April 1965): 1 and 4.
82. King's own account appears in "Behind the Selma March," *Saturday Review* 48 (3 April 1965): 16–17 and 57, at 17, where he wrote that "none of us anticipated" or even "imagined that they would use the brutal methods to which they actually resorted." Also see Coretta Scott King, *My Life With Martin Luther King, Jr.* (New York: Holt, Rinehart & Winston, 1969), p. 259. King's April version differs a bit from that which he apparently offered to the press on Sunday evening, March 7. As the *Times* reported it, King "said he and staff members of the Southern Christian Leadership Conference . . . had agreed last night [Saturday, March 6] that he should not lead the march because they had learned troopers would block it." King's Sunday statement went on to say, though, that he had nonetheless not expected any violence (*New York Times*, 8 March 1965, p. 20). While that apparent lack of consistency raises some questions, various other accounts make it clear that by Sunday morning at the latest the movement leaders in Selma expected to be met with tear gas and clubs. See Warren Hinckle and David Welsh, "Five Battles of Selma," *Ramparts* 4 (June 1965): 19–52, at 26; and Forman, *Sammy Younge, Jr.*, p. 75. The view that King avoided the march because of the personal danger to him is put forward by two writers whose accounts of other events in the campaign are unusually accurate. Paul Good later related, "Dr. King had been advised by Attorney General Katzenbach not to take part," and Jim Bishop wrote that King had told his wife "that he had not led the march because he had been warned that there was a plot to kill him in the melee." Bishop notes that King's claim that no violence was expected is rather dubious, especially given the presence of the movement ambulances. See Paul Good, "Beyond the Bridge," *Reporter* 32 (8 April 1965): 23–26; and Bishop, *The Days of Martin Luther King, Jr.*, p. 385. Also see William Robert Miller, *Martin Luther King, Jr.* (New York: Avon, 1969), p. 220. Fager, who admits that his version is more sympathetic to King than are others, argues

> people close to him . . . persuaded him to stay away. It appears they may actually have finessed him away from it, assuring him that the march would be a cakewalk which would be stopped without either violence or much public impact, and that he could just as well spend the day resting at home and preparing himself for the second try, which would probably be more eventful. From that distance, having been gone several days, King probably was unaware of the atmosphere of tension that had enveloped Dallas County and shown itself the day before when the whites marched. So he allowed himself to be dissuaded from coming (*Selma 1965*, p. 92).

Also see Raines, *My Soul Is Rested*, p. 385, and Earl and Miriam Selby, *Odyssey* (New York: G. P. Putnam's Sons, 1971), p. 79.
83. Roy Reed, *New York Times*, 8 March 1965, p. 1. Also see Hinckle and Welsh, "Five Battles of Selma," pp. 26–27.

84.   See Hinckle and Welsh, "Five Battles of Selma," pp. 27–29, as well as Reed's story and Fager's account of the aftermath.

Chapter 3

1.   Charles Fager, *Selma 1965* (New York: Charles Scribner's Sons, 1974), pp. 97–98; White House Daily Diary, 7 March 1965, LBJ Library. On the juxtaposition of the Selma coverage and the Nuremberg movie, see Warren Hinckle and David Welsh, "Five Battles of Selma," *Ramparts* 4 (June 1965): 19–52, at 36, who call it "one of those extraordinary coincidences that can move men to memorable deeds. . . The hideous parallel between Auschwitz and Selma was obvious, even to the insensitive. Were it not for this accident of programming, Selma, Alabama, might just have been news, but never history. The pictures from Selma were unpleasant; the juxtaposition of the Nazi Storm Troopers and the Alabama State Troopers made them unbearable." On CBS's film, and the shooting of it, see Nelson Benton's comments in Howell Raines, *My Soul Is Rested* (New York: G.P. Putnam's Sons, 1977), p. 386.

2.   *Washington Post*, 8 March 1965, p. 1; *New York Times*, 8 March 1965, p. 1. For one example of the AP version, see the *Hartford Courant*, 8 March 1965, which also ran a photo of the attack across the entire width of the top of p. 1.

3.   U.S. Congress, Senate, *Congressional Record* 111 (pt. 4, 8 March 1965), pp. 4311, 4335, and 4350–52.

4.   Nan Robertson, *New York Times*, 9 March 1965, pp. 1 and 24; Reports on Legislation, 8 March 1965, Justice Department, LBJ Library.

5.   Fager, *Selma 1965*, p. 101. Hinckle and Welsh, "Five Battles of Selma," p. 30, give what purports to be a description of the session, but incorrectly place it on Tuesday morning. See Roy Reed, *New York Times*, 9 March 1965, p. 1. Publicly, Wallace refused to criticize the troopers' actions and insisted that the marchers had to be stopped for their own safety. Privately, though, Wallace was reported to have been angered at the lack of appreciation Lingo and Clark showed for the predictable public relations results of the clash. Gubernatorial press secretary Bill Jones, writing a year later, said the Wallace staff and the governor himself, who allegedly had ordered Lingo to stay away from the scene, were surprised when the initial news reached them Sunday afternoon. "What happened there wasn't supposed to happen," Jones claimed. *The Wallace Story* (Northport: American Southern Publishing Co., 1966), pp. 360–63 and 368–70. Major Cloud's subsequent version, which Jones relates, throws little real light on the question. Several informed parties have concluded explicitly that Wallace himself was culpable. John Herbers quoted "a reliable source" as saying that "the plan to use clubs and gas had been worked out in a meeting in the Governor's office in Montgomery" (*New York Times*, 9 March 1965, p. 23). Also see the very straightforward conclusion which Judge Frank M. Johnson, Jr., arrived at in *Williams* v. *Wallace*, 240 F. Supp. 100 (1965).

Aside from Wallace's personal culpability and subsequent failure to own up, two other possible explanations exist. First, Clark and Lingo, who were reported to have had a falling out with the governor, may well have decided to "teach the demonstrators a lesson" on their own initiative, without hinting of their intent to Wallace, Smitherman, or Baker, all of whom the two officers plausibly could have had a desire to spite. See Paul Good, *Washington Post*, 18 January 1965, p. A3; and William Chapman, *Washington Post*, 17 March 1965, p. A14. Second, since Major Cloud himself and Clark's chief deputy, L.C. Crocker, had pledged personally to Baker early on Sunday that there would be no violence, it is plausible that the troopers and possemen "let go"—and rioted—on their own initiative, without any explicit directions from Lingo or Clark. Nevertheless, Cloud was the man who ordered them forward. Jones later concluded, rather lamely, "No one seems to know what caused the fiasco."

6. Louis Martin to Marvin Watson, 8 March 1965, and Watson's attached notes, LBJ Library, WHCF, Ex HU 2/ST 1, Box 24.

7. James Forman, *Sammy Younge, Jr.* (New York: Grove Press, 1968), pp. 76–78.

8. George B. Leonard, "Midnight Plane to Alabama," *Nation* 200 (10 May 1965): 502–5. Also see Fager, *Selma 1965*, p. 99. Leonard's account, which goes on to describe his spur-of-the-moment flight to Alabama and other people he met on the way who, like him, had been motivated to go by their reactions to the news, is perhaps the most fascinating item in all of the Selma literature.

9. Many accounts have been referred to in constructing this narrative of the events of March 8 and 9. Perhaps the two most informative and persuasive are Jim Bishop, *The Days of Martin Luther King, Jr.* (New York: G.P. Putnam's Sons, 1971), pp. 386–88; and David L. Lewis, *King: A Critical Biography* (New York: Praeger, 1970), pp. 278–82 and 392. Also see Forman, *Sammy Younge, Jr.*, pp. 77–78; Alan F. Westin and Barry Mahoney, *The Trial of Martin Luther King* (New York: Thomas Y. Crowell, 1974), pp. 172–74; Fager, *Selma 1965*, pp. 101–2 and 105; Andrew Kopkind, "Selma: 'Ain't Gonna Let Nobody Turn Me 'Round,' " *New Republic* 152 (20 March 1965): 7–9; John Herbers, *New York Times*, 10 March 1965, p. 22; Dean Peerman and Martin E. Marty, "Selma: Sustaining the Momentum," *Christian Century* 82 (24 March 1965): 358–60; Max L. Stackhouse, "The Ethics of Selma," *Commonweal* 82 (9 April 1965): 75–77; and Hinckle and Welsh, "Five Battles of Selma," p. 32.

King himself, despite his own remarks on Tuesday and two days later in court, subsequently asserted that "no prearranged agreement existed" and that any story which argued that one had was "a perversion of the facts" ("Behind the Selma March," *Saturday Review* 48 [3 April 1965]: 16–17 and 57). Lewis, who investigated the controversy in some detail, concludes however that King's version was "a transparent misrepresentation of the facts." CRS official Fred Miller, Lewis writes, claims to have given Andrew Young a map of the scenario, and Lewis goes on to say that "the memoranda in the files of the CRS prove conclusively" that King "had agreed to curtail the march." Also see Steven F. Lawson, *Black Ballots: Voting Rights in the South, 1944–1969* (New York: Columbia University Press, 1976), pp. 311 and 420–21. The desires expressed by King in his Monday morning talk with Louis Martin might well be considered circumstantial evidence as to just what his intentions were. While the overall picture of this controversy emerges somewhat more clearly than those concerning King's Sunday absence and the actual instigator(s) of the attack, it must be acknowledged that King had no easy way out of his Tuesday morning choice. Balancing two constituencies with opposite desires—the SNCCers who were demanding a march, and the administration leaders who were warning that they could not condone his action if he were to violate Judge Johnson's order—King made a substantial, and defensible, effort to avoid greatly offending either. His final actions appear to indicate that King feared the loss of the administration's good-will more than he feared a controversy or split within the movement's ranks. Administration officials were quite happy with the course that in the end King chose to follow. King might also have reckoned, in considering the public opinion consequences, that the "moral impact of the march . . . would have been greatly diminished if the court order had been violated." Such at least is the result Judge Johnson later claimed would have occurred. See Frank M. Johnson, Jr., "Civil Disobedience and the Law," *Tulane Law Review* 44 (December 1969): 1–13, at 10.

Nevertheless, King's decision became the target of some very harsh criticism within the movement, and some observers later were to trace the actual break-up of the movement, first widely recognized in 1966, back to the anger Forman and SNCC felt on March 9. See Eldridge Cleaver, *Soul On Ice* (New York: McGraw-Hill, 1968), p. 74; and John Herbers, *The Lost Priority* (New York: Funk & Wagnalls, 1970), p. 78. Also see Godfrey Hodgson, *America In Our Time* (Garden City, N.Y.: Doubleday, 1976), p. 219. Lingo and Clark told newsmen that King had agreed not to march to Montgomery, but that *they* had had no agreement with him. Participant-observer accounts of Tuesday's brief march and of a preparatory meeting of the Selma teenagers are Wayne H. Cowan, "Selma at First Hand," *Christianity and Crisis* 25 (5 April 1965): 67–69; and Al Ulmer, "Ain't Gonna Let Nobody Turn Me Round," *New South* 20 (March 1965): 11–13. On the teenagers, also see Pat Watters, "Why the Negro Children March," *New York Times Magazine*, 21 March 1965, pp. 29–30 and 118–20.

10. *Washington Post*, 9 March 1965, p. A16. Also see *Washington Star*, 8 March 1965, and *New York Times*, 9 March 1965, p. 34. Other Tuesday morning papers which ran similar editorials were the *New York Daily News*, the *New York Herald Tribune*, and the *Baltimore Sun*. Montgomery's *Alabama Journal* had reacted angrily on March 8. Wallace's press secretary, Bill Jones, spoke of the deluge as "an editorial barrage of condemnations seldom matched in American journalism history" (*The Wallace Story*, p. 363).

11. See *New York Times*, 9 March 1965, p. 23; Robert C. Albright, *Washington Post*, 9 March 1965, p. A2. On the reaction among the clergy, also see John Cogley, "The Clergy Heeds A New Call," *New York Times Magazine*, 2 May 1965, p. 42; and Charles L. Palms, "A Harlem Priest Reports on Selma," *Catholic World* 201 (June 1965): 171–76. See as well Jeffrey K. Hadden, "Ideological Conflict Between Protestant Clergy and Laity on Civil Rights," *Social Science Quarterly* 49 (December 1968): 674–83. A number of the state and local resolutions of protest, which in most cases coupled a call for voting rights

legislation with expressions of anger, were printed subsequently in the *Congressional Record*. See pp. 5406, 5416, 5472–73, 5878, 5915, 6192, and 6487 of volume 111.

12.   U.S. Congress, House, *Congressional Record* 111 (pt. 4, 9 March 1965), pp. 4452–54. Those who signed the Conyers telegram were Republicans Paul A. Fino, Seymour Halpern, Frank J. Horton, John V. Lindsay, and Ogden R. Reid of New York; Elford A. Cederberg and James Harvey of Michigan; James C. Cleveland of New Hampshire; Robert McClory of Illinois; Charles McC. Mathias of Maryland; and F. Bradford Morse of Massachusetts. The Democrats were Thomas L. Ashley, Wayne L. Hays and Charles A. Vanik of Ohio; Jonathan B. Bingham, Hugh L. Carey, John G. Dow, Leonard Farbstein, Jacob L. Gilbert, Richard D. McCarthy, Adam Clayton Powell, Joseph Y. Resnick, Benjamin Rosenthal, William F. Ryan, James H. Scheuer, Samuel S. Stratton and Herbert Tenzer of New York; George E. Brown, Jr., Jeffrey Cohelan, James C. Corman, Ken W. Dyal, Don Edwards, Augustus F. Hawkins, James Roosevelt, and Edward R. Roybal of California; Raymond F. Clevenger, John Conyers, Jr., Charles C. Diggs, Jr., John C. Dingell, Billie S. Farnum, John C. Mackie, Lucien N. Nedzi, James G. O'Hara, Paul H. Todd, Jr., and Weston E. Vivian of Michigan; John Brademas, Andrew Jacobs, Jr., and Ray J. Madden of Indiana; Emilio Q. Daddario and William L. St. Onge of Connecticut; Paul J. Krebs and Frank Thompson, Jr., of New Jersey; Robert W. Kastenmeier and Henry S. Reuss of Wisconsin; William S. Moorhead and Robert N.C. Nix of Pennsylvania; Spark M. Matsunaga and Patsy Mink of Hawaii; John A. Blatnik of Minnesota; Richard Bolling of Missouri; Edith Green of Oregon; Thomas P. O'Neill of Massachusetts; and Teno Roncalio of Wyoming.

13.   *Congressional Record* 111 (pt. 4, 9 March 1965), p. 4443.

14.   White House Daily Diary, LBJ Library; George E. Reedy to Lyndon B. Johnson, LBJ Library, WHCF, Ex HU/ST 1; and Lyndon B. Johnson, *The Vantage Point—Perspectives of the Presidency* (New York: Holt, Rinehart & Winston, 1971), pp. 161–62. An example of the calls for Johnson to deploy federal troops is "The Power to Protect," *New Republic* 152 (20 March 1965): 5–6. Also see Eric F. Goldman, *The Tragedy of Lyndon Johnson* (New York: Alfred A. Knopf, 1969), pp. 369–70; and the impressions reportedly gathered by Speaker John McCormack on Tuesday, in Richard B. Stolley, "Inside the White House: Pressures Build Up to the Momentous Speech," *Life* 58 (26 March 1965): 34–35. A number of writers have noted that Johnson was "out of sympathy with the politics of demonstration." See Rowland Evans and Robert Novak, *Lyndon B. Johnson: The Exercise of Power* (New York: New American Library, 1966), p. 494; and Goldman, *The Tragedy of Lyndon Johnson*, p. 312.

15.   *New York Times*, 10 March 1965, p. 23.

16.   For the details of the assault on Reeb and the subsequent delay in getting him to an adequate hospital, see Fager, *Selma 1965*, pp. 108–9; and Jack Mendelsohn, *The Martyrs* (New York: Harper & Row, 1966), pp. 153–75.

17.   Jack Rosenthal to Jack Valenti, 10 March 1965, LBJ Library, Busby Papers, Box 3; Lawrence O'Brien to Lyndon B. Johnson, 10 March 1965, LBJ

Library, WHCF, Ex LE/HU 2; and Joseph Loftus, *New York Times*, 11 March 1965, p. 19. The two draft statements are in the Busby Papers, Box 3. On Mansfield and Dirksen and their concerns, see Tom Wicker, *New York Times*, 21 March 1965, p. E5; and Neil MacNeil, *Dirksen: Portrait of a Public Man* (New York: World Publishing Co., 1970), pp. 253–54.

18. See Hinckle and Welsh, "Five Battles of Selma," pp. 32–33; William Robert Miller, *Martin Luther King, Jr.* (New York: Avon, 1968), p. 223; and Forman, *Sammy Younge, Jr.*, pp. 79–80.

19. See *Washington Post*, 11 March 1965, p. 1; *New York Times*, 11 March 1965, p. 1; and *Hartford Courant*, 11 March 1965, p. 1. Also see Sister Thomas Marguerite Flanigan, "Nuns at Selma," *America* 112 (3 April 1965): 454–56.

20. Jack Valenti to Lyndon B. Johnson, 11 March 1965, LBJ Library, Appointment File. Also on Thursday morning, Assistant Attorney General Norbert Schlei passed along to Lee White a report that St. John Barrett, one of Ramsey Clark's assistants, had prepared listing the various federal personnel assigned to the Selma situation. These included nine Civil Rights Division attorneys in Selma, plus two more in Montgomery, as well as three CRS officials and sixteen U.S. deputy marshalls. While Barrett and Schlei reported that the FBI refused to inform Justice of how many agents it had in the Selma area or what they were doing, Valenti's Thursday morning notes indicate twenty-five. Norbert A. Schlei to Lee C. White, 11 March 1965, LBJ Library, White Papers, Box 5.

21. Nicholas deB. Katzenbach to Lyndon B. Johnson, 11 March 1965, LBJ Library, Appointment File; White House Daily Diary, LBJ Library. News of the troop alert, which had involved seven hundred men in the predawn hours of Tuesday, first appeared in the national press on Saturday morning. See Tom Wicker, *New York Times*, 13 March 1965, p. 1. In regard to the contents of the "talking paper," it appears quite clear that it was the administration's intent to support King against any charges of a "deal" in an effort to prevent his discreditation within the civil rights movement. Given King's efforts on Tuesday morning to avoid offending the administration—when the president and the Justice Department desperately wanted to avoid being put in a position of having to take sides in a confrontation between King and Judge Johnson—the strategy is easily understandable, as it is also within the context of larger possible concerns, such as the administration's preference for having King, a perhaps not obsequious but nevertheless malleable figure, as opposed to someone less "reasonable," as the nation's leading civil rights spokesman.

22. *New York Times*, 12 March 1965, p. 18. Also see Tom Wicker, *New York Times*, 21 March 1965, p. E5.

23. "Issues to Be Resolved on the Voting Legislation," 11 March 1965, LBJ Library, Justice Department Administrative History, Volume 7, Part Xa.

24. Ben Franklin, *New York Times*, 12 March 1965, p. 1.

25. White House Daily Diary, LBJ Library; Tom Wicker, *New York Times*, 12 March 1965, pp. 1 and 12. A number of movement observers were to note the substantially greater attention and reaction that followed Reeb's death as compared to that experienced in the wake of Jimmie Lee Jackson's murder in Feb-

ruary. While some chose to attribute this difference to an unconscious national racism—white civil rights deaths received far greater attention than those of blacks—the increased saliency of Selma at the time of Reeb's passing certainly was a factor as well. See "Reaction to Murder . . . A National Disgrace," *Southern Patriot* 23 (April 1965): 3; David Riley, "Who Is Jimmie Lee Jackson," *New Republic* 152 (3 April 1965): 8–9; and Mendelsohn, *The Martyrs*, pp. 150–51.

26. *New York Times*, 12 March 1965, p. 18; White House Daily Diary, LBJ Library; Tom Wicker, *New York Times*, 13 March 1965, p. 1; Lee C. White to Lyndon B. Johnson, 12 March 1965, Appointment File, LBJ Library.

27. E.W. Kenworthy, *New York Times*, 13 March 1965, p. 10; "Mansfield–Dirksen (Being Redrafted) 3/12/65 (p.m.)," LBJ Library, Moyers Papers, Box 7. Also see MacNeil, *Dirksen*, p. 254.

28. William Chapman, *Washington Post*, 13 March 1965, p. 8; Ben Franklin, *New York Times*, 13 March 1965, p. 10.

29. Jones, *The Wallace Story*, pp. 375–78; George C. Wallace to Lyndon B. Johnson, 12 March 1965, LBJ Library, WHCF, Ex HU 2/ST 1; Ramsey Clark to Bill D. Moyers, 13 March 1965, LBJ Library, Moyers Papers, Box 7; Johnson, *The Vantage Point*, p. 162; White House Daily Diary, LBJ Library; *Public Papers of the Presidents, Lyndon B. Johnson, 1965* (Washington: USGPO, 1966), pp. 274–81.

30. Ben Franklin, *New York Times*, 14 March 1965, pp. 1 and 66; William Chapman, *Washington Post*, 14 March 1965, p. 9; Hinckle and Welsh, "Five Battles of Selma," pp. 41–45.

31. Martin Luther King, Jr., "Civil Right No. 1—The Right to Vote," *New York Times Magazine*, 14 March 1965, pp. 26–27 and 94–95.

32. White House Daily Diary and Appointment File, 14 March 1965, LBJ Library; Johnson, *The Vantage Point*, p. 164; Goldman, *The Tragedy of Lyndon Johnson*, p. 378. The major source is Jack Valenti's very detailed notes of the meeting, which are in the Appointment File. These were also used by whoever created the account of the meeting that appears in *The Vantage Point*, which makes Johnson appear much more eager to go before a joint session than the actual notes show he truly was. King was unable to get to Washington for the Monday evening speech.

33. Coretta Scott King, *My Life With Martin Luther King, Jr.* (New York: Holt, Rinehart & Winston, 1969), p. 263; Ben Franklin, *New York Times*, 16 March 1965, p. 31; Daniel Berrigan, "Selma and Sharpeville," *Commonweal* 82 (9 April 1965): 71–75; and John Herbers, *New York Times*, 17 March 1965, p. 28.

34. Barefoot Sanders to William McCulloch, 15 March 1965, LBJ Library, Justice Department Administrative History, Volume 7, Part Xa. On the continued study of the bill's actual wording, also see William L. Taylor, staff director of the Civil Rights Commission, to Phillip Sam Hughes of the BOB, 15 March 1965, and Lee C. White to Ramsey Clark, 17 March 1965, LBJ Library, White Papers, Box 3.

35. U.S. Congress, House, *Congressional Record* 111 (pt. 4, 15 March 1965), pp. 5017–19.

36. See "Draft 1 Goodwin, 3/15," LBJ Library, Moyers Papers, Box 7. Goodwin's own papers at the Johnson Library contain nothing in regard to this speech. Also see Tom Wicker, *New York Times*, 16 March 1965, p. 1; and *Public Papers of the Presidents, Lyndon B. Johnson, 1965*, pp. 281–87. A second "special message," the one drafted by Horace Busby, was sent up quietly with the legislation itself. See *Public Papers*, pp. 287–91.

37. Goldman, *The Tragedy of Lyndon Johnson*, p. 320; Evans and Novak, *Lyndon B. Johnson: The Exercise of Power*, p. 497; Doris Kearns, *New York Times*, 15 April 1976, p. 35; and Bayard Rustin and Tom Kahn, "Johnson So Far: Civil Rights," *Commentary* 39 (June 1965): 43–46, at 44. Also see Abie Miller, *The Negro and the Great Society* (New York: Vantage Press, 1965), p. 144; Irving Howe, "What Is New About Selma?" *Dissent* 12 (Spring 1965): 147–48; Lewis, *King: A Critical Biography*, p. 285; "A Continuing Battle," *New Republic* 152 (27 March 1965): 5–6; and Jack Gould, *New York Times*, 17 March 1965, p. 91. King himself termed the speech "one of the most eloquent, unequivocal, and passionate pleas for human rights ever made by a President of the United States" ("Behind the Selma March," p. 16).

38. Carroll Kilpatrick, *Washington Post*, 16 March 1965, p. 1; William O. Douglas to Lyndon B. Johnson, 16 March 1965, LBJ Library, Busby Papers, Box 3; White House Daily Diary, LBJ Library; E.W. Kenworthy, *New York Times*, 17 March 1965, p. 1.

39. Ben Franklin, *New York Times*, 17 March 1965, p. 26; Roy Reed, *New York Times*, 17 March 1965, pp. 1 and 26; Forman, *Sammy Younge, Jr.*, pp. 99–101; U.S. Congress, House, *Congressional Record* 111 (pt. 4, 16 March 1965), p. 5106; *New York Times*, 17 March 1965, p. 44; *Washington Post*, 17 March 1965, p. A20; and *Hartford Courant*, 17 March 1965, p. 18.

40. Charles Mohr, *New York Times*, 18 March 1965, p. 1; James R. Jones to Marvin Watson, and Watson to Lyndon B. Johnson, 17 March 1965, LBJ Library, WHCF, Ex LE/HU 2, Box 66.

41. *New York Times*, 18 March 1965, p. 21; U.S. Congress, House, *Congressional Record* 111 (pt. 4, 17 March 1965), pp. 5298–99 and 5307.

42. On the Montgomery meeting, see William M. Kunstler, *Deep In My Heart* (New York: William Morrow, 1966), pp. 354–55. On the Community Relations Service's efforts to improve the Montgomery situation in the wake of the March 16 attack, see LeRoy Collins to Lyndon B. Johnson, 24 March 1965, McPherson Papers, Box 5, LBJ Library.

43. *Williams* v. *Wallace*, 240 F. Supp. 100 (1965). Johnson himself was particularly fond in subsequent years of quoting what might be termed his "commensurity theorem." See "Civil Disobedience and the Law," Johnson's standard speech of the late 1960s, in *Tulane Law Review* 44 (December 1960): 1–13, at 4; *Vanderbilt Law Review* 22 (October 1969): 1089–1100, at 1092; and *University of Florida Law Review* 20 (Winter 1968): 267–77, at 276. The doctrine also had drawn some guarded comments by others. Burke Marshall termed it "the first articulation" of that "constitutional principle" and called the overall opinion "remarkable" without indicating clearly just why he thought so. See

"The Protest Movement and the Law," *Virginia Law Review* 51 (June 1965): 785–803, at 788–89. Nicholas Katzenbach was a bit more forthright, calling it "an unusual opinion" and stating that Johnson "had to interpret existing doctrine imaginatively in order to give the march from Selma to Montgomery the protection of a court order." Speaking of the commensurity theorem, Katzenbach said, "I question that rule as a practical measure of the applicability of the First Amendment." See "Protest, Politics and the First Amendment," *Tulane Law Review* 44 (April 1970): 439–51, at 443 and 445. Also see Elliot Zashin, "Civil Rights and Civil Disobedience: The Limits of Legalism," *Texas Law Review* 52 (January 1974): 285–301. Two public law scholars have written that Johnson's doctrine gave protection to the right to demonstrate "in terms broader than any American court had used before" (Westin and Mahoney, *The Trial of Martin Luther King*, p. 176). Some rather thoughtless criticism, which calls the theorem "a totally unworkable formula" and "absurd legal theory," appears in Steven Brill, "The Real Governor of Alabama," *New York* 9 (26 April 1976): 37–41, at 41.

44.   U.S. Congress, House, Committee on the Judiciary, *Voting Rights— Hearings Before Subcommittee No. 5*, 89th Congress, 1st session, 1965, pp. 1–5. Celler's second line bore close resemblance to an editorial observation made by the *New York Times* a day earlier on p. 44. The later quotations are from Barry E. Hawk and John J. Kirby, Jr., "Federal Protection of Negro Voting Rights," *Virginia Law Review* 51 (October 1965): 1051–1213, at 1212; and Alexander M. Bickel, "The Voting Rights Bill is Tough," *New Republic* 152 (3 April 1965): 16–18, at 18, and again in *Politics and the Warren Court* (New York: Harper & Row, 1965), p. 126. Also see William W. Van Alstyne, "The Right to Vote: Small Fruit of a Bold Promise," *Nation* 200 (19 April 1965): 411–13. A very poor essay which gives a sterile account of the bill's progress is James B. Spell, Jr., "The Voting Rights Act of 1965: A Summary of Its Legislative History," M.A. thesis, University of Richmond, 1966.

45.   Cabell Phillips, *New York Times*, 19 March 1965, p. 1; and Ben Franklin, p. 20. It was not until approximately March 16 that the first issues of news-magazines containing photos and stories about the events of March 7 began to appear. The first was the March 19 issue of *Life*, which more than made up for its lack of immediacy with numerous full-color photos of the assault on the marchers. A striking picture of the column descending the bridge just prior to the attack was on the cover. In its next issue, that of March 26, *Life* again devoted its cover to the Selma story, featuring a colorful photo of King, Reuther, and Archbishop Iakovos at the courthouse service in Reeb's memory on March 15. Comparable verbal and photographic coverage was supplied, with a similar delay, by *Newsweek*, *Time*, and *U.S. News & World Report*. In the only study of newspaper coverage of Selma which has been conducted, Donald R. Shanor surveyed the March 18 editions of 170 southern dailies. Shanor examined what editorial stance, if any, the paper took on voting rights legislation, and whether it ran syndicated columns which either supported or opposed its own position. See "Southern Editors and Selma," *Journalism Quarterly* 44 (Spring 1967): 133–35.

46. *New York Times*, 20 March 1965, pp. 1, 12, 13, and 20; White House Daily Diary, LBJ Library. For criticism of the trigger formula as "blunt and imperfect," see Robert B. McKay, "Racial Discrimination in the Electoral Process," *Annals of the American Academy of Political and Social Science* 407 (May 1973): 102–18, at 114. At the time, administration officials replied that those areas of discrimination missed by the trigger were few at most, and that the Justice Department, with most of its voting rights litigation bypassed by the bill's trigger, could easily focus its litigative efforts—which the 1965 bill explicitly cited as an additional enforcement tool—on whichever cases did remain after the 1965 act's major provisions had dealt with the great majority of recalcitrant counties. The best account of the small, intermittent, SNCC-sponsored demonstrations in Montgomery which received very little press coverage is in Judge Johnson's opinions in *Forman* v. *City of Montgomery*, 245 F. Supp. 17, and *Johnson* v. *City of Montgomery*, 245 F. Supp. 25. In these decisions the judge refused to remove the cases of the arrested protestors from city to federal courts.

47. For good accounts of the actual march and its mood, see Andrew Kopkind, "A Walk in Alabama," *New Republic* 152 (3 April 1965): 7–8; Renata Adler, "Letter From Selma," *New Yorker* 41 (10 April 1965): 121; Simeon Booker, "50,000 March on Montgomery," *Ebony* 20 (May 1965): 46; Christopher S. Wren, "Turning Point for the Church," *Look* 29 (18 May 1965): 32–37; W.C. Heinz and Bard Lindeman, "The Meaning of the Selma March: Great Day at Trickem Fork," *Saturday Evening Post* 238 (22 May 1965): 30–31 and 89–95; and Fager, *Selma 1965*, pp. 150–59.

48. *New York Times*, 23 March 1965, p. 29; E.W. Kenworthy, *New York Times*, 25 March 1965, p. 28, and 26 March 1965, p. 23; Barefoot Sanders to Nicholas deB. Katzenbach, 22 March 1965, LBJ Library, Justice Department Administrative History, Volume 7, Part Xa; U.S. Congress, Senate, Committee on the Judiciary, *Voting Rights—Hearings on S. 1564*, 89th Congress, 1st session, 1965; Archibald Cox to Nicholas deB. Katzenbach, 23 March 1965, LBJ Library, Justice Department Administrative History, Volume 7, Part Xa.

49. Roy Reed, *New York Times*, 25 March 1965, p. 27. For two participants' accounts of the entry into Montgomery, see Margaret Long, "Strictly Subjective," *New South* 20 (March 1965): 2 and 13–16; and Stanley Plastrik, "Marching on Montgomery," *Dissent* 12 (Spring 1965): 145–47. On the television coverage, see Fred. W. Friendly, *Due to Circumstances Beyond Our Control . . .* (New York: Random House, 1967), p. 171. For the full text of King's speech, an oration which cannot be appreciated fully when presented only in part, see *New York Times*, 26 March 1965, p. 22. On efforts to secure a peaceful and orderly reception for the marchers in Montgomery, see Collins to Johnson, 24 March 1965, McPherson Papers, Box 5. Also see Jones, *The Wallace Story*, p. 430.

50. For Rowe's account, as told to a ghostwriter, see Gary Thomas Rowe, Jr., *My Undercover Years With the Ku Klux Klan* (New York: Bantam, 1976). On President Johnson's television appearance, see Friendly, *Due to Circumstances*, pp. 172–73; and George P. Hunt, "The Racial Crisis and the News

Media," in Paul L. Fisher and Ralph L. Lowenstein, eds., *Race and the News Media* (New York: Praeger, 1967), p. 16. On Mrs. Liuzzo, who, like James Reeb, had been affected deeply by the television coverage of Bloody Sunday, see Mendelsohn, *The Martyrs*, pp. 176–95; and Don Whitehead, *Attack on Terror: The FBI Against the Ku Klux Klan in Mississippi* (New York: Funk & Wagnalls, 1970), pp. 305–10. For some surprising—and perhaps scarey—indications of some people's reactions to the Liuzzo murder, see Lyn Tornabene, "Murder in Alabama," *Ladies' Home Journal* 82 (July 1965): 42–44.

51.   For a good example of the columns critical of the administration bill, see Arthur Krock, *New York Times*, 23 March 1965, p. 38. On the legislative situation, see E.W. Kenworthy, *New York Times*, 27 March 1965, p. 12; Arthur Krock, *New York Times*, 28 March 1965, p. E11; E.W. Kenworthy, *New York Times*, 30 March 1965, p. 26; Edward M. Kennedy to Lee C. White, 30 March 1965, LBJ Library, White Papers, Box 3; Louis F. Claiborne, "Possible Substantive Changes in Voting Bill," 29 March 1965, LBJ Library, Justice Department Administrative History, Volume 7, Part Xa; Tom Wicker, *New York Times*, 29 March 1965, p. 28; and E.W. Kenworthy, *New York Times*, 31 March 1965, p. 18, and 2 April 1965, p. 24.

52.   Jones, *The Wallace Story*, p. 430; *New York Times*, 30 March 1965, pp. 1 and 46; Andrew Kopkind, "Boycotting Alabama," *New Republic* 152 (17 April 1965): 11–13; Martin Luther King, Jr., "The Civil Rights Struggle in the United States Today," *The Record of the Association of the Bar of the City of New York* 20 (May 1965, Supplement): 3–24, at 13–15 and 19–20; and *New York Times*, 3 April 1965, p. 14.

53.   E.W. Kenworthy, *New York Times*, 3 April 1965, p. 1, and 6 April 1965, p. 18; Reports on Legislation, 5 April 1965, Justice Department, LBJ Library; Archibald Cox to Nicholas deB. Katzenbach, 6 April 1965, and Barefoot Sanders to Stephen J. Pollak, 6 April 1965, LBJ Library, Justice Department Administrative History, Volume 7, Part Xa; *New York Times*, 8 April 1965, p. 28; and E.W. Kenworthy, *New York Times*, 9 April 1965, p. 6.

54.   E.W. Kenworthy, *New York Times*, 10 April 1965, p. 1; and Reports on Legislation, 12 April 1965, Justice Department, LBJ Library. Also see Alexander M. Bickel, "Amending the Voting Rights Bill," *New Republic* 152 (1 May 1965): 10–11. King spoke out strongly against the Dirksen escape clause in a speech on April 21 in New York, saying that its retention would "emasculate" the bill. See "The Civil Rights Struggle," pp. 13 and 20–21. Also see U.S. Congress, Senate Committee on the Judiciary, *Voting Rights Legislation—Report No. 162* (3 pts.), 89th Congress, 1st session, 1965. See in particular the joint views of the twelve-member majority, which include the observation, "Experience has shown that the case-by-case litigation approach will not solve the voting discrimination problem" and make reference to Dallas County as an example (pp. 6–8). In this same period of time both of New York's senators, as well as Mayor Wagner, were becoming interested in having added to the bill an amendment to provide for the registration of New York City's 500,000 to 600,000 Spanish-speaking residents of voting age. Dirksen was hostile to any such measure,

which would result in a growth in Democratic registration in the city, though Katzenbach was willing to accept such an amendment so long as its addition did not increase opposition to the entire bill. See Lee C. White to Lyndon B. Johnson, 8 April 1965, LBJ Library, WHCF, Ex LE/HU 2-7.

55. "Selma: Only A Beginning," *Southern Patriot* 23 (April 1965): 1 and 3; Fager, *Selma 1965*, pp. 172–73, 179, and 184–85; and Fred Graham, *New York Times*, 13 April 1965, p. 20, and 14 April 1965, p. 1. On the dissolution of Hare's injunction and the resolution of arrests made under it, see *Dallas County* v. *SNCC* and *State* v. *Allen*, 10 *Race Relations Law Reporter* 234. For the ruling against Sheriff Clark, see *U.S.* v. *Clark*, 249 F. Supp. 720 (1965). A subsequent order instructing that certain prosecutions in local court be dropped was entered on June 1, 1965. See 10 *Race Relations Law Reporter* 568. Also see *New York Times*, 17 April 1965, p. 1, and 18 April 1965, p. 53; U.S. Congress, House, *Congressional Record* 111 (pt. 5, 28 April 1965), p. 8695; and Fred Graham, *New York Times*, 20 April 1965, p. 25.

56. Those two proposals were also the only two items strongly opposed by the administration. For the reasons behind that opposition, see "Questions Concerning the Voting Rights Act of 1965 as Reported by the [Senate] Judiciary Committee," LBJ Library, Justice Department Administrative History, Volume 7, Part Xa. In regard to the poll tax ban, the department believed that there was no evidence of the tax's inherently discriminatory nature, especially given its uncontroversial use in Vermont. Dirksen's escape hatch provision would have allowed Louisiana, Virginia and South Carolina, on a statewide basis, and several dozen Virginia and North Carolina counties on a county-by-county basis, to receive exemption from the act's provisions, assuming that they could prove that no racial discrimination presently was being practiced in their electoral systems. As the Justicè Department memo argued in voicing opposition to the Illinois senator's proposal, "The bill should make clear that a momentary pause in discrimination is not sufficient to excuse the state or subdivision. The Dirksen escape hatch does not make this clear."

57. E.W. Kenworthy, *New York Times*, 23 April 1965, p. 16; Harold H. Greene to Stephen J. Pollak, 23 April 1965, LBJ Library, Justice Department Administrative History, Volume 7, Part Xa; *New York Times*, 24 April 1965, p. 12; Marjorie Hunter, *New York Times*, 26 April 1965, p. 1; Reports on Legislation, 26 April 1965, Justice Department, LBJ Library; Lawrence O'Brien to Lyndon B. Johnson, 26 April 1965, LBJ Library, WHCF, Ex LE/HU 2, Box 66; E.W. Kenworthy, *New York Times*, 27 April 1965, p. 19, 29 April 1965, p. 16, 30 April 1965, p. 1, 1 May 1965, p. 12, 4 May 1965, p. 58, 5 May 1965, p. 1, 8 May 1965, p. 14, and 9 May 1965, p. E6; Marjorie Hunter, *New York Times*, 10 May 1965, p. 1; and E.W. Kenworthy, *New York Times*, 12 May 1965, p. 1, and 13 May 1965, p. 10.

For the administration argument against the poll tax ban as of early May, see Nicholas deB. Katzenbach to Mike Mansfield, 7 May 1965, *Congressional Record* 111 at 9930. A much fuller articulation of the department's hesitancies concerning such a statutory ban is given in Nicholas deB. Katzenbach to Lyndon B. Johnson, 21 May 1965, LBJ Library, WHCF, Ex LE/HU 2, Box 66. In that memo the attorney general noted the earlier Supreme Court decisions that had upheld the tax and emphasized that any pure test of the constitutionality of the tax per se would focus on its use in Vermont as well as in Mississippi. Katzenbach stressed the importance of avoiding any Supreme Court ruling against any portion of the act as passed, but also emphasized a more immediate concern as well. "A decision to support this approach and oppose the flat ban also appeared advisable as the best means [of] assuring the necessary votes for cloture," the attorney general wrote the president. Dirksen's continued support of the bill, Katzenbach said, "is necessary to assure those votes" for cloture, and was dependent upon administration opposition to a flat ban. "If we had not opposed the flat ban," Katzenbach went on, "I believe Senator Dirksen, Senators Aiken and Prouty of Vermont, and other Republicans would probably be lost for cloture. With only 45 Democratic votes, we could not prevail without these Republicans." Also see MacNeil, *Dirksen*, pp. 255–56, and Andrew Kopkind, "Birth of A Bill," *New Republic* 152 (15 May 1965): 11–13. Katzenbach's fears about the constitutional infirmity of any poll tax ban echoed those of scholarly analysts. See two brief articles by Alexander M. Bickel: "Congress and the Poll Tax," *New Republic* 152 (24 April 1965): 11–12; and "Voting Rights Bill—Third Edition," *New Republic* 152 (22 May 1965): 13–14.

58.   Reports on Legislation, 10 May 1965, Justice Department, LBJ Library; E.W. Kenworthy, *New York Times*, 14 May 1965, p. 18; Marjorie Hunter, *New York Times*, 17 May 1965, p. 19; E.W. Kenworthy, *New York Times*, 20 May 1965, p. 1; Warren Weaver, *New York Times*, 21 May 1965, p. 1; E.W. Kenworthy, *New York Times*, 22 May 1965, p. 1, 25 May 1965, p. 23, 26 May 1965, p. 1, and 27 May 1965, p. 1. Also see Congressional Quarterly, "Senate Passes Voting Bill," *Weekly Report*, 28 May 1965, pp. 1007–9, and "Voting Rights," *Weekly Report*, 4 June 1965, pp. 1052–57. For criticism of the Puerto Rican amendment, see Alexander M. Bickel, "The Kennedy-Javits Voting Amendment," *New Republic* 152 (5 June 1965): 10. On Dirksen's efforts to persuade Republican senators to support cloture, and Hickenlooper's attempts to frustrate Dirksen, see MacNeil, *Dirksen*, pp. 257–59. Four senators who had opposed the 1964 act—Hickenlooper, Gore, Cotton, and Simpson—voted for the 1965 act on May 26. Neither Russell Long nor any of the other southern senators who had been considered possible "switches"—e.g., Smathers and Fulbright—supported the bill that day.

59.   *New York Times*, 27 April 1965, p. 22, 29 April 1965, p. 16; Paul Montgomery, *New York Times*, 3 May 1965, p. 28, and 4 May 1965, p. 58; Roy Reed, *New York Times*, 4 May 1965, p. 58, 8 May 1965, p. 1, 11 May 1965, p. 25; *New York Times*, 12 May 1965, p. 27; Roy Reed, *New York Times*, 16 May 1965, p. 72; Ben Franklin, *New York Times*, 24 May 1965, p. 19, 25 May 1965, p. 1; *New York Times*, 30 May 1965, p. 36, and 1 June 1965, p. 23. Also see Gay Talese, "Where's the Spirit of Selma Now?" *New York Times Magazine*, 30 May 1965, pp. 8–9, 41, and 44–45. On the Wilkins' trial in Hayneville, also see Murray Kempton, "Trial of the Klansman," *New Republic* 152 (22 May 1965): 10–13.

60. See U.S. Congress, House, Committee on the Judiciary, *Voting Rights Act of 1965—Report No. 439*, 89th Congress, 1st session, 1965. Also see *New York Times*, 3 June 1965, p. 23; E.W. Kenworthy, *New York Times*, 27 May 1965, p. 1; Reports on Legislation, 7 June 1965, 14 June 1965, and 18 June 1965, Justice Department, LBJ Library; and *New York Times*, 25 June 1965, p. 20. The substantial delay begot protestations from the LCCR, which asked Johnson to use his influence to end the "unconscionable delay." See Clarence Mitchell and Arnold Aronson to Lyndon B. Johnson, 22 June 1965, LBJ Library, WHCF, Gen LE/HU 2-7, Box 72. Also see Aronson's memo to member organizations, 24 June 1965, LBJ Library, White Papers, Box 3, and White's June 25 response to Mitchell's and Aronson's letter, LBJ Library, WHCF, Gen LE/HU 2–7, Box 72.

61. Reports on Legislation, 28 June 1965, 6 July 1965, and 12 July 1965, Justice Department, LBJ Library; E.W. Kenworthy, *New York Times*, 6 July 1965, p. 1, 7 July 1965, p. 18; *New York Times*, 8 July 1965, p. 14; Lyndon B. Johnson (by Bill D. Moyers) to Walter P. Reuther, 7 July 1965, LBJ Library, WHCF, Ex LE/HU 2-7; E.W. Kenworthy, *New York Times*, 9 July 1965, p. 10, 10 July 1965, p. 1; and *Public Papers of the Presidents, Lyndon B. Johnson, 1965*, pp. 731–32. Also see Goldman, *The Tragedy of Lyndon Johnson*, p. 389; Congressional Quarterly, "House Passes Voting Rights Bill," *Weekly Report*, 16 July 1965, pp. 1361–63; and Alexander M. Bickel, "House and Senate Voting Bills," *New Republic* 153 (24 July 1965): 8.

62. Fager, *Selma 1965*, pp. 196–98; *New York Times*, 7 July 1965, p. 1, and 8 July 1965, p. 21; Haynes Johnson, *Washington Evening Star*, 26 July 1965 (in *Congressional Record* 111 at 18453); *New York Times*, 13 June 1965, p. 73; Elwyn A. Smith, "Stalemate in Selma," *Christian Century* 82 (25 August 1965): 1031–33; and John Doar to Joseph A. Califano, Jr., 9 August 1965, Dallas County "justification memo," LBJ Library, WHCF, Ex HU 2-7, Box 55.

63. On Jackson, see Paul Montgomery, *New York Times*, 15 June 1965, p. 1, 16 June 1965, p. 1, 17 June 1965, p. 21, 18 June 1965, p. 24, and 19 June 1965, p. 14; and *Congressional Record* 111 at 13725. For an overview of Mississippi's quiet summer, see Elizabeth Sutherland, "Summer of Discontent," *Nation* 201 (11 October 1965): 212–15. On Bogalusa, see Roy Reed, *New York Times*, 9 July 1965, p. 1, 11 July 1965, p. 1, 12 July 1965, p. 1, 13 July 1965, p. 1, 14 July 1965, p. 1, 15 July 1965, p. 1, 27 July 1965, p. 1, 28 July 1965, p. 40, and 30 July 1965, p. 1. Also see Paul Good, "Klantown, USA," *Nation* 200 (1 February 1965): 110–13; John Doar and Dorothy Landsberg, "The Performance of the FBI in Investigating Violations of Federal Laws Protecting the Right to Vote—1960–1967," in U.S. Congress, Senate, Select Committee to Study Governmental Operations with Respect to Intelligence Activities, *Hearings on Intelligence Activities, Federal Bureau of Investigation*, 94th Congress, 1st session, 1975, pp. 888–991, at 942–46; and Judge Wisdom's wide-ranging opinion in *U.S. v. Original Knights of the Ku Klux Klan*, 230 F. Supp. 330 (1965).

On Americus and Sumter County, see Gene Roberts, *New York Times*, 28 July 1965, p. 40; and *New York Times*, 1 August 1965, p. 1. Less press attention was given to a series of demonstrations in Greensboro, Alabama. See *New York*

Times, 27 July 1965, p. 18, and 1 August 1965, p. 58; Roy Reed, *New York Times*, 2 August 1965, p. 15; and *New York Times*, 3 August 1965, p. 19. An excellent overview of the 1965 summer in the South, and the absence of any well-publicized movement effort, is given in Gene Roberts' page-one story in the August 1 *Times*. A number of writers have sounded the theme that the movement "somehow fell apart after Selma," in large part because of the basic differences between the SCLC and SNCC which had been highlighted in the aftermath of March 9. See Pat Watters, *Down To Now* (New York: Pantheon, 1971), pp. 330, 323, and 345; Forman, *Sammy Younge, Jr.*, pp. 75 and 99; and Debbie Louis, *And We Are Not Saved* (Garden City, N.Y.: Doubleday, 1970), pp. 221–23 and 230–31. Also see Pat Watters, *Encounter With The Future* (Atlanta: Southern Regional Council, 1965); Jack Newfield, *A Prophetic Minority* (New York: New American Library, 1966), pp. 99–112; Robert H. Brisbane, *Black Activism* (Valley Forge: Judson Press, 1974), pp. 125–48; Nick Kotz and Mary Lynn Kotz, *A Passion For Equality* (New York: W.W. Norton, 1977), pp. 148–49; Anne Braden, "The Southern Freedom Movement in Perspective," *Monthly Review* 17 (July–August 1965): 1–93, at 1; Gene Roberts, "The Story of Snick: From 'Freedom High' to 'Black Power,' " *New York Times Magazine*, 25 September 1966, p. 27; and Allen J. Matusow, "From Civil Rights to Black Power: The Case of SNCC, 1960–1966," in Barton J. Bernstein and Allen J. Matusow, eds., *Twentieth-Century America: Recent Interpretations*, 2nd ed. (New York: Harcourt Brace Jovanovich, 1972), pp. 494–520. An excellent recent analysis of SNCC's demise, marred only by several errors concerning the Voting Rights Act, is Emily Stoper, "The Student Nonviolent Coordinating Committee: Rise and Fall of A Redemptive Organization," *Journal of Black Studies* 8 (September 1977): 13–34.

Also during the summer both the Alabama and Mississippi legislatures revised their states' voter qualifications, changes which were of little practical importance once the Voting Rights Act became law. See *New York Times*, 24 June 1965, p. 15, and 23 July 1965, p. 26.

64. Reports on Legislation, 19 July 1965, 26 July 1965, and 2 August 1965, Justice Department, LBJ Library; Mike Manatos to Lawrence O'Brien, 26 July 1965, LBJ Library, Manatos Papers, Box 8; and E.W. Kenworthy, *New York Times*, 30 July 1965, p. 1, and 4 August 1965, p. 1. An angry Representative Cramer secured a copy of the Katzenbach letter and made it public. See *Congressional Record* 111 (4 August 1965), p. 19444. Also see Congressional Quarterly, "Voting Rights," *Weekly Report*, 13 August 1965, pp. 1595–97. For two brief and not terribly informative articles on the civil rights voting behavior of southern representatives, see Thomas A. Flinn and Harold L. Wolman, "Constituency and Roll Call Voting: The Case of Southern Democratic Congressmen," *Midwest Journal of Political Science* 10 (May 1966): 192–99; and Joe R. Feagin, "Civil Rights Voting by Southern Congressmen," *Journal of Politics* 34 (May 1972): 484–99.

65. *Public Papers of the Presidents, Lyndon B. Johnson, 1965*, pp. 840–43. For the complete text of the act as signed into law, plus a brief outline of its

provisions, see U.S. Commission on Civil Rights, *The Voting Rights Act of 1965* (Washington: USGPO, 1965). One provision rather largely ignored at the time was that the final version specified a five-year lifetime for some provisions, rather than the ten years that administration drafters had suggested initially. On the elaborate White House planning of the signing ceremony, see Jack Valenti to Lyndon B. Johnson, 16 July 1965, Jack Valenti to Horace Busby, 20 July 1965, Horace Busby to Marvin Watson, 4 August 1965, and Horace Busby to Lyndon B. Johnson, 4 August 1965, LBJ Library, WHCF, Ex LE/HU 2, Box 66.

Chapter 4

1. See Alan F. Westin and Barry Mahoney, *The Trial of Martin Luther King* (New York: Thomas Y. Crowell, 1974), p. 177; Pat Watters and Reese Cleghorn, *Climbing Jacob's Ladder: The Arrival of Negroes in Southern Politics* (New York: Harcourt, Brace & World, 1967), p. 57; John Herbers, *The Black Dilemma* (New York: John Day, 1973), p. 27; Irving Howe, "What is New About Selma?" *Dissent* 12 (Spring 1965): 147; and Thomas R. Dye, *The Politics of Equality* (Indianapolis: Bobbs-Merrill, 1971), pp. 55 and 122.

2. See Doris Kearns, *Lyndon Johnson and the American Dream* (New York: Harper & Row, 1976), p. 228; and Eric F. Goldman, *The Tragedy of Lyndon Johnson* (New York: Alfred A. Knopf, 1969), p. 318.

3. See Bayard Rustin and Tom Kahn, "Johnson So Far: Civil Rights," *Commentary* 39 (June 1965): 43–46, at 43.

4. Kearns, *Lyndon Johnson*, pp. x, 53, 230, 299, and 308. Also see Doris Kearns, "Lyndon Johnson's Political Personality," *Political Science Quarterly* 91 (Fall 1976): 385–409; Steven F. Lawson and Mark I. Gelfand, "Consensus and Civil Rights: Lyndon B. Johnson and the Black Franchise," *Prologue* 8 (Summer 1976): 65–76, at 66–68; and Monroe Billington, "Lyndon B. Johnson and Blacks: The Early Years," *Journal of Negro History* 62 (January 1977): 26–42, at 27 and 42.

5. See Lee C. White to Bill D. Moyers, 30 December 1964, LBJ Library, White Papers, Box 3.

6. See Nicholas deB. Katzenbach to Lyndon B. Johnson, 28 December 1964; "Constitutional Amendment, Draft 1/8/65;" James L. Morrison to Norbert A. Schlei, 15 February 1965; Archibald Cox to Nicholas deB. Katzenbach, 23 February 1965; and "An Act," 5 March 1965; all in Justice Department Administrative History, Volume 7, Part Xa, LBJ Library. Also see Reports on Legislation, 15 February 1965, Justice Department, LBJ Library; and Nicholas deB. Katzenbach to Lee C. White and Bill D. Moyers, 1 March 1965, LBJ Library, Busby Papers, Box 3.

7. See Claude Sitton, "Racial Coverage: Planning and Logistics," in Paul L. Fisher and Ralph L. Lowenstein, eds., *Race and the News Media* (New York: Praeger, 1967), p. 77; August Meier, "On the Role of Martin Luther King," *New Politics* 4 (Winter 1965): 52–59, at 53; Westin and Mahoney, *The Trial of Martin Luther King*, pp. 2, 156, and 285. Also see John Herbers, *New York Times*, 14 February 1965, p. E5, who quotes the SCLC's Andrew Young as speaking of how the 1964 act "was written in Birmingham."

8. *New York Times*, 4 April 1963, p. 24; Foster Hailey, *New York Times*, 5 April 1963, p. 16, 6 April 1963, p. 20, 7 April 1963, p. 55, 8 April 1963, p. 31, 9 April 1963, p. 53, 10 April 1963, p. 29, 11 April 1963, p. 21, 12 April 1963, p. 1, 13 April 1963, p. 1, and 14 April 1963, p. 1; and Jack Raymond, *New York Times*, 14 April 1963, p. 46. For an excellent background piece on the city, written before the SCLC arrived in town, see Joe David Brown, "Birmingham, Alabama: A City in Fear," *Saturday Evening Post* 236 (2 March 1963): 11–19. Also see Reese Cleghorn, "Bustling Birmingham," *New Republic* 148 (20 April 1963): 9.

9. Foster Hailey, *New York Times*, 15 April 1963, p. 1, 16 April 1963, p. 1, 17 April 1963, p. 22, 18 April 1963, p. 21, 19 April 1963, p. 9; *New York Times*, 19 April 1963, p. 9, and 20 April 1963, p. 12; Foster Hailey, *New York Times*, 21 April 1963, p. 21, 23 April 1963, p. 20; *New York Times*, 24 April 1963, p. 19, 25 April 1963, p. 20, 27 April 1963, p. 9, and 29 April 1963, p. 15.

10. *New York Times*, 4 May 1963; *Washington Post*, 4 May 1963. See also *Hartford Courant*, 4 May 1963, p. 1. The one particular photo which each paper used at the top of p. 1 also was later used extensively by the newsmagazines. See *Newsweek*, 13 May 1963, p. 27; and *Time*, 10 May 1963, p. 19. Also see *Life*, 17 May 1963, pp. 26–36.

11. Arthur M. Schlesinger, *A Thousand Days: John F. Kennedy in the White House* (Boston: Houghton Mifflin, 1965), p. 959; James C. Harvey, *Civil Rights During the Kennedy Administration* (Hattiesburg: University & College Press of Mississippi, 1971), p. 56; and *Washington Post*, 5 May 1963, p. A13. Also see Edwin Guthman, *We Band of Brothers* (New York: Harper & Row, 1971), p. 213; Theodore Sorensen, *Kennedy* (New York: Harper & Row, 1965), p. 494; and James H. Laue, "The Movement, Negro Challenge to The Myth," *New South* 18 (July–August 1963): 9–17.

12. *New York Times*, 5 May 1963, pp. 1 and E10; *Washington Post*, 5 May 1963, p. 1.

13. *New York Times*, 7 May 1963, pp. 1 and 33; *Washington Post* 7 May 1963, pp. 1, 4, and 16. On Sunday's and Monday's marches, also see Michael Dorman, *We Shall Overcome* (New York: Delacorte Press, 1964), pp. 150–53. On the foreign coverage of Birmingham, see p. 14 of May 10's *Times*.

14. Claude Sitton, *New York Times*, 8 May 1963, pp. 1 and 28; *Washington Post*, 8 May 1963, p. 1. Also see Dorman, *We Shall Overcome*, pp. 153–54.

15. U.S. Congress, House, Committee on the Judiciary, *Civil Rights—Hearings Before Subcommittee No. 5*, 88th Congress, 1st session, 1963, p. 907; *Public Papers of the Presidents, John F. Kennedy, 1963* (Washington: USGPO, 1964), pp. 372–78.

16. The best accounts of the negotiations are Vincent Harding, "A Beginning in Birmingham," *Reporter* 28 (6 June 1963): 13–19; and Dorman, *We Shall Overcome*, pp. 148–50, 154–56, 177–78, 182, and 186. Also see William M. Kunstler, *Deep In My Heart* (New York: William Morrow, 1966), pp. 173–96, who details the agreement on pp. 191–92; Howell Raines, *My Soul Is Rested* (New York: G.P. Putnam's Sons, 1977), pp. 157–61; James Reston, *New York Times*, 10 May 1963, p. 32; William V. Shannon, "The Crisis in Birmingham," *Commonweal* 78

(24 May 1963): 238–39; and Jean Stein, *American Journey: The Times of Robert Kennedy* (New York: Harcourt Brace Jovanovich, 1970), pp. 114–18.

17. *Public Papers of the Presidents, John F. Kennedy, 1963*, pp. 397–98; *New York Times*, 13 May 1963, pp. 1 and 25; *Washington Post*, 13 May 1963, pp. 1 and 4. Also see Dorman, *We Shall Overcome*, pp. 167–74; and Stephen C. Rose, "Test for Nonviolence," *Christian Century* 80 (29 May 1963): 714–16.

18. Paul Duke, *Wall Street Journal*, 15 May 1963, p. 1. On Monday's events, see Dorman, *We Shall Overcome*, pp. 175–76.

19. A full account of the passage of the 1964 act lies far beyond the scope of this work. Unfortunately, no comprehensive work on that topic has yet been published. In the meantime, in addition to Congressional Quarterly's *Weekly Reports*, see CQ's *Revolution in Civil Rights*, 3rd ed. (Washington: Congressional Quarterly Service, 1967), and *Legislators and Lobbyists* (Washington: Congressional Quarterly Service, 1965), parts 1 and 7. An account that provides little more than a survey of what is contained in the various CQ publications is Clifford M. Lytle, "The History of the Civil Rights Bill of 1964," *Journal of Negro History* 51 (October 1966): 275–96. Two far more valuable accounts are Alexander M. Bickel, "The Civil Rights Act of 1964," *Commentary* 38 (August 1964): 33–39; and James L. Sundquist, *Politics and Policy—The Eisenhower, Kennedy and Johnson Years* (Washington: Brookings Institution, 1968), pp. 259–71. Three other instructive sources are Joseph W. Sullivan, *Wall Street Journal*, 3 February 1964, pp. 1 and 12; Hubert H. Humphrey, *Beyond Civil Rights: A New Day of Equality* (New York: Random House, 1968), pp. 80–97; and Robert Byrd's comments of June 19, 1964 in *Congressional Record* 110 at 14482. An account of the bill's progress through the end of the Kennedy administration appears in Carl M. Brauer, *John F. Kennedy and the Second Reconstruction* (New York: Columbia University Press, 1977), pp. 247–51, 263–85, 290–92, and 303–10. Also see John F. Manley, "The U.S. Civil Rights Act of 1964," *Contemporary Review* 206 (January 1965): 10–13; Keith Hindell, "Civil Rights Breaks the Cloture Barrier," *Political Quarterly* 36 (April–June 1965): 142–53; James C. Harvey, *Black Civil Rights During the Johnson Administration* (Jackson: University & College Press of Mississippi, 1973), pp. 8–20; Arthur I. Waskow, *From Race Riot To Sit-in* (Garden City, N.Y.: Doubleday, 1966), p. 250; Ben Franklin, *New York Times*, 10 April 1964, pp. 1 and 23; Neil MacNeil, *Dirksen: Portrait of a Public Man* (New York: World Publishing Co., 1970), pp. 218–19 and 223–38; and Robert A. Dahl, *Pluralist Democracy in the United States: Conflict and Consent* (Chicago: Rand McNally, 1967), pp. 422–26.

20. Concerning the impact of Birmingham on John F. Kennedy, see Anthony Lewis, "Since the Supreme Court Spoke," *New York Times Magazine*, 10 May 1964, p. 91; Schlesinger, *A Thousand Days*, p. 969; Louis Harris, *The Anguish of Change* (New York: W.W. Norton, 1973), pp. 15–16; Brauer, *John F. Kennedy*, pp. 230 and 246–47; and Harold Fleming, "The Federal Executive and Civil Rights: 1961–1965," *Daedalus* 94 (Fall 1965): 921–48, at 941–42. Gary Orfield has suggested somewhat unclearly that the introduction in Congress of a number of bills aimed at eliminating federal support of segregated schools was somehow a

"response" to Birmingham. Since school desegregation never was touched upon during the Birmingham campaign, Orfield's suggestion seems curious. Such actions instead may have been influenced by the federal-state standoff at Tuscaloosa and Huntsville. See *The Reconstruction of Southern Education* (New York: Wiley-Interscience, 1969), p. 33.

21. On the impact of the March on Washington of August 28, 1963, see the stories by James Reston, Warren Weaver, and E.W. Kenworthy in the *New York Times* of August 29; Congressional Quarterly, "March on Washington," *Weekly Report*, 30 August 1963, pp. 1495–96 and 1527; and Humphrey, *Beyond Civil Rights*, pp. 171–72. For comments on the degree of change in Birmingham in the years after 1963, see Paul Good, "Birmingham Two Years Later," *Reporter* 33 (2 December 1965): 21–27; and Fred L. Shuttlesworth, "Birmingham Revisited," *Ebony* 26 (August 1971): 114–18.

22. Eight sets of relevant remarks expressed neither clear support of nor clear opposition to the Selma protestors and their goal of equal voting rights. No claim is made that the *Congressional Record* contains a complete record of all public comments on Birmingham and Selma made by members of Congress. Any number of newspaper stories concerning dinner speeches and various passing remarks would disprove such an assertion. Neither is it claimed that the *Record* is a precise and accurate account of what *actually* transpired on the floor of either house of Congress, as informed observers well know. It is true, however, that the compilation of statements contained in the *Record* offers an excellent resource for determining just what events, and what facets thereof, had an impact upon the members of Congress, and what the relative quantitative differences in such impact were.

23. During the Birmingham campaign some news publications characterized Dr. King as simply the "outside agitator" that southern segregationists accused him of being. See the interesting piece of editorial journalism in *Time* 81 (19 April 1963): 30–31.

24. Several writers have stressed the importance of these characteristics, and the resulting effects, to what is perhaps an excessive degree. They are important, however. See Jack Mendelsohn, *The Martyrs* (New York: Harper & Row, 1966), p. 173, concerning Reeb; and Monroe Lee Billington, *The American South* (New York: Charles Scribner's Sons, 1971), p. 406, in regard to Mrs. Liuzzo.

25. A number of observers have commented upon the need for a protest to make its goals clear and for an easily visible connection to exist between acts of protest and what is being demonstrated against if a direct action campaign is to succeed. We shall touch upon this again in chapter 7. See Burke Marshall, "The Protest Movement and the Law," *Virginia Law Review* 51 (June 1965): 785–803, at 786; Frank M. Johnson, Jr., "Civil Disobedience and the Law," *University of Florida Law Review* 20 (Winter 1968): 267–77, at 273; and Bo Wirmark, "Nonviolent Methods and the American Civil Rights Movement, 1955–1965," *Journal of Peace Research* 11 (1974): 115–32, at 119.

26. Many writers have voiced the opinion that southern law-enforcement officials such as Clark and Connor assisted rather than hindered the movement

through their violent behavior. While such observations are basically correct, they often are rather simplistic. Additional important perspectives on this point will be touched on in chapters 5 and 7. Perhaps the most well-known statement of this view was that often attributed to President Kennedy. As Burke Marshall later wrote, "Everyone took to heart the truth in President Kennedy's remark to the civil rights leaders at the time of the March on Washington that no man had done more by his individual actions to further the cause of civil rights than Eugene 'Bull' Connor" ("The Protest Movement and the Law," p. 793). Also see Leslie W. Dunbar, *A Republic of Equals* (Ann Arbor: University of Michigan Press, 1966), p. 80.

27.   Lucian W. Pye, "Political Culture," *International Encyclopedia of the Social Sciences* 12 (1968): 218–25, at 218; Sidney Verba, "Comparative Political Culture," in Pye and Verba, eds., *Political Culture and Political Development* (Princeton: Princeton University Press, 1965), pp. 513 and 516. Also see V.O. Key, *Public Opinion and American Democracy* (New York: Alfred A. Knopf, 1961), p. 275.

28.   Herbert McClosky, "Consensus and Ideology in American Politics," *American Political Science Review* 58 (June 1964): 361–82; Donald J. Devine, *The Political Culture of the United States* (Boston: Little, Brown, 1972); and William C. Mitchell, *The American Polity* (New York: Free Press, 1962), pp. 104–39 and 376–80.

29.   James W. Prothro and Charles M. Grigg, "Fundamental Principles of Democracy: Bases of Agreement and Disagreement," *Journal of Politics* 22 (May 1960): 276–94, at 291; and Frank W. Westie, "The American Dilemma: An Empirical Test," *American Sociological Review* 30 (August 1965): 527–38, at 537.

30.   McClosky, "Consensus and Ideology," pp. 363 and 366; and Samuel A. Stouffer, *Communism, Conformity, and Civil Liberties* (New York: John Wiley, 1955), p. 27. Also see Robert A. Dahl, *Who Governs?* (New Haven: Yale University Press, 1961), p. 319.

31.   A number of reputable scholarly efforts have concerned themselves with whether regional variations exist. See Samuel C. Patterson, "The Political Cultures of the American States," *Journal of Politics* 34 (February 1968): 187–209; and John Gillin, "National and Regional Cultural Values in the United States," *Social Forces* 34 (December 1955): 107–13, for two examples of this literature.

32.   Richard Merelman, "Learning and Legitimacy," *American Political Science Review* 60 (September 1966): 548–61; Roger W. Cobb and Charles D. Elder, "The Political Uses of Symbolism," *American Politics Quarterly* 1 (July 1973): 305–38, "Symbolic Identifications and Political Behavior," *American Politics Quarterly* 4 (July 1976): 305–32, and *Participation in American Politics: The Dynamics of Agenda-Building* (Boston: Allyn & Bacon, 1972), pp. 78, 131, 135, and 137. Also see Murray Edelman, *The Symbolic Uses of Politics* (Urbana: University of Illinois Press, 1964).

33.   Walter M. Gerson, "Violence as an American Value Theme," in Otto N. Larsen, ed., *Violence and the Mass Media* (New York: Harper & Row, 1968), p.

154. Also see David L. Lange, Robert K. Baker, and Sandra J. Ball, *Mass Media and Violence* (Washington: USGPO, 1969), pp. 91 and 94; Peter K. Eisinger, "Protest Behavior and the Integration of Urban Political Systems," *Journal of Politics* 33 (November 1971): 980-1007, at 992; and Monica D. Blumenthal et al., *Justifying Violence: Attitudes of American Men* (Ann Arbor: Institute for Social Research, University of Michigan, 1972), pp. 25 and 246. A number of writers have expounded the theme that violence is not viewed as negatively by southerners as it is by other Americans. While this may well be true, it does not concern us directly here. See W.J. Cash, *The Mind of the South* (New York: Alfred A. Knopf, 1941), esp. pp. 113-21; Erskine Caldwell, "The Deep South's Other Venerable Tradition," *New York Times Magazine*, 11 July 1965, pp. 10-14; Gillin, "National and Regional Cultural Values," p. 112; Sheldon Hackney, "Southern Violence," *American Historical Review* 74 (February 1969): 906-25; and John Shelton Reed, "To Live—and Die—in Dixie: A Contribution to the Study of Southern Violence," *Political Science Quarterly* 86 (September 1971): 429-43, which also appears as chapter 5 in Reed's *The Enduring South* (Lexington, Mass.: D.C. Heath, 1972).

34. Alan Lincoln and George Levinger, "Observers' Evaluations of the Victim and the Attacker in an Aggressive Incident," *Journal of Personality and Social Psychology* 22 (May 1972): 202-10, at 208. Unfortunately, the "observers" that Lincoln and Levinger employed were all college students, a group rather atypical of the country's entire population.

35. See Clarence M. Case, *Nonviolent Coercion: A Study in Methods of Social Pressure* (New York: Century Co., 1923), pp. 226-27, 397, and esp. 399; Orrin E. Klapp, *Symbolic Leaders* (Chicago: Aldine, 1964), pp. 86-87; Harvey Seifert, *Conquest By Suffering* (Philadelphia: Westminster Press, 1965), pp. 61 and 70; Sidney I. Perloe et al., "The Effect of Nonviolent Action on Social Attitudes," *Sociological Inquiry* 38 (Winter 1968): 13-21, at 17; Gene Sharp, *The Politics of Nonviolent Action* (Boston: Porter Sargent, 1973), pp. 544, 546, 601, 634, 657-58, 665, and 690; and Herbert M. Hyman, "Mass Communication and Socialization," *Public Opinion Quarterly* 37 (Winter 1973-1974): 524-40, at 531. Also see Leroy H. Pelton, *The Psychology of Nonviolence* (New York: Pergamon Press, 1974), p. 143; and Thomas R. Frazier, "An Analysis of Nonviolent Coercion as Used by the Sit-in Movement," *Phylon* 29 (Spring 1968): 27-40, at 39.

36. Lincoln and Levinger, "Observers' Evaluations," p. 208; Blumenthal et al., *Justifying Violence*, p. 251; and Monica D. Blumenthal et al., *More About Justifying Violence* (Ann Arbor: Institute for Social Research, University of Michigan, 1975), pp. 195 and 220.

37. A good example of this can be seen in the two editorials that the *Wall Street Journal* published on the situation in Birmingham. While even in response to Selma that paper was very "even-handed" in its comments about Alabama officials and the marchers, in the two pieces on Birmingham, one entitled "The Mob's Blind Force," not one mention was made of police dogs, fire hoses, or other tactics of the lawmen, while repeated mention was made of how blacks had

thrown stones and the dangers of "mob rule." The criticism of the demonstrators far outweighed what little there was of state and city officials, and one might well wonder why the *Journal* did not call for "a plague on both your houses" rather than just rail at the blacks. See 9 May 1963, p. 12, and 14 May 1963, p. 16.

38. See Blumenthal et al., *Justifying Violence*, p. 249; and Angus Campbell, *White Attitudes Toward Black People* (Ann Arbor: Institute for Social Research, University of Michigan, 1971), p. 16. Also see Blumenthal et al., *More About Justifying Violence*, p. 184; Peter K. Eisinger, "Racial Differences in Protest Participation," *American Political Science Review* 68 (June 1974): 592–606, at 593; Amitai Etzioni, *Demonstration Democracy* (New York: Gordon & Breach, 1970), pp. 9–11; Bayard Rustin, *Strategies For Freedom* (New York: Columbia University Press, 1976), pp. 48–49; and Cobb and Elder, "Symbolic Identifications," p. 324.

39. Hazel Erskine, "The Polls: Demonstrations and Race Riots," *Public Opinion Quarterly* 31 (Winter 1967–1968): 655–77, at 656–57; William Brink and Louis Harris, *The Negro Revolution* (New York: Simon & Schuster, 1964), p. 145. For data that indicates that individuals with higher levels of education, as well as several other characteristics, are much more likely to endorse others' rights to protest, see Marvin E. Olsen, "Perceived Legitimacy of Social Protest Actions," *Social Problems* 15 (Fall 1967): 297–310. Also see Ralph H. Turner, "The Public Perception of Protest," *American Sociological Review* 34 (December 1969): 815–31.

40. Erskine, "The Polls: Demonstrations and Race Riots," p. 659.

41. Hazel Erskine, "The Polls: Speed of Racial Integration," *Public Opinion Quarterly* 32 (Fall 1968): 513–24; Paul B. Sheatsley, "White Attitudes Toward the Negro," *Daedalus* 95 (Winter 1966): 217–38, at 234; and Erskine, "The Polls: Demonstrations and Race Riots," p. 657. Also see George H. Gallup, *The Gallup Poll*, volume 3, 1959–1971 (New York: Random House, 1972), pp. 1867, 1933, 1939, and 1955, which provides more accurate dating than do the other sources.

42. Olsen, "Perceived Legitimacy," p. 299.

43. Daniel C. Thompson, "The Rise of the Negro Protest," *Annals of the American Academy of Political and Social Science* 357 (January 1965): 18–29, at 20. Also see Sidney Verba et al., *Caste, Race and Politics* (Beverly Hills, Calif.: Sage Publications, 1971), pp. 22 and 183.

44. William Brink and Louis Harris, *Black and White* (New York: Simon & Schuster, 1967), pp. 127 and 136. Also see Herbert H. Hyman and Paul B. Sheatsley, "Attitudes Toward Desegregation," *Scientific American* 211 (July 1964): 16–23; and Sundquist, *Politics and Policy*, pp. 496–98.

45. For two expressions of journalistic views which support this position, see the *Montgomery Advertiser*, 17 May 1960, which stated in its editorial: "Negro voters and Negroes butting their way into white schools where they are not wanted are organically different matters" (quoted by Charles V. Hamilton, "Southern Judges and Negro Voting Rights: The Judicial Approach to the Solu-

tion of Controversial Social Problems," *Wisconsin Law Review* 1965 [Fall]: 72–102, at 101) and E.W. Kenworthy, *New York Times*, 26 May 1965, p. 1, who termed voting discrimination "the least defensible" of all discrimination.

46.   Brink and Harris, *The Negro Revolution*, p. 142; and Sheatsley, "White Attitudes," pp. 238 and 231. Also see Charles F. Cnudde, *Democracy in the American South* (Chicago: Markham, 1971), p. 57; and Harrell R. Rodgers, Jr., and Charles S. Bullock III, *Law and Social Change: Civil Rights Laws and Their Consequences* (New York: McGraw-Hill, 1972), p. 180.

47.   Gallup, *The Gallup Poll*, vol. 3, pp. 1933–34; and Sheatsley, "White Attitudes," p. 235. One other data resource concerning public opinion on voting rights legislation is the results of the polls a number of congressmen conducted as a part of their early 1965 newsletters. While no one has ever claimed that the names on such mailing lists represent a balanced cross-sample of even that member's own constituency, the results obtained in early 1965 mirror the same support levels obtained in the national surveys. Eighty-eight percent of some 3,000 respondents to Connecticut Democrat John Monagan's April newsletter poll reported that they favored "federal legislation to guarantee the right of voting registration for every citizen," while 81.5 percent of the approximately 10,000 individuals responding to Iowa's Bert Bandstra said that they favored "additional legislation to insure that all Americans, in all parts of the country, are not denied the right to vote." Three other such queries produced support levels ranging from 65 to 77 percent. A very informative contrast is offered, however, by the results of New York Republican Henry Smith's inquiry which asked if the respondent favored the "elimination of all literacy tests for voters." Only 14.1 percent of 19,000 respondents answered Yes, while 83 percent indicated No. Once again we can see that the phrasing of the question can produce any of a variety of results merely on the basis of whether positive symbols—the right to vote—or negative symbols—illiterate voting—are invoked. See U.S. Congress, House, *Congressional Record* 111, at pp. 10068, 16708, 11865, 12199, 19299 and 11164.

48.   Erskine, "The Polls: Demonstrations and Race Riots," p. 661.

49.   Donald Von Eschen et al., "The Conditions of Direct Action in a Democratic Society," *Western Political Quarterly* 22 (June 1969): 309–25, at 319 and 322, and "The Disintegration of the Negro Non-violent Movement," *Journal of Peace Research* 6 (1969): 215–34, at 227. Consider in this regard the comment attributed to a moderately conservative Republican representative in early 1964 concerning some provisions of the then pending civil rights bill: "I still don't like the idea of turning the Attorney General loose to correct all the abuses in our society with Federal court injunctions, but as long as you have George Wallaces holding office in the South it's clear the Negroes need some help" (Joseph Sullivan, *Wall Street Journal*, 3 February 1964, pp. 1 and 12). On the importance of legitimacy, also see the letters of Daniel Bell, Carl Kaysen, and Oscar Handlin that appear in the *Correspondent* 33 (Winter 1965): 103–4. They were in response to Arthur I. Waskow's " 'Creative Disorder' in the Racial Struggle," *Correspondent* 32 (Autumn 1964): 61–73. Note also Gaston V. Rimlinger, "The

Legitimation of Protest: A Comparative Study in Labor History," *Comparative Studies in Society and History* 2 (April 1960): 329–43.

50.   Von Eschen et al., "The Disintegration of the Negro Nonviolent Movement," p. 226. Also see Dye, *The Politics of Equality*, pp. 120, 122 and 124; and Paul H. Douglas, *In the Fullness of Time* (New York: Harcourt Brace Jovanovich, 1972), p. 298.

Chapter 5

1.   G. Ray Funkhouser, "The Issues of the Sixties: An Exploratory Study in the Dynamics of Public Opinion," *Public Opinion Quarterly* 37 (Spring 1973): 62–75, at 62.

2.   "Last night I sat in my living room," Morse told his colleagues, "and viewed on my television screen the pictures of the brutality of the Alabama police. . . . As I watched the television screen last night and saw Negro women beaten to the ground; when I observed the nature of the blows that were struck on the heads and the bodies of Negroes by white, bigoted, racist policemen, I shuddered to think that that could come to pass in any state of my country in the year 1965" (U.S. Congress, Senate, *Congressional Record* 111 [pt. 4, 9 March 1965], pp. 4562–63).

3.   See, for example, William Peters, "The Visible and Invisible Images," in Paul L. Fisher and Ralph L. Lowenstein, eds., *Race and the News Media* (New York: Praeger, 1967), p. 81; William B. Monroe, Jr., "Television: The Chosen Instrument of the Revolution," in Fisher and Lowenstein, eds., *Race and the News Media*, p. 89; Joseph L. Brechner, "Were Broadcasters Color Blind?" in Fisher and Lowenstein, eds., *Race and the News Media*, p. 100; William A. Wood, *Electronic Journalism* (New York: Columbia University Press, 1967), pp. 89, 100, and 106; Gary Orfield, *The Reconstruction of Southern Education* (New York: Wiley-Interscience, 1969), pp. 33 and 265; and Bayard Rustin, *Strategies For Freedom* (New York: Columbia University Press, 1976), pp. 44–45.

4.   Amitai Etzioni, *Demonstration Democracy* (New York: Gordon & Breach, 1970, p. 12.

5.   James Reston, "Washington: The Rising Spirit of Protest," *New York Times*, 19 March 1965, p. 34; and Russell Baker, "Stomach-Bulge Defense," *New York Times*, 5 April 1975, p. 29. Also see William Small, *To Kill A Messenger* (New York: Hastings House, 1970), pp. 43–44; and Benjamin Muse, *The American Negro Revolution—1963–1967* (Bloomington: Indiana University Press, 1968), p. 169. Somewhat similar observations have been made concerning the possible impact of television coverage of the Vietnam War. See James Reston, *New York Times*, 30 April 1975, p. 37; and Jerome H. Skolnick, ed., *The Politics of Protest* (New York: Simon & Schuster, 1969), p. 42. For a report that indicates that such coverage affected at least one important senator, see *New York Times*, 27 February 1975, p. 3. For a not terribly enlightening scholarly inquiry on the topic, see Timothy P. Meyer, "Some Effects of Real Newsfilm Violence on the Behavior of Viewers," *Journal of Broadcasting* 15 (Summer 1971): 275–85.

6. "Cruelty occurs most readily," one scholar has written, "in sequestered areas in which the domination of the powerful is inescapable and impregnable, at least for the moment." Implicit in that analysis is the presumption that cruelty is viewed negatively by the larger or external society and will be attacked by it when such behavior is brought to its attention. Hence, as John Herbers noted, "Justice is more apt to prevail in the light of publicity." See Philip P. Hallie, *The Paradox of Cruelty* (Middletown: Wesleyan University Press, 1969), p. 68; and John Herbers, "The Reporter in the Deep South," in Louis M. Lyons, ed., *Reporting the News* (New York: Atheneum, 1968), p. 226. In earlier years, however, such local victims had no medium by which their plight could be publicized to those who might become their allies. See William A. Gamson, *The Strategy of Social Protest* (Homewood: Dorsey Press, 1975), pp. 81–82 and 87; and the comments of Charles Evers in Jack Lyle, ed., *The Black American and the Press* (Los Angeles: Ward Ritchie Press, 1968), p. 69. Also see Pat Watters and Reese Cleghorn, *Climbing Jacob's Ladder: The Arrival of Negroes in Southern Politics* (New York: Harcourt, Brace & World, 1967), p. 173, who quote Charles Sherrod, director of the VEP's southwest Georgia effort, as saying, "One of the reasons the white man with the segregationist attitude has been somewhat successful in blocking the black man in the past has much to do with the effectiveness of isolation."

7. Edward Jay Epstein, *News From Nowhere* (New York: Random House, 1973), p. 219; and Robert E. Kintner, "Televising the Real World," *Harper's* 230 (June 1965): 94–98, at 95. Also see Clarence Mitchell, "The Warren Court and Congress: A Civil Rights Partnership," *Nebraska Law Review* 48 (1968): 91–128, at 103; Alphonso Pinkney, *The Committed* (New Haven: College & University Press, 1968), p. 90; William Brink and Louis Harris, *Black and White* (New York: Simon & Schuster, 1967), p. 10; and Harry Holloway, *The Politics of the Southern Negro* (New York: Random House, 1969), p. 332.

8. See David L. Lange, Robert K. Baker, and Sandra J. Ball, *Mass Media and Violence* (Washington: USGPO, 1969), p. 139; Holloway, *The Politics of the Southern Negro*, p. 335; Etzioni, *Demonstration Democracy*, p. 21; Robert MacNeil, *The People Machine—The Influence of Television on American Politics* (New York: Harper & Row, 1968), p. 73; and Gary L. Wamsley and Richard A. Pride, "Television Network News: Re-thinking the Iceberg Problem," *Western Political Quarterly* 25 (September 1972): 434–50, at 439.

9. MacNeil, *The People Machine*, pp. 8 and 71. Also see Michael J. Robinson, "Television and American Politics: 1956–1976," *Public Interest* 48 (Summer 1977): 3–39, at 12–13.

10. Bruce L.R. Smith, "The Politics of Protest: How Effective is Violence?" *Proceedings of the Academy of Political Science* 29 (March 1968): 115–33, at 117. Also see James L. Sundquist, *Politics and Policy—The Eisenhower, Kennedy, and Johnson Years* (Washington: Brookings Institution, 1968), p. 281, who noted that by 1966 "the image of the Negro . . . was no longer that of the praying, long-suffering nonviolent victim of Southern sheriffs; it was of a defiant young hoodlum shouting 'black power' and hurling 'Molotov cocktails' in an urban slum."

11.   Lyle, ed., *The Black American and the Press*, pp. 40–41. Also see Orfield, *The Reconstruction of Southern Education*, p. 142.

12.   Wamsley and Pride, "Television Network News," p. 438.

13.   Monroe, "Television: The Chosen Instrument of the Revolution," p. 84.

14.   Henry Fairlie, "Can You Believe Your Eyes?" *Horizon* 9 (Spring 1967): 24–27, at 25. Also see Robert S. Frank, *Message Dimensions of Television News* (Lexington, Mass.: D.C. Heath, 1973), p. 13; Herbert H. Hyman, "Mass Communication and Socialization," *Public Opinion Quarterly* 37 (Winter 1973–1974): 524–40, at 529; and Etzioni, *Demonstration Democracy*, pp. 13–14.

15.   *Time*, 19 March 1965, p. 25. Also see Willard Clopton, *Washington Post*, 15 March 1965, pp. 1 and 6.

16.   Louis Lusky, "The King Dream: Fantasy or Prophecy?" *Columbia Law Review* 68 (June 1968): 1029–39, at 1034.

17.   See Kintner, "Television the Real World," p. 95; Anthony Lewis, "Since the Supreme Court Spoke," *New York Times Magazine*, 10 May 1964, p. 91; and Anthony Lewis, "Moral Bankruptcy," *New York Times*, 16 December 1974, p. 33.

18.   CBS indicated that for news broadcasts prior to March 1967, when it began to preserve transcripts, "we have neither transcripts nor the broadcasts themselves." Vanderbilt University's archive of CBS Evening News broadcasts dates from 1968, and CBS itself began to retain video cassette copies of the shows at the beginning of 1974. NBC News stated that it too "does not make transcripts of its regularly scheduled news programs." It has retained, however, a transcript of at least one important news special, a three-hour documentary entitled "The American Revolution of '63," which was broadcast on Monday evening, September 2, 1963. The program included a segment on May's events in Birmingham which featured both the officials' use of dogs and hoses on May 3 and 4 and the rioting that followed the bombings on May 11. References to the throwing of various debris by blacks during the earlier marches also were made, and the Birmingham segment ended with a "talking head" of Commissioner Connor denouncing blacks and their supporters as "lazy . . . indolent . . . beatniks . . . and bleeding hearts." The show also included a report on the voter registration barriers which blacks faced in Greenwood, Mississippi. The final half hour of the program was devoted to the March on Washington, which had occurred four days earlier, and to various congressional comments concerning the pending civil rights proposals. Produced by Chet Hagan and Robert Northshield and anchored by Frank McGee, the show was viewed by an estimated 11 million Americans, which, it might be noted, was far fewer than the 70 million who watched Johnson's address of March 15. See Kintner, "Televising the Real World," p. 94.

Film clips of events such as March 7 do exist and have been included in a number of documentary programs and films, such as Ely Landau's "King—A Film Record—Montgomery to Memphis." However, as CBS put it, "The context in which they were broadcast can no longer be established" (John W. Kiermaier, Vice-President for Corporate Responsibility, CBS, letter to author,

11 December 1974; and Milton Brown, Coordinator, News Information Services, NBC, letter to author, 2 December 1974). Also see Funkhouser, "The Issues of the Sixties," p. 64; and Wamsley and Pride, "Television Network News," p. 441, n. 43.

19.   Also see the discussion at, and preceding, n. 10 in chapter 4.

20.   Arthur I. Waskow, *From Race-Riot To Sit-in* (Garden City, N.Y.: Doubleday, 1966), p. 234.

21.   *Washington Post*, 16 May 1963, p. A22.

22.   U.S. Congress, House, Committee on the Judiciary, *Civil Rights— Hearings Before Subcommittee No. 5*, 88th Congress, 1st session, 1963, p. 1936.

23.   For a similar formulation of this same distinction, see Raymond A. Bauer et al., *American Business and Public Policy—The Politics of Foreign Trade* (New York: Atherton Press, 1963), p. 404.

24.   David R. Mayhew, *Congress: The Electoral Connection* (New Haven: Yale University Press, 1974), pp. 5, 13, and 49.

25.   Warren E. Miller and Donald E. Stokes, "Constituency Influence in Congress," *American Political Science Review* 57 (March 1963): 45–56.

26.   Charles F. Cnudde and Donald J. McCrone, "The Linkage Between Constituency Attitudes and Congressional Voting Behavior: A Causal Model," *American Political Science Review* 60 (March 1966): 66–72. Also see Hugh Donald Forbes and Edward R. Tufte, "A Note of Caution in Causal Modelling," *American Political Science Review* 62 (December 1968): 1258–64.

27.   Cnudde and McCrone, "The Linkage Between Constituency Attitudes and Congressional Voting Behavior," p. 69. A similar view also has been expressed by Aage R. Clausen, who has asserted that "constituency influence is dominant" on "civil liberties" legislation. See *How Congressmen Decide: A Policy Focus* (New York: St. Martin's Press, 1973), pp. 234 and 221. A dissent from this position has been voiced by Jack R. Van Der Slik, who has written that for Republican representatives in the Eighty-eighth Congress "variations in the constituency variables considered do not explain variations in Negro rights voting." Van Der Slik's apparent conclusion that something more than constituency influence is involved in congressional position taking on civil rights matters can be viewed as lending some limited support to the "personal feelings" hypothesis advanced here. See "Constituency Characteristics and Roll Call Voting on Negro Rights in the Eighty-Eighth Congress," *Social Science Quarterly* 49 (December 1968): 720–31, at 730. A somewhat relevant discussion of the question also appears in James N. Rosenau, *Citizenship Between Elections* (New York: Free Press, 1974), who advances the argument that certain segments of the populace, namely the "Attentive Public" and even more so the "Mobilizable Public," are particularly influential. See pp. 8, and especially 12 and 55, for statements relating this model to civil rights legislation.

28.   All population figures used in these computations come from the U.S. Department of Commerce, Bureau of the Census, *Congressional District Data Book* (Washington: USGPO, 1963) and seven supplements to that volume which were issued in 1964 and 1965 to cover states which had been reapportioned for

the Eighty-ninth Congress. The 7.6 percent black figure is preferable to the national figure of 10.5 percent black because eight Southern states—Alabama, Arkansas, Georgia, Louisiana, Mississippi, North Carolina, South Carolina, and Virginia—had no member of Congress who spoke out in favor of the movement or voting rights. Hence the population figures for these eight states were removed from the national totals, and the black population percentage for the remainder of the nation—7.6—was calculated. This process, and the percentage resulting from it, supplies a more suitable basis for comparison with the population percentages of those districts whose members did speak out than would a nationwide figure which failed to take into account the fact the hundreds of thousands of blacks in those eight states were without any hope of direct congressional representation on this issue.

29. See Clausen, *How Congressmen Decide*, p. 235.

30. Thirty-one of the 155 entered the Congress for the first time in January 1965, while two representatives who had served in earlier years but not in the Eighty-eighth Congress—Illinois' Sidney Yates and Ohio's Walter Moeller—returned at that same time.

31. U.S. Congress, Senate, *Congressional Record* 111 (pt. 4, 9 March 1965), pp. 4545–46. Arthur Waskow relates a somewhat earlier story concerning Colorado representative Byron Rogers which is very similar to that told by Representative O'Hara in 1965. See *From Race-Riot To Sit-in*, p. 252.

32. On Edwards's experiences, see *New York Times*, 9 July 1964, p. 14.

33. Bauer et al., *American Business and Public Policy*, p. 415. Aside from this volume, little literature exists which has sought to determine the influence of "the mail" on congressmen's policy positions and decisions. Likewise, data on the volume and source of congressional mail over time or at any one time on any issue or issues is virtually nonexistent and would be a worthy topic for inquiry. No member released any figures concerning the mail he or she received in February and March concerning Selma and voting rights.

34. U.S. Congress, Senate, *Congressional Record* 111 (p. 4, 10 March 1965), pp. 4638–39.

35. Bauer et al., *American Business and Public Policy*, pp. 415–16.

Chapter 6

1. See Stephen Pollak to John Doar, 3 June 1965; Alan G. Marer to Stephen Pollak, 11 June 1965; Stephen Pollak to Alan G. Marer and Frank Schwelb, 11 June 1965; Stephen Pollak to Nicholas deB. Katzenbach, 11 June 1965; St. John Barrett to Stephen Pollak, 15 June 1965; and John Doar to S.A. Andretta, 9 July 1965; all in Volume 7, Part Xa of the Justice Department Administrative History, LBJ Library. Also see John Doar to J. Ross Eckler (by Alan G. Marer), 13 July 1965; and Stephen Eilperin and Alan G. Marer to Stephen Pollak, 14 July 1965; also both in Volume 7, Part Xa.

2. See John Doar to Stephen Pollak, 14 July 1965; and Stephen Pollak to John Doar, 20 July 1965; both in Volume 7, Part Xa of the Justice Department Administrative History, LBJ Library.

3. See Stephen Pollak to John Doar, 26 July 1965, Justice Department Administrative History, Volume 7, Part Xa, LBJ Library.

4. See Alan G. Marer to John Doar, 2 August 1965, in Volume 7, Part Xa; and Nicholas deB. Katzenbach and John W. Macy to Lyndon B. Johnson, *Weekly Compilation of Presidential Documents*, 9 August 1965, pp. 51–52.

5. See Bayard Rustin and Tom Kahn, "Johnson So Far: Civil Rights," *Commentary* 39 (June 1965): 43–6, at 44.

6. John Herbers, *New York Times*, 4 August 1965, p. 17.

7. In addition to Justice Department documents in Volume 7, Part Xa, see Congressional Quarterly, "Voting Rights," *Weekly Report*, 13 August 1965, p. 1595; and John Herbers and Roy Reed, *New York Times*, 8 August 1965, p. 1. Also see John Doar to Joseph A. Califano, Jr., 9 August 1965, LBJ Library, White House Central Files, Ex HU 2-7, Box 55; 30 *Federal Register* 9897; and John Herbers, *New York Times*, 10 August 1965, p. 1.

8. See Gene Roberts, *New York Times*, 11 August 1965, p. 1; and John Herbers, *New York Times*, 12 August 1965, p. 15. On the first day's scene in Selma, see Fred Powledge's story on Sheriff Clark's reaction in the *Times* of 11 August, p. 20, and Janet Wells's profile of the first federal registrant, "Why Mrs. Mauldin Registered First," *VEP News* 3 (March 1969): 2–3.

9. John W. Macy to Lyndon B. Johnson, 14 August 1965, *Weekly Compilation of Presidential Documents*, p. 92.

10. John Herbers, *New York Times*, 13 August 1965, p. 13; John W. Macy to Lyndon B. Johnson, 21 August 1965, *Weekly Compilation of Presidential Documents*, pp. 125–26.

11. See Nan Robertson, *New York Times*, 22 August 1965, p. 45; and Richard Claude, *The Supreme Court and the Electoral Process* (Baltimore: Johns Hopkins Press, 1970), p. 119. Perez's effort continued to be successful; by mid-1966 statistics indicated that examiners had added 1,404 whites and 1,203 blacks to Plaquemines's voting rolls. On Perez's actions in regard to voting rights, see James Conaway, *Judge: The Life and Times of Leander Perez* (New York: Alfred A. Knopf, 1973), pp. 144–51 and 154–61; and Glen Jeansonne, *Leander Perez: Boss of the Delta* (Baton Rouge: Louisiana State University Press, 1977), pp. 242–52.

12. John Herbers, *New York Times*, 26 August 1965, p. 21. On the Louisiana gains, see Jules Witcover, "Who's Afraid of Those New Negro Voters?" *New Republic* 153 (30 October 1965): 10.

13. John Herbers, *New York Times*, 12 September 1965, p. 68. Also see Paul Good, "Beyond the Voting Rights Act," *Reporter* 33 (7 October 1965): 25–29.

14. See *Perez* v. *Rhiddlehoover*, 247 F. Supp. 65; and *New York Times*, 1 September 1965, p. 20.

15. *New York Times*, 8 September 1965, p. 28; 12 September 1965, p. 68; and 19 October 1965, p. 24. Also see *Reynolds* v. *Katzenbach*, 248 F. Supp. 593; *Dent* v. *Duncan*, 360 F.2d 33; *Annual Report of the Attorney General, 1966*, pp. 186–90; and Alexander M. Bickel, "The Voting Rights Cases," *Supreme Court Review* 1966, pp. 79–102, at 80–81.

16. See Tom Wicker, *New York Times*, 16 September 1965, p. 1; and John Herbers, *The Lost Priority* (New York: Funk & Wagnalls, 1970), pp. xi, 127, and 169–73.

17. See John Herbers, *New York Times*, 30 October 1965, p. 1. Also see Gene Roberts, *New York Times*, 25 October 1965, p. 1; and John W. Macy to Lee C. White, 3 November 1965, LBJ Library, White Papers, Box 3.

18. See Neil Maxwell, *Wall Street Journal*, 20 December 1965, p. 1.

19. See John Herbers, *New York Times*, 17 October 1965, p. 1, and 31 October 1965, p. E4; Nicholas deB. Katzenbach to Lyndon B. Johnson, 2 November 1965, LBJ Library, White Papers, Box 6; John Herbers, *New York Times*, 19 November 1965, p. 1, and 1 December 1965, p. 33; and August Meier, "The Dilemmas of Negro Protest Strategy," *New South* 21 (Spring 1966): 1–18, at 13.

20. See U.S. Commission on Civil Rights, *The Voting Rights Act . . . the first months* (Washington: USGPO, 1965), esp. p. 3; and Nicholas deB. Katzenbach to William L. Taylor, 4 December 1965, LBJ Library, White Papers, Box 3. Also see John Herbers, *New York Times*, 30 October 1965, p. 1, and 5 December 1965, p. 1. For further criticism of the department's policy on assigning examiners, see William L. Higgs, "LBJ and the Negro Vote: Case of the Missing Registrars," *Nation* 201 (13 December 1965): 460–62.

21. John W. Macy to Lyndon B. Johnson, 3 January 1966, LBJ Library, White Papers, Box 6; Nicholas deB. Katzenbach to "local officials," 8 January 1966, LBJ Library, Justice Department Administrative History, Volume 7, Part Xa.

22. Pat Watters and Reese Cleghorn, *Climbing Jacob's Ladder: The Arrival of Negroes in Southern Politics* (New York: Harcourt, Brace & World, 1967), p. 262.

23. See *New South* 21 (Spring 1966): 55–60. A copy of the text of the address also is in the Sparks Papers, Box 2, LBJ Library. Also see John Herbers, *New York Times*, 1 March 1966, p. 43. Justice's underlying belief, as John Doar articulated it in February 1967, was that there had been "a remarkable amount of compliance by local officials." U.S. Congress, House, Committee on Appropriations, *Hearings on Department of Justice Appropriations for 1968*, 90th Congress, 1st session, 1967, p. 368.

24. Southern Regional Council, *The Effects of Federal Examiners and Organized Registration Campaigns on Negro Voter Registration* (Atlanta: SRC, 1966). A second effect of the use of examiners, who primarily were sent to counties in which blacks constituted a high percentage of the population, was that the old rule that the lower the black population percentage, the higher the percentage of blacks who were registered voters was reversed. By 1967, counties with substantial black populations had black registration rates higher than those of counties in which blacks constituted a lesser percentage of the population. See Johnnie Daniel, "Negro Political Behavior and Community Political and Socioeconomic Structural Factors," *Social Forces* 47 (March 1969): 274–81, esp. p. 276; and Paul E. Joubert and Ben M. Crouch, "Mississippi Blacks and the

Voting Rights Act of 1965," *Journal of Negro Education* 46 (Spring 1977): 157–67, esp. pp. 163–64. Also see Joubert's M.A. thesis, "The Effects of the Voting Rights Act of 1965 on Negro Voter Registration in Mississippi," Mississippi State University, 1969, whose limited findings support the SRC's argument about the importance of examiners.

25. *South Carolina* v. *Katzenbach*, 383 U.S. 301. Also see Robert B. Semple, *New York Times*, 22 October 1965, p. 1; and Fred Graham, *New York Times*, 6 November 1965, p. 1. For commentary upon the Court's opinion in *South Carolina* and the constitutionality of the act, see Armand Derfner, "Racial Discrimination and the Right to Vote," *Vanderbilt Law Review* 26 (April 1973): 523–84, at 552; Alexander M. Bickel, "The Voting Rights Cases," pp. 80–93; Warren M. Christopher, "The Constitutionality of the Voting Rights Act of 1965," *Stanford Law Review* 18 (October 1965): 1–26, at 15–24; Archibald Cox, "Constitutionality of the Proposed Voting Rights Act of 1965," *Houston Law Review* 3 (Spring-Summer 1965): 1–10; Ronald J. Cristal, "The 1965 Voting Rights Act and State Literacy Tests," *Albany Law Review* 30 (January 1966): 112–23; Comment, "Voting Rights Act of 1965," *Duke Law Journal* 1966 (Spring): 463–83; *St. John's Law Review* 41 (October 1966): 270–78; and Charles E. Rice, "The Voting Rights Act of 1965: Some Dissenting Observations," *Kansas Law Review* 15 (December 1966): 159–65.

26. *Harper* v. *Virginia State Board of Elections*, 383 U.S. 663. See Bickel, "The Voting Rights Cases," pp. 93–95. The department previously had secured decisions from three-judge district courts in Alabama and Texas invalidating the poll tax in each of those two states. See, e.g., *U.S.* v. *Texas*, 252 F. Supp. 234, affirmed per curiam 384 U.S. 155 (1966).

27. *Katzenbach* v. *Morgan*, 384 U.S. 641. Two three-judge courts, one in Washington and one in New York, had issued differing opinions on the constitutionality of 4(e). See Warren Weaver, *New York Times*, 16 November 1965, p. 1; and Edward Ranzal, *New York Times*, 9 December 1965, p. 1. In December the Justice Department had brought an action, *U.S.* v. *Harvey*, alleging that black citizens registered by federal examiners in West Feliciana Parish had been evicted from their homes and land because of their registration, a violation of section 11(b) of the act. After the issuance of a partial temporary restraining order, the district court eventually found for the defendants and the department chose not to appeal the decision. See *New York Times*, 24 December 1965, p. 42; and *Annual Report of the Attorney General, 1966*, pp. 190–91.

28. See Gene Roberts, *New York Times*, 14 April 1966, p. 27, and 17 April 1966, p. 63; and Roy Reed, *New York Times*, 6 March 1966, p. 76, and 3 May 1966, p. 33. Also see Gene Roberts, "A Remarkable Thing is Happening in Wilcox County, Alabama," *New York Times Magazine*, 17 April 1966, p. 26.

29. See *U.S.* v. *Executive Committee of the Democratic Party of Dallas County, Alabama*, 254 F. Supp. 537. Also see Gene Roberts, *New York Times*, 3 May 1966, p. 1, and 4 May 1966, p. 1; Roy Reed, *New York Times*, 4 May 1966, p. 28, and 5 May 1966, p. 1; Gene Roberts, *New York Times*, 5 May 1966, p. 30; Roy Reed, *New York Times*, 6 May 1966, p. 1; *New York Times*, 7 May 1966, p.

1; Gene Roberts, *New York Times*, 8 May 1966, p. 1, and 18 May 1966, p. 24; and *New York Times*, 26 May 1966, p. 44. Clark continued to have other problems with Judge Thomas growing out of the events of early 1965. See *Boynton* v. *Clark*, 10 *Race Relations Law Reporter* 1472 and 12 *Race Relations Law Reporter* 620; and *Clark* v. *Boynton*, 362 F.2d 992. Also see *New York Times*, 28 February 1967, p. 40, and the far more wide-ranging discussion of Dallas County in Paul Good, *The American Serfs* (New York: G.P. Putnam's Sons, 1968), pp. 54–70. On election problems in other counties, see John Beecher, "Sword in the Heart of Dixie," *Nation* 202 (23 May 1966): 611–14.

30.   Earl Black, *Southern Governors and Civil Rights* (Cambridge, Mass.: Harvard University Press, 1976), p. 184.

31.   See Southern Regional Council, *What Happened in the South, 1966* (Atlanta: SRC, 1966); Felix Belair, *New York Times*, 6 November 1966, p. 67; and *New York Times*, 10 November 1966, p. 30. Also see Reese Cleghorn and Pat Watters, "The Impact of Negro Votes on Southern Politics," *Reporter* 36 (26 January 1967): 24–25 and 31–32; and John Beecher, "Despite Negro Opposition, A Negro Might Make It," *New Republic* 155 (2 July 1966): 11–12. Comments by black candidates themselves appear in Julian Bond, *Black Candidates—Southern Campaign Experiences* (Atlanta: Voter Education Project, Southern Regional Council, 1968); and Mervyn M. Dymally, ed., *The Black Politician: His Struggle for Power* (Belmont: Duxbury Press, 1971).

32.   Numan V. Bartley and Hugh Davis Graham, *Southern Politics and the Second Reconstruction* (Baltimore: Johns Hopkins Press, 1975), pp. 109–11 and 188.

33.   By far the best discussion of this oft-ignored topic is Earl Black and Merle Black, "The Changing Setting of Minority Politics in the American Deep South," *Politics* 73 (March 1973): 35–50. Also set Black and Black, "The Demographic Basis of Wallace Support in Alabama," *American Politics Quarterly* 1 (July 1973): 279–304, esp. pp. 290–92; Earl Black, *Southern Governors and Civil Rights*, p. 326; Russell J. Levesque, "White Response to Nonwhite Voter Registration in the Southern States," *Pacific Sociological Review* 15 (April 1972): 245–55; and a more recent study that focused on turnout, John L. Hammond, "Race and Electoral Mobilization: White Southerners, 1952–1968," *Public Opinion Quarterly* 41 (Spring 1977): 13–27. The overall white registration total in the eleven states grew from some 13 million in 1964 to 17.4 million in 1971. Over that same period of time, black registration increased from approximately 2 million in 1964 to 3.5 million in 1971. The black increase of some 1.5 million thus was far surpassed by the increase of 4.4 million in white registrants.

34.   See U.S. Commission on Civil Rights, *Political Participation* (Washington: USGPO, 1968), p. 12; *VEP News* 1 (September 1967): 2; Walter Rugaber, *New York Times*, 9 November 1967, p. 33; Charles N. Fortenberry and F. Glenn Abney, "Mississippi: Unreconstructed and Unredeemed," in William C. Havard, ed., *The Changing Politics of the South* (Baton Rouge: Louisiana State University Press, 1972), p. 487; Robert Analavage, *Southern Patriot* 25 (October 1967): 3; Robert Analavage and Mike Higson, *Southern Patriot* 25 (December

1967): 2–3; and Neal R. Peirce, *The Deep South States of America* (New York: W.W. Norton, 1974), p. 188. Problems of harassment and intimidation also had characterized some of the Mississippi municipal elections held in May of 1967. See *New York Times*, 2 May 1967, p. 23; and L. Thorne McCarty and Russell B. Stevenson, "The Voting Rights Act of 1965: An Evaluation," *Harvard Civil Rights—Civil Liberties Law Review* 3 (Spring 1968): 347–412, at 390–91.

35.   *VEP News* 1 (September 1967): 1. As the VEP director, Vernon Jordan, correctly emphasized, "Registration alone counts for little. In order to get real results, registration must be followed by voting" (*VEP News* 1 [August 1967]: 2).

36.   Donald R. Matthews and James W. Prothro, *Negroes and the New Southern Politics* (New York: Harcourt, Brace & World, 1966), p. 12. Also see pp. 120 and 134, and Ralph M. Goldman, "The Politics of Political Integration," *Journal of Negro Education* 33 (Winter 1964): 26–34, at 29–30.

37.   Anthony Orum, "A Reappraisal of the Social and Political Participation of Negroes," *American Journal of Sociology* 72 (July 1966): 32–46, at 44. For support of this finding, see Sidney Verba and Norman H. Nie, *Participation in America: Political Democracy and Social Equality* (New York: Harper & Row, 1972), p. 157. Also see Marvin E. Olsen, "Social and Political Participation of Blacks," *American Sociological Review* 35 (August 1970): 682–97.

38.   Verba and Nie, *Participation in America*, pp. 19 and 150.

39.   Lester M. Salamon and Stephen Van Evera, "Fear, Apathy, and Discrimination: A Test of Three Explanations of Political Participation," *American Political Science Review* 67 (December 1973): 1288–1306, at 1301. Also see Taylor Branch, "Black Fear: Law and Justice in Rural Georgia," *Washington Monthly* 1 (January 1970): 38–58.

40.   See David J. Garrow, "Fear, Apathy, and Discrimination: The Test of Time—Black Voting in South Carolina, 1970–1976," unpublished paper, Duke University, 1977. Using data more reliable than that available to Salamon and Van Evera from Mississippi, this inquiry produced very supportive results for 1970 election statistics. Results of applications using 1972, 1974, and 1976 data were so random, however, as to draw into doubt the workings of the model, and particularly Salamon's and Van Evera's claim that it would permit empirical measurement of changes in "fear" over time. See Salamon and Van Evera, "Fear Revisited: Rejoinder to 'Comment' by Sam Kernell," *American Political Science Review* 67 (December 1973): 1319–26, at 1324. Also see Sam Kernell, "Comment: A Re-evaluation of Black Voting in Mississippi," *American Political Science Review* 67 (December 1973): 1307–18.

41.   Derfner, "Racial Discrimination and the Right to Vote," p. 553. Also see Comment, "Voting Rights: A Case Study of Madison Parish, Louisiana," *University of Chicago Law Review* 38 (Summer 1971): 726–87, at 754 and 757. Section 5 appears as section 1973(c) of title 42 of the United States Code.

42.   By far the best accounting of these many and varied tactics is the Civil Rights Commission's report, *Political Participation*, esp. pp. 21–114. Also see McCarty and Stevenson, "The Voting Rights Act," pp. 387–90; and *New York Times*, 20 December 1967, p. 32.

43.   253 F. Supp. 915. Also see Robert B. McKay, "Racial Discrimination in the Electoral Process," *Annals of the American Academy of Political and Social Science* 407 (May 1973): 102–18.

44.   See *VEP News* 2 (February 1968): 3 for a full accounting as of the beginning of the year, and subsequent monthly issues throughout the year. Also see Douglas Kneeland, *New York Times*, 25 February 1968, p. 54; *VEP News* 3 (January 1969): 3; Janet Wells, *VEP News* 3 (May 1969): 1 and 4; Willadeane Clayton, *VEP News* 3 (July 1969): 1; and Joe R. Feagin and Harlan Hahn, "The Second Reconstruction: Black Political Strength in the South," *Social Science Quarterly* 51 (June 1970): 42–56; at 51. A particularly good account of the situation in one state, where blacks also had to cope with a statewide reregistration of all voters, is Pat Watters, "South Carolina," *Atlantic Monthly* 222 (September 1968): 20–28. A somewhat informative survey of black elected officials is Joe R. Feagin, "Black Elected Officials in the South: An Exploratory Analysis," in Jack R. Van Der Slik, ed., *Black Conflict With White America* (Columbus: Charles E. Merrill, 1970), pp. 107–22. Also see Lester M. Salamon, "Leadership and Modernization: The Emerging Black Political Elite in the American South," *Journal of Politics* 35 (August 1973): 615–46. In Alabama in early 1968 seven blacks ran for posts on the Selma city council, and three made it into a runoff before being defeated in a contest marked by a very high turnout and very little voting across racial lines. See *New York Times*, 6 March 1968, p. 16, and 3 April 1968, p. 34. Later in the year Jim Clark's political career ended when he drew only 18 percent of the vote in a statewide race for the chairmanship of the state public service commission.

45.   Marvin Rich, "Civil Rights Progress Out of the Spotlight," *Reporter* 38 (7 March 1968): 25–27, at 25. Southern blacks also won greater representation in the 1968 national conventions of the two major political parties, where 43 black Democrats and 4 black Republicans served as delegates and 50 black Democrats and 9 black Republicans as alternates. Of the twenty-two major party state organizations, however, only Arkansas Republicans appeared to be making a visible effort to increase black participation in party activities. See Janet Wells, *VEP News* 2 (July 1968): 1 and 3; U.S. Commission on Civil Rights, *Political Participation*, pp. 133–51; and Feagin and Hahn, "The Second Reconstruction," p. 52. With the exception of some scattered efforts in Alabama and Mississippi, black attempts to achieve political gains through separate or independent political parties, such as the United Citizens party in South Carolina and the National Democratic party of Alabama, proved unsuccessful. Some notable county-level successes, such as that of the Lowndes County Freedom Organization in Alabama, were obtained by that route, however. On the overall topic, see Carlyle C. Douglas, "Black Politics in the New South," *Ebony* 26 (January 1971): 27–34; Hanes Walton, Jr., *Black Political Parties* (New York: Free Press, 1972), chapters 3–5, esp. pp. 77–79; and Hanes Walton, Jr. and William H. Boone, "Black Political Parties: A Demographic Analysis," *Journal of Black Studies* 5 (September 1974): 86–95. On Lowndes County, see Jack Shepherd, "A Worker Hits the Freedom Road," *Look* 29 (16 November 1965): M8–M12; *Student Voice*

6 (20 December 1965): 2; Andrew Kopkind, "The Lair of the Black Panther," *New Republic* 155 (13 August 1966): 10–13; Margaret Long, "Black Power in the Black Belt," *Progressive* 30 (October 1966): 20–24; Robert Analavage, *Southern Patriot* 24 (October 1966): 3–4, (December 1966): 1 and 8, and 26 (April 1968): 3; Carl Braden, *Southern Patriot* 29 (February 1971): 1 and 8; John Corry, "A Visit to Lowndes County, Alabama," *New South* 27 (Winter 1972): 28–36; and David Campbell, "The Lowndes County Freedom Organization: An Appraisal," *New South* 27 (Winter 1972): 37–42.

46. On Greene County, see Ray Jenkins, "Majority Rule in the Black Belt: Greene County, Alabama," *New South* 24 (Fall 1969): 60–67; *VEP News* 3 (August 1969): 3; David S. Glick, "Black Power Enclave," *New Republic* 164 (16 January 1971): 11–12; "Judgement on the Judge," *New Republic* 164 (30 January 1971): 11–12; Milton Lee Boykin, "Black Political Participation in Greene County, Alabama: An Information-Efficacious Hypothesis," *Politics* 73 (March 1973): 51–64, esp. pp. 53–55; and Jules Loh, *Hartford Courant*, 6 October 1974, p. 37. On Evers's victory and the far less heartening results of Mississippi's other 1969 municipal elections, see Bruce W. Eggler, "A Long Way to Go in Mississippi," *New Republic* 160 (28 June 1969): 19–21.

47. In this regard, note Chandler Davidson's contention that it is not the election of black and liberal white officeholders that is important, but the provision of "substantive political benefits" to the black community that counts. *Biracial Politics* (Baton Rouge: Louisiana State University Press, 1972), p. 112.

48. William R. Keech, *The Impact of Negro Voting* (Chicago: Rand McNally, 1968).

49. A number of earlier studies indicate that Keech's observations concerning Durham, North Carolina, and Tuskegee, Alabama, cannot be generalized. In some southern locales blacks did receive improved municipal services in the wake of substantial black voting but well before blacks themselves were elected to office. See George C. Stoney, "Suffrage in the South, Part II," *Survey Graphic* 29 (March 1940): 163–67 and 204–5, at 205; Donald S. Strong, "The Rise of Negro Voting in Texas," *American Political Science Review* 42 (June 1948): 510–22, at 521; and Luther P. Jackson, "Race and Suffrage in the South Since 1940," *New South* 3 (June–July 1948): 1–26, at 22–23. Other studies, however, have produced observations very similar to Keech's. See Alfred B. Clubok, John M. DeGrove, and Charles D. Farris, "The Manipulated Negro Vote: Some Pre-Conditions and Consequences," *Journal of Politics* 26 (February 1964): 112–29, at 128; and Davidson, *Biracial Politics*, pp. 8 and 137–38. Also see Hugh Douglas Price, "The Negro and Florida Politics, 1944–1954," *Journal of Politics* 17 (May 1955): 198–220; and Hugh S. Whitaker, "A New Day: The Effects of Negro Enfranchisement in Selected Mississippi Counties," Ph.D. dissertation, Florida State University, 1965.

50. Frederick M. Wirt, *Politics of Southern Equality* (Chicago: Aldine, 1970), p. 168. Also see p. 314. Wirt's book is a case study of Panola County, Mississippi, a Black Belt area in which surprisingly little opposition was voiced from the early 1960s on to increases in black political participation. Clubok, DeGrove,

and Farris had witnessed similar changes in some of the Florida communities they had studied several years earlier. "The Manipulated Negro Vote," p. 128.

51. Matthews and Prothro, *Negroes and the New Southern Politics*, pp. 479–80.

52. See Comment, "Voting Rights: A Case Study of Madison Parish," pp. 754–55, where it is noted that because "the Act fails to extend *automatic*, administrative protection to every stage of the electoral process . . . the success of administrative sanctions depends upon strong executive pressure" (emphasis added).

53. See U.S. Congress, House, Committee on the Judiciary, *Voting Rights Act Extension—Hearings Before Subcommittee No. 5*, 91st Congress, 1st session, 1969, esp. pp. 42–53, 226, and 269–72; U.S. Congress, House, Committee on the Judiciary, *Extension of the Voting Rights Act of 1965—Report No. 397*, 91st Congress, 1st session, 1969; *Congressional Quarterly Weekly Report*, 25 July 1969, p. 1326, 1 August 1969, pp. 1411–15, and 8 August 1969, p. 1456; Gary Orfield, *Congressional Power and Social Change* (New York: Harcourt Brace Jovanovich, 1975), pp. 97–98; and Richard Harris, *Justice* (New York: E.P. Dutton, 1970), pp. 200–3. Also see "Controversy Over the Federal Voting Rights Act," *Congressional Digest* 48 (November 1969): 257–88.

54. See George C. Bradley and Richard T. Seymour, "When Voting Rights Are Denied," *Civil Rights Digest* 2 (Summer 1969): 1–5, which details the problems experienced by black voters, candidates, and poll watchers in the May 1969 Mississippi primaries, and John W. Lyon, "The Mississippi Ballot Box," *Saturday Review* 52 (17 May 1969): 20–21. Another excellent early 1969 piece which paints a further picture of the need for an undiluted extension of the Voting Rights Act is Vernon E. Jordan, Jr., "The Black Vote in Danger," *Civil Rights Digest* 2 (Spring 1969): 1–7. Jordan notes how the remaining voting discrimination problems are less visible than were those focused on prior to 1965, and that any notion that the 1965 act already had solved all the problems faced by southern blacks in the electoral arena was false. Jordan also sounded a call for more extensive use of federal examiners and observers, describing why it was that "black people in the South very much prefer going before a Federal examiner to going before a local registrar. There is a difference in attitude. There is a difference in setting: for many black people fear and dread the local county courthouse, which is for many of them a symbol of injustice and oppression. There is a difference, too, in procedure." Also see *VEP News* 3 (March 1969): 4–5.

55. See U.S. Congress, Senate, Committee on the Judiciary, *Amendments to the Voting Rights Act of 1965—Hearings Before the Subcommittee on Constitutional Rights*, 91st Congress, 1st and 2nd sessions, 1969–70; *Congressional Quarterly Weekly Report*, 1 August 1969, pp. 1411–15, and 29 August 1969, p. 1595. Initial House passage was necessary because a pro-voting rights majority could not be obtained in the Constitutional Rights Subcommittee.

56. *VEP News* 3 (October 1969): 3; *Congressional Quarterly Weekly Report*, 21 November 1969, p. 2340, 19 December 1969, pp. 2613–14, and 23 January 1970, p. 237; Orfield, *Congressional Power*, pp. 99–100; and Harris, *Justice*, pp. 205–8.

57.   Senate, Committee on the Judiciary, *Amendments to the Voting Rights Act of 1965*, esp. pp. 261–62 and 535; *Congressional Quarterly Weekly Report*, 6 March 1970, pp. 674–75; Orfield, *Congressional Power*, pp. 101–3; Richard Harris, *Decision* (New York: E.P. Dutton, 1971), pp. 85–86 and 97; *Congressional Quarterly Weekly Report*, 5 June 1970, p. 1487, 19 June 1970, p. 1570, and 26 June 1970, p. 1616. For the text of the Voting Rights Act as revised in 1970, see U.S. Commission on Civil Rights, *Summary and Text—The Voting Rights Act* (Washington: USGPO, 1971). On the eighteen-year-old vote provision, see Lewis J. Paper, "Legislative History of Title III of the Voting Rights Act of 1970," *Harvard Journal on Legislation* 8 (November 1970): 123–57. The 1970 act's extension of the literacy test suspension provision to the entire nation was upheld subsequently by the Supreme Court in *Oregon* v. *Mitchell*, 400 U.S. 112 (1970). For a discussion of that holding, see Frank Foster, "Constitutional Bases for Upholding the Voting Rights Act Amendments of 1970," *DePaul Law Review* 20 (Summer 1971): 1002–28.

For a complete listing of the areas which came under the updated trigger formula in terms of the 1968 turnout, see *New York Times*, 11 January 1975, p. 60. A number of jurisdictions covered by the section 4 trigger have taken advantage of the provision in 4(a) which allows a subdivision to remove itself from coverage if it can convince the Federal District Court in Washington that it has not used a "test or device" in a racially discriminatory manner in the previous five—extended to ten in 1970—years. Alaska, one Idaho and three Arizona counties, and Wake County, N.C. (Raleigh), have applied for such exemptions and received them with Justice Department concurrence. A second North Carolina county, however, attempted to secure such an exemption and was opposed by Justice. The Supreme Court ruled, in an important decision, that the county's long maintenance of segregated schools in which blacks had received inferior educations mandated that an exemption not be granted, for any reimposition of literacy tests would discriminate unfairly against those black citizens whom the county previously had provided with inadequate educations. See Owen M. Fiss, "*Gaston County* v. *United States*: Fruition of the Freezing Principle," *Supreme Court Review* 1969, pp. 379–445, esp. 412–17; 395 U.S. 285 (1969); and U.S. Commission on Civil Rights, *The Voting Rights Act: Ten Years After* (Washington: USGPO, 1975), p. 13. Several years later the state of Virginia applied for such an exemption and was rejected on the same grounds. See *Virginia* v. *U.S.*, 386 F. Supp. 1319 (1974), affirmed per curiam 420 U.S. 901 (1975).

58.   Comment, "Voting Rights: A Case Study of Madison Parish," p. 755. Also see Charles V. Hamilton, *The Bench and The Ballot: Southern Federal Judges and Black Voters* (New York: Oxford University Press, 1973), pp. 241 and 245; Allan Wolk, *The Presidency and Black Civil Rights—Eisenhower to Nixon* (Rutherford, N.J.: Fairleigh Dickinson University Press, 1971), p. 80; "Voting Rights," *Civil Rights Digest* 4 (December 1971): 29–33; and Leon E. Panetta and Peter Gall, *Bring Us Together—The Nixon Team and the Civil Rights Retreat* (Philadelphia: J.B. Lippincott, 1971).

59.   *Allen* v. *State Board of Elections*, 393 U.S. 547 (1969). Eight years later the Court ruled that a Justice Department decision not to object to a submitted

change within the specified sixty days could not be challenged in court. It further held that Justice could not interpose a valid objection after that period of time had expired. See *Morris* v. *Gressette*, 97 S. Ct. 2411 (1977), affirming 425 F. Supp. 331 (1976). Earlier cases following from *Allen* included *Fairly* v. *Patterson*, 282 F. Supp. 164; *Burton* v. *Patterson*, 281 F. Supp. 918; and *Whitley* v. *Williams*, 296 F. Supp. 754. A subsequent Alabama case, and a 1971 Mississippi one, also involved questions of the scope of section 5, questions which the Supreme Court answered by ruling that section 5's provisions applied to a wide variety of electorally related changes, including requirements imposed upon independent candidates and new parties, and annexations. See *Hadnott* v. *Amos*, 394 U.S. 358, and 320 F. Supp. 107; and *Perkins* v. *Matthews*, 301 F. Supp. 565 and 400 U.S. 379 (1971). An excellent discussion of these early cases is John J. Roman, "Section 5 of the Voting Rights Act: The Formation of an Extraordinary Federal Remedy," *The American University Law Review* 22 (Fall 1972): 111–33. An account of a subsequent 1972 case decided by a three-judge district court in the Middle District of Alabama which further enlarged the scope of section 5 is Kirke M. Hassan, "*MacGuire* v. *Amos*: Application of Section 5 of the Voting Rights Act to Political Parties," *Harvard Civil Rights—Civil Liberties Law Review* 8 (January 1973): 199–210. See 343 F. Supp. 119. *Allen*'s and *Perkins*'s holding that *local* federal district courts could consider only whether changes were covered by section 5, and not whether a change was allowable, which was a task reserved to the D.C. court or the Justice Department, subsequently was reiterated in *Connor* v. *Waller*, 421 U.S. 656 (1975), and *U.S.* v. *Board of Supervisors of Warren County*, 429 U.S. 642 (1977).

60.   See David H. Hunter, *The Shameful Blight: The Survival of Racial Discrimination in Voting in the South* (Washington: Washington Research Project, 1972), p. 10. Also see David H. Hunter, *Federal Review of Voting Changes: How to Use Section 5 of the Voting Rights Act*, 2nd ed. (Washington: Joint Center for Political Studies, 1975), p. 51. A recent paper on Justice's section 5 activities which fails to acknowledge the important role played by Edwards's subcommittee in stimulating the department's policy change is Howard Ball, Dale A. Krane, and Thomas P. Lauth, Jr., "Judicial Impact on the Enforcement of Voting Rights Policy By Attorneys in the Department of Justice," unpublished paper presented at the Annual Meeting of the Southern Political Science Association, New Orleans, La., November 3-5, 1977.

61.   See U.S. Congress, House, Committee on the Judiciary, *The Enforcement of the Voting Rights Act—Hearings Before the Civil Rights Oversight Subcommittee*, 92nd Congress, 1st session, 1971; 36 *Federal Register* 18186; Hunter, *Federal Review of Voting Changes*, pp. 10–11; and Roman, "Section 5 of the Voting Rights Act," p. 126. One effect of these events was an increase in the number of submitted changes objected to by the Justice Department. In calendar 1971 it forbade the implementation of more than fifty changes, more than twice the number that it had blocked in the previous five years combined. Ball, Krane, and Lauth suggest that the number of objections is not greater than it is because of the extensive preliminary bargaining between Justice and submitting jurisdic-

tions that precedes the formal submission of most reported changes ("Judicial Impact," pp. 21-23).

62. U.S. Congress, House, Committee on the Judiciary, *Enforcement of the Voting Rights Act of 1965 in Mississippi—A Report of the Civil Rights Oversight Subcommittee*, 92nd Congress, 2nd session, 1972, esp. p. 5. Also see Hunter, *The Shameful Blight*, esp. pp. 45–47, and 73–92. See as well the Civil Rights Commission's excellent study, *The Voting Rights Act: Ten Years After*, esp. pp. 329, 337, and 345–46. Three years later in 1975, Justice still had not devised a comprehensive solution to the problem of unsubmitted changes. See the colloquy between Representative Yvonne B. Burke and Deputy Assistant Attorney General K. William O'Connor, U.S. Congress, House, Committee on Appropriations, *Hearings on Department of Justice Appropriations for 1976*, 94th Congress, 1st session, 1975, pp. 773–75. Also see the criticisms made in a 1978 General Accounting Office report, *Voting Rights Act—Enforcement Needs Strengthening* (Washington: USGPO, 1978), pp. 10–20.

63. The leading student of the shifting racial positions of southern gubernatorial candidates is Earl Black. See "Southern Governors and Political Change: Campaign Stances on Racial Segregation and Economic Development, 1950–69," *Journal of Politics* 33 (August 1971): 703–34; and *Southern Governors and Civil Rights*. Also see David R. Colburn and Richard K. Scher, "Race Relations and Florida Gubernatorial Politics Since the *Brown* Decision," *Florida Historical Quarterly* 55 (October 1976): 153–69; and Edwin M. Yoder, "Southern Governors and the New State Politics," in H. Brandt Ayers and Thomas H. Naylor, eds., *You Can't Eat Magnolias* (New York: McGraw-Hill, 1972), pp. 160–66, plus the inaugural address excerpts appearing on pages 358–67 of that volume. Also worth noting is Tod A. Baker and Robert P. Steed, "Southern Political Elites and Social Change: An Exploratory Study," *Politics* 74 (March 1974): 27–37. A number of volumes have sought to survey and depict southern politics in the years since 1965. The most insightful of these is Neal Peirce's *The Deep South States of America*, which covers seven of the eleven states. The other four—North Carolina, Tennessee, Texas, and Virginia—are covered in two others of Peirce's volumes. Similar efforts are Havard, ed., *The Changing Politics of the South*; Bartley and Graham, *Southern Politics and the Second Reconstruction*, and Jack Bass and Walter DeVries, *The Transformation of Southern Politics* (New York: Basic Books, 1976).

64. On the racial character of the Wallace runoff campaign, see Ray Jenkins, "Standing For It Again in Alabama," *New South* 25 (Summer 1970): 26–30; Black, *Southern Governors and Civil Rights*, p. 57; and Black and Black, "The Demographic Basis of Wallace Support in Alabama," p. 300.

65. On the Louisiana race, see Charles E. Grenier and Perry H. Howard, "The Edwards Victory," *Louisiana Review* 1 (Summer 1972): 31–42; and Bartley and Graham, *Southern Politics and the Second Reconstruction*, pp. 155–56.

66. Bartley and Graham, *Southern Politics and the Second Reconstruction*, p. 154; *In the Public Interest* 1 (August 1971): 1–4, and (March 1972): 5.

67. Jerry W. DeLaughter, "Black Political Participation in Mississippi: The 1971 General Election," *In the Public Interest* 2 (June 1972): 2–4 and 6; F. Glenn Abney, "Factors Related to Negro Voter Turnout in Mississippi," *Journal of Politics* 36 (November 1974): 1057–63; and Jason Berry, *Amazing Grace* (New York: Saturday Review Press, 1973), pp. 325–26. Also see Thomas Powers, "Letter From A Lost Campaign," *Harper's* 244 (March 1972): 22–31.

68. See Neil Maxwell, *Wall Street Journal*, 22 June 1971, p. 1; *VEP News* 5 (April–June 1971): 1 and 4; Berry, *Amazing Grace*, passim; and Lester M. Salamon, "Mississippi Post-mortem: The 1971 Elections," *New South* 27 (Winter 1972): 43–47.

69. See DeLaughter, "Black Political Participation in Mississippi," p. 3; and Abney, "Factors Related to Negro Voter Turnout," p. 1062.

70. See Neil Maxwell, *Wall Street Journal*, 2 November 1971, p. 1; and Salamon, "Mississippi Post-mortem," p. 45.

71. See Salamon, "Mississippi Post-mortem," p. 45; and Berry, *Amazing Grace*, passim.

72. U.S. Commission on Civil Rights, *The Voting Rights Act: Ten Years After*, pp. 35–37.

73. Ibid., pp. 32–33 and 395–97. Examiners also continued to be active in several other previously designated counties, such as Madison and Humphreys in Mississippi in 1971. See *VEP News* 5 (July–September 1971): 1. All told, however, while from 1965 through 1968 examiners had listed 168,208 new voters, in the period 1969 through 1974 the federal officials added only 2,068 in all covered jurisdictions, including the two newly designated counties in 1974. See U.S. Congress, House, Committee on the Judiciary, *Extension of the Voting Rights Act—Hearings Before the Subcommittee on Civil and Constitutional Rights*, 94th Congress, 1st session, 1975, p. 218.

74. See Stanley A. Halpin, Jr., and Richard L. Engstrom, "Racial Gerrymandering and Southern State Legislative Redistricting: Attorney General Determinations Under the Voting Rights Act," *Journal of Public Law* 22 (1973): 37–66; and Frank R. Parker, "County Redistricting in Mississippi: Case Studies in Racial Gerrymandering," *Mississippi Law Journal* 44 (June 1973): 391–424. Also see Joseph F. Gilliland, "Racial Gerrymandering in the Deep South," *Alabama Law Review* 22 (Spring 1970): 319–48.

75. See *Bussie* v. *Governor of Louisiana*, 333 F. Supp. 452, and 457 F.2d 796; *Taylor* v. *McKeithen*, 407 U.S. 191; and Halpin and Engstrom, "Racial Gerrymandering," pp. 52–57.

76. See *Georgia* v. *United States*, 411 U.S. 526 (1973); Halpin and Engstrom, "Racial Gerrymandering," pp. 62–63; and *Indiana Law Review* 7 (January 1974): 579–91.

77. *Connor* v. *Johnson*, 265 F. Supp. 492, 386 U.S. 483 (1967), 330 F. Supp. 506, 402 U.S. 690 (1971). *Connor* also was important in that in its 1971 opinion the Supreme Court ruled that a redistricting plan decreed by a federal district court was *not* subject to section 5 review, a holding which drew strong criticism from voting rights attorneys. See Hunter, *The Shameful Blight*, pp. 151–55.

Despite that, however, repeated efforts to devise an acceptable redistricting of the Mississippi state legislature all proved unavailing. In May 1977 the Supreme Court, in *Connor* v. *Finch*, 97 S. Ct. 1828, invalidated the *sixth* attempt on the grounds that population deviations from district to district were too large to be acceptable. The first three unsuccessful plans had been prepared by the state legislature itself, and the second three by the Federal District Court for the Southern District of Mississippi. The best overview of *Connor* v. *Johnson*, its progeny, and the redistricting efforts up through the 1975 plan is Thomas Vocino, John H. Morris, and D. Steve Gill, "The Population Apportionment Principle: Its Development and Application to Mississippi's State and Local Legislative Bodies," *Mississippi Law Journal* 47 (November 1976): 943–78, esp. 952–68.

78. *Whitcomb* v. *Chavis*, 403 U.S. 124 (1971). Two earlier holdings appear at 305 F. Supp. 1364 (1969) and 307 F. Supp. 1362. A pre-1971 discussion of the case is Note, "*Chavis* v. *Whitcomb*: Apportionment, Gerrymandering, and Black Voting Rights," *Rutgers Law Review* 24 (Spring 1970): 521–50. Commentaries which discuss the 1971 Supreme Court opinion are Walter L. Carpeneti, "Legislative Apportionment: Multi-member Districts and Fair Representation," *University of Pennsylvania Law Review* 120 (April 1972): 666–700, at 678–85; Robert B. Washington, Jr., "Fair and Effective Representation Revisited—The Shades of *Chavis* v. *Whitcomb*," *Howard Law Journal* 17 (1972): 382–400, esp. 387–93; Halpin and Engstrom, "Racial Gerrymandering," pp. 43–46; and Armand Derfner, "Multi-Member Districts and Black Voters," *Black Law Journal* 2 (1972): 120–28, at 121–23.

79. *Sims* v. *Amos*, 336 F. Supp. 924, affirmed 409 U.S. 942 (1972). Also see 365 F. Supp. 215; *Wallace* v. *Sims*, 415 U.S. 902 (1974); and U.S. Commission on Civil Rights, *The Voting Rights Act: Ten Years After*, pp. 239–41. Derfner argues a view somewhat similar to the case law in stating that multimember districts will be much more discriminatory against blacks in locales where blacks commonly are excluded from successful electoral coalitions—i.e., much of the South—than in areas where they often are not—e.g. Indiana. In areas where blacks are not a politically isolated minority, multimember districts may not be harmful to their interests. As Derfner has said, "The critical question involves the comparison between control over a few officials and less influence over a greater number" ("Multi-Member Districts and Black Voters," p. 127).

80. The Texas case was *Graves* v. *Barnes*, 378 F. Supp. 640. Notable subsequent Supreme Court rulings which reflected negative views of multimember districting schemes include *White* v. *Regester*, 412 U.S. 755 (1973), and *East Carroll Parish School Board* v. *Marshall*, 424 U.S. 636 (1976). The *East Carroll* decision was the culmination of proceedings which previously had been conducted under the name of *Zimmer* v. *McKeithen*. See 467 F.2d 1381 (1972) and 485 F.2d 1297 (1973). Discussions of this complex and evolving—some would say confusing—area of the law include Christopher E. Peters, "At-Large Election of Parish Officials," *Alabama Law Review* 26 (Fall 1973): 163–76; *Harvard Law Review* 87 (June 1974): 1851–60; Paul W. Bonapfel, "Minority Challenges to At-Large Elections: The Dilution Problem," *Georgia Law Review* 10 (Winter

1976): 353–90; and Robert L. Bell, *Howard Law Journal* 19 (Spring 1976): 177–89.

81. *Dunston* v. *Scott*, 336 F. Supp. 206 (1972); and *Stevenson* v. *West*, 413 U.S. 902 (1973).

82. *City of Petersburg* v. *U.S.*, 354 F. Supp. 1021 (1972), affirmed 410 U.S. 962 (1973); *City of Richmond* v. *U.S.*, 376 F. Supp. 1344 (1974), reversed 422 U.S. 358 (1975). Also see *Holt* v. *City of Richmond*, 334 F. Supp. 228 (1971), reversed 459 F.2d 1093, cert. denied 408 U.S. 931 (1972). Petersburg too elected a black majority council and a black mayor in its first elections held under the new ward system. An excellent account of the Petersburg election is Carey E. Stronach, "Anatomy of a Black Victory," *Nation* 217 (27 August 1973): 146–48. Discussions of these cases appear in William J. Wernz, " 'Discriminatory Purpose,' 'Changes,' and 'Dilution': Recent Judicial Interpretations of Section 5 of the Voting Rights Act," *Notre Dame Lawyer* 51 (December 1975): 333–51, at 336–41; James W. Ozos, "Judicial Review of Municipal Annexations Under Section 5 of the Voting Rights Act," *Urban Law Annual* 12 (1976): 311–20; Brian A. Powers, "Annexations and the Voting Rights Act," *North Carolina Law Review* 54 (January 1976): 206–16; Craig S. Cooley, Wade W. Massie, and Carl M. Rizzo, "Securing A Valid Annexation in Virginia: State and Federal Requirements," *University of Richmond Law Review* 10 (Spring 1976): 557–96, at 575–95; Joseph F. Zimmerman, "The Federal Voting Rights Act: Its Impact on Annexation," *National Civic Review* 66 (June 1977): 278–83; and *Georgia Law Review* 10 (Fall 1975): 261–74, esp. pp. 264 and 270. Press accounts of the Richmond developments include Robert G. Holland, *Raleigh News and Observer*, 27 February 1977, p. IV–2; *New York Times*, 3 March 1977, p. 36, 7 March 1977, p. 22, and 9 March 1977, p. 14; Robert G. Holland, *Raleigh News and Observer*, 13 March 1977, p. IV–2; B.D. Ayres, Jr., *New York Times*, 30 July 1977, p. 6; and Robert G. Holland, *Raleigh News and Observer*, 7 August 1977, p. IV–2. Also see Hunter, *The Shameful Blight*, pp. 132–35; *Annual Report of the Attorney General, 1973*, pp. 70–71; and Armand Derfner and Joseph Taylor, *Focus* 1 (July 1973): 3. A less encouraging result was obtained from litigation concerning councilmanic redistricting in New Orleans. See *Beer* v. *United States*, 374 F. Supp. 363 (1974), reversed 425 U.S. 130 (1976), and note in particular Justice Marshall's dissent. Like Richmond and Petersburg, New Orleans too soon elected a black mayor, Ernest N. Morial. See John Pope, *Washington Post*, 14 November 1977, p. A6; and Bill Rushton, "New Orleans Elects Black Mayor," *Southern Exposure* 6 (1978): 5–7. A more recent redistricting case whose final outcome was favorable to the black plaintiffs involved the Jackson, Mississippi metropolitan area. See the *en banc* ruling of the Fifth Circuit Court of Appeals in *Kirksey* v. *Board of Supervisors of Hinds County*, 554 F.2d 139 (1977), which the Supreme Court declined to review (46 *USLW* 3354).

83. See Parker, "County Redistricting in Mississippi," pp. 412, 414, and 418. Early in 1977, in *United Jewish Organizations of Williamsburgh, Inc.* v. *Carey*, 430 U.S. 144, the Supreme Court, in a notable decision, upheld the use of race-conscious redistricting in the Williamsburgh area of Brooklyn, New York.

Faced with a redistricting of the state legislature, state officials, striving to obtain Justice Department approval under section 5's preclearance requirement, consciously had set out to create several black majority districts and in the process had divided a tightly knit Jewish community between two such districts. Local Jewish groups objected to the plan and attempted to block it in the courts. Their complaint was dismissed by the district court, which in turn was upheld by the Second Circuit Court of Appeals and the Supreme Court. Discussions of the case prior to the final Supreme Court holding include William J. Bowman, *Georgetown Law Journal* 63 (July 1975): 1321–35; Christine M. McEvoy, *Suffolk University Law Review* 9 (Summer 1975): 1496–1511; and Note, "Proportional Representation By Race: The Constitutionality of Benign Racial Districting," *Michigan Law Review* 74 (March 1976): 820–41. The appellate court's opinion appears at 510 F.2d 512 (1975).

84. See John Lewis and Archie E. Allen, "Black Voter Registration Efforts in the South," *Notre Dame Lawyer* 48 (October 1972): 105–32, at 114.

85. See John Dean, *The Making of a Black Mayor* (Washington: Joint Center for Political Studies, 1973), for an account of the successful race of A.J. Cooper.

86. See *New York Times*, 9 August 1972, p. 16; and Roy Reed, *New York Times*, 22 March 1970, p. 44. Also see *Reese* v. *Dallas County*, 505 F.2d 879 (1974), reversed per curiam 421 U.S. 477 (1975), which concerned a Selma-based challenge to the format used for electing the five county commissioners. While the Fifth Circuit Court of Appeals, by an 8 to 6 vote, upheld the city residents' challenge, the Supreme Court held 8 to 0 that the circuit court majority had erred.

87. *In the Public Interest* 2 (August 1973): 3–11.

88. For a somewhat earlier picture which emphasized that actual black political control really existed only in Greene County and a small number of tiny, scattered towns, see Mack H. Jones, "Black Officeholders in Local Governments of the South: An Overview," *Politics* 71 (March 1971): 49–72. Also see James E. Conyers and Walter L. Wallace, *Black Elected Officials* (New York: Russell Sage Foundation, 1976), pp. 137–54. For later accounts that note several additional black victories, see David Campbell and Joe R. Feagin, "Black Politics in the South: A Descriptive Analysis," *Journal of Politics* 37 (February 1975): 129–62; and Charles S. Bullock III, "The Election of Blacks in the South: Preconditions and Consequences," *American Journal of Political Science* 19 (November 1975): 727–39.

89. On Busbee and his victories over segregationists Lester Maddox and Ronnie Thompson, and the supplantation of racial concerns by other issues, see B.D. Ayres, Jr., *New York Times*, 8 September 1974, p. E4. The decreasing attention to the politics of race throughout the South in the 1974 campaigns was noted by any number of observers. See the editorial comments of the *New York Times*, 5 September 1974, p. 36; and the stories by Roy Reed in the *Times* of 27 September 1974, p. 37; and 25 February 1975, pp. 37 and 70. Also see Albert R. Hunt, *Wall Street Journal*, 22 October 1974, pp. 1 and 37.

90. B.D. Ayres, Jr., *New York Times*, 14 July 1974, p. 37. Despite the heavi-

314 NOTES TO PAGES 206–207

ly publicized endorsements of Wallace by Hobson City's mayor, J.L. Stringer, where Wallace received 76 percent of the almost all-black vote, and Tuskegee's mayor, Johnny Ford, where Wallace got 32 percent of the black vote, outside of those two towns the incumbent governor received only some 7 to 9 percent of the black vote in his Democratic primary race against a little-known state senator, Gene McLain of Huntsville. See Emory O. Jackson, *Focus* 2 (June 1974): 3. Also see Ray Jenkins, "Blacks For Wallace," *New Republic* 170 (25 May 1974): 11–12; Charles Fulwood, "Blacks For Wallace," *Ramparts* 13 (November 1974): 13–14; and Manning Marable, "Tuskegee, Alabama: The Politics of Illusion in the New South," *Black Scholar* 8 (May 1977): 13–24. Subsequent to the election, Wallace added a young Selma black man to his staff. See B.D. Ayres, Jr., *New York Times*, 21 January 1975, p. 14; and *New York Times*, 1 February 1975, p. 21.

91. See *New York Times*, 20 February 1976, p. 26. The important federal appointment was that of Matthew Perry to a seat on the U.S. Court of Military Appeals. In May 1978 the Senate approved President Carter's nomination of New Orleans magistrate Robert F. Collins to the federal district court there. Collins will be the first modern-day black federal judge in the Deep South. See Bill Peterson, *Washington Post*, 3 November 1977, p. A3, *New York Times*, 7 November 1977, p. 20, and *Raleigh News and Observer*, 18 May 1978, p. 7.

92. See the UPI story in the *New York Times* of 1 March 1974, p. 12; as well as an AP article in the *Hartford Courant* of 28 October 1974, p. 23. For the election results, see the account by Ayres in the *Times* of 11 November 1974, p. 30, as well as an item in the *Times* of 1 December 1974, p. 33. Also see the editorial reaction to the results voiced by the *Times*, which stated, "The election gave real support to the conventional wisdom that the Voting Rights Act of 1965 was the most successful law enacted during the period of legislative creativity called 'The Great Society' " (18 November 1974, p. 23). The *Times* also noted, as the Civil Rights Commission was to do in a January 1975 report, that racially motivated irregularities still had occurred in the 1974 elections in some scattered locations. Some two hundred federal observers were used in six counties, four in Alabama, one in Georgia, and one in Mississippi. See *The Voting Rights Act: Ten Years After*, chapters 4–7 passim, esp. pp. 174 and 189; Ernest Holsendolph, *New York Times*, 24 January 1975, p. 37; *Washington Post*, 6 November 1974, p. A11; and *Time*, 27 January 1975, p. 12.

93. See B.D. Ayres, Jr., *New York Times*, 15 June 1975, p. 24; *New York Times*, 5 August 1975, p. 34, and 7 August 1975, p. 20; R.W. Apple, Jr., *New York Times*, 18 August 1975, p. 40; Roy Reed, *New York Times*, 23 August 1975, p. 14, and 20 October 1975, p. 1; *New York Times*, 30 December 1975, p. 15; Thomas A. Johnson, *New York Times*, 4 January 1976, p. 32; and *New York Times*, 2 March 1976, p. 20.

94. See U.S. Congress, House, Committee on the Judiciary, *Extension of the Voting Rights Act*, 1975, p. 3; *New York Times*, 15 January 1975, p. 15; Ernest Holsendolph, *New York Times*, 24 January 1975, p. 37; *New York Times*, 27 February 1975, p. 14, and 6 March 1975, p. 24; and Joseph Taylor, *Focus* 3 (February 1975): 3.

95. See U.S. Congress, House, Committee on the Judiciary, *Extension of the Voting Rights Act*, 1975, pp. 140–41, 167–69, and 725. Also see Roy Reed, *New York Times*, 25 February 1975, pp. 37 and 70; and Richard E. Cohen, *National Journal Reports*, 26 October 1974, pp. 1606–13.

96. See U.S. Congress, Senate, Committee on the Judiciary, *Extension of the Voting Rights Act of 1965—Hearings Before the Subcommittee on Constitutional Rights*, 94th Congress, 1st session, 1975; *Congressional Quarterly Weekly Report*, 8 March 1975, pp. 489–92; Ernest Holsendolph, *New York Times*, 10 April 1975, p. 7; and Martha V. Gottron, *Congressional Quarterly Weekly Report*, 12 April 1975, pp. 761 and 768. Also see "Controversy Over the Voting Rights Act Extension," *Congressional Digest* 54 (June–July 1975): 163–92.

97. *New York Times*, 18 April 1975, p. 5, and 30 April 1975, p. 13; *Hartford Courant*, 19 April 1975, p. 46; and *Congressional Quarterly Weekly Report*, 26 April 1975, p. 876. The approval of the language minorities provisions, whose sponsors—such as Democrats Herman Badillo of New York, Barbara Jordan of Texas, and Edward Roybal of California—sought to allow for increased political participation by Puerto Rican Americans in the Northeast and by Mexican-Americans in the Southwest, produced a flurry of efforts in Texas to find some way to escape such federal coverage. See Ernest Holsendolph, *New York Times*, 23 April 1975, p. 15; and Kaye Northcutt, *New York Times*, 11 May 1975, p. E5.

98. See *New York Times*, 3 May 1975, p. 32; Martha V. Gottron, *Congressional Quarterly Weekly Report*, 3 May 1975, pp. 925–26, and 17 May 1975, pp. 1042–44; and U.S. Congress, House, Committee on the Judiciary, *Voting Rights Act Extension—Report No. 196*, 94th Congress, 1st session, 1975.

99. See *New York Times*, 4 June 1975, p. 17; Ernest Holsendolph, *New York Times*, 5 June 1975, p. 25; and Diantha Johnson, *Congressional Quarterly Weekly Report*, 7 June 1975, pp. 1200–3. On the growing moderation of the South's representatives in Congress, see Roy Reed, *New York Times*, 10 February 1976, pp. 1 and 22; and Michael J. Malbin, *National Journal Reports*, 20 March 1976, pp. 370–74. Malbin notes how the voting records of those southern representatives and senators elected prior to 1966 remain far more conservative than those of their colleagues who have entered the Congress since the Voting Rights Act first became law. Also see Bass and DeVries, *The Transformation of Southern Politics*, pp. 369–83.

100. *New York Times*, 13 June 1975, p. 9; *Congressional Quarterly Weekly Report*, 14 June 1975, p. 1232; *National Journal Reports*, 5 July 1975, p. 1008; Ernest Holsendolph, *New York Times*, 18 July 1975, p. 33; *New York Times*, 19 July 1975, p. 20, 20 July 1975, p. 16, and 22 July 1975, p. 50; Martha V. Gottron, *Congressional Quarterly Weekly Report*, 26 July 1975, pp. 1595–99; Richard L. Madden, *New York Times*, 24 July 1975, p. 1, 25 July 1975, p. 28, and 29 July 1975, p. 1; *National Journal Reports*, 2 August 1975, p. 1124; and Martha V. Gottron, *Congressional Quarterly Weekly Report*, 2 August 1975, pp. 1666–67. On Ford's unsuccessful and quickly and quietly forgotten attempt to work a "southern strategy" of his own by "nationalizing" and weakening the measure, see Rowland Evans and Robert Novak, *Middletown Press*, 29 May 1975, p. 14; and *Atlantic Monthly* 236 (November 1975): 14.

For detailed accounts the provisions of the Voting Rights Act as amended in 1975—and the language minorities provisions are rather complex—see U.S. Commission on Civil Rights, *Using the Voting Rights Act* (Washington: USGPO, 1976), esp. p. 5; and David H. Hunter, "The 1975 Voting Rights Act and Language Minorities," *Catholic University Law Review* 25 (Winter 1976): 250–70. Hunter correctly points out that the 1975 act suffers both from some sloppy drafting and from "the lack in Congress of a clear notion of the problem to be remedied" in regard to language minorities. Congress, Hunter notes, gave "greater attention to assuring that a bill showing concern for the voting problems of Mexican Americans would pass than to carefully delineating these problems (and those of other minority groups) and drafting a bill to meet them" (pp. 268–69). Also see U.S. Congress, Senate, Committee on the Judiciary, *Voting Rights Act Extension—Report No. 295*, 94th Congress, 1st session, 1975, pp. 24–39. On the initial Justice Department moves to enforce the act's new provisions, see *National Journal Reports*, 6 September 1975, p. 1285; *New York Times*, 31 August 1975, p. 38, and 22 April 1976, p. 25; Assistant Attorney General Pottinger's testimony in U.S. Congress, House, Committee on Appropriations, *Hearings on Department of Justice Appropriations for 1977*, 94th Congress, 2nd session, 1976, pp. 209–11; and John Crewdson, *New York Times*, 1 May 1976, p. 10. The state of Texas challenged the language provisions in the federal courts without any success; in June 1977 the Supreme Court held that Texas was subject to the provisions of the 1975 Act. See *Briscoe* v. *Bell*, 97 S. Ct. 2428, affirming 535 F.2d 1259. On developments in San Antonio, where a federally stimulated shift to single-member city council districts led to Chicano gains, see *New York Times*, 17 January 1977, p. 48, and 4 April 1977, p. 25.

101. *Raleigh News and Observer*, 13 May 1976, p. 20. One year later that figure had increased further to 2,129, but even that total represented only 2.6 percent of all of the South's elected officials. Of the South's 1,781 state legislators, approximately 106 were black. Fifteen years earlier there had been only one. See *Raleigh News and Observer*, 12 June 1977, p. VI–6; and B.D. Ayres, Jr., *New York Times*, 21 February 1977, p. 14.

102. Young's appointment as United Nations ambassador in the Carter administration early in 1977 reduced southern black representation in the U.S. House of Representatives from three to two, as Atlanta's city council president, Wyche F. Fowler, Jr., a moderate-to-liberal white, defeated former VEP director John Lewis in the race for Young's Fifth District seat. On the Fowler-Lewis race, see *New York Times*, 15 March 1977, p. 15; *Raleigh News and Observer*, 16 March 1977, p. 3; *New York Times*, 17 March 1977, p. A18; Pat Watters, *Raleigh News and Observer*, 27 March 1977, p. IV–2; and Wayne King, *New York Times*, 5 April 1977, p. 16, and 7 April 1977, p. 33.

103. U.S. Congress, House, Committee on the Judiciary, *Extension of the Voting Rights Act*, 1975, p. 664. One excellent analysis has found that black members of county governing boards in the rural South have had an impact that is "at best negligible" in regard to reordering governmental priorities. See Mack H. Jones, "Black Officeholding and Political Development in the Rural South," *Review of Black Political Economy* 6 (Summer 1976): 375–407, esp. p. 401. Jones

strongly criticizes what he sees as these officials' failure to play an innovative role with respect to local governmental policy (pp. 402–4).

104. See Paul Delaney, *New York Times*, 1 June 1976, pp. 1 and 25; and Janet Wells, "Voting Rights in 1975," *Civil Rights Digest* 7 (Summer 1975): 13–19, which gives an excellent account of some of the continuing problems, particularly those involving election irregularities, and the additional enforcement efforts that could be made. Also see *New York Times*, 6 March 1975, p. 24; and Jerry DeMuth, "Powerless Politics: Blacks and Voting Rights," *America* 133 (27 September 1975): 170, which reports some different figures. For a profile of blacks' political plight in one very heavily black county, see B.D. Ayres, Jr., *New York Times*, 3 December 1976, p. A18, on Calhoun County, South Carolina. Also see Warren Brown's story on Terrell County, Georgia, *Washington Post*, 3 September 1977, pp. A1 and A12. As Brown's piece indicates, fear of white economic retaliation is still a major barrier to black voting in some areas of the rural South. Estimates of overall black registration in the South in late 1976 and early 1977 were 54 or 55 percent. See *Raleigh News and Observer*, 16 January 1977, p. 12, and 6 March 1977, p. 16.

105. Kenneth S. Colburn, *Southern Black Mayors: Local Problems and Federal Responses*, 2nd ed. (Washington: Joint Center for Political Studies, 1974), esp. pp. 2 and 16. Also see Roy Reed, *New York Times*, 11 March 1975, p. 21; Ernest Holsendolph, *New York Times*, 28 June 1976, p. 16; and George Goodman, Jr., *New York Times*, 3 September 1977, p. 5.

106. See Thomas A. Johnson, *New York Times*, 30 December 1975, p. 15; and Andrew Kopkind, "Lowndes County, Alabama: The Great Fear is Gone," *Ramparts* 13 (April 1975): 8–12 and 53–55. Also see Johnson's stories on two other jurisdictions in which blacks had experienced some political success, Fayette, Mississippi, and Hancock County, Georgia, in *New York Times*, 29 December 1975, p. 42, and 31 December 1975, p. 31. Other stories which touch upon this point include Reginald Stuart, *New York Times*, 31 May 1976, p. 1; Nancy Hicks, *New York Times*, 21 June 1976, p. 20; Roy Reed, *New York Times*, 24 January 1977, pp. 1 and 16; and Wayne King, *New York Times*, 6 February 1977, p. 24. A graphic portrayal of the poverty and economic dependence rampant in the Delta is Tony Dunbar, *Our Land Too* (New York: Pantheon, 1971), pp. 1–104, esp. 22–24, which focuses upon Humphreys County, Mississippi. Also see Jack E. White, Jr., "The Unchanged South," *Ebony* 26 (August 1971): 126–32.

107. See Thomas A. Johnson, *New York Times*, 7 January 1976, p. 20, and 2 June 1976, p. 19; Richard A. Schaffer, *Wall Street Journal*, 17 October 1974, pp. 1 and 35; and Black, *Southern Governors and Civil Rights*, p. 304. Professor Jones has argued that elected black county officials have had "only limited success" in increasing black citizens' share of governmental services and benefits in the rural South. See "Black Officeholding and Political Development in the Rural South," p. 404.

108. Hunter, *The Shameful Blight*, p. vi. Also see Nick Kotz, "The Other Side of the New South," *New Republic* 178 (25 March 1978): 16–19, and (1 April 1978): 18–23.

Chapter 7

1. As Lowi has observed, "To pluralists, social change in a pluralist system works in small increments" (*The End of Liberalism* [New York: W.W. Norton, 1969], p. 50). The most well-known exponent of the pluralist view is Robert Dahl, though a number of other scholars—such as David B. Truman and Earl Latham—are equally well associated with the pluralist perspective. See in particular Dahl's *Pluralist Democracy in the United States: Conflict and Consent* (Chicago: Rand McNally, 1967).

2. See in particular David Easton, "The New Revolution in Political Science," *American Political Science Review* 63 (December 1969): 1051–61, at 1057; and Samuel P. Huntington, "Paradigms of American Politics: Beyond the One, the Two, and the Many," *Political Science Quarterly* 89 (March 1974): 1–26, at 13. Also see Darryl Baskin, "American Pluralism: Theory, Practice, and Ideology," *Journal of Politics* 32 (February 1970): 71–95; and Michael Parenti, "Power and Pluralism: A View From the Bottom," *Journal of Politics* 32 (August 1970): 501–30. Perhaps the two most outspoken critics of pluralism in this regard are Lowi, who is mentioned above, and William A. Gamson. Both have challenged whether pluralism supplies an accurate description of American political interaction, and Gamson in particular has attacked what he regards as pluralism's failure to acknowledge that minority groups receive very little representation in the ongoing political system. See "Stable Unrepresentation in American Society," *American Behavioral Scientist* 12 (November-December 1968): 15–21; and *The Strategy of Social Protest* (Homewood: Dorsey Press, 1975), esp. chapters 1 and 8. Also see Chandler Davidson, *Biracial Politics* (Baton Rouge: Louisiana State University Press, 1972), pp. 8, 25, and 51; and Charles V. Hamilton, "Blacks and the Crisis in Political Participation," *Public Interest* 34 (Winter 1974): 188–210.

3. See especially Michael Lipsky, "Protest As A Political Resource," *American Political Science Review* 62 (December 1968): 1144–58, at 1157; and Lipsky, *Protest in City Politics: Rent Strikes, Housing and the Power of the Poor* (Chicago: Rand McNally, 1969). Also see Pauli Murray, "Protest Against the Legal Status of the Negro," *Annals of the American Academy of Political and Social Science* 357 (January 1965): 55–64; Edie N. Goldenberg, *Making the Papers* (Lexington, Mass.: D.C. Heath, 1975), esp. p. 1; James Q. Wilson, *Political Organizations* (New York: Basic Books, 1973), pp. 283–84; Alan F. Westin and Barry Mahoney, *The Trial of Martin Luther King* (New York: Thomas Y. Crowell, 1974), p. 290; and April Carter, *Direct Action and Liberal Democracy* (New York: Harper & Row, 1973), p. 139.

4. See Clarence M. Case, *Nonviolent Coercion: A Study in Methods of Social Pressure* (New York: Century Co., 1923), esp. pp. 400 and 404–5. Also see the equally prescient comments by Edward Allsworth Ross in the introduction.

5. James S. Coleman, *Community Conflict* (New York: The Free Press, 1957), esp. pp. 10–12 and 25–26.

6. E.E. Schattschneider, *The Semisovereign People* (New York: Holt, Rine-

hart & Winston, 1960), pp. 3-7. Also see Schattschneider, "Intensity, Visibility, Direction and Scope," *American Political Science Reivew* 51 (December 1957): 933-42; and David B. Truman, *The Governmental Process* (New York: Alfred A. Knopf, 1951), pp. 362 and 422, for earlier references to what was to become the "socialization of conflict" perspective.

7.   James Q. Wilson, "The Strategy of Protest: Problems of Negro Civic Action," *Journal of Conflict Resolution* 5 (September 1961): 291-303, at 293.

8.   Harvey Seifert, *Conquest Through Suffering* (Philadelphia: Westminster Press, 1965). The classic work on nonviolence devoted only limited attention to the role that third-party observers could play and even then saw that role as being primarily one of inducing shame in the protestors' immediate opponents. See Richard B. Gregg, *The Power of Nonviolence*, rev. ed. (New York: Schocken Books, 1959), esp. pp. 45-48, 53, 81, and 86. Even less attention is devoted to the matter in another well-known work. See William Robert Miller, *Nonviolence: A Christian Interpretation* (New York: Association Press, 1964). One writer on nonviolence who had adopted the tripartite view in 1962, although his manuscript was not published until 1968, was George R. Lakey. See "The Sociological Mechanisms of Non-violent Action," *Peace Research Reviews* 2 (December 1969): 1-98. Lakey evinces an excellent awareness of the public's potential role in aiding nonviolent protestors and also notes that the "communication of images is an important part of any conflict." See esp. pp. 34 and 72.

9.   Seifert, *Conquest Through Suffering*, pp. 32-38, 56-64, 69-72, 116-17, and 142-45.

10.   Michael Lipsky, "Protest As A Political Resource"; "Rent Strikes: Poor Man's Weapon," *Transaction* 6 (February 1969): 10-15; and *Protest in City Politics*.

11.   Lipsky, *Protest in City Politics*, p. 187; and "Rent Strikes," p. 12. Although any number of futile efforts have been made to define "news," a majority of commentators have observed that that which is newsworthy is that which is novel. See David L. Lange, Robert K. Baker, and Sandra J. Ball, *Mass Media and Violence* (Washington: USGPO, 1969), pp. 88 and 139; Amitai Etzioni, *Demonstration Democracy* (New York: Gordon & Breach, 1970), p. 14; and Goldenberg, *Making the Papers*, pp. 28 and 120. As James Q. Wilson has emphasized, however, just what qualifies as "unusual" changes over time, and the newsworthiness of a tactic declines in proportion to its increasing use. As two other scholars recently have suggested, "The effectiveness of different forms of protest as a political resource may be inversely related to the frequency with which such activity occurs." See Wilson, *Political Organizations*, p. 287; and Bryan T. Downes and Kenneth R. Greene, "The Politics of Open Housing in Three Cities: Decision Maker Responses to Black Demands for Policy Change," *American Politics Quarterly* 1 (April 1973): 215-43, at 234. Also see Barrie Thorne, "Protest and the Problem of Credibility: Uses of Knowledge and Risk-Taking in the Draft Resistance Movement of the 1960s," *Social Problems* 23 (December 1975): 111-23, at 121; John Wilson, *Introduction to Social Movements* (New York: Basic Books, 1973), pp. 232-33 and 261; Peter K. Eisinger,

"Racial Differences in Protest Participation," *American Political Science Review* 68 (June 1974): 592–606, at 606, and *Patterns of Interracial Politics* (New York: Academic Press, 1976), p. 145; and Carter, *Direct Action and Liberal Democracy*, p. 54.

12. Lipsky, "Protest As A Political Resource," pp. 1146–47 and 1151; *Protest in City Politics*, p. 191; and "Rent Strikes," pp. 11 and 15.

13. Lipsky, *Protest in City Politics*, pp. 58, 63, and 68.

14. Wilson, *Political Organizations*, chapter 14; Ronald J. Terchek, "Protest and Bargaining," *Journal of Peace Research* 11 (1974): 133–44; and Paul D. Schumaker, "Policy Responsiveness to Protest-Group Demands," *Journal of Politics* 37 (May 1975): 488–521. Other writers also have reiterated the general dynamics involved. See, e.g., Anthony Oberschall, *Social Conflict and Social Movements* (Englewood Cliffs, N.J.: Prentice-Hall, 1973), esp. pp. 28–29, 214, 219, and 320–23. Two recent studies at welfare rights organizations also are within the Lipsky tradition. See Larry R. Jackson and William A. Johnson, *Protest by the Poor* (Lexington, Mass.: D.C. Heath, 1974), esp. p. 12; and Lawrence N. Bailis, *Bread or Justice* (Lexington, Mass.: D.C. Heath, 1974), pp. 125–39. Bailis attempts to articulate several conceptual distinctions which would set his work apart from Lipsky's, but fails in the effort, as his suggested distinctions are largely artificial. See in particular the concession made in the note on p. 129. For some commentary on the limitations of Lipsky's study, see Frances Fox Piven, "The Social Structuring of Political Protest," *Politics & Society* 6 (1976): 297–326, at 314.

15. See Roger W. Cobb and Charles D. Elder, *Participation in American Politics: The Dynamics of Agenda-Building* (Boston: Allyn & Bacon, 1972), esp. pp. 43 and 51–52.

16. See Carter, *Direct Action and Liberal Democracy*; and Gene Sharp, *The Politics of Nonviolent Action* (Boston: Porter Sargent, 1973), esp. p. 489. Also see Gene Sharp, *Exploring Nonviolent Alternatives* (Boston: Porter Sargent, 1970); Martin Oppenheimer and George Lakey, *A Manual For Direct Action* (Chicago: Quadrangle, 1965); George Lakey, *Exploring Nonviolent Action* (London: Housmans, 1970); and April Carter et al., *Non-violent Action: A Selected Bibliography* (London: Housmans, 1970).

17. As Earl Black, picking up on Schattschneider, has phrased it, "the activities of the civil rights movement in the early 1960s gradually expanded the arena of social conflict from small, isolated southern constituencies" (*Southern Governors and Civil Rights* [Cambridge: Harvard University Press, 1976], p. 324).

18. Martin Luther King, Jr., "Nonviolence and Racial Justice," *Christian Century* 74 (6 February 1957): 165–67. Also see *Stride Toward Freedom: The Montgomery Story* (New York: Harper & Brothers, 1958), chapter 6.

19. Judith Stiehm, "Nonviolence is Two," *Sociological Inquiry* 38 (Winter 1968): 23–29.

20. Martin Oppenheimer, "Towards A Sociological Understanding of Nonviolence," *Sociological Inquiry* 35 (Winter 1965): 123–31, at 124–25.

21. Paul E. Wehr, "Nonviolence and Differentiation in the Equal Rights

Movement," *Sociological Inquiry* 38 (Winter 1968): 65–76, at 67. Also see Theodore Paullin, *Introduction to Non-violence* (Philadelphia: Pacifist Research Bureau, 1944), pp. 25 and 55; and Gene Sharp, "The Meanings of Non-violence: A Typology (Revised)," *Journal of Conflict Resolution* 3 (March 1959): 41–66, at 43 and 56–59.

22. The Montgomery boycott had been resistance in the form of noncooperation, rather than the nonviolent persuasion that King articulated in his writings of the late 1950s. Montgomery had witnessed a strategy of withdrawal, rather than the positive physical resistance which the sit-ins and marches of the very early 1960s represented. Hence, Albany was King's first true test of the doctrine he had put forward several years earlier. No comprehensive account of the Albany campaign exists, but a number of writings contain valuable discussions of it. See Reese Cleghorn, "Epilogue in Albany," *New Republic* 149 (20 July 1963): 15–18; David L. Lewis, *King: A Critical Biography* (New York: Praeger, 1970), pp. 140–70; Howard Zinn, *The Southern Mystique* (New York: Alfred A. Knopf, 1964), pp. 147–213; James Forman, *The Making of Black Revolutionaries* (New York: Macmillan, 1972), pp. 247–62, William M. Kunstler, *Deep In My Heart* (New York: William Morrow, 1966), pp. 93–131; Carl M. Brauer, *John F. Kennedy and the Second Reconstruction* (New York: Columbia University Press, 1977), pp. 154–56 and 168–79; Edward Peeks, *The Long Struggle For Black Power* (New York: Charles Scribner's Sons, 1971), pp. 344–48; Howell Raines, *My Soul Is Rested* (New York: G.P. Putnam's Sons, 1977), pp. 361–66; Slater King, "The Bloody Battleground of Albany," *Freedomways* 4 (Winter 1964): 93–101, and "Our Main Battle in Albany," *Freedomways* 5 (Summer 1965): 417–23; Vincent Harding and Staughton Lynd, "Albany, Georgia," *The Crisis* 70 (February 1963): 69–78; and Wyatt T. Walker, "Albany, Failure or First Step?" *New South* 18 (June 1963): 3–8. Also see Anne Braden, "The Southern Freedom Movement in Perspective," *Monthly Review* 17 (July–August 1965): 1–93, at 44–45; Staughton Lynd, "Freedom Riders to the Polls," *Nation* 195 (28 July 1962): 29–32, at 30; Howard Zinn, "Kennedy: The Reluctant Emancipator," *Nation* 195 (1 December 1962): 373–76; and Reese Cleghorn, "Martin Luther King, Apostle of Crisis," *Saturday Evening Post* 236 (15 June 1963): 15–19, at 18.

23. Others have endorsed this intepretation as well. See Howard Hubbard, "Five Long Hot Summers and How They Grew," *Public Interest* 12 (Summer 1968): 3–24, at 5.

24. Another was that the goals of the Albany effort had been too vague and diffuse. In a late 1964 interview King acknowledged that the Albany campaign had suffered from a lack of specificity, and he added, "We have never since scattered our efforts in a general attack on segregation, but have focused upon specific, symbolic objectives." As was noted in chapter 4, the Selma campaign was considerably more specific and focused than had been the Birmingham one, or the St. Augustine effort. See Martin Luther King, Jr., "Playboy Interview," *Playboy* 12 (January 1965): 65–78, at 66. Also see Martin Luther King, Jr., "The Civil Rights Struggle in the United States Today," *The Record of the Associa-*

tion of the Bar of the City of New York 20 (May 1965, Supplement): 3–24, at 24, where King twice stresses how goals must be clearly defined and stated.

25. Over time King came to appreciate more and more the view of coercion which Reinhold Niebuhr had articulated in *Moral Man and Immoral Society* (New York: Charles Scribner's Sons, 1932). What Niebuhr wrote of Gandhi in 1932 is equally applicable to King: "He came finally to realise the necessity of some type of physical coercion upon the foes of his people's freedom, as every political leader must" (p. 242). Also see King, *Where Do We Go From Here: Chaos or Community?* (Boston: Beacon Press, 1967), pp. 90 and 128–29. Many discussions of nonviolent action evince only an awareness of the persuasive, and not the coercive, possibilities. See Charles C. Walker, *Organizing For Nonviolent Direct Action* (Delhi: Navchetan Press, n.d.); and Herbert Kelman, *A Time To Speak* (San Francisco: Jossey-Bass, 1968), pp. 231–60. For articulations of the differences between persuasion and coercion, see Lewis M. Killian, *The Impossible Revolution* 2nd ed. (New York: Random House, 1975), pp. 64–68; Ralph H. Turner, "Determinants of Social Movement Strategies," in Tamotsu Shibutani, ed., *Human Nature and Collective Behavior* (Englewood Cliffs, N.J.: Prentice-Hall, 1970), pp. 145–64, at 159–63; and Judith Stiehm, *Nonviolent Power* (Lexington, Mass.: D.C. Heath, 1972), pp. 19–21 and 27. Two other discussions of "coercion" are David H. Bayley, "The Pedagogy of Democracy: Coercive Public Protest in India," *American Political Science Review* 56 (September 1962): 663–72; and Anthony De Crespigny, "The Nature and Methods of Nonviolent Coercion," *Political Studies* 12 (June 1964): 256–65. De Crespigny includes as "coercive" several types of activity which involve "withdrawal" rather than active, forceful coercion.

26. Oppenheimer, "Toward A Sociological Understanding," pp. 125–26. A somewhat similar observation has been made by a scholar who studied CORE in the 1960s. "The conversion of businessmen and politicians through the moral power of nonviolence was so rare as to be insignificant. Leaders of direct action groups knew this and planned their campaigns accordingly. Yet these same leaders usually expressed, and half believed, the 'official' version of nonviolence." See Inge Powell Bell, *CORE and the Strategy of Nonviolence* (New York: Random House, 1968), p. 37, and especially chapter 3. The truth of Bell's remark is no less applicable to the SCLC leadership than to that of CORE.

27. Indicative in this regard is a somewhat earlier remark by King. "Violence," one journalist has quoted him as saying, "is immoral. But, more than that it is impractical" (Michael Dorman, *We Shall Overcome* [New York: Delacorte Press, 1964], p. 176). Similar practical priorities, I would argue, also apparently guided the tactical choices the SCLC made in St. Augustine in 1964. See Robert W. Hartley, "A Long, Hot Summer: The St. Augustine Racial Disorders of 1964," M.A. thesis, Stetson University, 1972, pp. 47–48, 55, 64, 73, 75, and esp. 87 and 90–91. Also see Paul Good, *The Trouble I've Seen* (Washington: Howard University Press, 1975), p. 87, and the other works cited in note 10 of chapter 2.

28. One writer who has indicated some awareness of it is Bo Wirmark, who has spoken of a "development in King's thinking." ("The Changing Ideology of

Nonviolence," *Gandhi Marg* 12 [April 1968]: 146–55, at 150, and "Nonviolent Methods and the American Civil Rights Movement, 1955–1965," *Journal of Peace Research* 11 [1974] 115–32; at 126–27). Two helpful analyses of King's thought are Kenneth L. Smith and Ira G. Zepp, Jr., *Search for the Beloved Community: The Thinking of Martin Luther King, Jr.* (Valley Forge: Judson Press, 1974); and John W. Rathbun, "Martin Luther King: The Theology of Social Action," *American Quarterly* 20 (Spring 1968): 38–53. Both works unfortunately fail to couple their analyses of King's published writings with a consideration of his actual political conduct and experiences. Hence they fail to see King's evolution toward an increasingly Niebuhrian view of man and society. Smith and Zepp, however, do exhibit several inklings of such a realization (pp. 85, 90, and 137). A considerably less valuable work is Hanes Walton, Jr., *The Political Philosophy of Martin Luther King, Jr.* (Westport: Greenwood Publishing Co., 1971). Walton fails to see that King's adoption of nonviolence was aimed at something more than merely "bringing about a change of heart in his opponent." See esp. pp. 62, 66, and 107. Also see Warren E. Steinkraus, "Martin Luther King's Personalism and Non-violence," *Journal of the History of Ideas* 34 (January–March 1973): 97–111.

29. See Fred Powledge, *New York Times*, 5 November 1964, pp. 1 and 33.

30. See John Herbers, *New York Times*, 3 January 1965, pp. 1 and 20; and Paul Good, *Washington Post*, 3 January 1965, p. A9.

31. Charles E. Fager, *Selma 1965* (New York: Charles Scribner's Sons, 1974), pp. 31 and 34.

32. King never fully articulated the shift which his own actions indicated had occurred, and he never revised or extended the intellectual autobiography which chapter 6 of *Stride Toward Freedom* represented. Hence his stance in the mid-1960s can be critiqued in much the same way that Niebuhr had analyzed Gandhi in *Moral Man and Immoral Society*. Both men employed nonviolent coercion while speaking of their actions as if they were merely nonviolent persuasion. King himself had at one time misread Niebuhr's discussion of Gandhi. See *Moral Man*, pp. 240–56; and *Stride Toward Freedom*, pp. 80–82.

33. Martin Luther King, Jr., "Let Justice Roll Down," *Nation* 200 (15 March 1965): 269–74, at 270. This piece reflects much more clearly than most of King's writings his strong belief that sympathetic white support would be necessary for the movement to achieve its goals. "Pressure," he wrote at that same time, was necessary for getting "American institutions to function," and "continued creative action" aimed at sharpening "the conscience of the nation" was necessary if that pressure was to be obtained. See "Civil Rights No. 1—The Right to Vote," *New York Times Magazine*, 15 March 1965, p. 26.

34. Martin Luther King, Jr., *Why We Can't Wait* (New York: New American Library, 1964), p. 37.

35. King, *Where Do We Go From Here*, pp. 51 and 158. Also see King's "The Last Steep Ascent," *Nation* 202 (14 March 1966): 288–92; *The Trumpet of Conscience* (New York: Harper & Row, 1968), p. 54; and "Playboy Interview," p. 68.

36. Martin Luther King, Jr., "Behind the Selma March," *Saturday Review*

48 (3 April 1965): 16–17 and 57. For a virulently harsh criticism of the movement that takes note of King's four points, see Frank S. Meyer, "The Violence of Nonviolence," *National Review* 17 (20 April 1965): 327. The *Saturday Review* piece also served as a lightning rod for the most outlandish right-wing fantasies. See Alan Stang, "The King and His Communists," *American Opinion* 8 (October 1965): 1–14, at 1–3.

37. King, *The Trumpet of Conscience*, p. 5.

38. Tom Kahn and August Meier, "Recent Trends in the Civil Rights Movement," *New Politics* 3 (Spring 1964): 34–53, at 49. On the little-noted Danville campaign, in which King's personal involvement was very brief, see Len Holt, *An Act of Conscience* (Boston: Beacon Press, 1965); Kunstler, *Deep In My Heart*, pp. 211–32; and James W. Ely, Jr., "Negro Demonstrations and the Law: Danville as a Test Case," *Vanderbilt Law Review* 27 (October 1974): 927–68.

39. Note King's statement shortly after Selma: "We realize that we must exercise caution so that our direct action program is not conducted in a manner that might be *considered* provocative or an invitation to violence" (emphasis added). Read quite literally, and with that added emphasis in mind, King's statement is very accurate. Without any deception, it avoids acknowledging the actual SCLC strategy. "Behind the Selma March," pp. 16–17.

40. As Lewis Coser has observed, "Modes of control involving the extralegal uses of violence worked well as long as the acts in question could be committed with a minimum of publicity and visibility. They became suicidal when they were performed under the glare of television cameras and under the observation of reporters for national newspapers and magazines" ("Some Social Functions of Violence," *Annals of the American Academy of Political and Social Science* 364 [March 1966]: 8–18, at 16). While some southern law-enforcement officials, such as Jim Clark, failed to appreciate just how "suicidal" such conduct would be when performed in a "visible" arena, many others did realize that fact and acted accordingly. Hence, a number of writers have noted how the presence of the national media served to restrain demonstrators' opponents and furnished many such activists with a form of protection from physical assault. See William B. Monroe, Jr., "Television: The Chosen Instrument of the Revolution," in Paul L. Fisher and Ralph L. Lowenstein, eds., *Race and the News Media* (New York: Praeger, 1967), pp. 83–97, at 88–89; August Meier and Elliott Rudwick, *CORE: A Study in the Civil Rights Movement* (New York: Oxford University Press, 1973), p. 274; Frederic Solomon and Jacob R. Fishman, "The Psychosocial Meaning of Nonviolence in Student Civil Rights Activities," *Psychiatry* 27 (May 1964): 91–99, at 98; and Good, *The Trouble I've Seen*, p. 53.

41. As Inge Powell Bell has written about another civil rights organization facing similar questions, "The assumption underlying CORE's propaganda style was clearly that its audience was sufficiently committed to the American creed and that they only needed to have the contrast between the real and the ideal made dramatic enough to justify drastic action and to call forth strong commitments" (*CORE and the Strategy of Nonviolence*, p. 30).

42. The most truly moral course, it can be argued, is to resist injustice by the most effective means available. This, in essence, is the course that the SCLC took. Resistance to evil, Niebuhr has emphasized, *must* be effective. "It may be necessary at times," he wrote, "to sacrifice a degree of moral purity for political effectiveness" (*Moral Man*, p. 244). This too is what the SCLC leadership chose to do. Also see Arthur I. Waskow, "Nonviolence and Creative Disorder," *Christian Century* 82 (13 October 1965): 1253–55.

43. Jan Howard, "The Provocation of Violence: A Civil Rights Tactic?" *Dissent* 13 (January–February 1966): 94–99.

44. See August Meier, "On the Role of Martin Luther King," *New Politics* 4 (Winter 1965): 52–59. Meier did write, however, that "contrary to the official nonviolent direct action philosophy, demonstrations have secured their results not by changing the hearts of the oppressors through a display of nonviolent love, but through the national and international pressures generated by the publicity arising from mass arrests and incidents of violence. And no one has employed this strategy of securing publicity through mass arrests and precipitating violence from white hoodlums and law enforcement officers more than King himself." King "is precisely most successful," Meier continued, giving King more than the benefit of doubt, "when, contrary to his deepest wishes, his demonstrations precipitate violence from Southern whites against Negro and white demonstrators" (p. 53). Although seemingly aware of what the SCLC strategy in fact was, Meier was unwilling to admit that it was being pursued consciously by the SCLC hierarchy. Aside from this point, the Meier piece is an excellent discussion of King's role in communicating blacks' aspirations to white America and in making direct action "respectable." Also see Kenneth B. Clark, "The Civil Rights Movement: Momentum and Organization," *Daedalus* 95 (Winter 1966): 239–67, at 255 and 257, for some very similar comments.

45. Howard, "The Provocation of Violence," p. 98.

46. John Herbers, *New York Times*, 28 March 1965, p. E6. Also see Howard, "The Provocation of Violence," p. 98, who relates a very similar story.

47. Hubbard, "Five Long Hot Summers," p. 7. As a somewhat hostile biographer of King wrote at about that same time, "Segregationist violence was the sine qua non of the success of King's nonviolence." Referring to Selma, the biographer wrote that "King *needed* Clark—*needed* a brutal response by the Sheriff of Dallas County—to secure Federal legislation." Clark, as a number of other writers also have noted, "obligingly fell into every baited trap King set for him." Lionel Lokos, *House Divided: The Life and Legacy of Martin Luther King* (New Rochelle, N.Y.: Arlington House, 1968), p. 161. Also see Kenneth Crawford, *Newsweek*, 1 March 1965, p. 39, who wrote even prior to March 7 that Clark, "with his quick temper and lack of restraining judgment, has been almost the ideal patsy for King's demonstrators in Selma. At various times he has been goaded into using his club and his fists but never his head. He has been so grossly inept. . . ." See as well Wilson, *Introduction to Social Movements*, p. 251.

48. Hubbard, "Five Long Hot Summers," p. 7. Also see Carter, *Direct*

Action and Liberal Democracy, p. 86; Lipsky, "Rent Strikes," p. 11; and Oberschall, *Social Conflict and Social Movements*, p. 303.

49.   Also see Donald von Eschen et al., "The Conditions of Direct Action in a Democratic Society," *Western Political Quarterly* 22 (June 1969): 309–25, at 324.

50.   See Roy Reed, *New York Times*, 17 March 1965, p. 1; and Monroe, "Televison: The Chosen Instrument of the Revolution," p. 90.

51.   On the advisability of specific, straightforward goals, see Goldenberg, *Making the Papers*, p. 30; and Lipsky, *Protest in City Politics*, pp. 195–97. On the benefits to be derived from religious overtones and ministerial status, see Coser, "Some Social Functions of Violence," p. 17.

52.   See Pat Watters, "The Negroes Enter Southern Politics," *Dissent* 13 (July–August 1966): 361–68, at 361; and Bayard Rustin, *Strategies For Freedom* (New York: Columbia University Press, 1976), esp. pp. 41 and 72. Also see Clark, "The Civil Rights Movement," pp. 256–57.

53.   Lipsky, *Protest in City Politics*, p. 182.

54.   For references to such newsworthy incidents, see Irving J. Cohen, "La Huelga! Delano and After," *Monthly Labor Review* 91 (June 1968): 13–16; and Harry Bernstein, "Duel in the Sun—Union-Busting, Teamster Style," *Progressive* 37 (July 1973): 17–20. Both pieces note that the UFW too has sought to benefit from association with religious themes and personages. For narrative accounts of the UFW's struggle from the mid-1960s through the early 1970s, see Eugene Nelson, *Huelga* (Delano, Calif.: Farm Worker Press, 1966); John Gregory Dunne, *Delano: The Story of the California Grape Strike* (New York: Farrar, Straus & Giroux, 1967); Peter Matthiessen, *Sal Si Puedes: Cesar Chavez and the New American Revolution* (New York: Random House, 1970); Mark Day, *Forty Acres* (New York: Praeger, 1971); and Jacques E. Levy, *Cesar Chavez* (New York: W.W. Norton, 1975). An excellent article on the UFW's status as of the end of 1977 is Helen Dewar, *Washington Post*, 30 January 1978, p. 1. Scholars should avail themselves of Beverly Fodell's excellent *Cesar Chavez and the United Farm Workers: A Selective Bibliography* (Detroit: Wayne State University Press, 1974).

55.   John P. Robinson, "Public Reaction to Political Protest: Chicago 1968," *Public Opinion Quarterly* 34 (Spring 1970): 1–9. Also see Neil Hickey, "Television in Turmoil," and Reuven Frank, "Chicago: A Post-Mortem," in Barry G. Cole, ed., *Television* (New York: Free Press, 1970), pp. 87–105 and 106–15. As Coser has noted, public acceptance or rejection of police violence is largely determined by how the public perceives and feels about those at whom the official force is aimed. See "Some Social Functions of Violence," pp. 16–17.

56.   See Robert A. Dahl, *Who Governs?* (New Haven: Yale University Press, 1961), pp. 322 and 324. Also see Gunnar Myrdal, *An American Dilemma* (New York: Harper & Brothers, 1944), p. 1; Tilman C. Cothran, "The Negro Protest Against Segregation in the South," *Annals of the American Academy of Political and Social Science* 357 (January 1965): 65–72, at 72; James H. Laue, "The Changing Character of Negro Protest," *Annals of the American Academy of*

Political and Social Science 357 (January 1965): 119–26, at 124; Dwaine Marvick, "The Political Socialization of the American Negro," *Annals of the American Academy of Political and Social Science* 361 (September 1965): 112–27, at 123; Donald R. Matthews and James W. Prothro, *Negroes and the New Southern Politics* (New York: Harcourt, Brace & World, 1966), p. 476; Reese Cleghorn and Pat Watters, "The Impact of Negro Votes on Southern Politics," *Reporter* 36 (26 January 1967): 24–25 and 31–32, at 32; Joseph S. Himes, "The Functions of Racial Conflict," *Social Forces* 45 (September 1966): 1–10, at 5, "A Theory of Racial Conflict," *Social Forces* 50 (September 1971): 53–60; at 56, and *Racial Conflict in American Society* (Columbus: Charles E. Merrill, 1973), pp. 16, 64, and 193; Tom Kahn, "Direct Action and Democratic Values," *Dissent* 13 (January–February 1966): 22–30, at 25; and Myrdal's comments in Jack Lyle, ed., *The Black American and the Press* (Los Angeles: Ward Ritchie Press, 1968), pp. 7–8.

57.   Richard M. Merelman, "Learning and Legitimacy," *American Political Science Review* 60 (September 1966): 548–61, at 553 and 559–60. Also see Roger W. Cobb and Charles D. Elder, "Symbolic Identifications and Political Behavior," *American Politics Quarterly* 4 (July 1976): 305–32, at 327; and Cobb and Elder, "The Political Uses of Symbolism," *American Politics Quarterly* 1 (July 1973): 305–38, at 324–25 and 332.

58.   As several writers recently have suggested, the number of causes inherently unable to employ such means of appeal may be greater than earlier authors admitted. As Willis Hawley has put it, the more basic the change demanded, the less likely it is that audience support for it can be accumulated. "The advocates of fundamental change," he has written, "will invariably face more substantial constraints than groups that place less substantial demands on the prevailing allocation of resources and privilege." See his review of Lipsky's *Protest in City Politics*, in *American Political Science Review* 64 (December 1970): 1256–58. Also see Terchek, "Protest and Bargaining," pp. 139 and 142; Turner, "Determinants of Social Movement Strategies," pp. 151–53; and Bailis, *Bread or Justice*, pp. 132 and 137–38. See as well Frances Fox Piven and Richard A. Cloward, *Poor People's Movements* (New York: Pantheon, 1977), who argue that often there are deeply rooted and insurmountable barriers to the emergence of protest. See pp. xiii, 3, 7, 14, 23, and 35–37. Prevailing social conditions are determinative, they argue, and in the absence of "profound social dislocation," protest will not take place. Needless to say, Piven's and Cloward's contention that elites respond only to punitive disruption is more than contradicted by the story told here in chapters 2 and 3. Their subsequent assertion that the "fundamental cause" of the voting rights triumph "was economic change" (p. 252) is as absurd as it is erroneous.

59.   For a number of different definitions of just what constitutes "protest," see Lipsky, *Protest in City Politics*, p. 2; Wilson, *Political Organizations*, p. 282; Schumaker, "Policy Responsiveness to Protest Group Demands," p. 490; and Piven and Cloward, *Poor People's Movements*, p. 23n.

60.   See Charles O. Jones, *Clean Air: The Policies and Politics of Pollution*

Control (Pittsburgh: University of Pittsburgh Press, 1975), p. 166; Mark Nadel, *The Politics of Consumer Protection* (Indianapolis: Bobbs-Merrill, 1971), pp. 242–47; and *New York Times*, 10 January 1975, p. 42, and John Hess, *New York Times*, 20 May 1976, p. 65. Also see Richard M. Kovak, "Urban Renewal Controversies," *Public Administration Review* 32 (July–August 1972): 359–72, at 369; and William Robbins, *New York Times*, 19 December 1974, p. 3.

61.   As Schattschneider wrote in 1960, "Everywhere the trends toward privatization and socialization of conflict have been disguised as tendencies toward the centralization or decentralization, localization or nationalization of politics" (*The Semisovereign People*, p. 12). As we noted earlier, concerning civil rights "localization" and "privatization" were much the same thing. Also see Matthews and Prothro, *Negroes and the New Southern Politics*, p. 476.

62.   For an excellent instance of this, see Lesley Oelsner, *New York Times*, 15 May 1976, p. 1, and 19 May 1976, p. 1.

63.   See Harold C. Fleming, "The Federal Executive and Civil Rights: 1961–1965," *Daedalus* 94 (Fall 1965): 921–48, at 945; and David Mars, "The Federal Government and Protest," *Annals of the American Academy of Political and Social Science* 382 (March 1969): 120–30.

Index

329

White primary (*continued*)
  Carolina, 242 *n*12
White v. *Regester*, 311 *n*80
Whitley v. *Williams*, 308 *n*59
Wicker, Tom, 97, 106
Wiggins, Charles, 208
Wilcox County, Ala., 105, 182, 230, 249 *n*44, 256 *n*70, 301 *n*28
Wiley, Alexander, 177
Wilkins, Collie Leroy, 127, 283 *n*59
Wilkins, Roy, 67, 68, 105, 115
Williams, Harrison, 143
Williams, Hosea, 48, 62, 112, 119; and Bloody Sunday, 73–74; and March 9 events, 83–84
Williams, John, 124
Williams, John Bell, 97, 110, 193
Williamsburg County, S.C., 237 *n*8
Williams v. *Wallace*, 111–12, 272 *n*5, 278 *n*43

Willis, Edwin, 120
Wilson, James Q., 214, 219
Winter, William, 207
Wisdom, John Minor, 23, 263 *n*6, 284 *n*63
Wolff, Lester, 56
Women, 78, 147–48

Yale Law Journal, 17, 22
Yarborough, Ralph W., 81, 141, 173
Yates, Sidney, 298 *n*30
Young, Andrew: and January *1965* events in Selma, 39, 40, 44, 267 *n*37; and February protests, 48, 49–50, 60; and Bloody Sunday, 76; and March 9 events, 83, 273 *n*9; in Congress, 205–06, 210, 316 *n*102; quoted, 230, 286 *n*7
Young, Whitney, 105, 119
Youngblood, Rufus, 93

Zimmer v. *McKeithen*, 311 *n*80